Boundaries of Contagion

BOUNDARIES OF CONTAGION

How Ethnic Politics Have Shaped
Government Responses to AIDS

Evan S. Lieberman

PRINCETON UNIVERSITY PRESS

PRINCETON & OXFORD

Published by Princeton University Press, 41 William Street, Princeton, New Jersey 08540

In the United Kingdom: Princeton University Press, 6 Oxford Street, Woodstock, Oxfordshire OX20 1TW

ISBN: 978-0-691-13286-0

ISBN (pbk.): 978-0-691-14019-3

Library of Congress Control Number: 2008942192

British Library Cataloging-in-Publication Data is available

This book has been composed in Adobe Garamond

Printed on acid-free paper ∞

press.princeton.edu

Printed in the United States of America

10 9 8 7 6 5 4 3 2 1

For Gideon and Jonah

CONTENTS

ILLUSTRATIONS

FIGURES

TABLES

ABBREVIATIONS

AIDS	acquired immunodeficiency syndrome
API	AIDS Program Effort Index
ART	antiretroviral drug therapy
ARV	antiretroviral drug
BJP	Bharatiya Janata Party (India)
CCM	Country Coordinating Mechanism
CDC	Centers for Disease Control (United States)
CSW	commercial sex worker
DFID	Department for International Development (United Kingdom)
ELF	Ethnolinguistic Fractionalization index
GFATM	Global Fund to fight AIDS, Tuberculosis and Malaria
HAART	highly active antiretroviral therapy
HIV	human immunodeficiency virus
MDG	Millennium Development Goal
MSM	men who have sex with men
NAPWA	National Association of People Living With AIDS (South Africa)
PEPFAR	President's Emergency Plan for AIDS Relief (United States)
PMTCT	prevention of mother-to-child transmission
ST	scheduled tribe (India)
SUS	Sistema Único de Saúde (Brazil)
TAC	Treatment Action Campaign (South Africa)
UNAIDS	Joint United Nations Program on HIV/AIDS
UNDP	United Nations Development Programme
UNGASS	United Nations General Assembly Special Session
UNICEF	United Nations Children's Fund
USAID	United States Agency for International Development
UP	Uttar Pradesh (India)
VCT	voluntary counseling and testing
WHO	World Health Organization

During the past quarter-century, the worldwide spread of the human immunodeficiency virus (HIV) has created one of the deadliest epidemics in human history. Despite widely available biomedical knowledge about how to prevent transmission of the virus, and technologies and resources to treat people living with HIV/AIDS, government responses have varied greatly. While some national governments have acted aggressively, others have done little or responded late. This book provides an explanation for divergent responses to the common threat, shedding light not just on the dynamics of this major policy problem, but on the politics of responding to shared problems and of building state capacity more generally. The focus is on the low- and middle-income countries, where more than 90 percent of the world's HIV infections are contained.

The central claim is that in addition to a country's resources and capacity and the severity of its epidemic, the aggressiveness of its response can be explained by the relative strength and fragmentation of internal ethnic group boundaries. Strong ethnic boundaries create disincentives for political leaders to act on the problem as a shared threat to the nation. In such ethnically divided societies, groups are less likely to perceive the threat of infection as a shared risk, and the politics of HIV/AIDS are much more likely to become an impossible game of blame and shame-avoidance, making it far less likely that government leaders will act. Alternatively, the most aggressive responses tend to occur in countries where group boundaries are weak. When the "us-them" dynamic is absent from politics, political entrepreneurs are more likely to perceive and to frame the epidemic as a shared threat that demands the mobilization of public resources.

Before turning to comparative analysis of those responses, the book explores the critical international dimension of policymaking in an increasingly integrated world. In a chapter on the role of global governance, efforts to guide policy and human behavior are detailed as a pressure on government action that has been increasing over the past twenty years. The best-practice guidelines formulated by international organizations— the "Geneva Consensus"—provide a template for government action around the world. As rich countries and institutions have actively disseminated this model, committing financial and other resources, the significant cross-country variation becomes increasingly puzzling.

The comparative analysis is based on an explicitly mixed-method research design. It combines "model-building" structured comparative analysis of the impact of racial boundaries on AIDS policy in Brazil and South Africa; a "model-testing" case study of ethnic boundaries and AIDS policies in India, including a statistical analysis of Indian state-level responses; and a cross-national statistical analysis of the determinants of AIDS policy across developing countries. The book draws on a vast array of evidence, including analysis of published documents, government and nongovernment statistical data, newspaper reports, and interviews with policymakers and political actors carried out around the world.

The completion of this book takes me full circle to the start of an intellectual journey that began in 1991, during my junior year at Princeton University. I had the extraordinary opportunity to participate in a Woodrow Wilson School seminar on the political transition under way in South Africa. Our professor, Ambassador Donald Easum, was a career diplomat who had retired from the post of assistant secretary for African affairs, and he created an extraordinary course that opened my eyes to the drama and possibilities of politics. Easum took our group on a fact-finding tour of South Africa that summer, and the trip changed my life forever. I am eternally in his debt for his efforts and inspiration.

Like most others at the time, I was paying more attention to Nelson Mandela, the African National Congress, ongoing violence, and the prospects for democracy in South Africa than I was to the growing AIDS epidemic. Nonetheless, I distinctly remember walking through the decrepit squatter camp of Alexandra, which lies nearby the wealthiest suburbs of Johannesburg, when our tour guide led us to the shack of a *sangoma* (traditional healer or "witch doctor"). The man showed us some hanging herbs that were for sale, one of which he proclaimed was a cure for AIDS. At the time, it seemed fairly innocuous—the words of an eccentric man, and a splash of the "exotic" for a New Yorker who had never before traveled to Africa. I did not fathom that disputes about the nature of this disease and how it ought to be treated would become central to the politics and human development of the country.

I returned to South Africa a few times after that 1991 trip, and my wife, Amy, and I returned for a yearlong stay between 1997 and 1998, a period during which I worked on my doctoral research, and she served as an arts educator. On a trip home for the winter holidays, I found myself telling our families about the amazing and positive transformations in postapartheid South Africa. It was a beautiful country, still glowing from the postapartheid "honeymoon," and the future seemed bright.

But my wife's aunt, Jane, who had long been involved in AIDS issues in the United States, challenged me to explain why the South African government was doing such a bad job on HIV/AIDS. Why weren't the leaders taking action to prevent the spread of HIV from mothers to children during the process of childbirth? I had no good answers for her. But the puzzle continued to haunt me as I read news reports about growing levels of HIV infection in the country. Why on earth wasn't the South African government doing more when the know-how and the resources were obviously available?

I stayed focused on my dissertation research, but I began to sense that AIDS might be the biggest threat to South Africa's future development. When we returned from South Africa, Amy and I lived in New York City, and I began to meet with renowned AIDS doctors and activists—including Arthur Amman and David Ho—who voiced their absolute ire at the South African government for not doing more. Particularly surprising to me was that the country that had been the "failing" or "pathological" exemplar in my doctoral research on tax policy—Brazil—was emerging as the leading light on AIDS control. I had been trained to make big comparisons about counterintuitive outcomes, and here was one staring me in the face. Even before I had completed my dissertation, I had decided that the study of AIDS and AIDS policy would be at the heart of my next major research project, and the fruits of that inquiry are contained in this book.

This is primarily a scholarly book in the sense that I engage existing theories of politics and use established research methods to test my own and competing explanations. But my hope is that this work will be of interest to a wider audience, as the concerns are indeed, widely relevant. As a courtesy to those not concerned with the scholarly debates, I have relegated, as much as possible, direct references to the scholarly literature to footnotes. And while this is a book that addresses subjects about which I feel passionate, it is not an impassioned analysis. I am not concerned with identifying "heroes" and "villains," although they make for good stories that can contribute in their own right to political change. Instead, I take a social scientific approach that identifies claims and evaluates which ones have the most support in the available evidence. While this approach lacks the drama of some others, it gets at the real story behind government responses to the greatest development challenge of my generation. It also uncovers more general political and social dynamics that can shed light on other policy problems.

The extent of my debts on this book is almost embarrassing. Moreover, I reneged on a promise I made to myself to keep better track of who has helped in what ways, knowing that one day I would be writing this section. Undoubtedly, I have omitted the names of some good friends and colleagues, and I apologize in advance for the unintended slight.

Soon after I first realized that I wanted to study AIDS in comparative perspective, I became aware that I knew little about health and health care policy. I was fortunate enough to be awarded a Robert Wood Johnson Health Policy postdoctoral fellowship at Yale University, and I am grateful to both institutions' generous support of my training. At Yale, I found myself surrounded by a group of extremely smart and engaging colleagues. I was mentored by Ted Marmor and Mark Schlesinger, who provided a foundation for understanding human health as a product of many competing social, biological, and environmental factors, not the least of which were political ideas and policies. Michael Merson, who at the time directed Yale's Center for AIDS Research, and is one of the world's leading authorities on AIDS, was exceptionally generous with his time, and I am grateful that one of his grants provided seed money for my initial research. During that period, Kim Blankenship, Ian Shapiro, Andrea Campbell, Vincent Hutchings, Mark Suchman, Abigail Saguy, Darrick Hamilton, Bradley Herring, Kimberly DaCosta, Eric Oliver, Taeku Lee, Gary McKissick, Kimberly Morgan, and Jennifer Klein all provided valuable feedback on proposals and ideas.

I benefited from extended discussions or interviews with well over two hundred political activists, party leaders, government officials, diplomats, and individuals working at pharmaceutical corporations or as public health professionals, academics, or think tank analysts in the United States, Canada, South Africa, Thailand, Uganda, South Africa, Brazil, and India. There were too many to name here, and because in most cases I promised I would keep their identities confidential, I use that as a blanket policy for all. I truly appreciate their time and insights.

I began a faculty position in the Department of Politics at Princeton in 2002, and I am grateful for the financial, intellectual, and professional support I have received. Specifically, the Woodrow Wilson School, the Center for Health and Wellbeing, the Bobst Center, the Princeton Institute for International and Regional Studies, and the University Committee for Research in the Humanities and Social Sciences have all provided generous funding. Chris Mackie helped to set up crucial databases for managing volumes of data collection, and Wangyal Shawa is largely responsible for producing the beautiful maps in chapters 5 and 6, and I thank both of them for their help. Anne-Marie Slaughter and Christina Paxson have been extremely supportive of my work, including efforts to bring AIDS-related guest speakers and programming to campus.

While at Princeton, various colleagues, students, and visitors have provided wonderful feedback and intellectual inspiration. Chris Achen, Mark Beissinger, Nancy Bermeo, João Biehl, Joshua Busby, Miguel Centeno, Sarah Chartock, Joshua Clinton, Christina Davis, Angus Deaton, Kent Eaton, Helen Epstein, Martin Gilens, Patrick Heller, Eric Thun, Grigore Pop-Eleches, Amaney Jamal, Jeffrey Herbst, Karen Long Jusko, Robert Keohane, Helen Milner, Rachel Riedl, Eric Thun, Joshua Tucker, Bruce Western, Jennifer Widner, and Deborah Yashar provided comments on working papers, chapters, and discrete ideas and analyses. Prerna Singh taught me a great deal about Indian politics and society, helped me to arrange much of my brief field research in that country, and has provided valuable feedback along the way, especially for chapter 5. Atul Kohli, Tali Mendelberg, and Jonas Pontusson all provided detailed and thoughtful comments on the entire manuscript.

My largest specific intellectual debt is to Varun Gauri, who is acknowledged as a coauthor of chapter 4, based on our study published in 2006 in *Studies in Comparative International Development*. I learned a great deal from that partnership, and the fruits of that effort were central to the development of the theories and empirical approach taken in this book.

During the 2006–7 academic year, I was a visitor at New York University's Wagner School of Public Policy, which was a wonderful place to do some thinking and writing, and I am grateful to John Gershman for helping to make that possible, along with Jason Furman, Jonathan Morduch, Victor Rodwin, and Rogan Kersh, and others who were delightful colleagues.

I have also benefited from comments from Catherine Boone, John Gerring, Margaret Levi, Peter Lewis, James McGuire, Vicki Murillo, Ken Shadlen, Eric Voeten, and Nicolas Van de Walle. Mentors from my graduate alma mater, the University of California, Berkeley, including David Collier, Ruth Collier, and Robert Price all provided helpful comments at early stages of this research. Richard Parker, whose name appears as both noted scholar and political actor in these pages, has been extremely encouraging and has provided fantastic feedback. Nicoli Nattrass and Jeremy Seekings provided thoughtful critiques and helpful suggestions at various stages of the research. John Gerring and Marc Morjé Howard each read multiple versions of multiple chapters and working papers and they have both been great friends and colleagues from start to finish.

I received feedback on working papers and chapters at a number of conferences and seminars. In 2003, I joined the Laboratory in Comparative Ethnic Politics (LiCEP) working group, and I am grateful to all members of that group, both for their comments on my work and for setting high standards of scholarship: Kanchan Chandra, Christian Davenport, James Fearon, Karen Ferree, Elise Giuliani, Michael Hechter, Macartan Humphreys, Stathis Kalyvas, Nelson Kasfir, David Laitin, Ian Lustick, Dan Posner, Nicholas Sambanis, Ken Scheve, Pieter Van der houten, Jeremy Weinstein, Steven Wilkinson, Jason Wittenberg, and Libby Wood.

I further benefited from comments received during presentations and conferences both from formal discussants and audience members, including at the Africa Centre in Mtubatuba, South Africa, the University of Cape Town, the Robert Wood Johnson Policy Scholars conference in Aspen, meetings of the American Political Science Association, the International Political Science Association, the Center for the Study of Democratic Politics at Princeton, the Princeton Comparative Politics Working Group, the Harvard Center for European Studies, the Watson Institute at Brown University, the Center for Latin American Studies at UC Berkeley, Stanford University, the University of Pennsylvania, Georgetown University, George Washington University, Yale University, Columbia University, the Mailman School of Public Health, the Johns Hopkins School of Advanced International Studies, the NYU Wagner School of Public Policy, the World Bank, and the University of Toronto.

I have been helped by research assistants—students at Yale and Princeton—who were a pleasure to work with. Many of them will not see the fruits of their labor in this book, because I sent quite a few down proverbial wild goose chases, but their good work is appreciated nonetheless. These include Eleni Azarias, Rashad Badr, Victoria Chang, Sarah Chartock, Stefana Constantinescu, Nalini Gupta, Rachel Jrade, Eva Kaye, Paulina Kubiak, Rebecca Lowry, Justin Mirabal, Dipali Mukhopadhyay, Petra Nahmias, Viany Orozco, Ryan Sheely, and Christina Shim.

I am grateful to Chuck Myers of Princeton University Press for having approached me to consider publishing this book, and for his encouragement and support along the way. Anonymous reviewers provided excellent feedback. Thanks also to Richard Isomaki for careful copyediting, Dimitri Karetnikov for help with the tables and figures, and everyone involved in production and distribution at the Press!

It is no surprise that a work that has been such a central part of my professional life also intruded into and made demands upon my own personal life. Not to sound ungrateful to them, but this book would have been completed much sooner, and perhaps with greater acumen, had it not been for the additions of Gideon and Jonah. The trade-off was certainly worthwhile—they have each made my life more full than I could ever have imagined, and for that, this book is dedicated to them.

I am extremely lucky to have a wonderful family. My parents and my in-laws and many other relatives have cheered me on in my endeavors, and helped us to care for the boys during this period, which in turn provided opportunities for me to complete my research. Without Amy, it would be hard to imagine how almost anything would be possible. She is always a fantastic sounding board for my ideas, and a source of steadfast encouragement and love. Listening to me as I wrestled with ideas and evidence all of these years cannot have been all fun, but she always did this with a smile. You will all be called on again for similar support for the next project.

Parts of chapter 4 previously appeared in Varun Gauri and Evan S. Lieberman, "Boundary Politics and Government Responses to HIV/AIDS in Brazil and South Africa," in volume 31, issue 3 of the journal *Studies in Comparative International Development*, published by Spring Science and Business Media LLC, New York, USA. This and other articles published in this journal can be found at www.springerlink.com. Parts of chapter 6 previously appeared in Evan S. Lieberman, "Ethnic Politics, Risk, and Policy-Making: A Cross-National Statistical Analysis of Government Responses to HIV/AIDS," in volume 30, issue 12 of the journal *Comparative Political Studies*, published by Sage Publications.

Boundaries of Contagion

1 ⁊ Introduction

"AIDS knows no boundaries." For much of the history of the AIDS epidemic, activists and officials around the world have repeated this incantation. As one diplomat described AIDS, "It discriminates against no ethnicity, no gender, no age, no race, no religion. It is a global problem that threatens us all."[1] From a strictly biomedical standpoint the claim is accurate. In 2006, UNAIDS, the lead international organization for AIDS control, estimated that approximately 65 million people—men and women, young and old, rich and poor, black and white, Christian and Muslim, from every continent and virtually every country—had been infected with the human immunodeficiency virus (HIV) between 1981 and 2006. An estimated 25 million people had died from the constellation of infections and ailments that comprise the syndrome known as AIDS. If ever there was a crisis that revealed the shared vulnerability of humanity, this was it.[2]

And yet, because the transmission of HIV is a social phenomenon as well as a biological one, boundaries have proven to be incredibly important. At almost every level, leaders and ordinary citizens have interpreted the deaths and illnesses associated with the global pandemic in terms of ethnic and national groups. In 1988, the Panos Institute produced a small volume

---

[1] William J. Burns (U.S. Ambassador to Russia), "AIDS Kills Irrespective of Nationality," *Izvestiya*, December 1, 2005, posted at http://moscow.usembassy.gov/embassy/print_statement.php?record_id=24 (consulted June 12, 2006). Virtually identical phrasings have been articulated by activists and leaders throughout the history of the epidemic.

[2] UNAIDS 2006, 4.

entitled *Blaming Others: Prejudice, Race, and Worldwide AIDS*,[3] which contained news reports and short essays identifying the worldwide prejudice associated with AIDS. In a thoroughgoing scholarly analysis, Cathy Cohen has documented how race has influenced the politics of AIDS in the United States, arguing that the historical marginalization of African-Americans produced a deafening quiet in political reactions to this stigmatized disease.[4] The renowned scholar-activist-medical practitioner Paul Farmer has chronicled the dynamics of blame associated with prevalence of AIDS among Haitians, which in myriad ways has been associated with the politics of race.[5] Throughout the history of the epidemic, even as millions fell ill and died, leaders and ordinary citizens have claimed that AIDS was a "foreign" scourge and someone else's problem. Although evidence of global contagion was reported soon after HIV was isolated, many government leaders and citizens around the world clung to the idea that geographic, social, and political boundaries would insulate them from the contagion. Such ideas often stifled aggressive action against the disease. Unlike microbes, people are keenly aware of boundaries, and successful political leaders—elected and otherwise—manipulate group boundaries to maintain support and stay in power. Tragically, the will to political survival has often led to the underprovision of public policies that might have meant human survival in the face of a viral pandemic. Since AIDS was perhaps the single most important threat to human development in low- and middle-income countries at the start of the twenty-first century,[6] the substantive implications are enormous.

To argue that AIDS has been associated with a politics of blame and group prejudice is hardly a novel proposition.[7] This book breaks new ground by offering a more careful analysis of how and why the boundaries that divide groups from one another have affected patterns of policymaking around the world. In so doing, it provides more general insights about the relationship between ethnic politics, policymaking, and development. Specifically, it helps to explain why some governments have been more ag-

[3] Sabatier et al. 1988.

[4] Cohen 1999.

[5] See, for example, Farmer 1992.

[6] HIV/AIDS was the leading cause of death and disease burden among adults aged 15–59 in 2002 as reported in WHO 2003.

[7] For example, UNAIDS executive director Pieter Piot commented in a September 5, 2001, UNAIDS press release, "People with HIV/AIDS from minority ethnic groups are often blamed for their condition." Others have noted that HIV has often been disproportionately problematic among "those people who were marginalized, stigmatized, and discriminated against—before HIV arrived" (Mann and Tarantola 1996, 464).

gressive in responding to AIDS than others, and it estimates the effects of boundaries on policies relative to other influences. My analyses reveal that the relationship between ethnicity and public policy is channeled largely through political competition over the social status of ethnic groups and the propensity to view risks as pooled, a departure from the existing literature on the effects of ethnic diversity and ethnic competition, which has emphasized problems of coordination; exogenously determined, heterogeneous preferences; rent-seeking behavior; and patterns of distrust.

Although the next chapter will more fully elaborate propositions linking boundaries to policies, a brief preview is in order. Boundaries are institutions that separate groups of people from one another. These include the internationally recognized borders that give shape to more than two hundred states and a few dozen territories around the world, and also the formal and informal practices and markers that reinforce a sense of group difference within and across countries. Boundaries vary tremendously in the degree to which they are recognized and enforced in their various manifestations. In some contexts, boundaries make group membership relevant and clear to almost everyone involved, whereas in other contexts, boundaries are shifting, ambiguous, and permeable. In the former, group identities are more fixed, while in the latter, they are more fluid and undifferentiated.

In a wide-ranging set of investigations, I have found that when countries have strong, internal boundaries dividing societies into substantial and recognizable *ethnic* groups, the epidemic is also likely to be understood in ethnic terms. In turn, this frame of reference becomes a political constraint on national policies to combat AIDS. In countries so divided, discourses about the risk of being infected and affected by AIDS are infused with ideas about ethnic difference. Ethnic conflicts intensify the near-universal political dynamic of assigning blame and attaching shame to information about the epidemic. As citizens and political leaders seek to avoid the group shame associated with a stigmatized problem, the effect is a dampening of potential support for AIDS policies, leading to weaker and slower responses. While AIDS may aptly be labeled the first disease of the era of globalization,[8] the persistence of state-level boundaries has meant that even within regions sharing common social and economic characteristics, resources and responses have been profoundly mediated by those in charge of national states. And those leaders have been sensitive to the politics that surround any major policy issue.

---

[8] Altman 1999; Barnett and Whiteside 2002.

To be certain, other factors have been critically important for policy-making. The extent of the epidemic in countries and regions; the resources available to the government; and the overall pressure to adopt policies from international actors and networks of activists have all been influential and are components of a general model of AIDS policymaking. Individual personalities and accidental historical circumstances have also shaped responses. But I approach the analysis of government responses to AIDS as a social scientist, in the sense that I identify general patterns and relationships that go beyond the particularities of any individual country's circumstances. In this regard, boundaries have been a central and underexplained influence on AIDS politics and policymaking, with dramatic implications for the course of human development. While I consider other drivers of politics and policymaking, I put a spotlight on the effect of boundaries.

This is a book about AIDS, but it is also about global politics and the interlayered process by which political actors attempt to govern and to transform people's lives through large-scale public policies. While the focus is on AIDS, this study is not an exhaustive account of the epidemic or of AIDS-related policies. It is not a book about why HIV/AIDS has hit some countries harder than others or which practices have been most effective for stopping it. In fact, I do not even assume that the most "aggressive" responses were the best responses from the perspective of maximizing human welfare. Generally speaking, for any given country more AIDS control was probably better than less, but my investigation does not rely on this assumption.

The more narrowly defined question I take on is this: Why have some national governments responded to AIDS more quickly and more broadly than others? More fundamentally, this is a question about the political origins of government effort, and the conditions under which a country's leaders are willing to take a stand on a politically sensitive issue for the sake of the longer-term development and well-being of its population. By focusing on boundary politics, I take up long-standing questions in the study of comparative politics concerning the effects of ethnic politics on the provision of public goods, and on development more generally. I attempt to wed political science theory and method to the study of public health. In so doing, I am inevitably drawn in to debates about the origins of authority and societal transformation.

In political science a puzzle exists when outcomes diverge from expectations. In this sense AIDS policy is a puzzle, for there is reason to have expected much more convergence in government responses to AIDS than we find.[9] While cross-country differences in policies on issues ranging from national health insurance to industrial development can be ascribed to accidents of history, including the timing of certain problems in particular countries,[10] AIDS has confronted countries worldwide more or less simultaneously, smack in the middle of an era of heightened global integration. In the relatively short span of two decades, HIV reached virtually every country in the world. Knowledge about how to prevent the transmission of HIV, and how to improve and to extend the lives of HIV-positive individuals, was identified early on, and has been disseminated around the world. Nonetheless, national governments have adopted a wide range of responses to the AIDS crisis, with dramatic consequences for the affected societies. To be certain, rates of infection and the resources available explain some of the cross-country variation. But even in a relatively rich, technically competent, and high-prevalence country like South Africa, the government responded slowly, and life expectancy has declined to levels not seen since the 1950s, largely because of AIDS-related deaths. In other countries, such as Brazil, the epidemic has been contained, and its effects are managed as well as, and in some cases better than, they are in the world's richest countries. Why have governments equipped with similar resources and similar information respond to the same biomedical phenomenon in such different ways?

The remainder of this chapter provides greater context for this and related questions by situating the problems of AIDS and AIDS policy in broader scholarly and policy-oriented concerns about states, governance, and globalization. I also detail the design of the research and provide an overview of the remainder of the book.

The Puzzle of Explaining Government Policy

The challenge of explaining responses to AIDS forces us to think more generally about why governments differ in their provision of public policies, public goods, and public resources that address the general welfare. What governments do, often in coordination with other partners, can have a huge impact on human development and well-being, particularly in the case of threats to public health. In the face of highly infectious and deadly diseases, such as the fever caused by the Ebola virus, governments

---

[9] For discussions of the factors that may drive or impede cross-national policy convergence, see Bennett 1991; Drezner 2001; Simmons and Elkins 2004; Dobbin 2007.

[10] See, for example, Gershenkron 1962 and Tuohy 1999.

in even the poorest of countries have been critical to rapid containment. But most public health threats do not receive such immediate and deliberate attention, particularly in resource-poor settings. In the absence of authorities who take responsibility for providing information and resources, disease can ravage societies, as markets and voluntary action alone may fail to provide the required coverage and action. By examining how and why different governments address a common problem in different ways, we can investigate seminal questions about the political dynamics of resource allocation and social control.

Some readers will question my focus on states, particularly in a book about a problem for which nongovernment actors have been so important. To be certain, other actors, ranging from transnational organizations to small communities, also affect health and well-being in the context of a viral epidemic, and many of them are considered in the pages that follow. And yet in the contemporary era, national states are uniquely positioned to broadcast information and to affect the behavior of people: they control the lion's share of public resources, and they are a site of negotiation and competition over a society's priorities. So long as states play a central role in societies and economies, we ought to investigate how and why they respond to important problems.

A study of governments and AIDS provides a lens onto the relationships between states and societies that lie at the core of the study of comparative politics.[11] We should assume neither that states will always take the lead in public health epidemics or other major social problems, nor that they will be inconsequential, corrupt, or absent. Instead, we need to consider how and why states adopt varied approaches for particular concerns. AIDS has implied a dramatic role for governments, just at a moment in time when state power appeared to be in retreat.[12] Many of the strategies for curbing the pandemic require that states intervene in the most private of matters: sexual conduct, drug use, childbirth and breastfeeding. The nature of the problem requires that political authority focus on bodily fluids, especially blood and semen, substances more amenable to deep metaphor than economic calculation. In the case of AIDS, state authorities have literally asked for blood[13] in order to test for the presence of the virus. Just as Charles Tilly explained war-making as the basis for the

---

[11] Migdal 1994, 11.

[12] Strange 1996.

[13] The invention of HIV tests that do not require blood samples has certainly facilitated the challenge of testing in recent years.

extension of state authority,[14] AIDS has provided a new exigency for state power, as well as for the powers of global governance. Some have described HIV as a security concern in the face of an "invisible enemy," and analogies to war have persisted among policymakers and scholars alike.[15]

By focusing on the politics, policies, and actions of national states, I risk contributing to a reified notion of state authority, which in practice is contested and varied across time and space.[16] Yet I acknowledge this governmental weakness and unevenness, because it is central to the questions I pose. The AIDS pandemic has provided states an opportunity to assert authority in their own territories and on the world stage. In an international environment in which national states remain the presumptive sources of authority, even if such authority fails to materialize in practice, we require an understanding of what shapes the exercise of power. Heads of state recognized by the international community have been pressured to act and cajoled with resources, and my concern is to understand their responses to these pressures. Within the state, influential actors vary in their inclination to adopt policies, depending upon their domain of authority and other personal and professional influences. I assume a partial coherence and autonomy in the state as policymaker, in the sense that we can characterize a "state response" for a period of time, one that reflects the decisions of those at the top of the pyramid of political power. I consider divergent or conflicting responses (more or less aggressive than that of the central government) by particular ministries or localities, as independent political actors with a potential influence on government decisions.

Understanding the politics of AIDS requires that we think about the challenge of gaining compliance and consent more generally. Most AIDS-related policies involve asking citizens to do things that they find undesirable, including wearing condoms, refraining from sex, getting their blood tested, and so on, and the benefit is an uncertain future nonoccurrence (i.e., protection from possible infection). Only late in the epidemic has treatment been part of the policy menu for most low- and middle-income countries. As a result of this ratio of effort to reward, publicizing and implementing AIDS-related policies created by the state in the private lives of citizens can be costly in monetary and political terms. Governments

[14] Tilly 1992.

[15] Ostergard 2002, 341; Peterson 2002.

[16] See, for example, within-country analyses on the variations in state power by O'Donnell 1994 and Boone 2003.

introduce policies related to sex, sexuality, and drugs at their peril. If citizens resent the message, they can challenge the messenger. In this sense, the political bargain over establishing an aggressive policy on AIDS is an instance of the state's attempt to gain conformity and sacrifice more generally, as in taxation, military conscription,[17] and other areas of social transformation, where states seek conformity through the imposition of new ideas, norms, and practices in order to promote "development." Vaccinations require succumbing to a shot from a uniformed medical worker, which may seem frightening.[18] Any major social policy, including the introduction of universal education, demands trade-offs and the reallocation of resources that might have been available for immediate consumption. Transformation often requires sacrifice, and in the development of public policy, actors may strike back when their moral or material interests are jeopardized.

A relatively simple explanation for cross-country differences in policy regimes is the catchall category of culture. That is, we could simply conclude that countries with "modern" cultures and values are more likely to embrace germ theories of disease and to use related technologies to combat viral spread. But if we were to classify cultures as modern according to their responses to AIDS, the proposition would be true by definition. It would be a tautology. Another approach would be to assess cultures in terms of potentially relevant beliefs, such as orientation toward "secular-modern" values,[19] but as it turns out, measures of those values don't do a good job of predicting which countries will take up AIDS policies aggressively and which will not.

As a political scientist, I am predisposed to look for the political underpinnings of choices in policy, especially in domains that might otherwise seem to be well guided by technical or biomedical science. I was therefore surprised to find that the comparative study of health and health policy in developing countries has received little attention from political scientists. Apart from a handful of important contributions, the study of AIDS and AIDS policy has been largely ignored.[20] The enormity of the HIV/AIDS

---

[17] See, for example, Levi 1988, 1997.

[18] Over time, vaccination policies seem less like sacrifices, once initial fears and stigmas associated with the procedure are overcome.

[19] See, for example, Inglehart and Welzel 2005, and their "cultural map of the world," available at www.worldvaluessurvey.org (consulted February 10, 2007).

[20] I review much of the existing literature on politics and policymaking on AIDS in the developing countries in chapter 2, as part of a discussion of alternative explanations. Pat-

pandemic is sufficient justification for anyone to devote time and attention to it. But AIDS is a social and political phenomenon, one of the most profound of the modern era, and deserves greater attention if we have a sincere interest in understanding how and why governments act, or ignore opportunities to act, to improve the human condition in their territories.

Explaining government responses to AIDS requires a comparative approach. Politics and policymaking rarely take place in a national vacuum, in isolation from the rest of the world. For a global problem, in an increasingly integrated world, with expansive global governance, external pressures shape the menu of possible responses and help determine which policies are selected from it. And yet transnational actors walk a delicate tightrope in exerting direct authority over peoples across the globe in a postcolonial era, when norms of sovereignty remain strong, even while many governments exercise little effective authority, and unmet needs are enormous. Any model of national government policymaking for an issue such as HIV/AIDS must take into account the role of transnational influences.

Thus, while the primary focus of this book is the effects of internal ethnic boundaries in national states, both the spread of the epidemic and the associated global response reflect the extraordinary movement of people, ideas, and resources across external or national boundaries. Perhaps no phenomenon reveals the interconnectedness of the world's peoples more than our very human susceptibility to disease, one that is passed on through behaviors associated with an innate desire and need for intimate contact—largely sexual contact and the process of childbirth. If national states are limited in their authority to transform people's lives, international organizations are even further restricted. In light of the now obvious potential to transmit disease across borders, societies depend on each other to contain the spread of infections, and donors have emerged with large sums of money to support national responses to AIDS. This global consensus heightens our expectation for action and universal conformity to scientific best practices. But in a world still largely governed by national states, "tackling" the global pandemic through deliberate policies and actions still requires state action, and this returns us to the question of why some governments act more aggressively than others.

---

terson 2006 is to my knowledge the only other explicitly comparative, book-length study of AIDS policy in the developing countries, carried out by a political scientist.

AIDS AS A LABORATORY FOR COMPARISON: POLITICS IN
  REALLY HARD TIMES

While the interplay of global and domestic pressures on policymaking
does complicate the task of providing a parsimonious explanation of government action on AIDS, the unfolding of the epidemic makes it valuable
as a case study of the politics of policymaking and state development.
From a social scientific perspective, the similarity of the problem for all of
the potential "subjects" (national governments) in the research implies a
rare degree of analytic control. A range of policies have been considered
by other scholars—policies on economic reform, pensions, health insurance, railroads, and labor, among others—but the set of developing countries affected by AIDS provides a unique laboratory in which to study the
possible determinants of policymaking.

Perhaps most important among the factors making it a valuable subject
of research is that the AIDS epidemic reached every region and virtually
every country in relatively short order. In a seminal work, *Politics in Hard
Times*, Peter Gourevitch argues that major transnational shocks and crises
are ripe for comparative social analysis:

> [They] are to countries what reagents are to compounds in chemistry:
> they provoke changes that reveal the connections between particulari-
> ties and the general. If the comparativist can find countries subject to
> the same stresses, it then becomes possible to see how countries differ
> or onverge and thereby to learn something about cause and effect.[21]

AIDS was a shock in the sense that it was unknown before the 1980s.
Existing social, economic, and political patterns can thus be treated as
largely exogenous, or independent, factors that might influence responses
to the disease. This is a critically important property because other social
scientific analyses of development outcomes—such as economic growth,
infant mortality, and more general social policy—may themselves be determinants of, as much as they are caused by, other macro-level variables.
While the AIDS pandemic also shapes these broader contexts, we can
carry out a "first-order" analysis of government responses and safely treat
these other factors as having been generated by processes independent of
the one we are trying to explain.

[21] Gourevitch 1986, 221.

The human immunodeficiency virus that causes the syndrome we now call AIDS existed prior to the 1980s. Blood samples taken in 1959 from the Belgian Congo (later Zaire, and more recently, the Democratic Republic of Congo) were later found to have been infected with HIV.[22] There may have been other infections in other parts of the world, and of course, such patterns are important for any full understanding of the spread of the virus. For the purposes of politics, however, the manifestation of these earliest infections was simply unexplained illness and death, generating no political response. The beginning of the history of AIDS is more appropriately dated to 1981, when the Centers for Disease Control (CDC) in Washington, D.C., reported the strange outbreak of a rare pneumonia and a rare skin cancer, Kaposi's sarcoma, among a handful of gay men in two cities in the United States. By 1985, a case had been reported in every world region, with virtually every country reporting a case by the early 1990s. The epidemic was initially reported among gay men in cosmopolitan cities in the wealthiest countries, but within a few years, the widest spread would occur in the developing countries, with most transmissions occurring through sexual contact between men and women.

Measuring and Interpreting the Size of the Epidemic

It is important to highlight at the outset how I measure and interpret the relative size of the epidemic across time and space. It is critical to clarify that I do *not* interpret either the share of the population (prevalence) or relative change in the numbers of new infections (incidence) as a proxy for the impact of government action. Doing so would require that we assume the consistent efficacy and immediacy of policies, neither of which I am prepared to do, given clear evidence to the contrary. Many other factors determine patterns of infection, and certain measures may have a counterintuitive relationship to a government's efforts to contain the disease. For example, effective treatment may boost the prevalence of AIDS relative to other countries because infected individuals live longer and remain potential sources of infection. A study of the impact of policies would require an entirely different form of research and analysis than what I have endeavored here.

[22] Iliffe 2006, 30.

Rather, the point of describing country-level trends in the epidemic is to provide some nuance to the claim that countries all faced the same shock. Regional and subregional patterns of infection have been distinctive, and any complete analysis must ultimately consider these differences. It certainly stands to reason (and I confirm empirically) that countries with bigger epidemics would respond more aggressively than countries with smaller ones.

Unfortunately, it has never been easy to identify reliable data on the number of people infected with HIV. Among other reasons, people have not wanted to get tested for the virus, they have not wanted to report their status, and governments and health facilities have not had the capacity to carry out testing. We do not know exactly how many people have been infected with the virus, but researchers and public authorities have estimated the number by extrapolating from smaller groups of people, just as in surveys of public opinion, and these estimates have been used for discussions of policy. In particular, the World Health Organization (WHO) and the United Nations AIDS agency (UNAIDS), as well as governments and ministries of health, have reported such data. While all surveys draw inferences from samples of a population, in the case of HIV/AIDS, the samples have been particularly *un*representative. (Only recently have governments authorized nationally representative surveys that actually *test* for HIV.) Most HIV data have been gathered from public health facilities, voluntary reporting, or focused collections of data among groups presumed to be at high risk for HIV. Not only are such groups not representative of the population at large, but inferences about how trends in these subpopulations are related to trends in the larger population have often been based on erroneous assumptions.

Late in 2007, UNAIDS announced significant revisions to its global estimates of the magnitude of the epidemic based on new data from surveys, as well as new models extrapolating from traditional samples of HIV infection. The estimated number of people living with HIV in 2007 was 33.2 million, whereas in 2006 the number had been estimated at 39.5 million. The report went to great lengths to explain that this difference was due mostly to revisions in the estimation procedures.[23] There is reason to believe that most estimates of prevalence previously reported could be improved with these recent procedures. In most cases, the relative ranking of country epidemics would not change, with the

---

[23] UNAIDS and WHO 2007, 3.

one important exception of India—a case discussed in more detail in chapter 5.

Such uncertainty about the size of the epidemic might seem to bedevil the entire social scientific enterprise of studying the AIDS pandemic in comparative perspective. In fact, this is not the case. For politics and policymaking what matters is not the actual number of infected people, but the information that is available to policymakers. For example, on the issue of environmental politics and policy, we do not know for certain what effect carbon dioxide emissions have on the ozone layer, climate change, or human development, and new evidence will almost surely suggest that scientists have under- or overestimated the precise threat. Nonetheless, contemporary political and policy action can be understood only in terms of what scientists have said up until the point that actions are taken. If we were trying to estimate a model of an outcome directly affected by the actual numbers of people infected with HIV, such as infant mortality or overall life expectancy, we would want the best available estimates, corrected retrospectively. Since politics and policy are the outcomes under investigation here, a better approach is to use estimates of HIV infections available during periods of policymaking.

As one source of data for comparative analysis, I have used time-varying estimates of infections provided in a WHO/UNAIDS map.[24] These data provide four consistent periods of estimates for almost all countries across the subject regions of Africa, Asia, and Latin America/Caribbean. These estimates are reported as wide uncertainty intervals, reflecting the low level of precise knowledge about numbers of infections, and I use the midpoints of these intervals as the basis of analysis. Again, if the goal of the analysis were to make predictions about health and epidemiological outcomes, this would be a faulty strategy, because we would want much more precise data. For the study of the politics of policymaking, however, these data provide the best estimates by technical experts on the relative size of the epidemics at different moments in time, which is the most relevant baseline for comparing policy responses. For 2003, more fine-grained data on HIV prevalence are available from UNAIDS 2006, and these correlate with the UNAIDS/WHO 2004 data at (Pearson's) $r = .96$. This suggests that even when using broad estimates of HIV prevalence, it is possible to sort out relative differences in the size of the epidemic extremely well, giving me confidence that we can use these data as the foun-

[24] UNAIDS/WHO 2004.

dation for comparing the epidemics faced by countries in the three developing regions.

These data are depicted graphically in figure 1.1. As measured by the share of the adult population[25] living with the virus (HIV prevalence), sub-Saharan Africa has been hit hardest, and by the mid-1980s, many countries in central Africa already had widespread epidemics. The African epidemic would become increasingly severe in the southern part of the continent, and by 2003, most southern African countries faced extreme epidemics.[26] Latin America, and especially several Caribbean countries, have faced epidemics, but no country in that region has faced an estimated prevalence in the double digits. Overall, HIV/AIDS has come latest to Asia, and there remains a great deal of variance in levels of infection in that region. A few countries in Southeast Asia, including Thailand, Vietnam, and Cambodia, were among the earliest to identify epidemics, and HIV has continued to spread throughout the region.

Implications of the Biology and Science of HIV and AIDS

For the most part, nuanced discussions of biology and immunology are absent from these pages, and I treat the AIDS pandemic as a single biomedical phenomenon. This is a necessary simplification of a complex reality. For example, there are multiple strains of the virus, and some are more virulent than others.[27] In the arenas where policies are set, however, these distinctions do not appear to have had any significant effect on the interpretations of AIDS, or on the range of prevention and treatment options available. Good clinicians know that individuals present viral loads and symptoms in a variety of ways and that best practice recommends approaches tailored to the individual. At the macro level of explaining government responses to AIDS, however, such subtleties do not figure prominently in the political calculus, and I do not consider them further.

[25] Infants and children also constitute a significant share of those infected by the epidemic, but because the most widespread testing and surveillance methods apply only to adults, no reliable cross-country epidemiological data exist for the youngest members of society, particularly for earlier years of the epidemic.

[26] See Epstein 2007 and Iliffe 2006 for discussions of why HIV has been so widespread in Africa, particularly in southern Africa.

[27] HIV-1 is more globally widespread, and HIV-2, which appears to cause less disease, is largely confined to West Africa. The reasons for these differences are not well understood (Smith 1998, 2).

Other facts and properties of the AIDS epidemic are worth highlighting because they shape the visible manifestations of an otherwise invisible virus, and have implications for politics and policymaking. First, as compared with many other viruses, there is a long interval (as long as seven to ten years or more) between infection and onset of the symptoms, a gap during which arguments over risk and the proper role of the state can flourish. In this sense, AIDS is a problem akin to environmental degradation or cardiovascular health, in that by the time one observes the manifestation of the problem, solutions are more costly and less effective than they would have been if it had been addressed earlier. Particularly where germ theories of disease are not universally accepted, a wide range of political interpretations of increased sickness and mortality may come into play, opening up contentious discussions of the proper role for government and "modern" science.[28] By contrast, in the case of fast-moving epidemics, such as SARS or Marburg, a swift government intervention, in coordination with international partners, is much easier to justify in political terms. While the time from infection to full-blown AIDS depends on factors including overall health and nutrition, in virtually any person who does not get tested, HIV is a silent killer that breaks down the immune system in an asymptomatic fashion over a very long time.

Second, the virus is contagious, but it is transmitted almost exclusively through intimate and deliberate acts. HIV gets transmitted through the blood, sexual fluids, and breast milk, primarily through extremely intimate human contact—particularly unprotected sexual relations and between mother and child, either through the process of delivery or breast-feeding. It can also be transmitted by the direct transfer of human blood, most often through blood transfusions or through the sharing of needles in medical facilities or among drug users. By far, sexual contact has been the predominant means of spread. Of particular importance, as compared with other viruses that are transmitted through breathing or sneezing or through food, these properties have important political implications because it is relatively easy to imagine and to discuss risk of infection as a matter of lifestyle. That is not to say that every individual has a full choice about lifestyle or sexual behavior—in particular, sexual violence against women is a leading route for infection—but the transmission routes allow citizens and political leaders to imagine infection as a choice (as contrasted, again, with SARS, for which infection may seem beyond one's control). Again, such characteris-

---

[28] See, for example, Ashforth's (2002) discussion of witchcraft in South Africa.

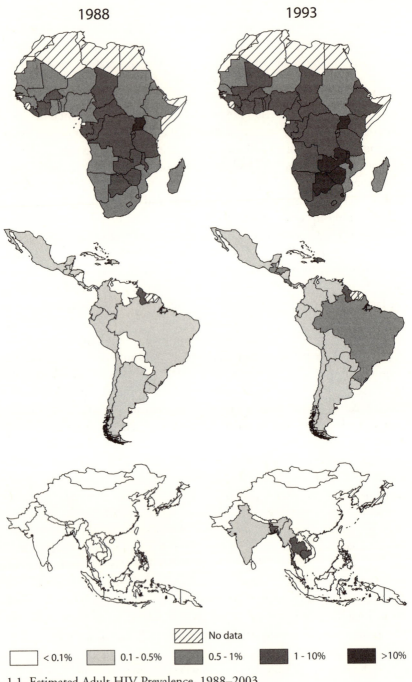

1.1. Estimated Adult HIV Prevalence, 1988–2003
Source: UNAIDS/WHO 2004.

1998   2003

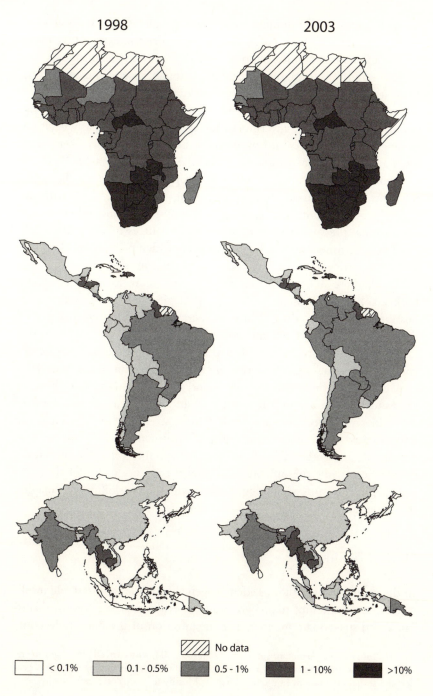

No data

< 0.1%   0.1 - 0.5%   0.5 - 1%   1 - 10%   >10%

tics do not make AIDS unique—other social problems such as poverty and unemployment are often understood in particular contexts to be choices, which can dampen political support for redistributive policymaking.

Because HIV is primarily transmitted through sexual contacts, and because it was first identified with homosexual contact, it has remained a stigmatized problem that elites and citizens have often preferred to ignore.[29] For that reason, government policymakers—particularly decision-making chief executives and ministers of health and finance—may view international best practices (what I describe in chapter 3 as the "Geneva Consensus") as a high-cost, low-benefit proposition, and may choose inaction as their preferred strategy. Increasing prevalence, along with domestic pressure from organized activists, physicians, and other groups, and external pressure from a wide variety of sources increases the likelihood of government action, but the impact of such pressures is likely mediated by particular social and institutional environments.

Third, there is neither a vaccination nor a cure for HIV or AIDS. Rather, as chapter 3 discusses, there are strategies for preventing the transmission of the virus, drug treatment therapies that improve and extend the lives of those infected, and policies for mitigating the impact of disease-related disability on the infected and their dependents. Despite ongoing scientific research, to date there is no viable plan to eradicate HIV or AIDS, as was the case for smallpox and polio. As a result, the effects of the pandemic can be mitigated, but HIV and AIDS will not be wiped off the planet until technologies derived from scientific breakthroughs are implemented. In fact, the availability of treatment options implies that people infected with HIV will live longer lives, increasing the prevalence of infection, while presumably increasing the quality of life of those infected. Thus, existing technologies allow only the possibility of managing the epidemic, not ending it.

OUTLINE OF THE BOOK

In the chapters that follow, I identify general theories and testable implications, and I attempt to analyze available evidence in a rigorous, skeptical, and dispassionate manner. The organization of the book reflects my

---

[29] See, for example, Aggleton, Parker, and Maluwa 2003, who correctly highlight the relationship between stigma and discrimination along dimensions including race, class, gender, and sexual orientation. In the next chapter, I justify my focus on race/ethnicity.

attempt to parse out theoretical claims from empirical analyses, and international dynamics from domestic ones. A brief overview will highlight how the analysis and evidence fit together, and provide guidance for those who may choose to skip ahead to a chapter of particular interest.

In chapter 2, I draw upon general theories of politics to develop propositions about how and why governments have responded to AIDS in different ways. I develop more fully the theoretical explanation linking boundary institutions to aggressive policies, through consideration of theories of ethnic politics, social identity, and the construction of risk. I also identify alternative hypotheses, including the effects of state capacities, regime types, and international influences, which help to guide the analyses, particularly by informing the choice of comparisons and control variables in the empirical analyses. While adjudicating among competing explanations of policy outcomes, I avoid investigation of the most proximate explanations. For example, it would be difficult to challenge the conclusion that a government adopted aggressive policies because those in charge of government policy acted aggressively, or that a particular president made AIDS a top priority. The relationship between cause and effect is so close that they are almost indistinguishable. "Leadership" cannot be understood as the "cause" since it is part of the outcome I am trying to explain. Instead, I attempt to make sense of key outcomes and seemingly anomalous events in terms of broader structures and factors, particularly ones that vary across space and time.

Chapter 3 details the globalized environment in which states have faced pressures to respond to AIDS. An elaborate international apparatus has developed to partner with and to cajole governments to respond to the epidemic aggressively and within guidelines. While the ultimate focus of the book is on politics and policymaking in developing countries, we cannot lose sight of the fact that most of the technology, resources, and push for AIDS policies has come from above, through massive efforts at global governance. My prior expectations for similarity in national responses is founded on research pointing to extensive consensus on best practice, as well as far-reaching efforts to disseminate that consensus to every country in the world.

In chapters 4, 5, and 6, I turn to the politics of policymaking in countries, through wide-ranging empirical analyses. The work was completed with a healthy awareness of the potential for bias or spurious findings in any particular approach, and with skepticism about how factors are measured and causal inferences drawn. I have tried to highlight the degree to which analytic findings are sensitive to particular interpretations. The research presented herein was a mixed-method enterprise, combining case study and statistical analyses. This approach allowed leverage over an eclectic array of data sources, and an ability to assess the robustness of my results. Only the most narrowly construed hypotheses are likely to have implications that can be decisively tested by any single research design or set of designs. And yet to the extent that the central explanation can help us to tell compelling narratives of particular countries, while providing a guide for estimating a robust statistical model of variance in AIDS policies, we can conclude that the general model provides real insights into the social and political dynamics of the problem.

Chapters 4 and 5 deploy case studies and structured comparisons[30] for generating and testing theoretical claims. While cross-country statistical analyses (discussed below) may be better suited to the estimation of the magnitude of effects, the generalizability of findings, and the analysis of multiple rival explanatory factors, case studies, conducted with attention to measurement in context, and to exploration of feasible causal pathways, also provide opportunities for evaluating general claims. We ought to be able to tell compelling narratives that link cause to effect, particularly for cases with extreme scores on the central explanatory variable. If we cannot identify a logic in the particularities of a case or set of cases that resonates with the more general theory, and if we cannot conclude that history would have unfolded differently with different scores on the explanatory variable, we lose confidence in our general claims.

On the other hand, we should not expect policymakers to specifically identify the political incentives and constraints on their actions in the terms presented in this book. Policymakers who have successfully addressed a problem such as AIDS are likely to highlight their own foresight and problem-solving skills, not the fact that they were unfettered by constraints faced by policymakers in ethnically divided countries. Most policymakers either defend their policies as appropriate and sufficient, or point to competing demands, or perhaps the morals and values of their culture, as constraints on further action. It is not appropriate to demand, as a test of a social scientific theory, that citizens or elites describe their

---

[30] For discussions of case study research, particularly in relation to multimethod research, see Gerring 2004, 2006; and George and Bennett 2005. I use a "nested" research design, that combines "model-building" and "model-testing" case studies with a statistical analysis, as outlined in Lieberman 2005.

behaviors with the theoretical framework.[31] If everyone were cognizant of the determinants of their behavior, there would be little need for social science. In fact, the policymaking literature has relied too much on actors as the source of explanations, when, of course, their perspectives are biased. My approach has been to look for traces of the consequences of ethnic-based conflict for AIDS policies, in the form of otherwise unexpected political resistance to them, comparing episodes where boundaries were weaker or stronger.

I examine boundary politics and AIDS policy in Brazil, India, and South Africa, cases that provide a wide range of variation in hypothesized cause and effect. Brazil has earned a reputation as an aggressive (and effective) responder to AIDS, whereas India and South Africa have been criticized for lackluster action. These countries are economic and political leaders in their respective world regions. Each has worn the dubious mantle of containing the largest numbers of infected citizens in its region, attracting a great deal of international attention. There would have been reason to expect aggressive responses to AIDS in all three countries because each had a significant viral outbreak, substantial industrial or governmental capacity, and a relatively open and democratic political regime. Compared with other countries at analogous levels of development and with similar epidemics, Brazil emerges as a relative overperformer and South Africa and India as underperformers. The goal of the analysis in this book is to see whether the location of these cases can be explained through a consistent political model of policymaking, or if they reflect unexplained "noise" associated with the random nature of social and political life.

The comparative analysis of AIDS policymaking in Brazil and South Africa presented in chapter 4 is a model-building analysis, in the sense that the explanation of differences in the outcome of interest was developed using "backward induction," subjecting the comparison to theoretically driven hypotheses about why Brazil developed a more aggressive response to AIDS than did South Africa. This puzzle was of particular interest because in my own prior research,[32] I was impressed by the simi-

---

[31] Hardin (1995, 12) makes a similar point in his discussion of rational choice theory—that even when people behave in a manner consistent with their own interests, they may not be able to describe it in such terms.

[32] Lieberman 2003. In chapter 4, I discuss why the outcomes for tax policy were exactly the opposite in Brazil and South Africa: South Africa developed the more progressive and efficient tax state, while Brazil's was more inefficient and regressive.

larities between the two countries in levels of economic development, social inequality, and racial diversity. These similarities formed the basis of fruitful comparative analyses. The importance of race politics in the discussions of AIDS in South Africa was evident to me prior to formal engagement with the materials in comparative perspective, and sustained comparative analysis suggested the mechanism linking "race" politics to aggressiveness on AIDS through the transmission of information and notions of risk. While the outstanding Brazilian response has been linked to many factors, including its democratic transition and vibrant civil society, those factors also appeared to be present in South Africa. What is striking in Brazil is that the weakly institutionalized category of race was not politicized for most of the history of AIDS, making possible a politics of national solidarity. In South Africa, discussions of risk, and a politics of blame and denial, broke down along racial lines, lowering demand for and supply of aggressive AIDS policies.

The Indian case was a model-testing analysis in the sense that investigation of the politics of AIDS largely followed the development of the theory. India shares similarities with Brazil and South Africa as a regionally dominant democracy facing an AIDS epidemic, with the capacity in the bureaucratic and private sectors to formulate a response. Like Brazil, it has a history of federalism. But like South Africa, India contains strong boundary institutions, and the national government did not respond aggressively to AIDS for most of the history of the epidemic. Beyond establishing this controlled correlational confirmation of the central hypothesis, the real test was to trace causal processes[33] and to see if I could find compelling evidence linking the hypothesized cause to effect. As I report in chapter 5, I found evidence connecting the country's ethnolinguistic, religious, and, especially, caste boundaries, to the politics of risk, and to patterns of blaming and shame avoidance, impeding a strong response. I also demonstrate with statistical evidence that variation in interethnic relations across Indian states helps to account for some of the variation in state-level responses to the pandemic in that country.

Analysis of all three countries is based on a wide range of case materials. First, I analyzed a vast library of documentation and data from governments and domestic and international nongovernmental organizations.

---

[33] Brady and Collier 2004 make a nice distinction between "dataset observations" and "causal process observations," but the strategy of "process tracing" is discussed elsewhere and extensively in the qualitative methodological literature, in addition to other forms of within-case causal analysis (e.g., Mahoney 1999).

The domestic and foreign presses have covered politics and policymaking extensively in all of these countries. Moreover, a significant secondary literature describes both politics and the AIDS epidemic in each country. I complemented these materials with targeted field research in Brazil, India, and South Africa (as well as brief stints in Uganda and Thailand) to gain additional information through open-ended, semistructured interviews and brief consultations with political elites, decision makers, activists, and bureaucrats; and to obtain additional materials not otherwise available. I attended dozens of lectures and seminars on these cases, including the two most recent international AIDS conferences (Bangkok 2004; Toronto 2006), where I listened to presentations and met with dozens of scholars, care-providers, government officials, and representatives of international organization doing work in these countries. For the most part, however, I don't detail insider accounts of AIDS politics and policymaking. In general, insiders have good access to data and to facts, which I have gathered in volumes, but their analyses tend to support their own political or other agendas, noble or not. Instead, I have relied on nonreactive measures, guided by involved actors in the search for facts and data verifying their assessments with additional evidence. As much as possible, I have used widely available news reports, documents, and publicly available data in order to maintain transparency.

While comparative analysis of these three important countries provides insights into the dynamics of AIDS policymaking, especially the ways in which ethnic boundaries shape political dynamics, such analysis leaves key questions unanswered. To what degree does the book's central proposition "travel" to other countries? Does it apply only to large, regional powers? Does the explanation I offer wishfully interpret the facts? In chapter 6, I present statistical analyses of a multicountry dataset, which helps to answer such questions, to adjudicate among alternative hypotheses, and to obtain estimates of the magnitude of the impact of boundaries on policy.

The domain of analysis was limited to low- and middle-income countries. To be certain, the industrialized countries have differed in their response to AIDS as well, as historians and social scientists have expertly documented.[34] But on substantive, methodological, and practical grounds, there is good reason to focus on the poorer countries, where more than 90 percent of the world's infected population lives, and where, by definition, the resources and institutions available for dealing with any threat to pub-

[34] For example, Bayer 1991; Bayer and Kirp 1992; Baldwin 2005.

lic health, especially one as difficult as HIV, are limited. The analyses presented in chapter 6 are analogous to a significant body of empirical work that has tested the effects of ethnic fractionalization on the provision of public goods and development across countries.[35] However, because those studies have considered policies and outcomes developed over long periods of time, it is difficult to know whether they are causes or consequences of ethnic politics. Because HIV/AIDS is a new and historically specific phenomenon, we can be certain that the outcome of AIDS policy is not endogenous to the explanation of ethnic boundaries, even if we assume that AIDS and AIDS policy will affect ethnic demographics and politics over the longer term. Overall, the statistical results confirm the central hypothesis, while bringing to light important differences across world regions and policy areas.

In chapter 7, I conclude by highlighting the ways in which the findings resonate with debates about identity politics, particularly among normative theorists. Scholars such as Amartya Sen and Anthony Appiah have emphasized the intrinsic values of combining cultural diversity with malleable institutional approaches to identity, and Appiah in particular makes an ethical case for cosmopolitanism. My positive empirical analyses emphasize the potential implications of such an approach for development outcomes. Permeable ethnic boundaries facilitate perceptions of interconnectedness and may help authorities to gain sacrifices for the public good. By contrast, the rigid institutionalization of ethnic difference impedes the pooling of risks, and encourages competition instead of cooperation. If well-intentioned international actors want to promote cooperative governance of global public problems, they would do better to promote cosmopolitanism than to strengthen ethnic boundaries.

---

[35] See, for example, Easterly and Levine 1997; Alesina, Baqir, and Easterly 1999; Posner 2004.

2 ᚬ A Theory of Boundary Politics and Alternative Explanations

In this chapter, I develop a general theory of how boundary institutions influence the politics of public policymaking. I draw upon social scientific theories of social identity and risk in order to enrich our understanding of the potentially negative effects of ethnic heterogeneity on the provision of public goods[1] and development. Using this theory, I detail more specific propositions about the relationship between ethnic boundaries and the development of national AIDS policies, which are explored through comparative and historical analyses in chapters 4–6. I also highlight alternative explanations of policymaking, and of AIDS policy more specifically, as the basis for comparison with the propositions I advance here.

The focus on ethnic boundaries is rooted in scholarly research investigating the relationship between ethnicity and development. With few exceptions, the conclusion in this research has been that ethnic diversity is bad for the provision of public goods, particularly those suited for longer-term economic development.[2] The implication, particularly in the African

---

[1] A strict definition of a public good is an outcome that is *nonrivalrous* and *nonexcludable*. The elimination or minimization of an infectious disease epidemic can be understood as such a good, even if the discrete policies designed to produce that outcome (for example, public provision of drug treatments) are themselves not public goods.

[2] A host of country and area studies analyses had long asserted the challenges of weak nations and ethnic political competition for the formulation and administration of effective public policy. See, for example, Young and Turner 1985; Sandbrook 1989; and

context, has been that the mismatch between national state borders and ethnic group loyalties—generated from patterns of colonial rule and African state formation—has resulted in a relative underprovision of growth-enhancing public goods, public policies, and good governance. Although the mechanisms described vary across studies, ethnic politics is usually understood to be a harbinger of corruption and predation, with a dearth of civic loyalty and citizenship. Similar arguments have been used to explain the relative underprovision of social policies and public goods in the racially diverse United States, when compared with other advanced industrial states.[3] A study examining hypotheses about the determinants of life expectancy and public health spending found that ethnic heterogeneity was negatively associated with both outcomes.[4] More generally, some have pointed to the negative effects of ethnic diversity on trust and the development of social capital.[5]

This body of research suggests consistent patterns, but the theoretical arguments do not apply to all forms of public policies. One prominent study identifies two mechanisms that lead to the underprovision of public goods in the context of ethnic diversity: ethnic groups have different preferences for which goods the government ought to provide; and each ethnic group's utility derived from a given public good is reduced if other groups also use it.[6] But in the case of HIV/AIDS, these propositions do not appear to hold: there is no reason to believe that any group would have an intrinsic preference for AIDS policies *ex ante*—that is, before they were aware of the magnitude of the problem in their group relative to other groups. Once information about group differences in infection levels is known, it would make sense from a rationalist perspective if groups with higher infection levels advocated more aggressive policy, particularly targeted at themselves, but the evidence shows that they behave otherwise (as will be demonstrated in subsequent chapters). In fact, many potential beneficiaries of AIDS policies have resisted them. Moreover, it is difficult

---

Joseph 1987. More recently, this argument has been supported with econometric analyses presented in Easterly and Levine 1997; Alesina, Baqir, and Easterly 1999; Miguel 2004; and Posner 2004. In the previous chapter, I highlighted the potential empirical shortcomings of such studies—namely, the strong likelihood of endogeneity—but in this chapter, I focus on what is missing from the theoretical accounts.

[3] Alesina et al. 2003; Alesina and Glaeser 2004; Gilens 1995; Lieberman 1998.
[4] Ghobarah, Huth, and Russett 2004.
[5] Putnam 2007.
[6] Alesina, Baqir, and Easterly 1999, 1244.

to advance the claim that a group's utility for AIDS policies would be depleted if another group were taking advantage of them. On the contrary, AIDS policies can be understood as "solidarity goods," in the sense that their utility increases to the extent that more people use them.[7]

Arguments about the negative consequences of ethnic diversity and ethnic competition also highlight the connection between ethnic loyalties and rent-seeking behavior—the collection of state resources by political elites for distribution to their supporters.[8] This phenomenon might explain why any public good would be underprovided, as resources are depleted in the distribution of rents, consumed as private goods. But by this logic, ethnic leaders of highly infected groups should have been actively seeking AIDS-related funds and programs for their own group as soon as such moneys became available, and again this is not what happened for the first decades of the AIDS epidemic. In fact, many leaders initially rejected offers of financial assistance on HIV/AIDS, saying they did not need it.

More generally, while a large body of evidence connects ethnic competition to the underprovision of public goods and development-enhancing public policies, I am dissatisfied with existing theoretical accounts of the link between these variables. They rest on the assumption that political actors, including individual citizens, act with the single purpose of enriching themselves, without considering the origins of policy preferences or group loyalties. The theories do not resonate with the practice of ethnic politics as a competitive and emotional dynamic.

I am more convinced that ethnic political competition is driven by the pursuit of esteem and status, that social and political action is not strictly "rational-instrumental," but imbued with social meaning. The nub of my argument is that boundary institutions, which give meaning to and reinforce ethnic group identities, shape the preferences of citizens and elites through mechanisms of information and group esteem, which in turn affect the political costs and benefits of providing public goods. When internal boundaries are strong, almost any issue may be interpreted in terms of the groups divided by those boundaries, irrespective of common need and benefit. In the case of policies that address ongoing dangers to citizens—such as AIDS—perceptions of risk are easily differentiated across ethnic groups, and such groups are more likely to engage in status conflicts over blame and victimization. These dynamics counteract other

[7] For a discussion of solidarity goods, see Sunstein and Ullmann-Margalit 2001, 132.
[8] See, for example, Ekeh 1975; Joseph 1987.

pressures for aggressive policies. Unlike explanations of ethnic politics that are rooted in individual self-interest,[9] the theory advanced in this book specifies that groups may provide important emotional attachments, and that interests can be understood in group terms.[10]

In the remainder of the chapter, I develop the logical foundations of this argument. First, I describe the concept of ethnic boundaries. Second, I specify the effects of boundaries on the demand for and resistance to certain public policies. Third, I detail the implications of the argument for understanding the politics of AIDS policies, and finally, I identify alternative explanations.

ETHNIC BOUNDARIES

Many accounts of the effects of ethnic politics on public policy begin with ethnic conflict or ethnic groups, but I highlight ethnic boundaries, because group formation is as much an institutional phenomenon as it is a demographic one.[11] That is, groups can be socially or politically relevant only when an institutional framework—formally or informally constituted—is available for mobilizing the boundaries between groups. In this sense, I build on the work of those who claim that institutions structure both cognitions[12] and policy priorities,[13] interacting with other social, political, and economic pressures. Specifically, the social and political significance of social groups in the political arena depends upon the boundaries that separate groups from each other.[14] Boundaries "signify

---

[9] For example, Hardin 1995. See Varshney 2003 for a discussion of the Weberian conception of "value-rationality" as a contrast to purely instrumental rationality, which is epitomized in Hardin's work. Varshney's identification of "dignity" and "self-respect" as motivations for ethnic behavior resonate with the mechanisms I identify of "esteem" and "status," associated with social psychological theories of intergroup conflict.

[10] To be certain, at particular moments in time, particularly in the face of major regime or state boundary changes, individuals may undergo periods of reflection and self-conscious choice about the identities they would like to adopt given various material and other incentives, as documented by Laitin 1998. However, for most periods, I assume that individuals understand their repertoire of identities as being fixed and make decisions about moral and material concerns *given* those identities.

[11] Barth 1969 provides a seminal statement on the study of ethnic groups as a concern for boundaries, rather than cultural content.

[12] Knight 2002.

[13] Steinmo, Thelen, and Longstreth 1995.

[14] Hechter 2000, 23. See Lamont and Molnár 2002 for a review of the the concept of boundaries in the social sciences.

the point at which something becomes something else . . . at which 'we' end and 'they' begin."[15] In this sense, "group-ness" is contingent upon the formal and informal rules that determine group membership, providing guidelines about who is in and who is out, constituting distinctive social identities.

I focus on group boundaries because they help to explain the origins of policy preferences. Rather than assuming that groups naturally emerge out of some form of cultural heterogeneity, and that those cultures define the values underlying preferences, I argue that the boundaries themselves influence how policies are framed and interpreted by citizens and elites. The relative strength of boundaries is consequential for calculations about policies with benefits that may not be realized for a long time and that are, as benefits *for individuals*, hard to calculate.

Groups can be constituted in multiple ways, for example by boundaries of class, gender, or age, but I am primarily concerned with boundaries that constitute ethnic groups. Weber defines as ethnic "those human groups that entertain a subjective belief in common descent because of similarities of physical type or of customs or both, or because of memories of colonization and migration."[16] Affiliations tied to phenotype/race, caste, ancestral city, tribe, or religion can be considered ethnic when membership is recognized at birth and understood as largely immutable. Regional identities can be considered ethnic when they are explicitly rooted in a shared culture and homeland, for which the costs of assimilation are nontrivial.

Of course, the traits that normally demarcate ethnic groups, such as skin color or language, may overlap and reinforce other boundaries, such as class, but I am primarily concerned with the impact of explicitly ethnic boundaries. I add the definitional point that ethnicity is a subnational identity. That is, if a group identity is coterminous with the boundaries of the national state, I understand it to be a national identity, not an ethnic one. This distinction is important because the theory is primarily about competition within the polity in which decisions are made.[17]

---

[15] Migdal 2004, 5. See also Tilly 2005.

[16] Weber 1968, 389. Horowitz's (1985) characterization of ethnic groups largely follows from Weber's, and is the basis for most comparative analysis of ethnic political competition in subsequent decades.

[17] For example, "Haitian" is an ethnic identity in the Dominican Republic, but not in Haiti, where it is the national identity in a largely homogeneous society. A titular

Ethnic groups are distinct from many other social groups because, when ethnicity is salient, people are much more likely to say that their connections and identities are fixed (even as comparative and historical research shows conclusively that they are not), unalterable over the long term, highly visible to others, and defining of close social networks, particularly networks of marriage and sexual contact. Ethnic groups have almost always been linked through metaphors of shared blood, and biological commonality, and such metaphors have legitimized claims about group interests. By the fifteenth century the Spanish term *limpieza de sangre*, or "purity of blood," meant being ethnically pure, without intermixture with other groups.[18]

I do not want to overstate the distinctiveness of ethnicity as a social category. In most societies in the contemporary era, the properties I have described may be more likely to characterize ethnic boundaries than other sorts, but other boundaries may have similar properties and effects. Other traits serve as important bases for social and political organization, but they have not commanded the same consistent and deep attachment across societies in modern times. For example, the material interests of individuals are highly differentiated according to age and gender in many countries. And while the interests of, for example, women or the elderly are often considered in political arenas, generational and gendered cleavages do not rival ethnic divisions as sources of organized political conflict. This is case because the social boundaries between these groups are virtually impossible to maintain for long periods of time: one's age is constantly changing; and intimate contact across generations and gender is a feature of all societies. Gender identities may be perceived to be at least as fixed as ethnic ones, but the boundaries between men and women are obviously of a quite distinct nature, given the ubiquitous intimate and social contact between them, and the near-universal fact of shared households.

Income or "class" distinctions are better candidates for strong social boundaries, in the sense that group membership is widely recognized and organized. However, lower-income people often have aspirations to higher economic status that are utterly unlike their long-term expectations about ethnic identity. (Parents may openly hope that a child will transcend their

---

identity—e.g., "Estonian,"—can be an ethnic identity so long as there is a sufficiently large and recognizable group of ethnic others—e.g., "Russians."

[18] Poole 1999, 360.

economic status; they are unlikely to proclaim a hope for ethnic switching.) While distinctions of income, wealth, and occupation are potentially powerful foundations for strong social boundaries, in the developing world they have been only weakly mobilized.

I focus on ethnic groups because there is substantial and observable variation in ethnic boundaries across countries, because a body of research lends credibility to claims of the systematic consequences of ethnic politics, and because my initial observations about the determinants of AIDS policies suggested that ethnic boundaries would be consequential. During the last quarter of the twentieth century, ethnic claims and conflicts were prevalent, though highly varied, in all regions of the world. Nonetheless, other social boundaries can have similar effects, and I discuss the effects of boundaries of class, gender, and sexual orientation in the empirical chapters.

Origins, Strength, and Number of Boundaries

Ethnic boundaries are created through a wide-ranging set of formal and informal institutions, and much scholarly research has highlighted the importance of state policies and institutions,[19] which often have enduring, path-dependent effects. For example, colonial strategies to distinguish Hutu and Tutsis made these identities salient in the successor states of Rwanda and Burundi, even after independence. Countries have varied widely in the degree to which ethnic boundaries have been institutionalized.[20] Formal boundary institutions—those created and implemented by the state—are developed because states, in their efforts to monitor and to regulate large and diverse populations, often require information about group identities to allocate rights and responsibilities according to prevailing policy. Such information has been used for a range of purposes— to deny privileges to certain groups of citizens (e.g., race-based slavery), to rectify past injustices, or to keep track of the cultural and socioeconomic composition of the society. While national states in the modern state system attempt to control large territories by building a sense of

---

[19] Laitin 1986 discusses the Gramscian notion of hegemony to indicate how states can help to forge commonsense frameworks about which identities matter for political life. See also Marx 1998; Nobles 2000a; Posner 2005; Brass 1994.

[20] Lieberman and Singh 2006.

political unity, such aspirations often conflict with claims to difference originating from the forced or voluntary mixing of people who have different cultural and physical traits, with international norms about the recognition of group difference and human rights, and with patterns of mobilization and demographic change in societies. In the face of such contradictions, there may be pressures to create or modify boundary institutions to emphasize or diminish the salience of groups. Unlike political entrepreneurs, I do not emphasize the specific contents of particular boundaries (i.e., the "cultural" differences across groups) but rather the strength of boundaries and their implications for the size and distribution of groups.

Boundaries are "strong" when the same group labels and categories are used across institutional forms, and when state-sanctioned labels and categories correspond with everyday racial or ethnic divisions.[21] Under such conditions, there are likely to be constraints on crossing the boundary, that is, switching identities. At the extreme, social and political organization in the form of political parties, access to citizenship, rights to employment, and so on, may be explicitly organized around group labels. Repeated violence perpetrated by one ethnic group against another and consistent use of ethnic labels in the dissemination of information are indicators of strong ethnic boundaries. Even in a single polity, laws may apply differently to different groups, and informal and sometimes formal rules discouraging or prohibiting sexual contact across boundary lines are likely. In practice, strong social boundaries may appear as extreme forms of social conservativism, as additional rules are needed to control the sexual habits of individuals.

By contrast, boundary institutions are "weak" when group labels are not used; or when they are used inconsistently or flexibly, and these inconsistent or flexible uses by the state correspond with a fluid use of the labels in society. Boundary institutions are likely to be weakened to the extent that interethnic associations are prevalent throughout society.[22] Societies may be characterized by weak or nonexistent boundary institutions because of deliberate political strategies to break down group divisions, often as the product of a nation-building strategy, including the

---

[21] See, for example, Huddy 2001, 133, for evidence of the effect of category salience on group identification.

[22] Varshney 2002 describes the prevalence of such institutions in certain Indian localities as important outlets for the mitigation of ethnic tensions.

effective development of a single national language. Sometimes, these are violent, and may involve the forced assimilation of small or weak minority groups. Moreover, because I am concerned with *internal* (i.e. subnational) boundaries, in the cases of full exclusion of a group—in the form of a fully autonomous reservation, where those on the reservation are completely removed from politics and society, and do not make claims on the central government—I do not include such groups as part of the unit of analysis.

When applied to ethnicity, the strength of boundary institutions is tantamount to social or political salience.[23] As scholars have pointed out,[24] ethnic identities are sociopolitical constructions, and neither a diversity of traits (religion, phenotype, ancestral origin) nor self-conscious ethnic groups (blacks, Muslims, Irish-Americans) necessarily imply that ethnic identities determine political loyalties and policy preferences. Indeed, Karl Marx's insight—that differences in people's location in the mode of production are not tantamount to class consciousness—applies also to ethnic consciousness. For the purposes of the theory being developed here, the relative strength of boundaries can be assessed at the level for which policy gets made: the informal boundaries that separate Dominicans from Puerto Ricans might matter in local districts in New York City, but not at the national level.

If boundaries are at least moderately strong, they fragment society into two or more identifiable groups. In addition to the strength of the boundary institutions, it is also important to consider the degree of fragmentation, or relative size and distribution of ethnic groups in the political unit for which policy gets made.[25] A society is highly fragmented when relatively strong boundaries separate many discrete social groups. If a single group constitutes the vast majority of the population—say 90 percent or more—then irrespective of the strength of boundaries that separate ethnic minorities, that polity is not described as fragmented.

Societies can also be divided by multiple ethnic cleavages. Indeed, individuals often have multiple and overlapping ethnic identities, let alone

[23] See, for example, Price 1997. Posner 2004 highlights the need to consider "political relevance."

[24] Weber 1968; Kasfir 1979; Horowitz 1985.

[25] This way of conceptualizing the division of ethnic groups is the more standard form, as described by Alesina et al. 2003. However, I still emphasize here the role institutions or boundaries play in the creation of those groups, rather than treating them as social "facts."

nonethnic social identities. Moreover, a person's repertoire of personal traits and history may offer an even wider array of *possible* identities. For the purposes of the model developed here, some of these identities may be local in nature and hence irrelevant for the larger political arena. An individual might consider herself both Irish-American and white, and both those identities might inform her thinking about, and participation in, politics. However, the category of Irish-American does not form part of a divide that is particularly relevant to national politics, and so in a consideration of politics at that level, the boundary that separates Irish-Americans from others is extremely weak. White identity, on the other hand, is constituted by a generally recognized racial boundary that has been highly institutionalized in the American polity. There may be more than one set of relevant ethnic boundaries in a country. For example, in India religion, language, and caste are meaningful ethnic boundaries for national-level politics and policymaking. Thus, societies may be divided by boundary institutions of varied strength and have varied degrees of fractionalization, with the size and distribution of groups differing along one or more cleavages.

Finally, it is important to highlight the mutability of boundary institutions. Conflicts, new ideas, and demographic shifts can change external and internal boundaries.[26] Nonetheless, for particular moments and places we can characterize the quality of boundary institutions and assess their effects on social and political outcomes. The theory I develop here takes boundary institutions as exogenous, while recognizing that the origins of such institutions remain of considerable theoretical and empirical interest.[27]

---

[26] Laitin 1998, for example, highlights the identity conflicts that arose following the redrawing of the Soviet map. Tilly 2005, 137–46, identifies several hypothesized drivers of boundary change.

[27] My theory of the effects of boundaries can be isolated from the factors that give rise to them. However, from an empirical perspective, we ought to be concerned if the factors that give rise to ethnic boundaries are plausible rival explanations for the determinants of government AIDS policies. Most theories of the origins of ethnic boundaries are largely historical and highly contingent (e.g., Marx 1998; Brass 1994 as relevant to the case studies in this book), and thus not usefully advanced as alternative theories of aggressiveness on AIDS policy. One recent contribution (Michalapoulos 2007) argues that variation in land quality was a determining factor of ethnic diversity, and further contends that this initial distribution, and not ethnic diversity, led to lower rates of economic development in many countries, especially in sub-Saharan Africa. While this may be true for economic growth, I see no plausible link between these initial factor endowments and the politics of AIDS policy, and thus do not pursue this factor in the empirical research in subsequent chapters.

THE EFFECT OF BOUNDARIES ON POLICYMAKING

So far I have described only the variation in ethnic boundaries; now I turn to the question of how boundaries shape the politics of policymaking.[28] I begin by thinking about policymaking as possible flows of attention from those who make decisions in the government. Government leaders have the option of doing something about a virtually limitless menu of topics. In response to a chosen problem they can allocate resources, make or remove rules and regulations, communicate in official terms its importance, and so on. Leaders try to stay in office, and all else being equal, they attempt to make policies that will be received favorably by society, or by the relevant actors upon whose support leaders rely to stay in office. Every day they are pushed and prodded to create new policies, but resources are limited, and leaders direct their efforts based on strategic calculations about returns to those efforts, with particular attention to political returns. Good policies, policies that maximize human welfare and development at a reasonable price, do not always provide political returns. Even the most technically or programmatically oriented government leaders realize that to make a difference, they need to stay in office. Those who are out of office also try to gain support. No leader, whether in a democracy or other form of political regime, wants to face resistance, particularly from core supporters. As for policies that involve sacrifice by citizens, leaders are aware that "quasi-voluntary" compliance[29] from citizens is needed if policies are to be effective and not too costly to administer. Leaders require a

[28] In Lieberman 2003, I related identity and policy variables in an analogous, but distinctive manner, explaining the effects of "National Political Community" on the development of taxation systems. A key similarity between that argument and this one was the idea that when, through institutional means, a notion of community could be constructed that imagined itself as homogeneous, or not differentiated, it was easier for the state to gain cooperation and compliance, as demands for sacrifice were thought to benefit "us." Potential collective action problems could be overcome because institutions shaped preferences, including time horizons, for groups thought to be united in terms of a racial identity. Although much of the logic applies to the model developed here, the specification of the community/identity variable is distinct. In Lieberman 2003, for the historical period for which variation in the explanatory variable was considered, significant racial differentiation and discrimination were present in the cases studied, and what varied was the extent to which states could exclude particular groups from citizenship. For the contemporary period relevant to the policy problem considered in this book, I assume that full exclusion is not possible, and what varies is the degree to which racial and other group differences are made salient through domestic boundary institutions.

[29] Levi 1988, 1997.

compelling narrative of the need to enact such policies, one that shows what might happen in the *absence* of such sacrifices and that resonates with the popular imagination.

I highlight two ways in which boundary institutions structure the demand for public policies by shaping interpretation of the problem to be addressed: Boundaries may affect perceptions and discourses of risk in politics and society, and they may cause members of social groups to focus on the status implications of being associated with the problem targeted by the policy. Indeed, there are other ways in which public policies may be influenced by ethnic politics. For example, many policies do not address risk-related concerns; and many are not relevant for social status. But risk and status characterize a great many policies, and certainly characterize those that address the challenge of HIV/AIDS. These propositions are probabilistic in the sense that not all problems map onto ethnic boundaries, but when boundaries are strong, there is a good chance that problems and solutions will be considered in ethnic terms. This is not to say that explicit labels will be used in open political discourse, but that long-standing repertoires of identifying problems in stratified terms will be repeated, and that the prospects of identifying collective interests—a "public good"—may be jeopardized because of the propensity to categorize and differentiate costs and benefits.

Perceptions and Discourses of Risk

New policies and state capacities develop in response to new threats, for example, the threat of war.[30] The magnitude of such threats can appear objective when conveyed in technical terms, but scholars agree that risks are themselves social and political constructions.[31] Even if quantitative and scientific evidence is available, the perception of risk—beliefs about the likelihood of the negative consequences in a set of events—is fundamentally political. When policy is considered in the political arena, what matters most is how risk is *described*.

---

[30] Tilly 1975, 1992.

[31] Mary Douglas's brilliant works that identify risk as a social, political, and cultural construction have been enormously influential here. See, for example, Douglas 1992. More recently, Paul Slovic's research in risk analysis has helped to advance our identification of the distance between "objective" and "subjective" accounts of risk. See, for example, Slovic 1999; Slovic et al. 2004.

Influential members of society and polity may describe the same danger as small or large, as concentrated or widespread, as a random act of nature or the result of deliberate human behavior. Presented with the same facts, two actors may understand them in completely different ways and take different actions. In political contexts the idea of risk is more than a statement of the probability that something will happen; it is presented in a narrative that may include an explanation of why danger is imminent, who is threatened, and where blame for the danger is distributed.

Responses to a threat that involve the state's extension of authority need justification, typically through accounts of what would happen without intervention. As Constance Nathanson argues, "Adoption and implementation of public health policies require culturally credible constructions of risk to the public's health."[32] The dissemination of ideas about risk is easily politicized and may gain momentum from, or be derailed by, social and political conditions. Not all information circulates through public channels; individuals can observe directly the fate of others, and such experiences drive perceptions of risk, but this information is still mediated by influential actors and institutions. In this book, I focus on *discourses* of risk—that is, the open discussion of, and attention to, risk by political actors. Talk of threats among individuals is likely to correlate with their perceptions of risk, but the latter can influence policy only if they are publicly articulated.[33] Moreover, individual perceptions of risk are extremely difficult to measure.

Lacking good information about their own risk from public threats, individuals tend to seek information in terms of group membership, asking, "Are people like me going to suffer?" Information flows in many ways, but when boundaries are well institutionalized, group heuristics, that is, methods of understanding that rely on social categories, are important. More specifically, when they are short on information, people tend to think in ethnic terms. As Kanchan Chandra points out, contexts of "limited information . . . bias observers who are distinguishing between individuals toward schemes of ethnic categorization."[34] In the broader political arena, political elites and information brokers (the media and state

---

[32] Nathanson 1996, 611.

[33] By contrast, studies of individual behavior are more likely to focus on individual-level perceptions of risk because of the more obvious proximate connection.

[34] Chandra 2004, 33. Though Chandra as well as Posner 2005 demonstrate that people seek out ethnic information for elections, it is plausible that people will seek out such information for everyday risks.

agencies that collect and disseminate information) tend to discuss risks, costs, benefits, reputations, and behaviors in terms of established groups and identities—that is, not in terms of the behaviors that create risk, but in terms of groups associated with these behaviors. This tendency suggests that the social construction of groups has an impact on understandings of risk, and of political preferences more generally.[35]

When ethnic boundaries are strong, discourses of *shared* risk and reward *across* groups are less common. Truly external threats (for example, of a foreign war against the nation) may increase the salience of external boundaries and increase the propensity toward risk-pooling, but when social problems are understood in more local terms, strong boundary environments make this pooling less likely. For example, in an ethnically divided society it would probably be more difficult to gain national support for a policy providing relief from natural disasters if it were understood that the only group vulnerable to such disasters is an ethnic minority.

When the costs and benefits of addressing risks are unclear, boundary institutions provide convenient reference points for processing information. When internal boundary institutions are strong, preferences and strategies are likely to conform to these lines, and political entrepreneurs are likely to seize on these labels. In fact, their first instinct may be to look for differences between ethnic groups as a basis for political competition. Moreover, societies with strong boundary institutions have routine strategies for labeling and differentiating problems by social groups.

On the other hand, when internal boundaries are weakened—such as through nation-building strategies—ideas about collective welfare and interdependency are more likely to extend to the wider citizenry.[36] Unlike arguments that analyze nationhood or patriotism, however, I highlight the effects of *nation-dividing* institutions (internal boundaries) on preferences and policymaking. The distinction is important because in the theory presented here, weak subnational boundaries have similar effects regardless of national attachments, even though the strength of subnational ethnic loyalties tends to be inversely related to national ones.

---

[35] As Brubaker 2004, 70–71, describes, the creation and reification of ethnic categories facilitates cognition in making sense of experiences, events, and information.

[36] Miguel 2004, 338–39, makes a similar set of points about the development of "tastes" and interethnic contacts.

Strong boundary institutions may reduce intergroup contacts and exchanges, but, more important, such institutions promote the perception of limited cross-boundary contact. They reinforce the idea that ethnic groups are coherent, and that any problem or solution may be grasped in terms of those groups. When the state asks questions about ethnic identity and reports information or frames policies in such terms, citizens soon believe that social conditions and associated policies will affect them *as* members of groups, perhaps in conflict with the fortunes of other groups. In the case of health problems, state policies may include reporting on epidemiological and behavioral patterns of groups, which may lead citizens to believe that group labels are meaningful biologically or in some other deep sense. Even if social problems do not map onto existing group boundaries, or if officials opt against reporting data according to group categories (often because they would be politically explosive), those who manage information in societies with strong boundary institutions use group heuristics. Alternatively, when boundary institutions are weak or permeable,[37] individuals are more likely to believe that interethnic contact is common, and they can more easily imagine that risks are shared across groups. At the very least, information about the risks for any single group becomes costly to obtain, and pooled risks become more apparent.

Social Identity and Status

A second, related mechanism through which boundaries may influence preferences for public policies is the dynamic of *intergroup competition*. A consistent finding in social identity research is that people strive to maintain a positive social status, particularly through comparisons with relevant "outgroups."[38] Because of this in-group bias, when their identities are unfavorable, people try to leave their group, find a more positive identity for it, or "reverse the relative positions of the in-group and the outgroup on salient dimensions."[39] According to this theory, and in contrast to the instrumentalist paradigm that imagines ethnic groups as *vehicles* for achieving material or political objectives,[40] the status of the group itself is

[37] Lamont and Molnár, 2002, 186.
[38] Allport 1954 provided the seminal statements about group prejudice by advancing the idea that people have a strong tendency to form ingroup attachments, particularly relative to outgroups.
[39] Tajfel and Turner 1986, 19; see also Brown 2000, 747.
[40] See Bates 1974; Posner 2005.

valued. This understanding of human motivation has gained currency among social scientists, and even economists have relaxed the standard assumption that individuals maximize their utility and highlighted the reflexive nature of preferences and their basis in one's identity relative to others. George Akerlof and Rachel Kranton, for example, argue that identity can help account for seemingly irrational or self-destructive behavior, noting the importance of a sense of self relative to others.[41] These findings can be applied to policymaking, as ethnic political leaders often promote the image of their group as a moral community.[42] Under conditions of competition between groups, they are likely to interpret risks, costs, and benefits so as to increase their esteem relative to other groups. Group leaders attempt to avoid shame and to assign blame[43] to other groups. The very identification of risk—the chance that something bad may happen to oneself or one's group—may be experienced as a damaging social psychological phenomenon. Although denial of profound problems may do harm in the longer term, and may appear irrational to an instrumentalist theory that considers individuals in isolation, such personal and political responses are consistent with social identity theory. My point is not to claim that people are prone to individually self-destructive behavior. Rather, it is that the valued good of a group's esteem may trump the material interests of its members.

While one might interpret group conflict as a matter of competing interests rooted in material conditions, a powerful finding from social psychology is that such interests are not always the root of competition: "Not only are incompatible group interests not always sufficient to generate conflict . . . but there is a good deal of experimental evidence that these conditions are not always necessary for the development of competition and discrimination between groups."[44] Even when members of an ethnic group are not bound by a shared interest—through an ethnic division of labor, for example—"groupness," as given by formal and informal boundaries, can provide a framework for interpreting one's social reality.

Not all policies have implications for a group's social status, but some clearly do. When ethnic boundary institutions are strong, an ethnic group

---

[41] Akerlof and Kranton 2000, 2.

[42] See, for example, Davies 1982 on how ethnic jokes reveal underlying moral competition across social boundaries.

[43] Gilens 1995, for example, argues that part of white resistance to welfare policies in the United States is "blame" for inequality resulting from lack of black work effort.

[44] Tajfel and Turner 1986, 13.

is more likely to resist policies that emphasize its social pathologies. Leaders of the group identified with social problems may resist policies to address them, simply to avoid the shame of association. And other groups will try to distance themselves from the one linked to the threat.

In certain cases, it may be possible to interpret such behavior in instrumentalist terms, as the pursuit of a credible reputation, which determines other material rewards. Appearing morally or otherwise reputable may help group members to accrue other benefits, such as better-paying jobs. On the other hand, when social problems go unchecked because of shame avoidance, the strategy may backfire by increasing perceptions of a group's links to a threat, exacerbating differences between groups and the potential for further conflict. Thus, even when the analyst considers payoffs over a long time horizon, the evidence may not support a theory that understands group behavior as the maximizing of individual benefits. My point is that when boundary institutions are strong, esteem is likely to be paramount, with self-harm as a possible consequence. In particular, the likelihood that political leaders will publicize a threat may be strongly conditioned by its implications for social status.

Responses by Policymakers

If national policymakers (such as heads of state, cabinet members, and legislative leaders) tend to act in response to demands, and to avoid actions that generate resistance, the foregoing discussion highlights why they are likely to deal with stigmatized problems less aggressively in ethnically divided societies. In such societies, leaders of ethnic groups are, virtually by definition, critical sources of political support. For reasons already described, such leaders are likely to underplay stigmatized risks to their constituency and are unlikely to demand, and may even resist, policies that respond to them. Government leaders—anticipating such resistance—are less likely to promote such policies, and are more likely to minimize risks. They may use shame-avoidance to deflect attention. Specifically, they may blame marginalized groups who lack political value or those outside the polity (foreigners), as the source of the problem (if it is accepted as real) or as conspirators in manufacturing its myth (if it is not). In so doing, they may engage in scapegoating,[45] deflecting attention onto groups who are

---

[45] See Gibson and Howard 2007 for a discussion of "scapegoat theory" in social science research.

not part of ethnic boundary conflicts. All else being equal, policymakers will respond less aggressively to the problem than if ethnic competition were *not* present.

IMPLICATIONS FOR AIDS POLICY

In sum, ethnic boundaries are likely to restrict AIDS policymaking for several reasons.[46] First, viral threats like AIDS can easily be *interpreted* as a "selective bad" that affects certain groups and not others.[47] (Compare the threat of nuclear war, which would so obviously do harm without regard to ethnic boundaries.) Moreover, because of the stigma associated with HIV and AIDS,[48] we can assume that groups consider ties to the epidemic detrimental to their relative status. Because HIV is associated with blood, it takes on deep connotations for descent-based (ethnic) groups. Disease is often a marker of deviance or impurity, and the role of blood in the epidemic intensifies the stakes of infection. In a biological sense, blood may be infected or "pure." Socially and politically, the "purity" of a group is tantamount to cohesion and power, and to the self-esteem the group strives to attain.[49] From this perspective, accepting that AIDS affects one's own group may lower one's status: it reduces the value of one's social identity by contradicting the affirming narratives associated with social group competition—for example, the narrative of the innocent victim.[50]

Second, during much of the AIDS epidemic, most people in the developing world have lacked access to individualized information. Testing

[46] Barnett and Whiteside 2002 and UNAIDS 2005 both make references to the importance of "unity" and "social cohesion" in addressing the pandemic, and the latter highlights the negative effects of ethnic divisions. I attempt to theorize more systematically about and empirically examine such intuitions.

[47] I am grateful to an anonymous reviewer of the manuscript at Princeton University Press for suggesting the idea of "divisible" or "selective" bads.

[48] Gilmore and Somerville 1994; Aggleton, Parker, and Maluwa 2003.

[49] Brewer 1999 identifies notions of "moral superiority," "perceived threat," "common goals," "common values and social comparison," and "power politics" as factors that may contribute to ingroup love and outgroup hate.

[50] Although Cohen's (1999) account of black political responses to AIDS in the United States was not framed in terms of social identity theory, her analyses highlight the role of blaming and shame avoidance. While sympathetic to her account, I propose that the dynamics of group competition do not, as she contends, apply merely to the marginalized, but to groups with varying levels of economic and political power who seek to maintain a positive social identity.

has not been widely available, and most people have been reluctant to learn, let alone disclose, their HIV status. Thus they have not known whether they should be concerned with the risk of becoming infected or with the risks that come from already being infected. Under such circumstances, group identities provide a simple if highly imprecise way to gather information: either my group is at risk or it is not. Scholars have demonstrated that perceptions of risk, including infection with HIV, are structured by the social networks in which perceptions are embedded.[51] In turn, we should expect that preferences about policies that address the epidemic to be so structured. A central aspect of ethnic identification is common origin and common destiny. Future benefits are discounted if one believes they will go disproportionately to "them"; alternatively, these benefits are more valued if one thinks they will benefit "us," particularly if there are accepted rules for thinking about costs and benefits along ethnic lines.

Third, since early in the epidemic, HIV/AIDS has visibly affected both poor and rich. The rich countries were the first to be identified with AIDS, but then it exploded in the developing world. Unlike many other health problems, the relationship between HIV incidence and socioeconomic status is mixed: poverty creates vulnerabilities to infection, particularly for women, but the contacts associated with greater income and travel also tend to increase vulnerability.[52] That is not to exclude the effects of class politics, but to point out that AIDS policy is not explicitly downward redistributive, in the manner of poverty grants, or the provision of basic maternal health care. Therefore, we should not assume that interests or preferences for AIDS policy will line up along class lines.

Finally, because ethnic groups tend to be spatially concentrated, and because the epidemic tends to be initially concentrated in certain regions, an initial ethnic imbalance in infections and AIDS-related mortality and morbidity is likely. In the context of strong and multiple ethnic group boundaries, individuals located in groups not yet identified with (or less identified with) the pathogen are more likely to believe that their families, partners, and regular social contacts are insulated from "contaminated" ethnic groups. HIV is largely spread through direct, intimate contact, and

[51] Kohler, Behrman, and Watkins 2007.
[52] Fore example, Misrha et al. (2007) find in a study of eight sub-Saharan African countries that wealthier men and women are just as likely to be infected with HIV as poorer adults.

when ethnic boundaries are a social barrier, they can be understood as a prophylactic against contagion.

Are the effects of ethnic fragmentation linear? On this question scholars have reached conflicting conclusions. On the one hand, more fragmentation might increase the challenges of coordinating collective action; on the other, a multiplicity of groups might reduce the polarizing effects of differences between them, increasing cooperation among groups. In interpreting the risks and status implications of a largely hidden viral infection that affects a minority of the population, I predict a linear relationship. So long as the boundaries separating groups are strong, increased ethnic fragmentation is likely to multiply the effect of boundaries. A study by Bisin and Verdier presents a formal model and draws on empirical evidence to argue that as minority groups become smaller, they search more intently for homogamous marriage.[53] The logic is straightforward: given a desire to transmit one's own cultural traits to children, minorities prefer endogamy because in heterogamous marriages social pressures lead to more transmission of the majority group's traits. If this is true, in increasingly ethnically fragmented societies there will be greater efforts among a larger share of the population to practice endogamy, as a larger share of the population is from a minority group. Because my theory concerns the politics of policymaking, I address only normative preferences for endogamy and perceptions of the practice of endogamy, not the impact of endogamy per se.[54] Moreover, as levels of fragmentation increase, it becomes increasingly plausible for members of any single ethnic group to imagine the problem as belonging to some other group from which they are insulated. Fragmentation increases the number of distinctions that can be made between groups that are at risk and those that are not.

The central prediction from the preceding discussion is that ethnic boundaries will affect how AIDS is interpreted and combated in the political arena (see figure 2.1). It is not necessarily the case that groups will explicitly organize *as* ethnic groups to advocate or challenge the government's allocation of resources for AIDS (though they may sometimes do so). In fact, citizens and elites in societies with strong ethnic divisions often recognize that it is nonnormative to proclaim ethnic labels, even

---

[53] Bisin and Verdier 2000.

[54] As Hechter 1978, 305–6 points out, endogamy is an excellent indicator of the salience of ethnic group boundaries, but the impact of endogamy on politics is more a matter of perception, and I assume that where ethnic groups are politically salient, the norm of endogamy is promoted and perceived, even if not practiced universally.

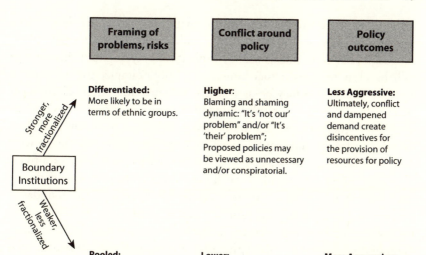

Framing of problems, risks	Conflict around policy	Policy outcomes
Differentiated: More likely to be in terms of ethnic groups.	**Higher:** Blaming and shaming dynamic: "It's 'not our' problem" and/or "It's 'their' problem"; Proposed policies may be viewed as unnecessary and/or conspiratorial.	**Less Aggressive:** Ultimately, conflict and dampened demand create disincentives for the provision of resources for policy
Pooled: More likely to be understood as national or general concern.	**Lower:** Potential denial not exacerbated by pre-existing divides and social competition.	**More Aggressive:** Other constraints still factor in, but identity based conflicts do not impede policy-making.

2.1. The Effect of Boundary Institutions on the Politics and Policies of Stigmatized Social Problems

while they are used to understand social and political environments.[55] Instead, euphemisms and heuristics communicate the ethnic correlates of information. Thus, we cannot test my argument by examining how people consciously and explicitly account for their own actions and preferences; we must look more generally at how policies and problems are framed and linked to broader patterns of ethnic group politics.[56]

Holding all else constant, in societies with *stronger* boundary institutions, information about the epidemic is more likely to be disseminated in terms of ethnic groups, either through official public health statistics, or informally, through news reports and rumors. In such societies some

[55] Posner 2005, 92–94, makes this case nicely in describing the reluctance of many Zambians to "admit" to the sustained importance of ethnic identities in social and political life. A virtual scholarly industry of designing clever survey and experimental methods has been developed to unmask ethnic and racial prejudice because of the difficulty in getting individuals to reveal it.

[56] Gilens 1995, for example, makes the point that in the United States, even when welfare policies are not explicitly targeted at blacks, white support for means-tested welfare policies declines among whites who hold negative views of blacks because of negative stereotypes they hold about this other ethnic group.

ethnic groups are likely to be identified with the virus earlier than others. Sometimes, such identification will be made implicitly or through "coded" language because of norms against explicit stereotyping, but the message will be clear to most actors nonetheless. For example, euphemisms of space or occupation may be used when there are clear ethnic divisions of geography or labor. As a result, individuals located in groups not yet identified with the pathogen are more likely to believe or to say that their families, partners, and regular social contacts are unlikely to mingle with infected individuals because the latter are located in stigmatized groups on the other side of the boundary. Such individuals come to believe that they are relatively safe or immune from the threat. Because social boundaries often have real or imagined bodily correlates, and because epidemics tend to inspire metaphors of physical difference,[57] groups with initially lower rates of disease tend to believe that their bodies and physical habits, such as hygiene, drug use, or promiscuity, are distinctive, and therefore make them impervious to infection. While these groups are unlikely to support prevention and treatment, they may support "contain and control" strategies, which isolate infected individuals and treat infection as a form of punishment.

Moreover, because ethnic competition is usually maintained through a discourse of moral hierarchies, in which groups claim to occupy spaces of relative virtue or cleanliness, a blood-borne viral infection becomes easy fodder for a politics of cultural difference. The primordial myths associated with ethnic identity and associated political mobilizations tie in closely with the very acts that lead to HIV transmission (such as sexual practices and childbirth), providing opportunities for ethnic entrepreneurs to mobilize along these lines either in favor of, or in opposition to, a coordinated government response. In a bitter irony, even among groups in which infection is more prevalent, such moral competition may lead ethnic elites to downplay the problem, anticipating the costs of self-stigmatization.[58] The existence of strong boundaries makes it more likely that internal blaming about the pathogenesis of the virus will ensue. In turn, this results in a tendency to deny known risks because of the shame entailed in recognizing them. Questions of victimization and blame almost always characterize political debates over public health policy.[59] So long as inequality in the impact of the epidemic across ethnic groups is perceived,

[57] Sontag 2001.
[58] Cohen 1999.
[59] Nathanson 1996.

there is likely to be less demand for government action across all groups in ethnically divided societies than in other societies, all else being equal.

Conversely, when boundary institutions are weak, information about ethnic group infection is less likely to be available, implying weak prospects for political entrepreneurs and citizens who might mobilize ideas about insulation from risk. Under such conditions, people are more likely to believe that risks are shared or pooled—a threat to all of "us." Regardless of actual risk or hazard, the stronger the sense of shared identity, the more likely it is that individuals will perceive themselves to be threatened when conationals are infected.

Strong ethnic boundaries, particularly when they fragment society into multiple groups, help structure elite and more general resistance to HIV/AIDS policies even when increasing levels of AIDS-related mortality and morbidity and external pressures from the international community (the latter are discussed in detail in the next chapter) provide greater incentives to accept such sacrifices. Governments that attempt to act on HIV/AIDS in the context of strong and multiple ethnic boundaries may inspire ethnically based political conflicts. If governments tailor their messages and policies to particular "high risk" ethnic groups, they will be seen as stigmatizing those groups, generating the resistance described above; if they opt for universal, as opposed to targeted, appeals, they may be challenged for being insensitive to group differences or for wasting resources by addressing "low risk" groups. In either case, the costs of action are likely to be higher than in societies where ethnicity is not politically salient, leading to less aggressive action.

Together, these tendencies toward greater resistance to government attention to the HIV/AIDS problem in societies with strong and multiple ethnic boundaries should lower the political benefits to policymakers of providing such policies. By contrast, in societies where individuals generally perceive high levels of interethnic contact (i.e., ethnic mixing), where there are no restrictions on how one chooses one's identity, or where people do not recognize ethnic group differences at all, epidemic outbreaks are more likely to be perceived as generally threatening, leading to greater demand for timely and expansive policy.

This model makes policy preferences endogenous to the nature of the ethnic political landscape.[60] Groups develop an understanding of their

---

[60] By contrast, most political-economy/rational choice models of policymaking take preferences as fixed. See, for example, Weingast 2002, 661; or for ethnic politics specifically, Hardin 1995.

needs and preferences in direct response to the presence or absence of other groups in the polity and society. Moreover, it is important to note that while the ethnic composition of the polity matters for my explanation, the group in power does not.[61] My argument suggests that even when ethnic "out-groups" with high levels of infection are in power, they will discount the severity of the problem so as to elevate their status relative to other groups under the conditions of strong ethnic boundaries.

The foregoing discussion outlines the likely effects of ethnic boundaries on politically sensitive policymakers. Of course, other actors and pressures factor into decisions about how much attention and resources to allocate. Chief executives are likely to face competing demands from technical experts in the state; from persons in state agencies with competing interests, and from external actors. Policy advocates inside and outside the state are likely to pressure decision-makers to see the benefits of a concerted response—in public health, economic, and political terms. Wherever the epidemic is large or concentrated, infected, sick, and dying individuals and their associates are likely to call for action. At times, chief executives and other leading policymakers are likely to be personally affected and impressed by the scope of the pandemic and the need for a response. In all of these cases, the increased severity of a threat is likely to increase the scope of government action. My central point is that boundary politics are likely to have a discernible effect in mediating those pressures.

When central governments are initially passive in the face of AIDS, and the epidemic proceeds unchecked, ethnic outsiders may charge the government with not merely irresponsible policy, but ethnically targeted and deliberate underprovision of needed goods and services. This may generate increases in subnational efforts to address AIDS, but it may reinforce the idea that risks are not evenly distributed across ethnic groups, leading to more classic distributional conflicts. Further conflict is likely to delay and jeopardize the rollout of aggressive policies at the national level.

I do not expect such boundary politics to have consistent effects indefinitely. Over time, external pressures and increased mortality and morbidity are likely to trump ethnically motivated political competition. Moreover,

---

[61] By contrast, Cohen 1999 discusses African-Americans as a marginalized group, and Horowitz 1985 makes the distinctions between "ranked" and "unranked" ethnic conflicts, but I relax those restrictions because I find that wherever ethnic group identities are salient, shame and blame figure into the political calculus.

when a social problem becomes so widespread that it loses its stigma, and obviously affects groups across boundary divides, the scope conditions for the theory will no longer apply. Nonetheless, if correct, this first-order effect may have long-term implications because the timing of interventions is paramount in curbing the spread of a deadly virus.

A Theoretical Example

Before turning in the next chapters to analysis of actual cases, in which the manifestation of politics, policy, and disease is complex, it is useful to elaborate the central propositions from the theory using a stylized example. Imagine two polities, A and B, which are identical in almost every way, including size and distribution of the population across four geographic regions (250 in each, for a total population of 1,000), and location of HIV infections. In region 1 is the largest number of infections in both polities (48); in region 2 is the next highest number, (10); and in regions 3 and 4, the fewest infections (1 in each). The one critical difference between the two polities is that in polity A, ethnic boundaries do not exist, whereas in polity B, they are strong and coterminous with regional boundaries. Thus, polity B is an example of an extremely divided society.

What should we expect to see in the political reactions to news of the epidemic, given the theory outlined above?

In polity A, region has no particular social or political significance, and it represents an arbitrary administrative grid. For that reason, people from each region give no emotive significance to their regional identities, and are much more likely to view the epidemic in "national" terms. Activists and public health workers are likely to act first to respond in regions 1 and 2, and pooling the calculated risks of infection across regions, they are likely to describe the problem of HIV in terms of a 60 / 1,000 = 6 percent prevalence. Therefore, a general sense of fear of being affected by the virus is likely to emerge, even in regions 3 and 4. There is much less likelihood of blaming the infected in region 1, simply because there is little language for talking about a particular group, and people in other regions have good reason to believe that the virus will spread to them. In the context of more uniformly distributed support for prevention, treatment, and rights policies, the state is more likely to provide them.

In polity B, despite an identical spatial distribution of infections, the political interpretation of the epidemic is likely to be much different.

Because the regional boundaries coincide with strong ethnic identities, and because people in polity B assume that there is little intimate contact across ethno-regions, risks are not described in the media or by elites as pooled. Rather, in regions 3 and 4, individuals understand their risk of infection in terms of what they know about their group—that is, that only 0.4 percent (1 / 250) are infected. Given this low rate, they have comparatively little reason to demand a strong national AIDS policy. At the other extreme, in region 1, the high prevalence, 28 of 250 people being infected (19.2 percent), is likely to prompt concern and attention. On the one hand, some in that region are likely to demand strong and immediate policies. On the other hand, ethnic leaders are likely to want to minimize the shame of having this problem in their community, and they may challenge the accuracy of the numbers. They may divide the infected from the rest of the ethnic group through new labels or discourses. Moreover, elites from regions 3 and 4 may resist spending national resources on a problem endemic to region 1—a problem "they brought on themselves"—and are likely to request that the region use its own resources to deal with the problem. In region 2, where the epidemic is significant (4 percent prevalence) but much less prevalent than in region 1, political actors are likely to emphasize that the problem belongs to region 1, not to region 2. Overall, while we may expect to see more targeted action in polity B, the national response is likely to be more aggressive in polity A.

ADDITIONAL AND ALTERNATIVE EXPLANATIONS

Even if boundary politics helps explain government responses to AIDS, this does not mean that other factors must be inconsequential. Nonetheless, it is important to assess the explanatory power of my argument relative to others. Moreover, if the number and strength of ethnic boundaries have observable effects on government responses, we need to know if the effects are independent, or if they wash away when we control for other factors. I specify alternative arguments as a guide to empirical analyses in the chapters to follow.

In order to anticipate these alternative explanations, I draw on insights from those who have made specific claims about the drivers of AIDS policy, and of public policymaking and development more generally. A theoretical literature exploring the determinants of government AIDS policies is still in the early stages of development, but there is some consensus about which influences are worth considering, and I examine four broad sets of factors:[62] political regimes; state capacities and institutions; culture; and nonethnic cleavages. Because international influences on AIDS policies have been so important, and form part of the larger explanation of the book, I detail those arguments in the next chapter.

Political Regimes

A central research agenda for students of the political economy of development has been the positive (or negative) effects of democracy on development.[63] In the case of AIDS policy, an obvious question is whether democratic states are more responsive than other political regimes.[64] Because regime changes are central to the political life of countries, many accounts of AIDS policy have highlighted the influence of a change in regime on the policy. For example, one observer writes about Nigeria, "The emergence of a democratic government in 1999 has prioritized the struggle to curb the growth of the pandemic."[65] Without theory and comparative analysis, however, it is hard to know whether the changes in policy were greater than they might have been in the absence of a new political regime, or why the relationship between policy and regime holds.

It is easy to advance conflicting theoretical propositions to explain these phenomena. One can imagine that democracies provide fertile conditions for pressing demands for action on AIDS and other threats. As Amartya Sen points out, no substantial famine has ever occurred in an independent and democratic country with a free press.[66] The explanations for this pattern, which include the freer flow of information in democracies, seem to apply to AIDS as well. Most social scientific research has

---

[62] These four are in addition to size of the epidemic and available resources, which I assume and verify are important drivers of responsiveness.

[63] See, for example, Przeworski et al. 2000; Kaufman 2003; Gerring, Thacker, and Alfaro 2006; McGuire 2006. For the case of taxation, see Cheibub 1998. Levi's (1988, 1997) arguments on the sources of consent and compliance suggest the value of democratic institutions.

[64] A question that has been raised by several scholars, including Boone and Batsell 1999; Patterson 2006; De Waal 2006; Bor 2007.

[65] Folayan 2004, 85.

[66] Sen 2001, 9.

considered more modest, probabilistic propositions about the impact of democracy, and two recent studies have found that in democracies the incidence of infant mortality is reduced.[67] The activism about AIDS and the dissemination of information by a wide range of actors in civil society in the United States are hard to imagine in a nondemocratic country. Conversely, the state's control of information on the AIDS epidemic (and the SARS epidemic) in China is hard to imagine in a democracy. In general, democracies provide opportunities for potentially marginalized actors to have a voice in the making of public policy, a particularly important characteristic in the case of AIDS. Advocates for action seem to have a stronger hand in a democracy.

Alternatively, there are reasons to believe that authoritarian governments might be more aggressive in response to AIDS. Erwin Ackerknecht's theory of state approaches to the prevention of infectious disease hypothesizes a negative relationship between democracy and aggressive public health policy. He argues that prophylactic policies that restrict individual liberties are associated with more authoritarian and absolutist political regimes.[68] One study of the effects of democracy on immunization coverage finds a negative effect—dampened, however, by declining levels of GDP per capita.[69] In the case of HIV/AIDS, we may hypothesize that increases in political rights are negatively correlated with the provision of policies to limit risky behavior in the private arenas in which HIV is transmitted. Given the negative valence of such policies, authoritarian regimes might be less sensitive to negative reactions from citizens. The glaring example of the strong AIDS program in Cuba, with the lowest infection levels in the Western hemisphere, provides prima facie evidence that authoritarian governments can be responsive to AIDS.

Thus, there are reasons to believe that the aggressiveness of a government's policy may be either positively or negatively associated with democratic regimes. And of course, it is possible that the effects are mixed.

While most analyses of the relationship between democracy and development are concerned with the formal process of selecting leaders, civil society also has an impact. Although an autonomous civil society is usually more prevalent in democracies, an authoritarian regime may allow

[67] Gerring 2006; McGuire 2006.
[68] As cited by Baldwin 1999.
[69] Gauri and Khaleghian 2002.

space in which nongovernment actors may organize; and conversely, some countries with free and fair elections have little in the way of civil society. Early analyses of AIDS policies found that civil society organizations were the ultimate drivers of aggressive policy in, for example, the United States and Brazil.[70] For the purposes of more general explanation, however, we need to ask if a vibrant civil society is sufficient to produce aggressive policies on AIDS, or at least makes them more likely.

State Capacities and Institutions

As I stated at the outset, I assume that those at the pinnacles of power act to maximize political returns at the lowest economic costs. This is not to say that political leaders don't care about human needs, but simply that given a wide range of social problems they might address, it is reasonable to predict that they will choose problems most likely to be popular, to be easily addressed, and to provoke little resistance. If this logic is correct, the political calculations about which policies to adopt vary according to the human and institutional capacities and proclivities in the state.

One popular argument on responsiveness by states concerns the effects of political leadership.[71] Put simply, this perspective suggests that the personal traits of the individuals at the helm of power determine the likelihood of an aggressive response. The intelligence, courage, and foresight of a president are more determinative than the political pressures and incentives he or she faces. Social scientists somewhat dismissively call this the "big man" theory of policymaking. Despite their dismissal, the theory demands attention simply for its popularity among policymakers and journalists. If we are to treat this theory as truly causal, we must be able to separate cause from effect. Doing so is possible, but not straightforward, and we cannot use leadership on AIDS as the measure of leadership—that would obviously be tautological. In comparing Brazil and South Africa, I consider the effect of presidential leadership because

---

[70] For example, Bayer and Kirp 1992; Parker 1994b; Headley and Siplon 2006.

[71] For example, Parkhurst and Lush 2004 consider political leadership in addition to bureaucratic structure, health care infrastructure, and nonstate actors as factors affecting AIDS policy.

it has become an important folk explanation, particularly in the case of South Africa.

Theories that specify the state as an explanatory variable may highlight the function and politics of elites in the state apparatus. For example, Van de Walle's account of responses by African government to economic crises focuses on three factors: persistent neopatrimonialism; elite beliefs; and (weak) state capacity.[72] Can this model explain AIDS policy? In the case of the first two factors, the problem is that no clear theoretical predictions emerge. If a government is corrupt, it might care little about public goods such as public health, or it might develop public health programs in order to attract and to distribute largesse. As for elite beliefs, the key question is, where do these come from? For a relatively new crisis such as HIV/AIDS, there are no patterns of intellectual development analogous to schools of economic thought in Van de Walle's account, that might lead some elites to reject international ideas about control of epidemics. When elite beliefs are shaped by other political calculations, the latter need to be examined thoroughly. I find that elites have been shaped both by socializing and by coercive international pressures (as described in chapter 3), but also by calculations relevant to boundary politics, as described above.

However, Van de Walle's third variable, state capacity, does lead to clear predictions that are relevant for all governments. Government leaders confronted the AIDS epidemic with state capacities that they inherited from histories of responses to other challenges. It is not tautological to argue, as Peter Baldwin does with respect to responses to AIDS in the advanced countries, that policies were a product of prior responses to earlier health epidemics.[73] Other scholars similarly hypothesize that health care infrastructure accounts for some of the variance in AIDS policies.[74] It stands to reason that stronger and more efficacious states, with more competent and professionalized technical staff, would be more responsive to AIDS, just as strong states respond to other public health problems. One can imagine this relationship holds for several reasons: First, it is likely to be easier and cheaper to initiate policies when related programs are already in place. Second, when citizens are accustomed to the state's addressing collective threats, they are more

[72] Van de Walle 2001, 49–50.
[73] Baldwin 2005.
[74] Nattrass 2006; Parkhurst and Lush 2004.

likely to press the state to act. Third, authoritative and effective states are more likely to include entrepreneurs who are willing and able to take on new functions. More specifically, the state's efforts in caring for the health of its population might predict the scope of its policies. Although aggressive responses typically recognize AIDS as more than just a medical problem, the health sector has taken a lead role in the formulation and implementation of HIV/AIDS policies. At the very least, states that allocate greater resources to health problems are likely to allocate greater resources to HIV/AIDS.

Even apart from available resources and general state capacities, countries that have tended to allocate greater resources to health might be expected to do more on AIDS. Previous commitments to health may predict prompt and high-level attention to new health problems. Such an explanation must be analyzed with particular care to constant causes[75] that may have generated both earlier responses and the responses to AIDS, complicating our inferences about which factor influenced AIDS policy.

In addition to bureaucratic capacities, states also have institutional features that structure national patterns of politics and decision-making.[76] Rules of political contestation, as distinct from existing endowments or preferences, can influence policy outcomes in predictable ways. Scholars have explained national differences in railroad policy, tax policy, conscription, health insurance, and social security through analysis of institutional variation across time and space.

To say that institutions matter, however, does not provide sufficient analytical guidance, because it is not clear which institutions matter most. Of course, my argument is largely concerned with state institutions that may strengthen ethnic boundaries, one institution being federalism if federal units are closely tied to particular ethnic groups (this is true in Canada, for example, but not in the United States). Federalism could have other independent effects on policymaking.[77] Scholars have hypothesized that federalism influenced the history of AIDS policy in the United States,[78]

---

[75] See Collier and Collier 1991.

[76] Steinmo, Thelen, and Longstreth 1995; and Bates et al. 1998.

[77] Pierson 1995 identifies a range of predictions about the potential effects of federalism on social policy, but notes that federalism is likely to interact with other variables, including policy properties, such that we must investigate the potential effects without any particular assumptions about the direction of the effect.

[78] Bayer and Kirp 1992.

Canada,[79] and Australia.[80] In each case, the authors identify features of the federal polity that influenced the relative strength of the country's political actors and affected the policies adopted, but they do not provide a general theory of the role of federalism. In a review of theories of public health, Nathanson hypothesizes that "public health policies contributing to mortality decline are more likely to be originated and implemented by strong, highly centralized states."[81] Based on research in other areas, one could imagine both positive and negative influences of federalism on the development of regimes in response to AIDS. Federalism can create political impediments to general welfare expenditures in the advanced industrialized countries,[82] and to progressive taxation in countries around the world.[83] Federalism can generate "veto points" for expansive public policies, and create political divisions between subnational units. By contrast, in the area of tobacco control, federalism has provided opportunities for political entrepreneurs to push for legislation at the subnational level, an important stepping stone for federal policies.[84] Based on this logic, we might expect more aggressive AIDS policies in federal polities than in unitary states.

I do not, however, take on certain other hypotheses about the effects of particular democratic institutions, such as parliamentary versus presidential systems of government, or proportional representation versus majoritarian electoral institutions. While these are plausible determinants of cross-country variation in many policies, I do not consider them for several reasons: First, such variation applies only to well-consolidated democracies, which would eliminate a large share of the cases I intend to consider. Second, such factors are themselves often strongly influenced by ethnic boundaries—for example, ethnically divided societies tend to adopt proportional representation—and we cannot disentangle such variables from the central variable of interest. Finally, and most important, I cannot logically adduce any reasons why such institutions ought to have systematic effects on AIDS policies, and none have been advanced in the literature.

[79] Rayside and Lindquist 1992.
[80] Ballard 1992.
[81] Nathanson 1996, 611. Parkhurst and Lush 2004 arrive at conflicting conclusions in their analysis of the effects of decentralization on AIDS policy in South Africa and Uganda.
[82] Crepaz 1998.
[83] Lieberman 2003.
[84] Marmor and Lieberman 2004.

Cultural Content

In cross-national analysis, "culture" can be an attractive variable for explaining outcomes, and the area of HIV/AIDS is no different: National responses to AIDS might be explainable by cultural norms and values about sexual relations,[85] childbirth and breastfeeding, and drug use. It would be hard to deny that such norms ought to be considered in understanding HIV transmission, but do norms and values influence the response of the state independently of their effect on prevalence? Defining and comparing the influence of culture is an extremely difficult task, demanding subjective interpretation. If we define culture in terms of specific attitudes about people with HIV/AIDS or norms of contraceptive use, our measure is so proximate to the outcome under investigation that it is difficult to know what causes what.

On the other hand, general norms about sex and sexuality are plausible candidates as influences on AIDS policymaking. One might predict, and many have argued, that aggressive AIDS policies are more likely in cultures that are more "relaxed" or liberal about sexuality and sexual orientation.[86] If indeed a key fear of government leaders is backlash against policies seen as violations of social norms—including prohibitions against condom use, discussion of premarital sex, homosexuality, or multiple sexual partners—then we might expect more aggressive AIDS policies where such mores are less strict.

An important and related influence on political life that can be considered here is religion. Religions take on different characteristics and practices in local settings, yet shared religious doctrine can propagate similar cultural values across national borders. Where religious and other norms and values weigh against open and public discussion of sexual topics such as condom use, homosexuality, and multiple sexual partners, it is more difficult to gain public support for an aggressive approach to HIV/AIDS. Moreover, in societies where religion is important, its direct influence on the state is likely to be strong (if not universally so.) Political leaders are more likely to be swayed by religious values, and religious

---

[85] For example, Siplon 2005 highlights patriarchy as a barrier to policymaking on AIDS.

[86] Berkman et al. (2005, 1168–69), for example, make this claim with respect to the Brazilian case.

leaders are more likely to influence state policy. In particular, Catholic and Muslim leaders have reiterated conservative views about sexual practices. Indeed, throughout the AIDS pandemic of the late twentieth century, Pope John Paul II objected to all forms of birth control, including condoms, which reduce the transmission of HIV. One could hypothesize that increasing rates of membership in these religions would lead to less aggressive responses to AIDS.

Other Cleavages

Finally, it is useful to distinguish the central hypothesis of this book—that strong *ethnic* boundaries constrain government responses to AIDS—from a related hypothesis: namely, that other boundaries, dividing nonethnic groups, affect policies.

The boundary politics I discuss in this book involve ethnic and national identities. Yet groups organized along gender lines, income or class, and age may be characterized by similar "us-them" dynamics. In the early years of the epidemic, particularly in the advanced countries, the relevant dimension of social conflict over AIDS concerned sexual orientation.[87] Nonetheless, for the problem of AIDS policy in the developing world, there is good reason to believe that these other cleavages are either less relevant or their effects can be understood in terms of broader patterns of boundary politics, closely tied to the boundaries that divide ethnic groups. Where states and societies have strong sanctions against exogamy, they are associated with controls on intimate contact, including prohibitions on same-sex contacts.

As in virtually all aspects of development, gender, or more precisely the relative imbalance in gendered power, is a variable in the dynamics of the AIDS epidemic. A few areas are worth highlighting: There are gendered divisions of labor, by which men leave the household for work, during which time they may have sexual relations, become infected, then return home to infect their wives. Unequal relations of power may make it difficult for women to insist that their husbands use condoms; in many contexts, women have little ability to regulate sexual advances.

---

[87] See, for example, the contributions in Bayer and Kirp 1992. Probably the single best account of the initial history of AIDS in the United States is Shilts 2000.

Because of different physiologies, men and women are at different risks for transmission; and men who have sex with men are at particularly high risk. Only women can pass on HIV to infants through birth and breast milk. In short, gender structures patterns of knowledge, behavior, risk, and impact of HIV/AIDS.

But again, these are issues of viral transmission, and the concern here is with national-level policymaking. If we push this line of explanation a bit, we might expect women to have a greater affinity for aggressive AIDS policies because of imbalances in household power and gender relations more generally, in addition to the specific consequences of policies meant to reduce HIV transmission from mothers to children. If so, a plausible hypothesis is that if women have more power in the polity, we should expect more aggressive AIDS policies.

Boundaries that reinforce a sense of group difference along lines of class[88] and along lines of sexual orientation are also important within and across countries, and there are instances in which these cleavages also explain government policies on AIDS. As stated earlier, it is plausible that these boundaries have effects analogous to ethnic boundaries. However, because I do not perceive these boundaries to be as well institutionalized or politicized in the developing world, nor to vary as widely across countries, I do not expect them to have as strong an effect as ethnic boundaries in explaining policies on AIDS.

CONCLUSION

In this chapter, I have provided theoretical accounts of how social boundaries might affect perceptions and discourses of risk in response to external shocks, and generate identity-based conflicts disproportionate to differences among groups in "objective" welfare or material interests. Such ideas lay the groundwork for an explanation of why government responses to AIDS vary systematically according to the strength and number of ethnic boundaries in countries. While most accounts of the adverse effects of ethnicity on public policy and development have focused on the heterogeneity of preferences in divided societies, on rent-seeking behavior, and

---

[88] Nattrass 2006, for example, hypothesizes that income inequalities structure political responses to AIDS.

on coordination problems, I emphasize challenges of pooling risk, and conflicts over social status.

I have highlighted a large number of possible explanations for differences in AIDS policy that guide the analysis to come. Before exploring the robustness of these explanations, however, it is necessary to consider the international environment in which responses to AIDS have been formulated and proposed, which is the subject of the next chapter.

3 ❧ Globalization and Global Governance of AIDS: The Geneva Consensus

The challenge of this book is to explain similarities and differences in national responses to a common problem, AIDS. As outlined in the previous chapter, my analysis focuses on domestic variables. But national governments are embedded in an international political economy, and particularly in low- and middle-income countries, the policymaking process takes place in the context of external pressures on governments. In the area of AIDS policy, we have witnessed extensive, steadfast, and concurrent international pressures on domestic policymaking. I label the best-practice recommendations in AIDS policy the *Geneva Consensus* because of the role of the UN agencies in framing it, though the architects of this consensus reside in governments, institutions, and networks around the globe. Because efforts to extend the global governance of AIDS, including offers of foreign aid, have been so far-reaching, national governments have not been as constrained by budgets as they have been in other areas, and they have shared a menu of options in facing the pandemic. Thus, before turning to analysis of cross-country variation in the chapters that follow, it is necessary to understand the context of efforts to exert global governance, because most of the impetus for advancing AIDS policy has been generated in that manner.

Scholars have long observed the influence of international actors and processes on domestic politics and policymaking.[1] Whereas debt, trade, economic growth, and security have obvious international dimensions, health-related policy has less often been explored by scholars as a basis for state formation and for the relations between states. A few quite powerful contributions, including Jared Diamond's magisterial book *Guns, Germs, and Steel*, Mark Harrison's *Disease in the Modern World*, William McNeil's *Plagues and Peoples*, Laurie Garrett's *Betrayal of Trust*, and other works written by journalists, historians, and public health experts[2] demonstrate that disease and the threat of disease have been intimately connected with the rise of modern states and the interconnectedness of people through time. Nonetheless, as Ilona Kickbusch points out, although health has come to the fore of world politics, there has been little *theoretical* analysis relating health policy to global governance.[3]

In this chapter, I begin to fill this lacuna for AIDS policy, by exploring the ways in which the institutions of global governance have spread their authority through national governments and other organizations around the world. Of course, the spread of HIV is itself an "international" phenomenon, but that diffusion is manifest in more obvious ways, through the movement of individuals across national boundaries, and the appearance of infection in virtually all countries. I focus on the spread of social, political, and economic pressures *in reaction to* the growing pandemic. I do not seek to test propositions about the origins or nature of policy diffusion as a general phenomenon because I consider AIDS policy alone. Instead, I use existing theories as a guide for investigating the role of international relations on the diffusion of policy, highlighting which theories are most closely aligned with the facts.

As a menu of possibilities, four key sets of theories have been advanced by scholars of international relations to account for the global spread of policies:[4]

1. Constructivist theories highlight the influence of epistemic communities and international organizations, which in turn define policies and

---

[1] As just a few of many examples, see Gourevitch 1978, 1986; Evans 1985; and Stallings 1992.

[2] For example, Walt 2006 and Merson 2006.

[3] Kickbusch 2003, 192.

[4] Dobbin, Simmons, and Garrett 2007 identify these four theories in their extensive review of the global diffusion of policies. I am grateful to Robert Keohane for pushing me to theorize further about the mechanisms of global governance and policy diffusion.

their goals. Constructivists suggest that elite actors and networks create new norms of appropriate policies and practices to be followed.

2. Theories of coercion identify pressures exerted by powerful states and international organizations that use carrot-and-stick approaches to induce conformity.

3. Competition theories account for diffusion through attempts by countries to appear attractive as potential recipients of trade, investment, and aid. Policies are spread not by norms but by material incentives.

4. Learning theories propose that policymakers change their strategies in the wake of evidence on the effects of a policy from their own experiences with it, or the experiences of other countries.

There is a degree of overlap in the implications of each paradigm. Moreover, as scholars have found for other issues, there are often multiple sources of diffusion. Nonetheless, these are distinctive theories of the global spread of particular policies and practices.

On balance, I am persuaded that in the case of AIDS policy, the first two theories—the social construction of policy norms and the coercive pressures of key states and organizations—identify the most important mechanisms of diffusion. As a starting point, it is important to recognize that diffusion has been quite far-reaching. Indeed, despite an extraordinary array of interpretations of the pathogenesis of the problem, the range of options considered in most high-level debates about appropriate action has been quite narrow. Through steady socialization and leveraged pressure, global actors have managed a consensus across countries on how the AIDS epidemic ought to be addressed. This is a far cry from suggesting that there has been uniform agreement—indeed a task of this book is to explore *variation*—but there is far more uniformity than we would have observed absent these global governance institutions.[5]

By comparison, competition seems not to have played an important role in diffusing policy. Early in the epidemic, many governments seemed to disavow AIDS strategies because their leaders did not want to publicize infections within their borders, hoping to sustain trade and tourism, as

[5] In this sense, my findings resonate strongly with Finnemore's (1996) analyses of how, for example, international organizations such as the World Bank have shaped the process by which states develop goals for development. The ideas of "development" and "poverty alleviation" were not simply natural prerogatives of states. The same is true for the goals used in addressing the threat of AIDS and infectious disease.

well as international reputation. As for learning, the record is perhaps less clear. It is almost inevitable that we would find evidence of learning in the diffusion of policy in response to a biomedical problem about which a great deal of scientific evidence is disseminated. Policymakers are themselves likely to explain their policies in terms of evidence and analysis that suggest learning. And yet the degree to which evidence and examples are trusted has been so embedded in social and political relations, that it would miss the mark to identify "learning," defined in largely technocratic terms, as the most influential mechanism. Scholars recognized as contributors to the learning paradigm[6] have identified examples of international organizations influencing target countries by pointing to particular best-practice or best-outcomes cases. However, because in subsequent chapters I am able to marshal evidence accounting for the political origins of policy adoption, I am doubtful that learning can be recognized as an autonomous and important source of policymaking.

The global response to AIDS provides a thoroughgoing example of global governance in terms of scope and participation by a wide range of actors. A few situational factors have contributed to the attention received by this problem: the sheer scope of the problem in terms of numbers of countries affected; the fact that the outcome is devastating illness and death; the fact that the wealthy and powerful, including celebrities, have suffered, and that they and their associates have been steadfast in mobilizing attention and resources. Other structural factors have also been influential, largely associated with the moment in historical time that the AIDS epidemic began to spread widely, including a truly global information network and the development of an extensive global governance regime.

By discussing the rise and impact of "global governance," I risk painting a false portrait of internal coherence. The core of wealthiest and most powerful countries and the range of global governance actors are not a unitary actor for most issues of international relations, and this is true for AIDS as well. And yet, as I chronicle, there has been more consensus than conflict on prescriptions for addressing HIV/AIDS. Fundamental political conflicts over interests and values—whether to expand or downsize the scope of national state authority; to adopt "rights-oriented" or "control" strategies; to promote "harm reduction" or "prohibition of risky behaviors"; to treat pharmaceutical patents as "intellectual property" or as

---

[6] Such as Haas, Nye, and Kahler, as cited by Dobbin, Simmons, and Garrett 2007, 461–62.

"essential medicines"—have been fought, but have also largely been re-solved, at the international level such that we can speak of a consensus. This has been achieved through deliberation and compromise, but also through cooperation-enhancing repeated interactions within particular institutions.[7] I do not claim that this pattern of consensus has been com-plete, or that it was predictable, but given this consistency, we have a use-ful "stylized fact" for understanding the trajectory of country-level AIDS policies: Thoroughgoing, global governance has been broadcast around the world to developing countries, with a largely consistent message and the provision of extensive resources.

By relating the efforts of international actors to exert global governance on AIDS, we can simultaneously describe the context of national-level policymaking and establish baselines for comparative analysis. From an analytical perspective, what is important is to observe the strength of ex-ternal pressures for aggressive AIDS policy across all developing countries. It is the combination of a shared *problem* and this shared set of policy op-tions and pressures that leaves us with expectations of a convergence on aggressive policy across countries.

In the remainder of this chapter, I provide a portrait of the rise of global governance of AIDS, highlighting its implications for the diffusion of pol-icy. First, I describe the foundations for the global governance of AIDS, that is, the rise of an asymmetric global governance regime in the health sector. As in other sectors of development and public policymaking, inter-national actors located largely in the advanced countries have established an extensive agenda for low- and middle-income countries. Then, I describe the emergence of the specific actors and institutions attempting to govern the AIDS pandemic from international seats of power, particularly Geneva, but also Washington and other world capitals. Finally, I detail the content of the best-practice guidelines articulated as the "Geneva Consensus," which will serve as a framework for comparing country-level responses.

THE RISE OF ASYMMETRIC GLOBAL HEALTH GOVERNANCE

Global governance can be defined as the exercise of power, persuasion, or authority by organizations and networks over a jurisdiction that spans at least two national states. The sources of such authority are diffuse: It may

---

[7] Keohane 1984, 244–45.

be exerted by individual states; by the multilateral bodies they have created, such as the United Nations, the World Bank, and the International
Monetary Fund (IMF); or by looser associations and networks of nonstate
actors, such as interlinked human rights organizations that set standards
and norms for behavior through coordinated campaigns. In the modern
state system, in which national states claim sovereignty and a monopoly
on the legitimate use of force, it is useful to differentiate global governance
from other forms of transnational authority—namely imperialism and occupation—which involve direct challenges to state authority on the basis
of military might. In the contemporary era, global governance tends to be
exerted with at least the tacit compliance of national states. The regulatory
and persuasive efforts of global networks on issues ranging from the environment, to human rights, to public health, have had a measurable impact
on policies and practices.[8] And yet, even as state actors participate in such
networks, they often choose not to abide by the mandates of supranational
authorities, claiming an absence of legitimacy to make and enforce rules.[9]

The character of global governance of AIDS during the past quarter-
century can be understood through identification of two important and
long-standing trends: the asymmetric development of power relations,
and the specific configuration of institutions and actors in the area of
public health.

Asymmetries of Power

Global governance has been asymmetric in the sense that the exercise of
authority has been disproportionately coordinated and exerted by the
wealthiest countries. As others have shown through insider accounts,[10]
careful reporting,[11] and scholarly analyses,[12] even as norms of "domination"
have been repudiated, wealthier governments and organized interests in
wealthier countries often disproportionately influence strategy and policy.
The nature of these relations is so deeply ingrained that it is sometimes difficult to recognize that this is just one of a set of possible historical out-

[8] See, for example, Slaughter 2004; contributions in Nye and Donahue 2000.
[9] Keohane 2002, 3.
[10] Stiglitz 2002 on the international financial institutions.
[11] Mallaby 2004 on the World Bank.
[12] Pop-Eleches (forthcoming) on the IMF.

comes that might have unfolded. Earlier strands of scholarship, notably from the dependency school, described countries not merely in terms of their relative levels of development, which tends to be the current practice, but as arrayed in a "core" and "periphery," emphasizing persistent relationships in a single "world system."[13] While no one denies the severe imbalances of wealth and power that persist across world regions, few observers describe the relations as purely extractive in the sense of the dependency school. For example, contemporary global governance has emerged prominently in the areas of human rights and democratization,[14] which only the most skeptical could interpret as wholly self-interested efforts by the wealthy core. Nonetheless, it is useful to characterize global governance as asymmetric in order to make clear that the interdependence associated with globalization does not imply an equal distribution of power and influence.[15]

Van de Walle's analysis of economic reform in Africa during the period 1979–99 epitomizes the tensions between asymmetric global governance and sovereign state policymaking in the developing world.[16] He describes the process of economic policy reform in African countries as responses to an "orthodox" agenda set by international donors. Such work is more nuanced than an earlier generation of dependency scholarship, both in its avoidance of a Marxist teleology, and in its recognition that there are important variations in the nature of these relationships and in their effects. Asymmetric global governance does not imply that all of the costs of exchange are borne by the poor countries, nor that all of the benefits are reaped by the rich countries. It does suggest, however, that the terms, goals, and assumptions in the making and reforming of policy originate

[13] Wallerstein 1974. Scholars concerned with understanding the determinants of public policymaking in the developing world have oscillated in their affinity for "domestic" and "international" explanations of state (in)action. Dependency theorists and neo-Marxists (e.g., Valenzuela and Valenzuela 1978; Cardoso and Faletto 1979) tended to see country-level policymaking in terms of international relations and global structures, affording little autonomy to domestic political economy. A subsequent generation of comparativists would err in the other direction, treating countries as if they were operating in isolation, and leading some such as Barbara Stallings to point out that "ideas about external influence have been too quickly abandoned" (1992, 43).

[14] See, for example, Keck and Sikkink 1998 and Risse-Kappen, Ropp, and Sikkink 1999.

[15] Dobbin, Simmons, and Garret 2007 and Keohane (personal communication) highlight the work of John Meyer and his students in describing emerging global consensus on appropriate actors, goals, and strategies, often as a diffusion of policies from the First World to the Third World.

[16] Van de Walle 2001.

largely in the advanced countries, and that ultimate control over the distribution of resources lies with a relatively small number of actors. This point is critical because it helps to explain how a menu of responses to complex issues can remain relatively bounded around the world. Global governance is far more oligarchic than democratic.

By the onset of the AIDS epidemic, almost every country in this study had gained its independence,[17] and the sovereignty of these states had been well established. And yet the imbalance of capacities and power between the poor countries and a small number of wealthy countries has been profound, with enormous consequences for the AIDS pandemic. The reasons for this imbalance are historical and institutional, but they are compounded by persistent inequalities in the distribution of resources. Approximately 80 percent of the measured global economy is located in the high-income countries, which contain less than 20 percent of the world's population. Richer countries provide resources in the form of aid and loans, which in poor countries represent as much as half of all government expenditures. Such aid dependency is a de facto source of influence. The rich countries contain the most important consumer markets, they possess advanced technologies ranging from communications to pharmaceuticals, and some have extraordinary military might. They are simultaneously donor countries, which give counsel and aid, and gatekeepers, barring people in poor countries from access to their markets, their intellectual property, and—with respect to potential immigrants—their borders. Although China and India, growing in both economic and military strength, are challenging a simple portrait of North-South imbalance, for most of the history of the AIDS epidemic, even these countries have acted as receivers, not deliverers of the Geneva Consensus. In short, the manifestation of global governance in terms of policy diffusion, particularly for the problem of HIV/AIDS, reflects a broadcasting of authority from places such as Geneva and Washington, D.C., not Delhi, São Paulo, or Abuja.

Global Health Governance: Legacies and New Imperatives

Beyond fundamental asymmetries, global responses to AIDS have been shaped by the inherited institutional legacy of the global governance of

---

[17] Namibia gained its independence from South Africa in 1990, and Eritrea from Ethiopia in 1993, but in these cases, the "colonizers" were neighboring countries that had gained their own independence in prior generations, not long-distance imperial powers.

health, including prior epidemic threats. This is no place for a comprehensive chronicling of public health threats and responses, but a capsule account may be of value.

In the face of the increasing contact with peoples around the world and growing understandings of how to prevent transmission of disease, individual states established policies and practices for curbing the spread of infections, including quarantine for incoming visitors and migrants. Preventive quarantine dates back to 1377, when the Rector of Ragusa (today Dubrovnik), implemented a thirty-day isolation period for ships suspected to be coming from places infected with the plague. The isolation period was extended to forty days—a *quaranta* (the basis of the term *quarantine*)—for land travelers.[18] Over time, with the growing trade and contact between peoples, leading to the unregulated exchange of viruses and bacteria, there were strong incentives to create more stable institutions to regulate the international relations of health. Moreover, states were becoming increasingly abusive in the quarantine practice,[19] and the negative externalities of an unregulated approach motivated calls for greater consistency in practices. Among the most notable modern institutions are those that originated during the mid-nineteenth century. The first official form of medical "diplomacy" was the 1851 International Sanitary Conference, in which European states met to discuss the threat of, and appropriate responses to, cholera, plague, and yellow fever, and other public health problems.[20] In the late nineteenth century, scientific discoveries cementing the validity of the germ theory of disease paved the way for the development of public health administrations at various levels of government.[21]

As viral threats came to be understood as transmittable, and as humans came in greater regular contact across states, new international institutions were created to address public health challenges. The 1899 and 1902 conferences on syphilis and other venereal diseases held in Brussels were the first international initiatives to control sexually transmitted diseases.[22] The first formal international medical organizations were established, the Pan American Sanitary Bureau in 1902 and the International Office of Public Hygiene in 1909.[23] A Health Section of the League of

---

[18] Gensini, Yacoub, and Conti 2004, 258.
[19] Gensini, Yacoub, and Conti 2004, 259.
[20] Fidler 2001, 843.
[21] Merson, Black, and Mills 2006, xxii.
[22] Weindling 1993, 94.
[23] Fidler 2001, 843.

Nations became the leading official institution for international health governance between the world wars. The movement of soldiers across borders inspired new fears of the rapid transmission of STDs, and as Paul Weindling points out, this generated new conflicts over state sovereignty, and the competing forces of "moralism" and "social medicine." Nonetheless, in 1923, the *Union Internationale contre le Péril Vénérien* (UIPV) was established, and despite various conflicts and challenges, managed to score a number of achievements, including international comparisons, a forum for meetings, and the coordination of policy ideas.[24] Eventually, the UIPV along with other international health organizations would be absorbed by the World Health Organization, established as an agency of the United Nations to carry the advances of modern medical science to "wherever local authorities would co-operate."[25] As of 2005, 192 countries were members—including every country in this study—and at least in principle, they collectively govern the organization through the World Health Assembly. The WHO was notable for leading efforts to curb the spread of polio and to eradicate smallpox in 1980. It is simultaneously a clearinghouse for information and resources, a center for control of disease, and an advocate for the establishment of local public health facilities of member nations.

Despite ambitious attempts to create viable global public health regimes, the results in gaining consistent compliance and cooperation have been decidedly mixed.[26] Many of the ideas associated with a public health authority are difficult to implement at any level because they demand a great deal of technical coordination and mandate behavioral change. In their attempts to govern certain behaviors on a global scale, international organizations such as the WHO and the UN face a problem in the very ideal such organizations have worked so hard to enforce: national sovereignty. Even in the extreme cases of civil war or state collapse, it is extremely difficult for an outside power to intervene directly in the affairs of a foreign territory. While the WHO may claim to govern the world's public health, it has been forced to organize its efforts in terms of existing state boundaries and authorities. Like virtually all contemporary institutions of global governance, it has no decisive powers to enforce its will when states choose not to comply.

[24] Weindling 1993, 96–98.
[25] McNeil 1998, 291.
[26] Fidler 2001, 846.

In recent years, several books and myriad articles have steadfastly criticized global health governance institutions, including the WHO, and rich countries, including the United States, for not doing enough to protect public health. The subtitle of one such volume is *How the U.S. Has Slept through the Global AIDS Pandemic, the Greatest Humanitarian Catastrophe of Our Time.*[27] In a thick volume entitled *Betrayal of Trust*, Laurie Garrett has expertly chronicled the weakness of public health institutions around the world. Such frustration on the part of advocates and humanitarians is understandable—inexcusable numbers of people fall ill and die each year even though knowledge and resources are globally and oftentimes nationally and locally available to keep them alive. But before we blame the leaders of international organizations, we should recognize that they exist between political rocks and hard places of constrained authority and limited resources.

Just as a tax collector sent to the hinterlands by the national government is likely to face resistance, representatives from global governance institutions must tread lightly. The WHO possesses no coercive powers, and its only claims to authority are the provision of material inducements and claims to legitimacy associated with technocratic competence and neutrality. It operates with a loosely democratic voting structure in which member nations vote on certain broad resolutions and declarations, but decisions about policy and practice are made by technical experts, most from the advanced countries, but also technocrats from developing countries with comparable training. Specific policy ideas and practices are not put up for referendum. Rich countries are influential because they contribute the resources for a relatively lean budget. Because the political stakes of health and health care have almost never been perceived to rival those of other state competencies associated with trade, finance, and defense, the WHO has not faced the public resistance that other international organizations, such as the WTO, the World Bank, or the IMF have met. Nonetheless, with such issues as tobacco use, immunization, and maternal health, within-country constituencies have prohibited the complete penetration of their borders by this global governance authority.

While the WHO has claimed the technical mantle in the health sector, other global governance institutions have weighed in. Increasingly health is understood as an outcome linked to poverty, security, and economic de-

[27]Behrman 2004.

velopment, which various actors have made issues in political campaigns for policy reform.[28] As a result, a wide range of international organizations have become involved in public health: the World Bank, the development arm of wealthy countries, such as the United Kingdom's DFID and the United States' USAID; other agencies of the United Nations, such as the United Nations Development Programme (UNDP) and the United Nations Children's Fund (UNICEF); and large international NGOs such as CARE, Population Services International, and Save the Children. In virtually all cases, the headquarters of the aid agency or international organization is based in a wealthy country, and the work of administering its goals is carried out by offices in the poor countries. While there are important differences in organizational structure between these institutions—for example, the majority of UNDP employees actually work in field offices in developing countries, while the majority of WHO employees work in Geneva—the global governance of health is asymmetric in the sense that ultimate authority resides in the wealthiest countries.

THE EMERGENCE OF THE GLOBAL RESPONSE TO AIDS

By the time AIDS was recognized as a global pandemic in the making, a fairly elaborate, asymmetric regime of global governance was already in place, including health governance institutions with a narrow focus. Governance of the AIDS epidemic was built upon these foundations, along with an emerging international network of disease-specific and human rights activists and NGOs. Akin to national states, global governance authorities often expand their scope in the face of new crises and exigencies. For example, after dozens of countries around the world had experienced years of low or negative growth rates in the late 1970s and 1980s, it became possible to speak of a global economic crisis. In response, international financial institutions began to promote what would be termed the "Washington Consensus"[29] on economic reform.

HIV/AIDS was initially understood as a problem almost exclusively confined to homosexual men in San Francisco, New York, and Paris—it was dubbed "Gay Cancer." Soon it would visibly affect the other mem-

---

[28]Taylor 2002. See especially Price-Smith 2002 and Ostergard 2002 for analyses of the security implications of AIDS epidemics.

[29]Williamson 1993.

bers of what came to be known as the "4-H club" of AIDS: hemophiliacs, heroine users, and Haitians. But within just a few years, as confirmed reports of AIDS cases struck every corner of the globe, epidemiologists, public health officials, and leading international actors understood that this was a truly global pandemic, extending well beyond these groups.

The virtually uncontrollable movement of peoples across national borders has been central to both the transmission of the virus and the institutional responses it has engendered. As Dennis Altman remarks, "AIDS ironically linked the least developed and the most developed regions of the world, and despite attempts to close borders to its spread (as in the restrictions on entry of HIV-positive people applied by many countries) the spread of the virus made a mockery of national sovereignty."[30] Until approximately 1985, medical researchers, public health bureaucrats, and concerned political actors struggled to identify the biomedical properties of the syndrome, and to develop medical and policy strategies to combat it. Starting in the mid-1980s more coordinated global action on HIV/AIDS began to emerge, the nascent development of a Geneva Consensus about what ought to be done.

Like the eradication of smallpox, or ongoing efforts to mitigate global environmental degradation, curbing the AIDS pandemic has been understood by leading global governance actors as a global public good,[31] with a high level of interdependency between countries. Indeed, the problem of infectious disease is well suited to the exertion of coordinated authority, and its rise is less theoretically problematic than for other areas of international cooperation where state interests are more likely to diverge.

Nonetheless, even for problems of infectious disease, the question, "How do states know what they want?"[32] has no obvious answer. We should not assume that an AIDS policy is a natural or neutral response to the problem. Indeed, as Martha Finnemore and other constructivists have argued, approaches to common problems often are shaped by goals and strategies articulated in the international arena. The very idea that disease is a social problem that can be addressed through distinctive policies is a

---

[30] Altman 1999, 564.

[31] A good that has nonrival, nonexcludable benefits that cut across borders. When seen in isolation, certain AIDS-related policies, especially treatment, are arguably not public goods, but as part of a larger strategic package for curbing the AIDS epidemic, they can be so considered. Specifically, World Bank 1999, 3, defines specific AIDS policies as being public goods.

[32] Finnemore 1996, 1.

thoroughly modern one, particularly when policies involve the regulation of highly personal, including sexual, behaviors. The very consideration of policies to address HIV/AIDS in national contexts has been shaped by actors and norms operating at the international level.

Lead Actors and Authorities

The initial efforts at global governance of AIDS were made largely within the existing formal institutions of the UN system, particularly the WHO. In numbers of international organizations involved, in amounts of aid, and in the sheer visibility of a public health problem in so many countries at the same time, global governance of AIDS has been far greater than for any public health problem in human history. For example, international donors spent approximately $98 million on the 1967–79 smallpox campaign,[33] a small fraction of a single year of donor funding for AIDS, estimated to be more than $3 billion in 2004.[34] Expenditures on polio eradication, guinea worm, TB control, and malaria control have all been far lower.[35] The 1918–20 Spanish influenza had a more devastating death toll—as many as 50 to 100 million lives of a much smaller world population were claimed—than AIDS has had in more than twenty-five years.[36] And yet most of the response to that epidemic was local and national, with minimal global coordination.

While the magnitude of the global response to AIDS has been largely a product of the wide-reaching scope of the pandemic, and the integrated era in which it has emerged, it has also drawn on the precedents and institutions of earlier global responses to public health crises. For example, while the creation of the WHO postdated the deadly flu pandemic of 1918–20, one of the organization's first tasks in 1948 was a response to the recent memory of that pandemic: the establishment of a global monitoring system, which today includes 110 laboratories in eighty-two countries.[37]

[33] Levine and What Works Working Group 2004, 18.
[34] Kates 2005, 10.
[35] Office of Development Studies 2002, 18. It is, of course, difficult to compare expenditure levels across problems because of the different costs for available interventions. If we are to consider these problems as global public goods, than the proper comparison is total spending—not spending per case—and on this count, AIDS spending has far outpaced these other diseases.
[36] Niall, Johnson, and Mueller 2002, 105.
[37] Barry 2004, 452.

Such initiatives proliferated in the decades to follow, and an international epistemic community was in place prior to the onset of the AIDS pandemic.[38] That community was accustomed to sharing ideas and using a common language to address public health problems. In the early 1980s, many global public health leaders were emboldened by recent success in eradicating smallpox, and declared that the same tools and approach would be used for AIDS.[39] But they would have to tread lightly, as the UN Charter provided no authorization to "intervene" in matters that were "essentially within the domestic jurisdiction of any state" (article 2.7).

Given its long-standing role in international health, the WHO was a natural leader for this emerging threat. As early as 1983, the WHO held international conferences on blood safety, prompted by the contamination of blood supplies. Under the leadership of Jonathan Mann—well known for his characterization of many public health problems and especially AIDS as issues of human rights—the WHO established the Special Program on AIDS in 1986, which in 1987 became the Global Program on AIDS (GPA). Mann tirelessly promoted the idea of a global AIDS strategy with this organization, though he resigned in 1990, citing inaction on the part of the UN and other international organizations. Nonetheless, the GPA, Mann, and others began to assist developing countries with national AIDS programs while mobilizing a response from potential donors.

As efforts intensified, the work of various organizations, particularly across the fragmented United Nations systems, overlapped and conflicted, and officials inside and outside the WHO complained of the GPA's ineffectiveness.[40] In particular, donor governments, in a period of disillusionment with international aid schemes more generally, demanded a streamlining of efforts and called for a consolidation. By 1993, plans were made to shift the responsibility of the GPA to a new bureaucracy. During a special session of the UN General Assembly, a resolution was passed to join the various UN agencies under a single umbrella, which would eventually become the Joint United Nations Programme on HIV/AIDS, better

[38] Susan Watkins (personal communication) points out that the international response to AIDS is both reminiscent of and built upon population control efforts of the 1970s and 1980s. Invitations to international meetings, proliferations of scholarships, and the movement of the issue into free-standing offices outside of the ministries of health established clear precedents and networks for addressing AIDS.

[39] Van Praag, Dehne, and Chandra-Mouli 2006, 595.

[40] This account draws largely on interviews with Michael Merson, and from Merson 2006. Merson was executive director of the GPA from 1990 to 1995.

known by its acronym, UNAIDS. The creation of such an organization was unprecedented, particularly as the UN system has tended toward fragmentation of power, rather than consolidation. The first meeting of the organization's board took place in Geneva in July 1995; it became fully operational in 1996; and the first director, Dr. Pieter Piot, has remained at the helm ever since. There were difficulties in the consolidation initially, including resistance from UN partner organizations that had already developed AIDS programs, such as the WHO and the UNDP. Nonetheless, the organization survived these initial fissures and has been the lead actor in the global campaign against HIV/AIDS, authoring and disseminating much of the Geneva Consensus. Today, UNAIDS partners include the WHO, UNDP, UNICEF, UN High Commissioner for Refugees, United Nations Office on Drugs and Crime, and the World Food Program, among others, all of which have made HIV/AIDS a substantial core of their respective institutional missions.

The World Bank is also a member of the UNAIDS partnership, but its action on HIV/AIDS and levels of spending have been so extensive that it is worth highlighting its role as a lead architect of the Geneva Consensus. Describing the World Bank's involvement in HIV/AIDS in the late 1980s and early 1990s, Sebastian Mallaby writes, "Other international agencies were no better at this time, but the Bank's failure on AIDS remains inexcusable," arguing that its participation in UNAIDS was virtually coerced.[41] However, a WHO leader who participated in the transition contradicts this view, arguing that the World Bank was a willing partner in the development of UNAIDS.[42] According to the Bank, it was the most expansive donor organization during the first decade of the global response: it made its first HIV/AIDS loan in 1986, and financed sixty-one projects in forty-one countries, for a total of $632 million as early as the end of 1996.[43] Given the Bank's limited involvement in global health prior to the onset of AIDS, its efforts on this issue have been extensive.

In carrying out global governance of AIDS, organizations such as the World Bank hardly hide the fact that they are trying to shape the nature of authority across national boundaries.[44] For example, the Bank has pub-

---

[41] Mallaby 2004, 318–19.

[42] Interview with former WHO official.

[43] World Bank 1999, 259.

[44] In a similar manner, Finnemore (1996) finds that UNESCO helped prompt the creation of science policy organizations as an "appropriate" or "necessary" role in member states.

lished and disseminated a document entitled *Turning Bureaucrats into Warriors: Preparing and Implementing Multi-sector HIV-AIDS Programs in Africa*,[45] which is a blueprint for how states should govern. It describes the application of conditions on loans to force the hand of government leaders[46] who resist taking on AIDS. International organizations, even those that had previously advocated reducing the role of the state, have recommended an important role for government in fighting HIV/AIDS. Their basis is the logic of public economics, by which health policies are public goods that would be underprovided in the market.[47]

In a state system that had already established institutions for global health governance, the onset of a virulent HIV/AIDS pandemic generated imperatives for the exercise of authority, ranging from empathy to preservation of national health, and even national security. Given the constant and rapid movement of people across borders, poor health is feared because it may contribute to state weakness and instability, jeopardizing economic and personal security in the North. In addition to scholars, both the United Nations Security Council in Resolution 1308 (2000) and the United States' National Security Council have made specific reference to such security threats. By 2001, there was clear consensus among the world's leading powers that efforts ought to be advanced on the problem of AIDS around the world.

In preparation for a 2001 United Nations General Assembly Special Session (UNGASS) on HIV/AIDS, the secretary-general announced the creation of a vehicle for generating the financial capital required to address the AIDS pandemic: The Global Fund to Fight AIDS, Tuberculosis and Malaria (GFATM). The GFATM was established as a response to the realities of an international environment characterized by strong state sovereignty: its mission has been to raise capital and to disperse funds almost exclusively at the country level, but not to implement any programs itself. Its mission is to support programs that reflect "national ownership." Located in Geneva, it has a lean program staff and employs an independent technical panel to review applications for funding. While the GFATM has the veneer of a neutral organization, just receiving and reviewing applications, it has strongly shaped the Geneva Consensus through its decisions on funding (discussed in the next section). In 2003, it approved 227

---

[45] Brown, Ayvalikli, and Mohammad 2004.
[46] World Bank 1999, 277.
[47] World Bank 1999, 39–44.

grants in 124 countries, and by the end of 2006, it had committed $6.8 billion across 136 countries.[48]

Beyond the UN agencies, other key actors have emerged as part of the apparatus of global governance prodding responses to the pandemic. All of the rich countries have made direct donations in addition to financial support for the multilateral organizations described above. In 2005, major donor government commitments to HIV/AIDS amounted to $4.3 billion, of which $3.5 billion was bilateral assistance.[49] (As a point of reference, total overseas development assistance provided by G7 countries was approximately $57.6 billion in 2004.)[50] Although the United States is among the least generous providers of overseas development assistance as share of GDP, AIDS activism and AIDS-based research helped make the United States the biggest financial supporter of AIDS research and direct development assistance for HIV/AIDS.[51] In a January 28, 2003, State of the Union speech, with a military confrontation with Iraq impending, and growing resentment toward the United States in its "war on terror," President George Bush announced a $15 billion President's Emergency Plan for AIDS Relief (PEPFAR).[52] PEPFAR provided resources through which bilateral development efforts, such as USAID's Global AIDS Program would be funded, with new centrally directed guidelines and targets. The cornerstone of the PEPFAR strategy has been to deliver ARV drugs to the most affected developing countries, and its emphasis on abstinence has been distinctive and widely criticized, but it carries out the full range of prevention and treatment programs advocated by most AIDS organizations. In May 2007, Bush announced a further five-year, $30 billion commitment for the AIDS program.

It is notable that perhaps the world's first "global tax" originated in response to AIDS (and to tuberculosis and malaria, which have gained attention in the era of AIDS because they increase susceptibility to infection and heighten symptoms). Long discussed by the French government, the

[48] www.theglobalfund.org (consulted January 5, 2007).

[49] Kates and Lief 2006, 9.

[50] Statistical annex of OECD 2005.

[51] According to Kates and Lief (2006, 10), in 2007, U.S. commitments amounted to 48.9 percent of all major donor government commitments on HIV/AIDS, and expenditure as share of gross national income was third among G7 industrialized countries, after Canada and the United Kingdom.

[52] Behrman 2004 chronicles the development of the PEPFAR, and in an interview, a top White House administrator involved with the program told me he believed the account was an accurate portrayal of its development.

"airline-ticket solidarity tax" was adopted by nineteen countries (as of late 2006) with the purpose of bringing low-cost medicines to developing countries through a purchasing facility housed in the WHO. Although the idea of an international tax to be used for pressing international needs has circulated since it was strongly advocated by Nobel laureate economist James Tobin, this new levy is the first actual manifestation and represents a milestone in global governance. National governments have concluded that it is politically viable to dedicate a new tax to primarily benefit people in other countries. The countries that have committed to the levy are from both the North and South, though most of the proceeds can be expected to come from wealthier countries. (In low-income countries, only the wealthiest people travel by air, making the tax progressive.)

It is critical to point out that unlike trade and many other areas subject to global governance in the postwar era, AIDS governance has not been a "club" model,[53] with backroom negotiations by health ministers from the wealthy states. On the contrary, by the mid-1990s it had become a far more open and transparent set of institutions. Private and nonprofit organizations have become central players in the global governance of HIV/AIDS, and they have helped to author and to support much of the Geneva Consensus. Throughout the epidemic, highly networked human rights and public health activists and academics—including those from Human Rights Watch, the Canadian HIV/AIDS Legal Network, and the François-Xavier Bagnoud Center for Health and Human Rights—played a role in the development of the Geneva Consensus. They have contributed to a larger epistemic community in the manner Anne-Marie Slaughter and others have described, linking biomedical researchers with lawyers, policymakers, and social scientists. Paul Farmer, a Harvard medical anthropologist, medical doctor, human rights activist, and NGO creator, and Richard Parker, a Columbia professor of socio-medical sciences active in Brazilian and international social science networks, are among the most prominent of a large number of people who have helped to develop and to advocate ideas about how to address the epidemic.

International NGOs such as Doctors Without Borders/Médecins Sans Frontières, Act Up, Catholic Relief Services, Family Health International, and CARE as well as international research and consulting organizations such as The Futures Group/Constella and McKinsey have all been involved in global efforts at AIDS control. Particularly in the early years of

---

[53] Keohane and Nye 2000a.

the epidemic, before most national governments and multilateral global institutions acted aggressively on AIDS, these organizations provided a patchwork global governance, with direct links at the grassroots level. Indeed, by the beginning of the twenty-first century, global public health finally arrived as an issue on the minds of the most powerful individuals on the planet. The wealthiest man on earth, Bill Gates, and one of the most powerful men on earth, Bill Clinton, have both made HIV/AIDS a concern of their charitable foundations and of their daily activities. The Gates Foundation's investment in global public health has been unprecedented and has been spent largely on specific research projects and interventions, but also in direct support of government efforts.

The head of the United Nations and presidents of several advanced industrialized countries, including the United States, the United Kingdom, and France, have all declared AIDS a global emergency in need of concerted attention. Famous figures from Hollywood to London to São Paulo, including the politically active rock star Bono, have stormed the globe championing greater attention to global inequality, poverty, and development. Health has become a concern in centers of international decision-making, even for those organizations and networks that have had little experience or mandate in this sector; in large part this development is due to international attention to the problem of AIDS. For example, in 2002, at the meetings at the World Economic Forum in Davos, Switzerland, the Global Health Initiative was launched to foster public-private partnerships on major health problems such as HIV/AIDS, tuberculosis, and malaria.

While the Geneva Consensus has been largely authored and supported by wealthy and powerful countries and individuals, select activists and technocrats from poor countries have played important roles. The failings of and resentment toward the "Washington Consensus," as well as notable movements to articulate a voice from the South, have created space for consultations within institutions that must be seen as at least partially democratic in their decision-making. The leaders of many developing countries, including Uganda's president Yoweri Museveni, South Africa's treatment activist Zachie Achmat, and Brazil's government AIDS program leader, Paulo Teixeira, have been actively involved as sources of ideas and leadership in global governance networks and formal structures. While smaller regional organizations do exist to coordinate responses in the developing world—such as the regional organizations of the WHO (PAHO) and regional parliamentary forums on HIV/AIDS—these are virtually all funded and organized by the international donor community.

Broadcasting Authority

Having identified the development of a network of actors and institutions involved in the global governance of AIDS, we can turn to the mechanisms through which such authority has been exerted. Recalling the theoretical paradigms identified at the outset of the chapter, two in particular have been important: the social construction of ideas, and direct or quasi-coercive influence. I refer to "quasi-coercive influence" because there have been no threats of military force against noncompliant states, and even other forms of sanctions have been largely implicit. And yet there is a degree of coercion in the sense that relatively poor and weak governments may be sensitive to the directives of aid and trade partners who can apply pressure for compliance through threats to reduce support.

The asymmetry of power in coordinating the global response to HIV/AIDS retains characteristics familiar from other policy areas. Given the strong norms of state sovereignty that govern the international system, it is quite remarkable that international organizations and especially single governments such as the United States have their own staff, offices, and resources in countries around the world, with the aim of directly shaping the knowledge, behavior, and health of people around the world. This is all the more exceptional given that HIV/AIDS concerns areas of human behavior that are private, and difficult and controversial for any authority to regulate.

Such direct exercise of authority is more the exception than the norm, however. Instead, the content of the Geneva Consensus has tended to be transmitted to national governments through direct consultations and meetings, but also indirectly to medical professionals, legislators, and civil society organizations in developing countries.[54] As in many other areas of global governance,[55] broad networks of professionals and government officials have been in constant communication and deliberation about new scientific findings, political interpretations, goals, and proposed actions.

Every developing country in Africa, Asia, and Latin America and the Caribbean is supported or coordinated by a regional WHO program on AIDS. As figure 3.1 shows, eighty-three of eighty-five countries considered in the analysis in chapter 6[56] have received direct financial and often

[54] World Bank 1999, 277.
[55] See Slaughter 2004.
[56] Countries with GDP/capita less than $8,000, populations greater than 500,000, in the regions of Africa, Asia, Latin America and the Caribbean.

3.1. World Bank, PEPFAR, and GFATM Coverage of AIDS-Related Assistance in Developing Countries

Number of major AIDS-related donor programs (World Bank AIDS Project; PEPFAR focus country; and/or Global Fund) operational in each country at least one year 1986–2006.

other assistance from at least one of the three largest AIDS funders—the GFATM, the World Bank, and PEPFAR—specifically for AIDS-related projects, and most of these countries have received funding from more than one.[57] The point is simply that all countries have been directly influenced by the Geneva Consensus, irrespective of their domestic conditions, which makes any differences in country-level responses all the more puzzling. In chapter 6, I will explore more fully some of the determinants of cross-country variation in levels of funding to governments for HIV/AIDS, but for now my point is simply to remark on how expansive and global these efforts have been.

Complementing such patterns of assistance, throughout the history of the epidemic, are forums for exchanging ideas about how to proceed. In particular, there have been highly visible international conferences on the pandemic. Since the mid-1980s, scientists, activists,[58] corporate representatives, and government bureaucrats and leaders from around the world have convened in order to discuss—but perhaps more importantly to disseminate—information about how to prevent HIV infections and to treat AIDS-related symptoms.

While these conferences are now hosted in locations around the world with varied themes and foci, the largest and politically most important conferences have been the international AIDS conferences, currently under the aegis of the International AIDS Society. The first was hosted in Atlanta, Georgia, home of the American Centers for Disease Control (CDC), and hosted by the WHO and the American Department of Health and Human Services. As shown in table 3.1, of the sixteen conferences held between 1985 and 2008, only three have been outside of the rich countries of the United States, Canada, Japan, and Western Europe. Of course, this may reflect the availability of airports and conference facilities as much as anything else. But even these factors highlight the manifestation of political and economic asymmetries.

The other important international focal meeting in the history of the pandemic was the spring 2001 United Nations General Assembly Special Session (UNGASS) on AIDS held in New York City, which was billed as

---

[57] Malaysia and Uruguay have not received such assistance. Both are relatively high income and have low adult HIV prevalence as compared with other countries in these regions.

[58] Keck and Sikkink's (1998) portrait of transnational activism well describes the dense networks that have driven the global AIDS agenda and the development of the Geneva Consensus.

TABLE 3.1
Locations of International AIDS Conferences (1985–2008)

	Global "North"			Global "South"		
	North America	Europe	Asia	Africa	Asia	Latin America
1985	Atlanta					
1986		Paris				
1987	Washington, D.C.					
1988		Stockholm				
1989	Montreal					
1990	San Francisco					
1991		Florence				
1992		Amsterdam				
1993		Berlin				
1994			Yokohama			
1996	Vancouver					
1998		Geneva				
1999						
2000		Barcelona				
2002				Durban		
2004					Bangkok	
2006	Toronto					
2008						Mexico City

an opportunity to jointly create new resolutions and to gather ideas for fighting the pandemic, but in reality was as much about broadcasting the Geneva Consensus and getting acceptance both from national governments and from the growing web of civil society organizations.

The social construction and coercion paradigms do a far better job than the learning paradigm in capturing the nature of AIDS-related policy diffusion. Someone who has attended international conferences on AIDS has a palpable sense of "key messages" being delivered by conference organizers and lead actors throughout the sessions of the conference. If policies generated at such conferences are adopted in developing countries, one cannot immediately infer that this is the result of independent, technical analyses of domestic circumstances and the impact of recommended AIDS control policies, but rather a socialization in the analyses promoted by the professional community. The conferences are highly social events, and in meetings and plenary sessions, the policies being promoted are not often directly challenged.

To identify one example, in the early stages of research for this book, I attended the "civil society" day of the 2001 UNGASS conference, when NGOs were invited to develop their own resolutions. It was billed as an opportunity for NGOs from poor countries to shape the global agenda on AIDS. The reality was something different. Representatives from organizations and countries from around the world—perhaps three or four hundred individuals in total—gathered in an open room with folding chairs set up. Announcements were made from a podium, and we were instructed to go to breakout sessions on education, human rights, finance, and so on. I attended the finance meeting, with approximately twenty-five individuals from various countries. We introduced ourselves, and because I said I was a researcher, someone suggested I serve as rapporteur. The others were largely from African countries, or Americans from organizations doing work in those countries. The Americans did much of the talking, and no one came with budgets or budget analyses. Nonetheless, within a few minutes, a consensus emerged that the UN resolution should call for $10 billion a year for the next ten years. How did we arrive at this figure? A bottom-up analysis of needs calculated by developing countries? In fact, this was the number Secretary-General Kofi Annan had suggested in the period leading up to the conference. I reported these findings to the larger group when it reconvened, and there was no call for more discussion from civil society organizations. What can I infer from my impromptu stint of participatory research? The meeting was as much a ritual as a forum for exchange of ideas. Decisions about policy and best practice are made by high-level experts and bureaucrats prior to a meeting, often in consultation with important NGOs. Leaders of the global governance regime perceive that civil society organizations, particularly with roots in the global South, must be consulted if the regime is to govern with authority. At least there must be the *appearance* of consultation.

Before, during, and after such international consultations and collaborations, a startling amount of documentation has been produced, with a host of guidelines: the content of the Geneva Consensus. Because of the period in which this epidemic has emerged—that is, particularly since the mid-1990s, parallel to the surge in Internet usage—the Geneva Consensus has been rapidly disseminated on websites and web-hosted documentation of best-practice guidelines. For example, since 1996, UNAIDS has maintained a "Best Practice" collection of documents to promote the general goals and strategies of the Geneva Consensus.[59] The 2001 UNGASS produced a "declaration of commitment" signed on June 27 by heads of state from around the world that brought together most of these recommendations and helped establish targets and monitoring indicators for country-level reporting. A follow-up 2006 UN meeting prompted governments and civil society actors to report back with data on progress (these data are analyzed in chapter 6).

While such meetings and consultations have socialized policymakers to accept the Geneva Consensus, the specific mechanisms of international funding for the epidemic have provided additional powerful inducements. In particular, the GFATM developed an application process that has required each country to develop a "Country Coordinating Mechanism" (CCM), to be broadly representative of stakeholders and actors in the country. The application forms for each funding round have been extremely detailed, with a great number of closed-ended questions that induce conformity for countries wishing to receive the funding. Given that the applications are reviewed in the Geneva headquarters of the organization, and that the WHO and UNAIDS are identified as lead partners, country applicants have strong incentives to propose to carry out what these organizations have touted as "best practice," what I describe as the content of the Geneva Consensus.

THE CONTENT OF THE GENEVA CONSENSUS

In the remainder of the chapter, I identify broad strands of the Geneva Consensus, the recommended policy strategies articulated by the international actors described above. While a much fuller inventory of policies

---

[59] As of September 2005, there were 156 titles in the UNAIDS "Best Practice" collection—recommendations for developing countries for fighting HIV/AIDS.

and recommendations could be identified, I have selected the most prominent policies with the most universal application. These are the benchmarks to which countries are held "accountable" in the global governance regime. In the absence of compliance, global governance authorities have used carrot-and-stick approaches, that is, greater encouragement and offers of additional assistance, public shaming, or cutting off resources. Because developing countries have expressed profound resentment over the conditionality clauses of structural adjustment packages that were part of the "Washington Consensus," there have been far fewer applications of such heavy-handed strategies with AIDS. Instead, global governance has been implemented more through persuasion; that is, international leaders have advanced frightening predictions of sickness, death, and economic collapse in the event that the epidemic is allowed to progress unchecked.

The benchmarks have also been used as targets intended to hold donors accountable, a sign of an era in which there has been concern for transparency and accountability in development assistance. The United Nations has promoted quantitative benchmarks in its articulation of the Millennium Development Goals (MDGs) for policies and outcomes, and the comparative analysis presented in subsequent chapters is framed by such prescriptions. I should point out, however, that by delineating "best practice" recommendations, I am not in fact endorsing any of them for their efficacy or appropriateness.[60] My research and analysis have not attempted to address these important concerns, which require a distinctive set of data and analyses.

Rather, this inventory helps to address three analytical goals: first, it provides a sharper and more detailed portrait of efforts at global governance of AIDS, allowing us to trace the international influences that shape domestic responses to the epidemic. Second, we can use this framework for comparing countries, in subsequent attempts to account for cross-country variance. And finally, by detailing some of the policies, we can anticipate the more specific political fault-lines that make governing this social problem challenging.

As a general rule, the consensus recommendation for AIDS policy has been to promote an aggressive response. That is, governments have been encouraged to be timely and expansive in their financial, human, and

---

[60] For example, Helen Epstein (2007) charges that many of the efforts of the West have not been as effective as locally generated and implemented solutions to the epidemic, including the "zero-grazing" campaigns of Uganda.

symbolic responses to the epidemic. While this recommendation may seem obvious, many other areas of policy are characterized by less agreement about best practice and the appropriate role for the state. For example, on taxation there has been disagreement about levels and types of taxes, and in the area of economic development, leading institutional actors disagree about what role the state ought to play. When it comes to pension reform or education policy, leading international actors have disagreed about the proper balance between state and market. On HIV/ AIDS there has been much more basic agreement that in the developing countries, more state involvement is better, though certainly not to the exclusion of nonstate actors, who have also been vigorously encouraged to participate.

I group the main sets of recommendations into four observable categories: general bureaucratic development, prevention, treatment, and rights orientation. Each has been associated with somewhat different global actors and initiatives, and each has had political implications. At least to a degree, each has been the product of a political battle, but one that was largely resolved in a manner that I can characterize as a "consensus." The resulting prescriptions have narrowed the range of likely policies adopted by national governments in the developing countries.

Bureaucratic Development

Since early in the pandemic, the Geneva Consensus has advocated development of strong state capacities for addressing AIDS at the national level. At least three components of a national response were broadcast as necessary: the establishment of an AIDS "program"; the visible representation of national leadership; and the commitment of financial resources.

An important constructivist insight is that AIDS was not obviously the responsibility of national states. Other more localized authorities, including traditional healers, traditional leaders, private doctors, and local governments might have been identified as lead actors in the absence of a coordinated diffusion of ideas about authority on this issue. Given the weakness of national public health systems, the relative weakness of states, and the widespread (albeit highly varied) trust in these other authorities, it is possible to imagine the counterfactual of a global AIDS strategy bypassing national state authorities altogether. In fact, the focus of the Geneva Consensus on state authority is in certain ways bitterly ironic, as international organizations such as the World Bank and the IMF had been trying to reduce the scope and power of national states in the 1980s as part of the Washington Consensus, and some scholars have concluded that service cuts demanded as part of structural adjustment programs have impeded the ability of governments to respond effectively to AIDS.[61]

Nonetheless the WHO, starting with its 1987 "global strategy" document created for the World Health Assembly of that year, prescribed a central role for national states, albeit in partnership with international and local actors. On the one hand, the mere establishment of policies or the creation of committees and programs requires little sacrifice. Governments produce endless such policies and initiatives, which can be created with relatively little publicity or legislative oversight. Thus it should not be surprising that by 1990 virtually every country in the world had established an AIDS program.[62] Given that only a handful of states in the developing world had confirmed significant numbers of HIV-infected individuals at that time, a great many of these states were responding to global governance pressures to act—even if those actions turned out to be largely superficial because states lacked understanding of and commitment to the problem. The AIDS strategy and policy documents associated with numerous developing countries were written almost verbatim by WHO representatives, and their acceptance was tantamount to the signing of a nonbinding international treaty.

The Geneva Consensus has also recommended a more visible and expansive development of government AIDS bureaucracies. This has included the coordination of AIDS-related policies across government sectors because, as was recognized early on, HIV/AIDS was not merely a biomedical, but a social phenomenon, affecting a wide variety of groups in different settings, with consequences for various government sectors. International health experts had also generally concluded that health has almost universally been a politically less central portfolio than ministries such as finance and security. To command resources and attention, other ministries would need to be involved. By 1992, the World Health Assembly was urging member states to include "multisectoral responses" and "commitment and leadership from the highest political level."[63] By

---

[61] Cheru 2002.

[62] Mann, Tarantola, and Netter 1992, 296–97. Iliffe (2006, 70) points out that because the WHO was bound by sovereignty agreements states were encouraged to invite WHO assistance; by June 1988, 151 countries had sought such assistance.

[63] WHO 1992.

the mid-1990s, the notion of the multisectoral response had become hegemonic, and government AIDS bureaucracies came to be evaluated by the simple question of whether they had some autonomy from the health ministry. Along these lines, the Geneva Consensus has long advocated direct participation by national executives in the form of visible displays of acknowledgment of the problem of AIDS within the country's borders and personal involvements in AIDS prevention.

The Geneva Consensus has encouraged developing countries to spend some of their own limited resources on AIDS, and also to avail themselves of grants and loans provided by the international community, in accordance with other tenets of the strategy. In support of the Geneva Consensus, there has been significant donor funding of HIV/AIDS, and the resource base has grown exponentially over time. Many observers and authors of the Geneva Consensus have highlighted funding shortfalls relative to need, particularly as an advocacy strategy, but the financial response has certainly been significant. In the mid-1980s, WHO leadership began soliciting contributions from donor countries in order to implement the unfolding global AIDS strategy.[64] In 1986, the total global outlay on HIV/AIDS from donor countries to developing countries was a mere $200,000;[65] by 1993 it had grown to $257 million;[66] and by 2003, it was $4.7 billion.[67] As of 2004, an estimated $6.1 billion was available for HIV/AIDS in low- and middle-income countries, approximately two-thirds of which was donor funding.[68]

The lion's share of donor resources has been channeled through national governments. In 1993, of $226 million in total funding from donor countries, $165 million went to national AIDS programs; $40.5 million to NGOs in developing countries; and $20.4 million to other sources.[69] Although major donors such as the World Bank, PEPFAR, and GFATM support many nongovernment programs in countries, they do this in careful negotiation with national governments sensitive to perceived infringements on their sovereignty. By the end of its sixth round of funding, 68 percent of GFATM disbursements went to national governments; and of the remaining, 19 percent went to NGOs and the private

---

[64] Kates 2005, 16.
[65] Mann, Tarantola, and Netter 1992, 511–12.
[66] Mann and Tarantola 1996, 380.
[67] From www.unaids.org (consulted September 15, 2005).
[68] WHO 1987.
[69] Mann and Tarantola 1996, 385.

sector, and 13 percent to multilateral organizations operating at the country level.[70]

A caricatured portrait of international development aid is one of developing country governments and societies in an endless quest for more resources and the pursuit of state enlargement. However, the case of AIDS highlights the limits of that view, as many countries have resisted such aid and the very development of AIDS-related state capacities. More visible strategies for bureaucratic development have sometimes been resisted because such moves would signal the AIDS epidemic in the country, something that many government leaders have tried to deny.

Finally, a core tenet of the Geneva Consensus on bureaucratic development has been the establishment of epidemiological monitoring and surveillance systems. As in other areas of state authority, monitoring has been a component of recommended AIDS strategies, and it has demanded new state intrusions into private lives in the sense that individuals would be required to submit to a blood test (later in the epidemic, other forms of testing would become available) and to receive potentially devastating information that might be revealed publicly. In the absence of treatment options, AIDS was understood early in the epidemic to be a death sentence, and often interpreted by local communities as evidence of immoral behavior.

Anticipating resistance to widespread testing—observed almost immediately in the rich countries where AIDS had presented itself most visibly early in the epidemic—the Geneva Consensus has recommended more limited intrusions in the form of sentinel surveillance of subpopulations,[71] and "voluntary counseling and testing" (VCT) sites, both of which were promoted because they were consistent with concerns to protect confidentiality and anonymity. In the wake of accounts of violence against people infected with HIV, Geneva Consensus authors have

---

[70] From http://www.theglobalfund.org/en/funds_raised/distribution/#sector_recipients (consulted March 5, 2008).

[71] For example, of women attending antenatal clinics, or of patients attending clinics for sexually transmitted infections. Historically, most estimates on HIV prevalence for developing countries have been generated from tests carried out at such sites, but because these groups are not representative of the general population (for example, by definition, pregnant women have recently been sexually active), many of these estimates have been extremely inaccurate, often overstating the extent of the epidemic within particular countries.

maintained a steadfast concern that such information be obtained in a protected manner.

Only more recently, particularly since the 2006 International AIDS Conference in Toronto, has more routine testing been proposed as an alternative strategy, owing to the low levels of take-up for voluntary testing, and the inadequacies of sentinel surveillance. However, this proposal has been vigorously challenged by those fearing an intrusive policy, one that might adversely affect citizens through public exposure of their HIV status. It is possible that routine testing will eventually become part of the Geneva Consensus, but this idea still lacks sufficient support from lead actors, including officials in UNAIDS and international human rights NGOs. At the 2006 conference, the Canadian HIV/AIDS Legal Network executive director, Joanne Csete, presented a talk, "Routine Testing: Are We Ready to Throw Human Rights Out of HIV Testing Policy?" Mary Robinson, former president of Ireland and head of the UN's Human Rights Commission, and Joseph Amon, head of Human Rights Watch's HIV/AIDS unit, have also publicly questioned the appropriateness of routine testing owing to concerns over human rights.

Beyond recommendations and ideas, some aspects of global governance have involved more direct exercise of authority. For example, the WHO, UNAIDS, and other Geneva Consensus actors have helped to implement specific procedures and guidelines, and created information systems for reporting and analyzing test data. National governments have been expected to report to international bureaucracies on standardized information concerning numbers of infections, levels of treatment, and AIDS-related deaths, and this information is then disseminated more widely. Not surprisingly, this information has been controversial, and many countries (including India, as described in chapter 5) have publicly debated international authorities about the quality of estimates that are produced with available data. Moreover, WHO officials have reported to me that they were unable to release subnational data on HIV infections because of the internal political conflicts they would engender at the country level. Nonetheless, the relevant global governance actors have managed to exert a great deal of authority across countries in collecting and legitimating the quality of information. At the 2006 International AIDS Conference, I asked an official from the Ethiopian government if he could share some HIV data, and he told me without any irony that the best source of his information for those data would be the (American) Centers for Disease Control website.

Prevention

Bureaucratic development has been promoted largely to carry out the two key tasks of prevention and treatment, which must be disentangled because they involve different state actions and have distinctive political implications. Prevention policies are those that aim to reduce the number of new infections by changing people's behaviors and by introducing specific barriers or safeguards. Because the virus is largely transmitted by individuals who have sex with multiple partners, through sex among men, and through the sharing of needles among those who inject drugs, and because such behaviors often violate norms articulated in laws and religions throughout the world, such behaviors have posed a political dilemma. Reaching a consensus has implied a degree of conflict and compromise between those who favor "harm reduction" and those who favor "prohibition / behavior change" approaches to public health. In the former case, it is generally assumed that certain behaviors will always be prevalent, and rather than pursue a futile effort to eliminate them, a more pragmatic strategy is to reduce damage to those who engage in them, and damage to others. In the latter case, harm reduction strategies are criticized as potentially "inducing" such behavior, and it is assumed that behaviors can be changed through more active prohibitions. In the case of IV drug use, for example, a harm reduction strategy is to offer clean needles and access to methadone clinics, whereas a prohibition / behavior change strategy is to punish drug use and distribution.

This divide has been at the core of political battles over HIV and AIDS policies, revolving around questions of acceptance of nonnormative behaviors that put people at risk of becoming infected. Early in the epidemic, many moral conservatives began to step up their condemnations of such behaviors, and to reject solutions that would reduce the likelihood of HIV transmission during them. Pope John Paul II, in particular, who reigned for almost the entire history of the epidemic until his death in 2005, was highly critical of condom policies and of homosexuality. Policy advocates would argue that such behaviors were simply normal and unstoppable human behaviors, and from a public health standpoint, the best strategy would be to make them safer. As the Geneva Consensus has been so deeply influenced by those championing human rights, a strong tendency toward the harm reduction approach has emerged.

Nonetheless, the implementation of prevention policies has proved politically and logistically difficult. Sexual intercourse and childbirth are private acts, not easily subject to government regulation. Sexual prevention campaigns are akin to other state-imposed collective action campaigns: getting people to transform their personal behaviors in ways that are against the norm. But such prevention strategies have been among the most controversial of the Geneva Consensus prescriptions at all levels of governance. As Helen Epstein points out, "If sex were an entirely rational process, the species would have died out long ago. But the delirious, illogical nature of sex makes setting a realistic HIV prevention policy very difficult."[72]

A 1987 WHO resolution on the global epidemic made no direct mention of sexual transmission, but the 1992 document did, referring to "safer sexual practices," and the 1994 "Paris Declaration" of forty-two government leaders advocated "promotion of and access to various culturally acceptable prevention strategies and products, including condoms and treatment of sexually transmitted diseases." By the time UNAIDS was formed, the lead architects were unambiguously promoting condom use, arguing in a report, "Condom use is a critical element in a comprehensive, effective and sustainable approach to HIV prevention and treatment . . . The male latex condom is the single, most efficient, available technology to reduce the sexual transmission of HIV and other sexually transmitted infections."

The alternatives to the promotion of the use of condoms—harm reduction that assumes people will have sexual relations with multiple partners—are strategies that aim to eliminate such behavior. For example, the socially conservative Bush administration has put more emphasis on "abstinence" and "being faithful" than have other authors of the Geneva Consensus. Indeed, religious leaders have argued that no sex before marriage and no "adultery" is the best prevention strategy. Many religious conservatives, especially but not exclusively in the United States, described HIV and AIDS as punishments against those who were libertine or unfaithful. Evangelical preacher Jerry Falwell famously proclaimed that AIDS was a "punishment from God" against those deviating from religious norms.

While this conflict is unlikely ever to be completely resolved, the synthetic "A, B, C" approach—to encourage *A*bstinence and *B*eing faithful, and if "that does not work" or is not possible, to use *C*ondoms—has emerged as a compromise consensus. Publicly, no prominent international AIDS figures supporting harm reduction have completely rejected the A and B approaches, but instead have questioned their efficacy and practical-

---

[72]Epstein 2005.

ity. In the case of the U.S. government, which has been the lead international actor favoring behavior change over harm reduction—representatives consistently note that the government is the leading international supplier of condoms.

It is also important to point out that as the death toll mounted, many religious conservatives who had associated the virus with "sinners" began to change their position. Starting around 2000, in the United States leading conservative figures such as Jesse Helms and Billy Graham proclaimed a need to take greater steps to prevent the spread of HIV and to treat those suffering with AIDS.[73]

Beyond sexual transmissions, three other modes of transmission have been consistently identified: "vertical" mother-to-child, blood transfusions, and needles shared among injecting drug users. The Geneva Consensus has included recommendations for each transmission route.

Before the idea of ARV treatment therapy became a consensus item, the use of these drugs was already promoted for prevention efforts. As the epidemic spread to women, and HIV-positive mothers began to give birth to HIV-positive children, biomedical researchers began to identify strategies to reduce the chances of such vertical transmission in a cost-effective manner. Drug regimes, including "short-course" and "long-course" therapies of zidovudine and nevirapine, were shown in the 1990s to reduce the likelihood of transmitting the virus from mother to child, and such therapies became central to "PMTCT"—prevention of mother-to-child transmission. Initially, many of the Geneva Consensus authors did not envision widespread adoption of these practices. In its landmark book, *Confronting AIDS*, published in 1999, the World Bank pointed out that "at roughly $3,000 per HIV infection averted, this approach to prevention does not compare favorably with other approaches . . . and would be affordable only in middle- or upper-income countries."[74] However, as costs began to drop, and proof of efficacy mounted, the tide turned. By the end of 1998, UNAIDS authored a report in its "best practice" collection that highlighted recommendations for PMTCT, while also indicating some of its social and political challenges. In 2000, the WHO issued recommendations on the use of antiretroviral drugs for preventing mother-to-child transmission of HIV,[75] and at the 2001 UNGASS, countries committed

[73] See Busby 2007 for an analysis of the rise of "moral action" on the part of actors who had previously appeared reluctant.
[74] World Bank 1999, 104.
[75] WHO 2004, iv.

to reduce the proportion of infants infected with HIV by 20 percent by 2005 and by 50 percent by 2010.[76] The other option for a PMTCT program was to provide mothers with infant formula in order to reduce transmission through breast-feeding. However, owing to the challenges of obtaining clean water in much of the developing world, a checkered history of failed infant formula schemes, the proven health benefits of breast milk, and the possibility of stigmatization of women not breast-feeding, there has been less agreement on this strategy.

Yet another distinctive strand of the prevention component of the Geneva Consensus has been regulation of the international blood supply. After massive numbers of hemophiliacs became infected with HIV through transfusions with tainted blood, panic ensued about blood safety, particularly in the advanced industrialized countries where the problem was most evident.[77] The establishment of blood safety guidelines was a natural course of action for lead actors authoring the Geneva Consensus, and while initially highly politicized, the implications of the recommendations have been far less contentious than the other prescriptions described above. The WHO held its first meeting on AIDS in 1983, and several recommendations were made that related directly to the safety of blood and blood products: The public and especially blood donors should be educated about AIDS; attempts should be made to exclude donors who were in groups at increased risk for AIDS; the use of blood and blood products should be limited to circumstances deemed to be essential.[78] By 1998, blood safety became one of the WHO's "strategic priorities."[79] As new technologies for testing donors and blood supplies became available, they were recommended as standards through international epistemic communities.

In practice, two issues have proved challenging: first is that in many countries, the commercial sale of blood and blood products is a substantial enterprise, and imperatives to keep costs low have often implied uneven screening procedures. Second, the interpretation of recommendations to avoid blood donors in "high risk" populations has caused political backlash.

[76] WHO 2004, 1.

[77] Contributors to Feldman and Bayer's (1999) edited volume on the tainted blood supply in the advanced industrialized countries describe how hemophiliacs mobilized against states and institutional blood suppliers to seek compensation, and forced a restructuring of the norms and practices of blood supply.

[78] Petricciani et al. 1987, x.

[79] Department of Blood Safety and Clinical Technology and the World Health Organization 1999.

Notwithstanding, by 2006 there was relatively little controversy over blood safety, and virtually all countries were committed to ensuring it, even if their governments could not always effectively enforce this goal. The level of sacrifice expected on the part of citizens is quite low. Without the development of international guidelines and protocols and the direct transmission of such information to developing countries by the WHO, it is difficult to imagine that blood would be nearly as safe as it is today.

The Geneva Consensus has included strategies for the reduction of HIV transmission through the sharing of needles by drug users. However, particularly because such drug use is criminalized in so many countries, there has been much less international enthusiasm and agreement with this strategy. Norms against IV drug use are much stronger than norms against having multiple sexual partners, making it far more difficult to arrive at political consensus on this strategy, despite widespread scientific evidence of its efficacy in reducing HIV transmission.

More recently, male circumcision has been found to reduce the likelihood of HIV transmission and is being promoted as a possibly important prevention strategy. Because of the recentness of the finding, however, it is not considered in the analyses that follow.

While it would be tempting to interpret the diffusion of ideas on prevention as evidence of learning, several facts suggest that what has been learned and repeated is the product of mediated power relationships. First, for virtually every prevention strategy, one can identify some conflicting evidence of its efficacy, which begs the question of which evidence drives the learning process. Second, there are clear examples of global governance leaders presenting, in a heavy-handed manner, evidence of particular "best practice" cases to other countries. For example, in 2005, the UNDP promoted Thailand as a country that could "share its know-how" on how to prevent transmission.[80] A limited body of evidence from best-practice cases is repeated to actors and policymakers around the world, providing a narrowed framework from within which policies have been made.

Treatment

The provision of drug treatment to people infected with HIV has become the most visible, and more recently, the most central component of the

---

[80] See, for example, http://www.undp.or.th/focusareas/hiv.html (consulted December 7, 2007).

Geneva Consensus. For much of the early history of the epidemic, it was widely assumed by global governance authorities that the only financially viable strategy for controlling the epidemic and its effects on illness and mortality in the developing world were through information-based and barrier methods of prevention. Beyond the limited application of drug treatment for opportunistic infections associated with AIDS, the costs of providing antiretroviral drugs (ARVs) were initially prohibitive, as annual costs per patient for these drugs were many times the per capita income of most low- and middle-income countries. Moreover, many leaders doubted the possibility of extending treatment to the developing countries simply because of logistical and cultural constraints: In 2001, USAID head Andrew Natsios made the infamous comment that drug treatment was impractical because treatment regimens required strict adherence to precise timing, and most Africans "don't know what Western time is . . . and if you say one o'clock in the afternoon, they don't know what you are talking about." The idea that long-term drug therapy ought to be provided to every person infected with HIV (at a clinical stage when such medication would be appropriate) was unimaginable to most global actors, let alone to policymakers and activists in the developing world, certainly in the early 1990s, and generally throughout that decade. But within a few years of the new millennium, "universal access" became a pillar of the Geneva Consensus.

One reason that ARV prices initially remained high was that they had patent protections, which limited competition and allowed pharmaceutical corporations to charge thousands of dollars for a year's supply of medication.[81] As of 1994, the Trade Related Aspects of Intellectual Property Rights (TRIPs) agreement, brokered within the World Trade Organization (WTO), mandated that countries provide and protect patents on pharmaceuticals. But even beyond patent protection, many developing countries lacked capacity to make competing generic drugs. In the face of what were initially only minor challenges, the wealthiest countries, especially the United States, vigorously supported the multinational drug companies' inclinations to prohibit the manufacture of generic versions of their drugs before the twenty-year monopoly expired on these profitable patents and without any substantial additional action to make those drugs available at reduced costs in very poor settings.

---

[81] Much of the following draws on Shadlen 2007.

In the late 1990s, however, international activism on AIDS had gathered momentum and helped to change the rules and norms of drug treatment access. The idea promoted by activists, including organizations born in strictly domestic contexts, was that certain medicines ought to be considered "essential medicines" and provided to all. The countervailing argument made by pharmaceutical corporations, their trade associations, and their defenders in governments and international organizations was that if patents were not protected, there would be no incentives for future research and development.[82] Ultimately, the battle was won by the AIDS activists.

No other aspect of the global politics of AIDS has galvanized so many actors. As with many other aspects of the global response to AIDS, a full historical accounting would require several books, not just a few paragraphs.[83] These actors managed to build upon existing human rights and other advocacy networks and to capitalize on increasingly hegemonic ideas of global equity, particularly in terms of basic health. Notably, in 1999, as Al Gore was announcing his candidacy for president of the United States, Act Up activists protested his support for the U.S. trade policy, which was to enforce patents on AIDS drugs in developing countries, and his opposition to "compulsory licensing," which would allow local companies to manufacture cheap generics. Protestors hounded him on the campaign trail, and this proved increasingly embarrassing. Government representatives in the United States and the other advanced countries, as well as pharmaceutical corporations such as Merck, Bristol-Myers Squibb, and Roche, faced protests and challenges. For them the contrast between people in poor countries who were dying of AIDS and people in the rich countries who lived relatively healthy and normal lives was a political and public relations fiasco.

In response to such pressures, new global initiatives emerged, all of which shared the now transformational idea that AIDS drugs ought not to be limited to people in the rich countries, or the richest people in the poor countries. Despite some lingering concerns about cost, adverse affects on behavior, and the development of drug resistance, all of the major funding organizations became convinced of the need to distribute these drugs widely. Most recently, donor efforts on HIV/AIDS have become virtually synonymous with drug treatment.

[82] Beigbeder 2007, 196–98.
[83] For an excellent account of the specific activist organizations who helped shape new global patterns of AIDS treatment, see Smith and Siplon 2006.

Again, it is important to emphasize that global governance institutions do not operate as a unit, and it is relatively easy to find internal conflicts and contradictions. On the one hand, international institutions such as the WTO, largely controlled by the governments of the wealthiest countries, initially helped major corporations in those countries to extend and to protect their patents. On the other hand, in their efforts to promote treatment access, officials from a different international organization—the WHO—encouraged governments to circumvent such rules. For example, Dr. Bernard Fabre-Teste, WHO's adviser for the disease in the Western Pacific region, said in 2005 that poor countries should consider using international treaties or take unilateral action to sidestep existing patents on key antiretroviral drugs, which help prevent the AIDS virus from reproducing in the body.[84] In particular, agreements reached in 2003 as part of the Doha Round of WTO negotiations provided loopholes for countries facing a public health emergency to issue "compulsory licenses" to manufacture generic versions of patented drugs.

The WHO and the United Nations have promoted major campaigns such as Access for All, and Three by Five—the goal to get three million people, mostly in the developing world, on ARV treatment by 2005. Although the results fell far short of the goals, the program helped cement the idea that widespread access to ARVs was possible in the developing countries. According to UN estimates, between 2003 and 2006, the number of people on ARVs in developing countries more than tripled to 1.3 million, and between 250,000 and 350,000 deaths were averted worldwide.[85]

The U.S. government initially acted as a constraint on treatment access, taking the side of the multinational pharmaceutical corporations seeking patent protection, and effectively keeping treatment prices out of reach; but it then acted forcefully to advance treatment. One such act was was President Bill Clinton's executive order in the year 2000 to import and produce generic forms of HIV treatment. After leaving office, Clinton's foundation would spearhead efforts to find ways to reduce drug prices through negotiations and bulk purchases. Again, the imperatives of the Geneva Consensus have contradicted aspects of the neoliberal, property-rights-oriented Washington consensus, and such contradictions have created moments of confusion and conflict for international actors.

[84] "Bend Patent Laws to Fight AIDS: WHO," *Times of India*, September 23, 2005.
[85] Secretary-General, United Nations General Assembly 2006, III.27.

By creating benchmarks for treatment in terms of total numbers of people worldwide, authors of the Geneva Consensus reinforced the very notion of a global pandemic, answerable to global authorities. Whereas international activists had once vilified international organizations for maintaining legal and cost barriers to treatment, the efforts associated with treatment access have become so accepted that protest is largely muted. International activists continue to challenge drug companies for limiting access to key drugs through high prices or their efforts to maintain patent protections—booths at the 2004 and 2006 international AIDS conferences were defaced by protestors—but the reality is that "Big Pharma" is now actively participating in free or highly subsidized AIDS drug distribution programs around the world. Annual costs of antiretroviral drugs have fallen from well over ten thousand dollars, to just a few hundred dollars, to just over one hundred dollars per patient in some countries.[86]

While building consensus on AIDS treatment has involved learning, in the sense that successes and failures guided discussion and emulation, it is important to highlight that policy diffusion had been mediated by international institutions of global governance. As will be discussed in chapter 4, Brazil pioneered the provision of free treatment to its population, and shattered prior notions that this was impossible. As Tina Rosenberg explained in a widely cited 2001 *New York Times Magazine* article,

> One major reason that only Brazil offers free triple therapy is that, until now, there was no Brazil to show that it is possible. A year and a half ago, practically nobody was talking about using triple therapy in poor countries. Today, it is rare to find a meeting of international leaders where this idea is not discussed. International organizations like the United Nations AIDS agency, UNAIDS, and nongovernment groups like Médecins Sans Frontières are starting to help countries try to replicate Brazil's program. Brazil has offered to transfer all its technology and provide training in the practicalities of treating patients to other countries that want to make drugs and will supply them to patients free.[87]

The idea of a Brazilian "model," as well as other successful early initiatives at providing drug treatment, such as Partners In Health's work in Cange, Haiti and Médecins Sans Frontières' pilot programs, did provide concrete

---

[86] Fleet and Béchir 2006, 662.
[87] Rosenberg 2001.

evidence that effective treatment could be provided in resource-poor settings, reversing early skepticism.[88] While ideas have certainly been transmitted across developing countries, these models have been so strongly mediated by international organizations, particularly through negotiations over protocols, pricing, and implications for other trade negotiations, that it would be difficult to make a purely "learning" argument about the diffusion of policy. Ideas about treatment access were socially constructed; and once in place, powerful global governance actors provided resources and active pressures to provide treatment.

Rights Orientation

The fourth component of the Geneva Consensus has focused on the human rights orientation of government policies. To a large extent, the framing of HIV/AIDS as a human rights issue has pervaded the other components of the Geneva Consensus. Indeed, one of the strategies of key actors broadcasting the Geneva Consensus has been to make the (plausible) claim that all four of the strategies work together. Just as treatment has been advocated as a prevention strategy (the idea being that prevention requires that people know their status, and people would have no incentive to get tested if there was no hope for treatment), so too has increased protections for those infected with HIV and those thought to be especially vulnerable to infection. Because a body of international law protecting human rights already existed prior to the onset of the AIDS epidemic, and continued to expand during this period, activists have had a platform to advance AIDS policy on the grounds of protecting those rights. In this sense, the development of this approach has involved the social construction of the idea that pathogenesis was linked to rights violations. Moreover, international human rights lawyers and scholars put forth the argument that health inequalities were themselves violations that ought to be targeted not just by those in the field of health, but by those working in the field of rights.[89] Human rights lawyers could then use the threat of coercion to punish states for not complying with international treaties.

---

[88] D'Adesky 2004, 226.
[89] Gruskin, Hendriks, and Tomasevski 1996, 327.

Whereas public health measures were once concerned almost exclusively with the desire to prevent transmission to the healthy/noninfected population, and ordinary liberties and freedoms for "infected" individuals were routinely suspended, the AIDS epidemic has emerged during an era when there has been more agreement that the dignity and rights of those who are infected, or suspected of being infected, ought to be respected and protected. To be certain, the seeds of international consensus on rights were planted long before HIV/AIDS was recognized. In 1948, the Universal Declaration of Human Rights established in the UN General Assembly core principles, and in the decades to follow, a vast industry of government and nongovernment organizations and networks developed, providing norms and enforcement mechanisms for countries around the world. But just as more general forms of repression persist throughout the world, the idea that human rights ought to be given high priority in the field of global public health has not advanced without some conflict. For a problem of infectious disease, individual human rights can be seen to be in potential political conflict with "group" rights, and in public health, protecting the freedom and confidentiality of those infected or suspected of being infected with a contagious virus can be seen to be at odds with the larger public interest of limiting spread of the disease. But by the early 1990s, the link between human rights and action on AIDS became increasingly tight, such that virtually no global governance authority would contest it.

The onset of the AIDS epidemic followed the 1978 Alma-Ata Declaration at the International Conference on Primary Health Care, which proposed that the dissemination of full information and full participation from communities was necessary to improve public health.[90] Moreover, many individuals in the AIDS world came to the conclusion that if HIV-positive individuals were "punished" for their sero-status, this would create strong disincentives against being tested, disclosing their status, or changing their behavior in ways that might reveal their status. Unlike viruses that present symptoms and lead to mortality in much shorter course, the slow progression of HIV implies a greater need for individual testing of sero-status, and some quasi-voluntary cooperation in this regard. Beyond these "affinities" with a rights-based approach, it is also the case that some of the leading figures in the global campaign on HIV/AIDS, in-

---

[90] Van Praag, Dehne, and Chandra-Mouli 2006, 594.

cluding the late Jonathan Mann, who directed the WHO's global AIDS strategy from 1986 to 1990, and the medical anthropologist, physician, and founder of Partners In Health, Dr. Paul Farmer,[91] have been extraordinarily strong advocates of rights-based approaches.

In the area of HIV/AIDS, human rights activists have championed protections against violence and have promoted freedom of movement within and across borders, voluntary and confidential testing, and equal access to employment and public services. The traditional public health strategy of quarantine has been proscribed by the Geneva Consensus, but there has been some evidence of this practice in a few countries around the world, most notably early in the epidemic in Cuba. While debate has continued about the extent to which certain rights ought to be protected and certain practices mandated, the nature of the prophylaxis associated with HIV/AIDS are voluntary and difficult to monitor, quite unlike diseases such as yellow fever, which can be prevented by immunization. In general, authors of the Geneva Consensus have accepted the argument that a rights-based approach is likely to be more effective in securing widespread voluntary compliance. The idea that Cuba's strategy of quarantine might have been a key in that country's ability to maintain the lowest rate of infection in the Western Hemisphere is almost never discussed publicly among lead authors of the Geneva Consensus, as such a strategy falls outside the human rights approach.

Although the WHO has long been identified with more traditional public health strategies in the response to past epidemics, in the case of HIV/AIDS it has been a fairly consistent promoter of rights-based approaches. In 1985, the organization spoke out against the attempt by certain governments to close their borders to people infected with HIV, stating that "no country bound by the Regulations [of a 1969 statute] may refuse entry into its territory to a person who fails to provide a medical certificate stating that he or she is not carrying the AIDS virus."[92] To be certain, for much of the history of the epidemic, this norm has been violated by countries around the world, and continues to be violated by the United States. Beginning in the mid-1980s, with the launching of the GPA, international organizations called for sensitivity and nondiscrimination in approaches to HIV/AIDS. In the face of reports of inhumane

[91] See, for example, Farmer 2003.
[92] *Weekly Epidemiological Record* 60 (40) 1985, 311, as cited in Mann, Tarantola, and Netter 1992, 554–55.

treatment and restrictions in 1989, the UN appointed a Special Rapporteur to study AIDS-related discrimination.[93]

Another critical foundation of the rights orientation of the Geneva Consensus was the passage of the Americans with Disabilities Act of 1990, which went into effect in 1992, and provided legal recourse for persons with disabilities who were discriminated against in employment and in access to public and other services. Although neither HIV nor AIDS is mentioned explicitly in the act, statements of legislative intent by the sponsors prior to its passage as well as an addendum issued by the Equal Employment Opportunity Commission, which oversees the act, made clear that HIV infection was a protected condition,[94] and this set an important precedent in the United States and abroad. In countries around the world, individuals and organizations have used this precedent and have sued governments to provide prevention and treatment policies, on the grounds that in denying those policies, governments were depriving them of constitutional protections to basic human rights.

In 1992, the World Health Assembly detailed the link between a rights-oriented approach and the goals of improving public health, resolving

> to reinforce efforts to oppose discrimination against persons and specific groups known to be or suspected of being HIV-infected; and to ensure a humanitarian response of governments and individuals to people with HIV/AIDS and that public health is not undermined by discrimination and stigmatization.[95]

Despite the strong consensus on a rights-based approach in international organizations, it has had detractors in various polities. Amid fear of the epidemic, many governments, with the support of elites and citizens, have tried to maintain policies of mandatory testing of foreigners, and denial of entry to those infected with HIV. Owing to constant and widespread pressures to promote and to protect human rights, almost all countries have paid lip service to this component of the Geneva Consensus. However, in terms of actual mechanisms for protecting against violations, and implementing those mechanisms, there has been a great deal of variation across countries.

[93] Mann, Tarantola, and Netter 1992, 54.
[94] Mello 1999, 71.
[95] WHO 1992.

Broad Structural Interventions

Authors of the Geneva Consensus have highlighted broad structural problems in societies that leave large segments of the population highly vulnerable to HIV infection, and to more rapid development of AIDS-related symptoms once infected. As a result, part of the Geneva Consensus has promoted more general strategies to reduce poverty and inequality and to enhance gender-equity. However, because these policies are themselves so far-reaching, relate to policies that predated the onset of AIDS, and are caught up in a wide range of other political concerns, I do not discuss or analyze them further in this book.

The Limits of Consensus

The notion that all of the major actors participating in the global governance of AIDS have reached a Geneva Consensus on what should be done is a stylized fact that other observers are certain to challenge. As I have already noted, certain policies have not always received widespread support from international actors. One important schism is the divide between the U.S. government, particularly under the George W. Bush administration, and the rest of the advanced industrialized countries. Anti-American sentiment was palpable in the halls of the 2006 International AIDS Conference in Toronto, particularly in response to a few distinctive features of the U.S. policy under the Bush administration: a greater emphasis on "abstinence" programs than that pursued by other donors, the insistence that organizations receiving funding sign a pledge opposing commercial sex work, and a prohibition against funding needle-exchange programs. Disagreement about these points has been bitter, causing consternation among non-American Geneva Consensus authors and activists. Even the American Institute of Medicine's two-year evaluation of the PEPFAR program, which generally praised its efforts and results, highlighted what activists had long been saying—that the efforts were hamstrung by politically driven constraints on what should and should not be funded.[96] AIDS activists continue to challenge global governance actors and pharmaceutical corporations with rhetoric that might

---

[96] PEPFAR 2007.

leave one to think that they were worlds apart in approaches to the epidemic at the country level.

While I don't want to make light of these serious concerns, for the purposes of establishing context, these "nonconsensus" items amount to only a small share of the overall strategies being promoted. Otherwise, there has been remarkably little disagreement among donor governments and international public health experts about the menus of policies and strategies that ought to be pursued by governments around the world. The U.S. government has certainly limited the extent of its multilateral action on AIDS, preferring to deploy most of its resources through its own bilateral programs. In a March 2002 cable sent to USAID missions around the world, Natsios wrote, "USAID has been entrusted with increased resources to lead the international war against HIV/AIDS and to assist in meeting the 2007 international targets set by the global HIV/AIDS community."[97] Moreover, in comparing the policy documents distributed by the U.S. government and UNAIDS, I find an extraordinary degree of overlap in what is recommended. The international response to AIDS, from the perspective of what has been advocated and offered by major donors, international organizations, and other global actors, has largely been one of consensus.

Conclusion

An elaborate global governance structure has been brought to the developing countries to conform to policies and strategies for responding to AIDS. Unprecedented resources and tools have become available in a world of increased global integration. They have been disseminated through a wide-reaching consensus about how a deadly pandemic ought to be stopped, albeit a consensus that has shifted over time, in which pressure and politics have been necessary to develop prevailing ideas and standards. Asymmetric global governance implies that poor countries are unequal partners in a state system that privileges the interests of the wealthiest countries. Institutions, norms, and a sense of interdependency have helped to generate important initiatives for collective welfare in the face of a natural viral disaster. Such asymmetries imply that a limited menu of policies

[97] Excerpt from cable memorandum from Andrew Natsios, "Monitoring and Reporting on HIV/AIDS Programs," March 11, 2002, printed as annex C in the USAID Office of HIV/AIDS, "Expanded Response Guide to Core Indicators for Monitoring and Reporting on HIV/AIDS Programs," January 2003.

have been promoted owing to consensus on modern science among donor countries.

Has the Geneva Consensus, and the exertion of global governance more generally, been more effective in curtailing AIDS than we would have seen in the absence of such authority? It is impossible to answer this question definitively since every country in the world has been influenced by the Geneva Consensus, and we have no evidence of the counterfactual condition. Nonetheless, it is hard to imagine that the AIDS epidemic would be under greater control today without these international efforts on AIDS. Notwithstanding critiques of the emphases of particular donors, the potential diversion of resources from more fundamental public health and development to AIDS initiatives, and the crowding out of local solutions,[98] modern biomedical understandings of the virus, and resources to disseminate particular interventions have almost certainly had a strongly positive impact. We could not so easily arrive at such conclusions for international efforts to promote economic and human development more generally.

The tragic news, of course, is that the authors of the Geneva Consensus did not act faster and that the resources committed fall short of needs. The consensus is not universal; where adopted, it has not always been well implemented; and where implemented, it has not always had the desired consequences. In a 2006 report, the UN secretary-general stated:

Five years after the 2001 special session, the available evidence underscores the extraordinary diversity between countries and regions in implementing the response envisioned in the Declaration of Commitment. While select countries have reached key targets and milestones for 2005, set out in the Declaration of Commitment, many countries have failed to fulfil the pledges specified in the Declaration. Some countries have made great strides in expanding access to treatment but have made little progress in scaling up HIV prevention programs, while other countries that are now experiencing a reduction in national HIV prevalence are making only slow progress to ensure that treatment is available to those who need it.[99]

The record of global governance of HIV/AIDS has been uneven, and profound differences remain in the nature of country responses. Superfi-

---

[98] See, for example, Epstein 2007.
[99] Secretary-General, United Nations General Assembly 2006, I.6.

cial conformity in the adoption of policies belies profound differences in the scope and timing of implemented action. These differences have been consequential for the lives of the people in developing countries and are the subject of further investigation in the chapters that follow. The remainder of this book takes up the question of why some developing country governments, such as Brazil, have been so aggressive in adopting the Geneva Consensus, while others, such as South Africa and India, have been more passive. I put a spotlight on the powerful effects of boundary politics.

4 ☞ Race Boundaries and AIDS Policy
   in Brazil and South Africa

This chapter takes up the challenge of explaining divergent governmental responses to AIDS in Brazil and South Africa between 1982 and 2006.[1] If we expect similar responses from countries with similar social, political, and economic profiles, we would expect parallel courses of action from these two governments (see table 4.1). When they faced AIDS epidemics, both were in the process of democratic transition, upper-middle-income countries[2] with high levels of economic inequality. Their public health systems were, though uneven, relatively strong in comparison to the rest of the developing world, with a cadre of informed technocrats well aware of the looming consequences of an unchecked epidemic as well as the widely broadcast Geneva Consensus recommendations for addressing the challenge. Both possessed the capacity to manufacture pharmaceuticals, a local source of appropriate drug therapies. And yet the Brazilian federal government responded aggressively and has been recognized as a world

[1] This chapter is a substantially revised version of an article coauthored with Varun Gauri (senior economist, World Bank) in *Studies in Comparative International Development*. I am very grateful for that rewarding partnership, and Gauri should also be considered a coauthor of this chapter. However, since I carried out significant revisions of the article on my own, he is not responsible for any errors of fact or potential disagreements of interpretation that may have arisen across versions.

[2] See Heller 2001; Seidman 1994; Marx 1998; Lieberman 2003, as examples of comparative analyses of these cases.

TABLE 4.1
Comparing Brazil and South Africa

	Year	South Africa	Brazil
GDP/capita, $US	1990	$3,152	$3,092
Population	2000	44 million	174 million
GINI coefficient	c. 2000	.58	.58
Political Regime (Polity Score)	1983 → 2000	4 → 9 (not democracy → democracy)	−3 → 8 (not democracy → democracy)

Source: World Bank 2005; Marshall and Jaggers 2006 (Polity IV).

leader in AIDS prevention and care, while the South African government, for most of the epidemic, has been criticized as a laggard. What can account for these differences?

The explanation presented here highlights the impact of boundary institutions, particularly with respect to the ethnic cleavage of race. Both countries contain people from a wide diversity of backgrounds, including sizable African-descended and European-descended people, and one can identify "white," "black," and "mixed" race groups in both countries. However, these labels and the groups they imply are varied across the two countries. South Africa's history was marked by institutionalized white supremacy, culminating in an elaborate scheme to keep race groups apart from one another—apartheid government—which lasted from 1948 until the early 1990s. By contrast, in Brazil, a quite distinctive history of institution-building, one that for most of the twentieth century emphasized racial mixing and the blurring of boundaries, has limited the salience of racial labels and categories. While in practice, socioeconomic status is highly correlated with skin color in both countries, the political salience of race varies between the two, and this difference is critical for explaining contrasts in the politics of AIDS policy. Similar pressures have weighed on these governments to act on AIDS, but strong boundary institutions constrained action in South Africa. No analogous hindrance was present in Brazil, suggesting that the Brazilian model for AIDS policy emerged out of the combination of positive pressures and the absence of negative ones.

Brazil's response—though not necessarily the associated epidemiological outcomes—represents what could have been South Africa's.

Since much of the argument of the book was derived through a comparative investigation of these two countries, the paired analysis in this chapter cannot be considered, strictly speaking, a test of the argument. Nonetheless, the analysis provides evidence concerning the effects of ethnic boundaries, as well as the limits of other explanations of variation in the responses of two critical countries. I begin by comparing epidemiological trends and information about infections. Second, I compare the two countries' records on AIDS policy. Third, I consider explanations that have been put forward by other analysts and scholars to account for the different responses of the respective countries, and I analyze the strengths and weaknesses of those explanations in light of the cross-country comparison. On the basis of the comparative-historical analysis, I do not reject these accounts, which emphasize the role of public health and state capacities, mobilized actors in civil society, democratic institutions, international influences, and leadership. Rather, I suggest that they are incomplete, and fail to account for the large differences in governmental responses. Finally, I turn to the effects of race boundaries in those countries, and highlight the important ways in which boundary politics affected the framing of the epidemic, patterns of blaming and denial, and levels of political conflict and cooperation.

Comparing the Epidemics in Brazil and South Africa

The value of a paired comparison lies in the analytic equivalence of cases, and for a comparison of AIDS policymaking it is necessary to establish that the aggressiveness of responses cannot be entirely explained by the most obvious driver—that is, that governments responded proportionally to the size of the problem as it existed in each country and to the degree that it was recognized by local public health experts. Such a comparison requires some sensitivity to historical timing. South Africa's epidemic, measured by HIV prevalence, is today orders of magnitude larger than Brazil's, but this is partially explained by the very differences in policy investigated here. Moreover, since we would expect more expansive responses from countries with more severe epidemics, this simply compounds the puzzle. On the other hand, Brazil's epidemic emerged more visibly in terms of sickness and deaths earlier on, and this helps to account for that country's earlier responses, described in the next section. Nevertheless, even if we calibrate the comparison to the differences in visible onset, the South African response appears delayed and weak, particularly as the severity of its epidemic began to surpass Brazil's.

The first cases of AIDS were diagnosed in both countries in 1982.[3] In the first decade in Brazil, HIV/AIDS was perceived to be a disease of upper-class gay men,[4] and seemed to be following a "North American/ West European" epidemic pattern. Between 1980 and June 1992, 46.1 percent of AIDS cases were estimated to be the result of homosexual or bisexual contacts.[5] Commercial sex workers, the poor, and heterosexuals more generally were recognized as being affected only seven to ten years after the first diagnoses. South Africa also initially seemed to be avoiding a "typical, African-style heterosexual epidemic," and between 1982 and 1986, 87 percent of the diagnosed AIDS cases in South Africa were among homosexual or bisexual males.[6] According to another account, between 1982 and 1990, 43 percent of reported AIDS cases in South Africa were transmitted through men having sex with men.[7] However, by approximately 1989, South Africa was experiencing a "heterosexual epidemic,"[8] and heterosexual transmission also became the principal mode of transmission since the mid-1990s in Brazil.[9]

At least as important is to consider the size of the epidemics. There is some difficulty in comparing epidemiological data, especially for earlier years of the epidemic, because testing and monitoring mechanisms were not yet in place, and governments with better capacity tend to report more AIDS cases simply because they look for them. However, by 1990, the number of cumulative cases of diagnosed and reported AIDS was orders of magnitude higher in Brazil (8,993 cases) than in South Africa (345 cases),[10] which suggested a larger Brazilian epidemic, even taking into account its larger population. But by 1993, estimated infection rates were already slightly higher in South Africa than in Brazil.[11] Moreover, national HIV prevalence of less than 1 percent was interpreted as generally threatening

[3] Brazil reported its first case to the WHO in 1982, and South Africa in 1985.
[4] Herbert and Parker 1993, 9–10.
[5] Ministério de Saúde as cited in Herbert and Parker 1993, 12.
[6] Ngwena 1998, 120.
[7] Hamilton 1991.
[8] Van der Vliet 2001, 153.
[9] Garcia-Abreu, Noguer, and Cowgill 2003, 26. According to Berkman et al. (2005, 1163), in 2003, 66.1 percent of reported cases were due to heterosexual sex.
[10] UNAIDS Epidemiological Fact Sheets.
[11] UNAIDS/WHO 2004.

in Brazil, and even after South Africa began to report double-digit prevalence, political and policy responses were delayed. The symptomatic expression of AIDS may have been widely visible in Brazil a few years before it was in South Africa, but this can explain only a small portion of the difference in timing of their responses.[12]

When it comes to politics and policymaking, more important than the actual rates and levels of infection, which could not be known definitively, is the information available to experts and the general public. In the mid-1980s, newspapers in both countries reported warnings from epidemiologists and other public health experts of the possibility of a large number of deaths, and by the early 1990s, there was widespread concern among public health experts that the epidemic was poised to become "generalized" or "explosive."[13] It is chilling to find the accuracy of epidemiological predictions from earlier moments in the epidemic: In 1991, a South African research team predicted that under the most pessimistic scenario, 5.2 million South Africans would be infected by 2000,[14] a figure surpassed when UNAIDS estimated actual prevalence in 2003.

More than twenty years after the first cases were discovered, the threat and impact of AIDS were radically different between the two countries. According to the WHO, as of 2005, between 4.9 million and 6.1 million South Africans were infected with HIV, an adult prevalence of 18.8 percent, and approximately 320,000 people had died of AIDS-related causes.[15] In Brazil, between 340,000 and 790,000 were infected, and with a population approximately four times the size of South Africa's, this represented a 0.5 adult percent prevalence, and only about 14,000 people had died of AIDS. From this vantage point, the Brazilian government's emphasis on AIDS appears dramatic.

DIFFERENT POLICY RESPONSES

Before turning to the question of why the two governments have responded in different ways, it is necessary to detail the nature of the differ-

---

[12] Moreover, it is almost certainly the case that a lower proportion of actual AIDS cases were diagnosed in South Africa because of the very policy differences discussed in this chapter.

[13] Grundligh 2001; Galvão 2000, 192; Brooke 1993.

[14] Reports of the Medical Research Council and the University of the Witwatersrand, as cited by Xinhua News Agency, "Five Million South Africans Could Be Infected in Five Years," July 9, 1991.

[15] UNAIDS 2006, annex 2.

ences. As described in chapter 3, I consider four broad areas of government responses to HIV/AIDS: the construction of bureaucratic capacity, the broadcasting of prevention strategies, the provision of treatment and support to people who are HIV-positive, and human rights/nondiscrimination protections. I am interested in comparing the aggressiveness of government response in these areas, measured in terms of speed and scope. Overall, the South African response was slower and less robust than in Brazil, with perhaps the one exception being the timing of the securing of the blood supply.

Brazil established an AIDS bureaucracy earlier than South Africa (table 4.2), and it created a much larger agency that assumed authority in formulating policy by the end of the 1980s.[16] The federal government established a National AIDS Program in 1985, which was directed between 1986 and 1990 by a competent public health specialist who had worked briefly at the United States' CDC.[17] Though there was some retrenchment of the AIDS program during the tumultuous Collor administration (1990–92),[18] a period when the country suffered hyperinflation, the scope and visibility of the AIDS bureaucracy continued to expand in subsequent years. As of 2002, it had a program staff of almost five hundred. The federal government has routinely been the lead actor on AIDS innovations and policy strategies, and it is the central political authority on AIDS control. The organogram of the Brazil's National AIDS Program (Programa Nacional de DST e Aids) reveals a highly differentiated and specialized bureaucratic structure, with links to international organizations such as UNAIDS and the CDC as well as with civil society organizations.

By contrast, the development of an autonomous bureaucratic structure has faced a far rockier road in South Africa, and to a large extent, even as of 2006, one was still lacking. Most observers of the history of AIDS in South Africa agree that the period between 1982 and 1988 was one of extremely limited government activity,[19] with the only discernible action in the bureaucracy being the appointment of a small AIDS Advisory Group in 1985, which provided mostly biomedical consultations to government. In 1988, the government established an AIDS Unit and National Advisory Group in the department of health,[20] and according to

---

[16] See Okie 2006 for a more detailed discussion of the Brazilian policy response from a biomedical perspective.

[17] Parker 1994b, 34.

[18] Wogart and Calcagnotto 2006, 4.

[19] Van der Vliet 2001; Fourie 2006.

[20] Ngwena 1998, 129–30.

TABLE 4.2
Development of National AIDS Bureaucracies in Brazil and South Africa (1982–2006)

	South Africa	Brazil
Bureaucratic structure	Disjointed development, never truly autonomous.	Clearly emerged by 1988. Highly differentiated specialties.
Number of HIV/AIDS program staff	100 (2004)	476 (2002)
Appearance of HIV/AIDS as budget line item	2000	1988
Partnerships with NGOs	Mixed/conflictual: NGOs challenge, sue government.	Collaborative: Direct budgetary support to NGOs since 1993.
Monitoring and testing	Systematic antenatal clinic surveillance since 1990; little surveillance among risk groups.	Ad hoc monitoring among risk groups since 1989; systematic population based monitoring since 1998.

Note: More aggressive actions are shaded.

the government's response to a survey, a National AIDS Council had formed by 1989.[21] In 1992, the original AIDS unit was dismantled, and in 1994, a national AIDS program director was appointed, but in the department of health, not as an independent unit.[22] At the end of 1997, an "inter-ministerial committee on AIDS" was established and chaired by the deputy president;[23] by 1998 the National AIDS Program had just eighteen full-time staff members and seven consultants.[24] Although the South African National AIDS Council (SANAC) was established in 2000, which on paper appears as a model of the Geneva Consensus "multisectoral" approach, it has not been widely recognized as the authoritative decision-

[21] Mann and Tarantola 1996.
[22] Schneider and Stein 2001, 725.
[23] Government of South Africa, GFATM Proposal Round 2:9.
[24] Schneider 1998, 3.

maker on AIDS policy, and the minister of health has almost always been the lead policy actor on AIDS policy, often downplaying the severity of the crisis. Over time, government organograms have shifted from year to year, revealing the weak institutionalization of the national AIDS bureaucracy. As late as 2004, there were significant vacancies in its AIDS program, and health minister Manto Tshabalala-Msimang faced senior resignations in the health department, including the head of the AIDS program.[25] South Africa has a more widespread epidemic and far greater numbers of people infected with HIV than does Brazil, but by 2004, only about one hundred people were employed in the analogous government agency.

Comparing patterns of budgeting and expenditure exposes the far more aggressive approach of the Brazilian government. Brazil's national budget included a reference to AIDS control as early as 1988, when it was included in the program to control sexually transmitted diseases;[26] but it was not until the 1997 budget speech that AIDS was mentioned in the formal presentation of South Africa's budget, and not until 2000 that the budget included line items dedicated to expenditure on HIV/AIDS. Most of Brazil's expenditure on AIDS since the early 1990s has been allocated to treatment, but non-ARV expenditures are higher per capita than South Africa's, despite much lower rates of infection. And while the South African AIDS budget has increased dramatically in recent years, the Brazilian state dedicated far more resources to HIV/AIDS sooner. In 1996, the Brazilian government spent $0.81 per capita and the South African government just $0.36 even though infection levels in South Africa were already several times higher than in Brazil. By 2002–3, expenditures were more equal, as both countries spent more than $1.50 per capita, but the Brazilian federal government was spending at least thirteen times more than South Africa per HIV-positive individual.

When we compare the two countries in terms of surveillance capacities, there are clear differences in approach, but it is not possible to conclude that either country was more aggressive. The South African government established an annual, national antenatal surveillance testing policy in 1990, and conducted its first national baseline survey of knowledge and

[25] Claire Keeton, "Manto Faces Exodus of Top Staff: Departure of Two Senior Officials Will Add to Growing Number of Critical Vacancies in the Department," *Sunday Times,* May 30, 2004.

[26] Orçamento da União, Projeto da Lei, vol. 1, 1988.

behavior in 2000. In Brazil, national surveillance of sexually transmitted infections and antenatal clinics began in 1999 and 2000 respectively.[27]

Brazil has been more aggressive in the speed and scope of its prevention policies (table 4.3). Brazil implemented prevention programs targeted at the "general population" as early as 1987 and 1988, including outreach, condom promotion, and testing for HIV status. In 1989, Brazil's National AIDS Program launched a prevention campaign targeted at high-risk populations that included male and female sex workers. Between 1994 and 2000, thirty-five campaigns were broadcast on media including television during the national holiday of Carnival.[28] In the 1990s, the National AIDS Program expanded the number of targeted interventions aimed at reducing incidence among men having sex with men, sex workers, injecting drug users (including hundreds of harm reduction programs that included needle exchange), and children of HIV-positive pregnant women.[29] As early as 1994, the government was providing AZT to prevent vertical transmission from mother to child. And after years of distributing condoms, in August 2004, the government announced plans to distribute as many as 3 billion free condoms each year.[30] The government provision and promotion of condoms has resulted in sharp increases in condom use in Brazil.

The South African government has a long history of rolling out HIV/AIDS prevention programs, but they have been more muted and often poorly planned and implemented.[31] Policymaking has proceeded in fits and starts, with a great deal of backtracking. During the first four years of the epidemic, the government simply tried to calm mounting public concern about the epidemic, and did little to target the gay community, where HIV was most prevalent.[32] Free condoms were distributed beginning in 1988—actually seven years earlier than the Brazilian national government—but with little fanfare, and television advertising for condoms was restricted to premium channels. In the late 1980s and early 1990s, campaigns targeted at white schools were implemented at least two

[27] Garcia-Abreu, Noguer, and Cowgill 2003, 66.
[28] Levi and Vitória 2002, 2375.
[29] See Gauri, Beyrer, and Vaillancourt 2004; Portaria No. 236, May 2, 1985; a history of the Brazilian legislation is available at http://www.aids.gov.br/final/biblioteca/legislacao/prefacio.htm (consulted September 10, 2006).
[30] "Brazil: 3 Billion Free Condoms." New York Times, August 12, 2004.
[31] Schneider 2002, 147.
[32] Grundligh 2001, 126.

TABLE 4.3
National AIDS Prevention Policies in Brazil and South Africa

	South Africa	Brazil
Education and outreach	Epidemic already generalized before significant campaigns initiated; eventually quite extensive, but routinely criticized for inappropriate messages.	TV spots and workplace by 1988; school-based by 1992; targeted outreach programs (e.g., with MSM 1985, sex workers 1990, harm reduction/needle exchange 1996).
Condom distribution	More muted program with less outreach. Government distributes approximately 340–540 million in 2004 (7.5–12 units per capita).	Extensive, high-visibility government programs. Government announces distribution of 3 billion in 2004 (17 units per capita).
Prevention of mother-to-child transmission (PMTCT)	Initiated in 2001. Nevirapine provided only following legal battle. By 2005, coverage estimates range from 10%–70%.	Initiated in 1994. Launch of AZT 076 protocol. By 2005, coverage close to 100%.
Safety of blood supply	Deemed safe in 1985.	Mostly safe in 1988, clandestine blood market eliminated in 1998.

Note: More aggressive actions are shaded.

years before campaigns in black schools.[33] Efforts to respond to the key drivers of the epidemic—sexual transmission among migrant workers, such as miners and truckers, and commercial and transactional sex among young women—were late, so much so that by the time that major prevention efforts were launched, the epidemic had passed from "concentrated" to "generalized." In 1993, an AIDS education budget was slashed from 8.5 million rand to 3.5 million rand,[34] and in 1995, the year after the country recorded the world's biggest jump in level of infection—from 4.3

[33]Grundligh 2001, 137–38. I am mindful not to describe the outcome of AIDS policy too closely in terms of the central explanatory of boundary or ethnic politics. Yet it does not follow by definition that racially differentiated AIDS policies would be expected in an ethnically divided society.

[34]Grundligh 2001, 141.

percent of adults to 7.6 percent, there was still no national public safe-sex campaign.[35]

The South African government also famously resisted the use of ARV monotherapy for the prevention of mother-to-child transmission (PMTCT)—an inexpensive and effective strategy for reducing pediatric AIDS.[36] Although a few provincial governments and nongovernment organizations acted earlier to provide this prophylactic, the national government rolled out eighteen pilot sites only in 2001.[37] The country's High Court in a 2002 case ordered the government to provide nevirapine more widely, but that ruling had limited impact. While the program has expanded, there are conflicting accounts of what proportion of HIV-positive women have received the drug— over 70 percent in a government report, less than 15 percent in a UNAIDS report, both for the year 2004.[38]

A notable exception to the pattern of greater aggressiveness in Brazil is blood safety. The South African blood supply was judged safe as early as 1985, and WHO reports have consistently extolled the safety of the system. In Brazil, the minister of health requested the screening of the blood supply in 1987, and it was judged mostly safe by 1988. However, other accounts reveal inconsistencies in the state of the blood supply as late as the early 1990s, identifying the commercial aspects of blood supply, including a sizable black market.[39] By contrast, South Africa has a tradition of voluntary donations, with no sizable black market for blood.

The Brazilian government has forged much deeper and cooperative partnerships with NGOs than South Africa's. Although there were conflicts between the government and NGOs in the middle and late 1980s, after the return of the previous director of the National AIDS Program in 1992 and the beginning of the first major World Bank loan in 1993, the state began to transfer significant resources to NGOs for HIV/AIDS prevention, outreach, treatment, and support.[40] The Brazilian government has touted its close ties with NGOs at international meetings, and at the 2004 International AIDS Conference in Bangkok, one government official expressed to me the closeness of the connection, a best practice in the

---

[35] R. W. Johnson, "South Africa Hit by Rapid Spread of HIV Infection," *The Times*, August 30, 1995.

[36] See, for example, Nattrass 2004.

[37] Government of South Africa, GFATM Proposal Round 1, 2002, 22.

[38] http://www.avert.org/aidssouthafrica.htm (consulted December 13, 2006).

[39] Parker 1994b, 35.

[40] Teixeira 1997; Galvão 2000; World Bank Operations Evaluation Department 2004.

Geneva Consensus: "The relationship is so close," he said, "we do not know where government ends and civil society begins."

Ironically, in South Africa, the deepening of democracy has been associated with a souring of state–civil society relations in the area of AIDS. In South Africa, a national AIDS conference held in October 1992 led to the development of an umbrella government–civil society organization, the National AIDS Convention of South Africa (NACOSA).[41] Though at the time considered a milestone and the start of a deliberate and coordinated response, little was implemented as a result. As it became clear that the national government assigned low priority to AIDS policies, the distance between state and societal actors grew, with previous collaborations giving way to outright hostility, protests, international condemnations, and lawsuits. At international AIDS conferences, where Brazilian NGOs and government officials were touting their almost familial ties, South Africa's own civil society organizations were leading international protests against the South African government. Disputes concerning the use of prevention funds for a high-priced musical production, lack of commitment on the National AIDS Plan, and government support of a controversial, domestically developed AIDS drug all damaged state-NGO relations.[42] As late as 2006, the South African government attempted to exclude two of the country's most important civil society organizations—the Treatment Action Campaign (TAC) and the AIDS Law Project—from accreditation at the 2006 UNGASS meetings in New York, although the organizations were eventually accredited for the meeting following protests.[43]

Particularly in the area of treatment, Brazil has been a notable leader, and South Africa a laggard (table 4.4). By the end of 2005, between 85 and 100 percent of Brazilians in need of drug therapy were receiving drugs, while between 13 and 21 percent of South Africans in need were.[44] Brazil's public health system began to provide free AZT to all patients with clinical AIDS in 1991. On November 13, 1996, its Congress passed Law No. 9313, proposed by Senator José Sarney, which required the national public health system to provide all medically necessary pharmaceuticals

[41] Van der Vliet 2001, 160.

[42] Gumede 2005, 153; Van der Vliet 2001, 170.

[43] "TAC and ALP Excluded from UNGASS," press release, http://www.tac.org.za/ (consulted April 6, 2006).

[44] The lower estimates for each country are based on the WHO Three by Five Coverage Report, and the higher estimates are based on the results of a collaborative survey conducted jointly by USAID, UNAIDS, WHO, UNICEF, and Policy Project, all as reported in UNAIDS 2006, annex 3.

TABLE 4.4
National AIDS Drug Treatment Policies in Brazil and South Africa

	South Africa	Brazil
Monotherapy	Never implemented	Initiated in 1991 Universal and free AZT
Highly active antiret- roviral therapy (HAART)	Initiated in 2004	Initiated in 1996
On treatment (2005)	13%–21%	83%–100%

Source: UNAIDS 2006.
Note: More aggressive actions are shaded.

for AIDS patients, and Brazil began to provide HAART and the requisite laboratory monitoring support for patients with clinical AIDS late that year. Since that time, Brazil has become the icon of providing universal access, and has negotiated year after year with pharmaceutical companies to lower drug prices, while also issuing compulsory licenses for local production in order to make treatments available to those in need.

By contrast, the South African government never embraced the universal public provision of drug treatment. In 1992, while the country was still under white rule, the minister of health asserted that "sophisticated first world medical care could not only be unaffordable but it would also be inappropriate."[45] The government maintained this position well after 1994, and as the idea of providing ARV treatment in low- and middle-income countries began to figure in the Geneva Consensus, President Mbeki in 2001 questioned the toxicity of the drugs, suggesting they might be more dangerous than the disease. Such skepticism was reiterated by the health minister and other public officials, until the national government introduced a "comprehensive plan" for care and treatment in 2003.[46] Even once

[45] SAPA News, "Minister Reports AIDS Cases up 27 Per Cent over 1992," February 22, 1994, from BBC Summary of World Broadcasts.

[46] At the time of writing, some 200,000—230,000 South Africans with HIV were receiving AIDS treatment, about half in the public and half in the private sectors. The numbers currently treated are not indicative of the overall government response. Brazil treated more people sooner, and at a time when treatment costs were much higher; at the same time, more South Africans need treatment than in Brazil partly because prevention efforts were historically less aggressive there.

a plan was in place, however, the government's embrace of HAART was weak, and the rollout proceeded slowly. The minister of health has publicly advocated herbal and nutritional alternatives to drug treatment, including "beetroot, spinach, garlic and olive oil," and several of these food items were on display in the South African information booth at the 2006 International AIDS Conference. Though billions of rands were allocated in the budget for a treatment program, the health minister did little to purchase and distribute drugs and, in stark contrast with the Brazilians, did virtually nothing to negotiate with drug companies over prices,[47] despite a much larger need for the product.

Finally, in the area of rights, the Brazilian response has also been more aggressive, but perhaps only as measured in terms of timing, because by the end of 2006, the legislative frameworks for protecting rights in the two countries were not markedly different (table 4.5). In 1988, Brazil passed a law guaranteeing workers with HIV/AIDS the same rights afforded to those with other incapacitating illnesses and, in 1992, the government disallowed HIV testing before school admission and made it illegal to dismiss HIV-positive students, teachers, or school staff. In South Africa, a law regarding employment equity protection was not passed until 1995.[48] Quite contrary to a rights-based approach, the South African state initially reacted to the HIV/AIDS threat with coercive measures. In 1987, the government announced that it would deport all HIV-positive migrant workers, and it added HIV/AIDS to the list of "notifiable" diseases, requiring medical practitioners to report names of HIV-positive individuals to the public health authorities.[49] Although both of these acts were eventually repealed, they demonstrated the government's initial intent to be more repressive, using control and force, than supportive of the rights of the infected. After 1995, although discrimination in practice continues to be widespread, additional laws entrenched the rights of people with HIV, including the 1998 Employment Equity Act of 1998 and the Promotion of Equality and Prevention of Unfair Discrimination Act No. 4 of 2000.[50] The courts, especially with the support of Supreme Court justice and HIV-positive AIDS activist Edwin Cameron, have protected the rights of

[47] Nattrass 2007, 128–29.
[48] Garbus 2003, 75.
[49] Ngwena 1998, 119.
[50] Department of Health, RSA, "Republic of South Africa: Progress Report on Declaration of Commitment on HIV and AIDS," prepared for United Nations General Assembly Special Session on HIV and AIDS, March 2006, 17–19.

TABLE 4.5
AIDS-related Human Rights Policies in Brazil and South Africa

	South Africa	Brazil
Workplace nondiscrimination	1995 Employment equity law, includes HIV-positive citizens	1988 Law extends disability protection to HIV-posi-tive citizens
Other rights-related policies	Early 1980s (Negative/coercive) Forced deportation of HIV-positive migrants, but eventually repealed	1988 Establish guidelines for "ethical treatment" of people with HIV

Note: More aggressive actions are shaded.

people with HIV/AIDS, consistently interpreting legislation so as to expand social and protective rights.

By the end of 2006 the South African government seemed to be on a path toward greater conformity with the Geneva Consensus and more aggressive AIDS policies, with expanding budgets and stated commitments to prevention and treatment. But not entirely. Most notably, deputy health minister Nozizwe Madlala-Routledge tried to advance an aggressive new approach to AIDS in late 2006, particularly while the health minister was sidelined with her own illness. Madlala-Routledge acknowledged the validity of past criticisms of the government's AIDS policies, and encouraged government leaders to undergo public testing. Moreover, deputy president Phumzile Mlambo-Ngcuka was appointed to head the government's AIDS efforts, and announced a new strategy on World AIDS Day, December 1, 2006, which included massive increases in prevention and treatment programs, which were lauded by critics inside and outside the country.[51] As the new plans were being announced, the TAC general secretary Sipho Mthathi commented, "We are now witnessing the emergence of a united front of government, civil society, and communities in a common effort,"[52] which was a radical departure from more than a decade of growing animosity between the state and civil society actors. And yet in August 2007,

[51]Chris Otton, "South Africa Finetunes AIDS Policy to Shore Up Battered Image," Agence France-Presse, November 29, 2006.
[52]Clare Nullis, "Activists Praise New Government Policy as New Dawn of Unity," Associated Press, November 9, 2006.

Mbeki fired Madlala-Routledge on charges of taking an unauthorized trip to an AIDS conference in Spain; her dismissal was believed to be the result of her open contradiction of his stance on HIV/AIDS, and was interpreted by many as evidence that the government's change in direction on AIDS was not thoroughgoing. Fatima Hassan and Mark Heywood of the AIDS Law Project wrote in a letter published in the *Mail and Guardian* that the deputy minister should not have been fired, and redirected criticism at Tshabalala-Msimang: "The minister is still holding up the scaling up of ARV treatment by refusing provinces the authority to accredit ARV sites. And she remains uncensored for brazenly promoting the right to choose untested substances over proven medicines."[53]

Notwithstanding this row, the South African government's more aggressive five-year plan adopted in mid-2007 has been complemented by large and increasing financial outlays. Momentum to address AIDS seemed to be taking off by the end of 2007, but the puzzle of why it took so long relative to Brazil remains of theoretical and substantive importance.

PARTIAL AND ALTERNATIVE EXPLANATIONS OF POLICY DIVERGENCE

In almost every area, the Brazilian government was more aggressive in rolling out relevant AIDS programs and policies than the South African government, and in the case of treatment, it helped to establish a new benchmark for the Geneva Consensus. Some difference in the timing of the Brazilian response is attributable to the earlier appearance of AIDS-related illnesses and deaths, but this hardly accounts for the qualitative differences in approach. With the precedent of the Brazilian response to the epidemic, one could have expected more rapid adoption of such an approach by South Africa.

Interestingly, the one area in which the South African government clearly moved more aggressively was the blood supply—perhaps the only area in which the state could avoid the politics of stigma associated with human-to-human transmission, and thus was far less likely to meet resistance over the implications of or sacrifices associated with AIDS policies. This certainly suggests that rapid and effective action on AIDS was possible in South Africa when politics did not get in the way.

---

[53] Fatima Hassan and Mark Heywood, "The President Fired the Wrong Minister," *Mail and Guardian*, August 21, 2007.

But what accounts for the broader pattern of cross-country divergence on AIDS policy? I have already identified some of the similarities and differences in the initial progression of the epidemic, and pointed out the limits of epidemiological trends as the explanation for responses. In chapter 2, I identified alternative theoretical explanations of government policymaking, and in fact several of them have been marshaled by other scholars and analysts to make sense of these two contrasting cases. However, in more systematic comparative analyses, I find that state capacity, democratic institutions and civil society actors, international influences, and leadership provide only partial explanations of the policies in each country. In many instances, similar pressures appeared to have opposite effects, suggesting their limits as general explanatory factors. However, racial boundaries, discussed in the section that follows, provide a strong explanation of the differences in government policies and actions.

State Capacity and Public Health

One leading analysis of Brazil's remarkable response to AIDS highlights that country's state capacity, particularly in public health, as a foundation not available in many other developing countries.[54] It is true that general state capacity in Brazil is stronger than in many developing countries, and that it was important for the development of Brazil's aggressive response to AIDS. Moreover, Brazil's emergent National Unitary Health System (Sistema Único de Saúde, or SUS) was "a qualitative advance in the history of public health in Brazil," "emerged from a long tradition of advocacy for governmental responsibility for the health of the nation," and provided "a proper vehicle for the management of HIV."[55] Nonetheless, the authors also note that the history of public health in Brazil has been uneven, and that the response to AIDS was in many ways a *model* for development of the SUS, so the direction of causality in the relationship between Brazil's public health system and its AIDS response is not clear.

For the comparison being made here, it would be difficult to conclude that the Brazilian state is generally more efficacious than the South Afri-

---

[54] Berkman et al. 2005, 1166–67.
[55] Berkman et al. 2005, 1166.

can state, and we cannot explain the puzzle of this paired comparison by focusing on capacity. Whether we use overall levels of state taxation, direct collections of income tax,[56] percentage of paved roads, or ICRG country risk ratings[57] as proxies for overall state capacity, South Africa met or exceeded Brazil for most years between 1980 and 2002.

With respect to capacity in public health more specifically, both countries have mixed records, which would made it difficult to predict *ex ante* if either country would respond aggressively. Brazil's Oswaldo Cruz Foundation, which was founded in 1900 to address growing epidemic threats such as yellow fever and bubonic plague, has been a leading institution in public health; but Brazil has struggled with many other public health crises in the decades preceding the AIDS crisis, including high rates of child and maternal mortality, endemic malaria, and periodic outbreaks of dengue and cholera. The South African government has had many notable accomplishments, including free care to all pregnant women and all children aged six and under—which made the failure to initiate a PMTCT program surprising. Concurrent with the AIDS pandemic, the South African government has scored notable successes against malaria using DDT and combination therapy for treatment.[58] As contrasted with HIV, malaria is an infectious disease that does not contain the same social stigma because it is not transmitted through human contact. In the past twenty years, both countries launched reforms that made their general health care system accessible to poor and excluded groups: Brazil in 1990, with the inclusion of informal sector workers in the system formerly available only to those contributing payroll deductions; and South Africa in 1989–90, with the desegregation of the public system. An expert-based assessment of maternal and neonatal health services rated Brazil's program "weak," while South Africa's was "moderate."[59] Total expenditures for health have been comparable in recent decades, and when different, they have been higher in South Africa. Public sector health expenditures as a share of GDP were close to 4 percent in South Africa and close to 3 percent in Brazil between 1997 and 2001.[60] In short, based on the rest of the public health system, one could not have predicted the observed divergences in AIDS response.

[56] Lieberman 2003.
[57] World Bank 2005.
[58] Duffy and Mutabingwa 2005.
[59] Bulatao and Ross 2002.
[60] World Bank 2005.

Political Regimes and Civil Society

A second important explanation for Brazil's successes in AIDS policies is political regime variables. Scholars have highlighted the active role of a civil society operating at a moment of profound political transition, one emphasizing a more expansive view of social citizenship, and culminating in a transition to democratic rule.[61] Brazilian civil society was organized and active in the movement to restore democracy and to expand health care access, and it continued to play a role in motivating the state to respond aggressively to AIDS. The movement to restore democracy to Brazil and to hold the military regime accountable for human rights abuses spun off a movement to provide health care to underserved groups and regions (*movimiento sanitarista*), based in some of the largest cities, including São Paulo.[62] The legacy of the struggle against the military regime and its human rights abuses informed activism on AIDS. Influential former exiles and opponents of the military regime had contracted AIDS themselves and played roles in the mobilization to fight AIDS from the earliest years of the epidemic. The number of registered NGOs working on HIV/AIDS increased from 120 to 480 between 1993 and 1997,[63] and a review conducted for the World Bank in 2003 found 798 different NGOs working on HIV/AIDS in Brazil.

Political activism from "below" advanced an aggressive policy in Brazil. Gay activists in the state of São Paulo helped put AIDS on the state's public health agenda in 1983, just as the country was experiencing a democratic opening, or *abertura*, which provided political space for such organizations to mobilize.[64] In the years to come, other organizations would mobilize and partner with state officials to broaden the scope and impact of the policy response. In 1985, an alliance of gay men, human rights activists, and health professionals in São Paulo formed the AIDS Prevention and Support Group, and later in the decade other notable organizations such as the Brazilian Interdisciplinary AIDS Association, the Group for Life (Grupo Pela Vidda), and the Gay Group of Bahia emerged to apply pressure on the federal government to expand its response to HIV/AIDS.[65] The influence of

---

[61] See, for example, Berkman et al. 2005, 1163–66; Biehl 2004; Parker 2003, 156–64; Levi and Vitória 2002, 2377–78; Galvão 2000.

[62] Weyland 1995.

[63] Galvão 2000.

[64] Parker 2003, 146–47.

[65] Berkman et al. 2005, 1166.

Brazilian NGOs and civil society organizations was visible in their opposition to national AIDS policies under President Fernando Collor de Mello, which led to the return of the previous HIV/AIDS program director,[66] in their efforts to secure additional AIDS treatment funding in 1999, despite the recent devaluation and financial crisis, and in the routine movement of AIDS activists into government positions in recent years.

Brazilian civil society and AIDS NGOs played a role in lobbying Congress and the president's office to overcome resistance to World Bank loans for AIDS, and launched simultaneous street demonstrations in sixteen states in 1999 to secure additional funding for AIDS treatment despite a recent devaluation and financial crisis. Although several government programs suffered budget cuts in 1998, and although in the original proposal from the Ministry of Finance the largest cut fell on health care, the AIDS budget was not cut and was in fact listed in the "essential" programs to be protected. The number of Brazilian AIDS NGOs multiplied after the World Bank loan earmarked money to civil society for outreach, support, and prevention efforts; and their numbers in turn increased the political strength of the AIDS community in Brazil.

While acknowledging the facts that have led observers to highlight activism and the momentum associated with democratic transitions as key influences on policy in Brazil, broader comparative analysis is required in order to make more general theoretical statements about the likely effect of regime conditions. Should we expect a strong, well-organized civil society in the context of a relatively open democratic regime to be *sufficient* to apply necessary pressure to a government to act in the face of a deadly pandemic? Are such conditions *necessary*? Or, more restrictively, do they make such outcomes *more likely*? The Brazilian AIDS story seems to shed a positive light on the effects of democratic rule for the provision of public goods and policy responsiveness. But it would be a mistake to draw strong conclusions about general patterns from a single case.

Like Brazil, South Africa was part of the "third wave" of democratization,[67] and political change was under way there in the late 1970s, before the outbreak of the global AIDS pandemic. Given the multifaceted nature of political transitions, it is difficult to put precise dates on the onset of each, but it is clear that by 1994, both countries met most scholarly criteria for being a democracy. The relatively weak South African response in

---

[66] Teixeira 1997; Galvão 2000.
[67] Huntington 1991; Seidman 1994.

most aspects of AIDS policy has persisted well after significant political openings, including the completion of three free and fair multiparty national elections. This finding is striking when one considers that democratic transitions in both countries helped give rise to strong, extensive, and well-organized networks of civil society organizations, active on a range of issues, including HIV/AIDS policy. Indeed, both countries developed strong civil society organizations during a prior era of antiauthoritarian political challenges, and by the 1990s, citizens in both countries enjoyed significant civil liberties—somewhat greater in South Africa than in Brazil, according to the Freedom House surveys. While this analysis cannot rule out the possibility that the presence of a strong civil society may be an factor that increases the likelihood of an aggressive AIDS policy, the paired comparison demonstrates that even a truly vibrant network of nongovernment AIDS organizations is not sufficient to elicit an aggressive government response. Of course few factors deterministically influence any social or political phenomenon, but this is still an important conclusion given the assumption of many political actors and observers that the free flow of information in democratic societies will result in deliberate responses to objective threats to society.

Much as in Brazil, South African civil society has been vocal and well organized and has played a role in the establishment of democracy and the end of apartheid, but as discussed earlier, the trajectory of the government's response to the epidemic has been very different from Brazil's. As in much of the world, including Brazil, the South African AIDS NGO sector developed in response to the lack of state action. As Mary Crewe observed in 1992, "Much of the successful work in AIDS prevention is being taken on by NGOs and other important groups such as unions and the ANC." While there are no precise figures on the numbers of AIDS-related NGOs and organizations, medical groups, grassroots political organizations, and community-based service delivery organizations have operated individually and collectively since the mid-1980s in South Africa, initially in concert with antiapartheid organizations or in communities with poor service delivery. As of 2000, there were over six hundred NGOs working in the HIV/AIDS field,[68] and by 2004, the AIDS consortium website claimed over one thousand organizational members.[69]

---

[68] Van der Vliet 2001, 170.
[69] http://www.aidsconsortium.org.za/About.htm (consulted September 1, 2006).

In fact, there is perhaps no single individual who has drawn more attention on the global HIV/AIDS stage in recent years than South Africa's Zachie Achmat, the HIV-positive AIDS activist, who refused to take ARVs until they were made publicly available. Achmat has led the popular Treatment Action Campaign (TAC), which has mobilized court litigation, public relations campaigns, and civil disobedience against the South African government. TAC was launched on December 10, 1998, by Achmat and Mark Heywood, both long-standing ANC members, who were concerned to extend treatments to people living with HIV. Initially, they had thought that the major barrier to treatment access would be the major pharmaceutical companies, but they soon turned their attention to pressuring government in the wake of its weak policies and actions.[70] The TAC organized rallies across the country on March 21, 1999, calling for a national PMTCT plan,[71] and a February 2003 march of approximately ten thousand people on Parliament demanding a treatment plan.[72] Scholars and journalists have highlighted the remarkable creativity and organizational tenacity of TAC and the AIDS Law Project, and Achmat's and TAC's actions, along with those of associated NGOs and the generally strong AIDS civil society, ought to be credited with some of the more recent policy developments in South Africa, including plans for public provision of ARV drugs for PMTCT and of HAART. But from a comparative perspective, given the mobilization and visibility of such organizations, the relative insensitivity of government decision-makers to their efforts is striking, and sheds light on the *limits* to civil society actors' influence on policy. Perhaps the South African government's response would have been even more lackluster in the absence of such pressure, but it is not possible to conclude that a strong and active civil society is sufficient for a strong government response given that the relative size and mobilization of civil society actors has been at least as large as in Brazil.

Beyond the role of civil society, it is difficult to explain the trajectory of either country in terms of the formal trappings of democratic rule such as elections and legislative politics. AIDS has figured in such agendas minimally for most of the epidemic, and became a growing influence in South Africa only very late in the epidemic.

---

[70] Friedman and Mottiar 2005, 513–14.

[71] Nattrass 2007, 186.

[72] For a more detailed analysis of TAC as a social movement, see Friedman and Mottiar 2005. See also Nattrass 2007.

In Brazil, Herbert Daniel, a prominent gay activist who himself had AIDS, registered in 1989, but later withdrew, as a Green Party candidate for the presidency.[73] A review of online articles in a leading newspaper in the country, *A Folha de São Paulo*, found that neither former president Fernando Henrique Cardoso nor his major opponents were quoted making a reference to AIDS in the nine months preceding the 1994 and 1998 elections. One exception involves the candidacy of José Serra, who served as health minister in the latter part of Cardoso's presidency and used his past support for the country's successful AIDS program as a principal banner for his (unsuccessful) campaign in 2002. Indirect electoral politics might also have played a role in President Cardoso's decision to approve the law authorizing all necessary ARV drugs for AIDS patients in 1998. His ministers of finance and planning recommended that he veto the law because of its high cost and suggested that the distribution of publicly financed AIDS drugs be targeted to those with limited means, but Cardoso was in the midst of negotiations with Congress on the terms of a constitutional amendment permitting presidential reelection, and his reluctance to antagonize the influential senator and former president José Sarney, a key sponsor of the AIDS drugs legislation, might have played a role in his decision not to veto the law. However, both Cardoso's decision not to veto the law and Serra's candidacy occurred well after the Brazilian AIDS program had been consolidated and can hardly be an explanation of Brazil's initial policy.

Meanwhile, in South Africa, there was almost no discussion of HIV/AIDS policy in the first two postapartheid national election campaigns (1994 and 1999), and only some party-based challenge to HIV/AIDS policy during the 2004 election. If anything, the results of that election suggest what public opinion polls had been finding—that AIDS was not a central concern for voters. Just a few months before the election, the Democratic Alliance party said it would make AIDS a campaign issue,[74] and its leader, Tony Leon, has spoken often and publicly about AIDS. The leader of the Inkatha Freedom Party, Mangosuthu Buthelezi, who hails from the worst-affected province of Kwazulu-Natal and had two sons who died from AIDS, announced in March 2004 that he and his party had entered into an alliance with the Democratic Alliance—the "Coali-

[73] UPI, "Brazilian Election Fields 34 candidates," August 18, 1989. Also, http://www.greens.org/s-r/15/15-03.html (consulted December 14, 2006).

[74] Kaiser Daily HIV/AIDS Report, "South African President Mbeki Rejects Criticism from Opposition Parties over AIDS Policies," February 10, 2004.

tion for Change"—to support five key platforms, one of which was more aggressive AIDS policies. Indeed, both members of the coalition could make credible claims that their parties were viable agents for more progressive AIDS policies, as the provinces they had the opportunities to control during the postapartheid era—the Western Cape and KwaZulu-Natal—had the most aggressive AIDS policies.[75] In April 2004, just a week before the elections, Patricia de Lille, the vocal leader of an extremely small opposition party (Independent Democrats), took a public HIV test and urged Mbeki to do the same as a way of emphasizing the scope of the epidemic and the government's inaction, describing the country as "10 years behind from the rest of the world in terms of fighting the AIDS pandemic."[76] Thus, the 2004 election provided alternative positions on a more aggressive AIDS policy, but the voters spoke, and they did not vote for change. On the contrary, the ANC claimed just under 70 percent of the seats in the National Assembly, up from 66 percent in 1999 and 63 percent in 1994; and for the first time, it swept all nine provinces, including the Western Cape and KwaZulu-Natal.

The only significant evidence that plausibly links government action on HIV/AIDS to electoral politics was the fall 2003 announcement about the proposed ARV-based treatment program—an announcement that came approximately six months before the spring 2004 election. Given international and increasing domestic pressure from civil society organizations, the ANC leadership may have perceived slight vulnerability to this issue and chose to head it off by announcing a program. Nonetheless, despite the severity of the AIDS problem by 2004, no opposition political party managed to make the government's failings an issue compelling enough to attract votes.

Beyond electoral politics and openings for civil society activity, democracies are defined by their representative legislative institutions, which in turn debate the issues of concern to citizens. The historic 1994 election—generally regarded as the birthdate of South African democracy—was hardly a boon for discussion of national AIDS policy among democratically elected representatives. In fact, perhaps just the opposite is true: figure 4.1 plots the number of days that HIV or AIDS was discussed in the

---

[75] The predecessor to the Democratic Alliance, the Democratic Party, was in a short-lived coalition and subsequent alliance with the now defunct National Party between 1999 and 2001, which allowed it to participate in governing the Western Cape Province. The IFP won KwaZulu-Natal outright in 1994 and controlled in coalition with the ANC after the 1999 elections.

[76] Reuters, "S. Africa Opposition Maverick Takes HIV Test," April 5, 2004.

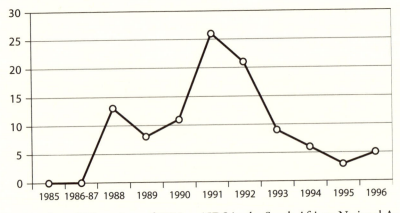

4.1. Number of Discussions of HIV or AIDS in the South African National Assembly, 1985–96
Source: South Africa Parliament, Hansard Indexes 1985–96.

legislature for the years 1985–96 (after which indexing of the Hansard parliamentary records was discontinued). After the unbanning of Nelson Mandela in 1990, legislative discussion of HIV and AIDS peaked in 1991, and indeed the 1991–92 period was an active period of AIDS policy discussion and the production of national proposals and plans. But by 1993, legislative discussion slowed considerably, and by 1995, the year following the first multiracial, postapartheid election, parliamentary discussion of AIDS reached the lowest level since the first parliamentary discussion of the topic in 1988.[77] Indeed, according to observers, it was the democratic transition itself that "crowded out" attention to AIDS. In a 2000 interview, president of the South African Medical Research Council Malegapuru Makgoba explained, "In the midst of the heroic efforts to build a new, pluralistic South Africa, the HIV epidemic simply became one challenge too many."[78] And again, from a purely idiographic standpoint, it may well be the case that democratic transition in South Africa overwhelmed rather than fueled the drive for a more aggressive AIDS policy. But the contrasting histories of Brazil and South Africa suggest the limited promise of a predictive theory of policymaking based on a country's political regime.

With the limits of democratic politics as a predictable influence on policy in view, it remains plausible that differences in the timing of demo-

[77] No indexing is available for speeches after 1996.
[78] Sparks 2003, 283.

cratic transitions in the two countries may explain some of the variance in policymaking.[79] The key "democratic" moment in Brazil was the 1988 constitution, and in South Africa, it was the 1994 election (Brazil's first direct presidential election was in 1989, and South Africa developed an interim constitution in 1993 and a final version in 1996). Thus, if democratic openings had a consistent effect on AIDS politics and policymaking, that would help to explain the delay in government response in South Africa, but it would not account for the very different dynamics described earlier in more than a decade of policymaking posttransition. The historical records do suggest that democratic transitions in both countries facilitated the protection of human rights for HIV-positive individuals. In the South African case, far more coercive measures that restricted the rights of many HIV-positive individuals and "high risk" groups were in place before the democratic transition, and rights-oriented protective legislation was drafted almost immediately after 1994. Overall, although democratic regime change provided an opening for the development of human rights protections, its impact on the other aspects of AIDS policy, particularly the ones requiring the greatest sacrifices and the most recognition of personal risk, was not consistent.

International Influences

Scholarly analyses of Brazilian AIDS policy have pointed to the role of external influences and assistance, and such analysis again motivates consideration of these factors as the sources of cross-country variation in policy outcomes. One study of the Brazilian AIDS "model" identifies international financial institutions, internationalizing economic policy, and international partnerships as critical to its development and success.[80] At first glance, such international factors seem to provide a plausible account of divergent country responses. For example, from 1993 to 2003 the World Bank lent Brazil US$325 million to respond to the HIV/AIDS epidemic, and the government's AIDS program has had relatively strong links with the WHO and PAHO since the late 1980s. At the same time, South Africa was an international pariah because of its apartheid govern-

---

[79] Thanks to Catherine Boone for suggesting that I not dismiss this "timing" variable too easily.

[80] Biehl 2004, 107.

ment, and had minimal contact with international organizations, including the WHO, until after the political transition in 1994.

The Geneva Consensus and broader international efforts have surely provided a common framework for political and policy responses. But international influences or the countries' positions in the international political economy cannot explain Brazil's relative aggressiveness, for several reasons. Most important, the two countries were more similar than different in their relations with the "core" countries during the second decade of the epidemic, and there was an interactive relationship between external assistance and domestic policy aggressiveness, not a unidirectional causality.

It is important to recognize that key moments in the Brazilian response to the epidemic *preceded* the World Bank loan. Before the loan was signed in 1993, Brazil had established a national program, a Brazilian president had mentioned AIDS in a public speech, the government had begun to purchase and distribute AIDS drugs, including AZT monotherapy free of charge, and the government was advancing the rights of AIDS patients. As described above, the government had issued human rights protections, including prohibiting the use of HIV tests in physical examinations of public sector workers. At the state and municipal levels, at least sixty-seven local laws and resolutions regarding HIV/AIDS had been approved by the end of 1992. These included requirements that motels and hotels provide condoms, guarantees of nondiscrimination for public sector workers and students, legal recognition and incorporation of AIDS NGOs, the reservation of hospital beds for AIDS patients, incorporation of information on HIV prevention in public and private school curricula, and compulsory HIV testing of prisoners.

Second, neither country has been a passive follower of international actors, including of the key architects of the Geneva Consensus. The South African government has defied international pressures, but the Brazilian government has also defied international actors when domestic political concerns were at stake. Declaring that "Brazil will not be a guinea pig" and impugning the expertise of the WHO, the minister of health refused to participate in WHO-led HIV vaccine trials, which resulted in the temporary isolation of the Brazilian AIDS program from the international community.[81] Both countries have taken opportunities to rebuff donors, especially the U.S. government, which has imposed restrictions on the use of AIDS-related funds.

---

[81] Teixeira 1997.

Finally, differences in foreign assistance on HIV/AIDS can be explained from the perspective of domestic policy. The Brazilians sought the loan from the World Bank; it was not one that the Brazilian government was forced or even persuaded to take on. At the time, the Brazilian government had decided not to borrow for the social sectors because the loans were not productive, and the hyperinflation of the early 1990s was complicating the development projects already under way. The decision to change course and pursue a World Bank loan was a result of the policy entrepreneurship of the National AIDS Program under the new government in 1992. After 1994, the South African government steadfastly rebuffed offers of aid and assistance, particularly from the World Bank. In more recent years, it has been noncooperative and even combative with both the U.S. government and the GFATM, even as it has begun to accept financial aid for dealing with the epidemic. In turn, the international community has applied steady pressure on the South African government for its weak response, with international activists, scholars, and international organizations being openly critical ever since the country's reluctance to provide nevirapine to HIV-positive, pregnant women. In his keynote speech at the 2006 International AIDS Conference, the UN special envoy for AIDS, Stephen Lewis, said South Africa's policies were "wrong, immoral, [and] indefensible," and its "theories more worthy of a lunatic fringe than of a concerned and compassionate state."[82]

Most other developing countries did not possess the financial and technical resources to chart a course autonomous from the core countries, and have been subjected to greater control in the context of asymmetric global governance. By contrast, both Brazil and South Africa—with among the highest level of per capita income and the largest economies in their respective regions—have been less beholden and their governments more capable of independent courses. Only in Brazil was this autonomy associated with aggressiveness of policy, implying the greater influence of domestic variables.

Leadership and the Ideas of Leaders

While I have analyzed structural influences on AIDS policymaking, individual actors and leaders also play an important role. It has become almost

---

[82] Agence France-Presse, "South African Health Minister Faces Axe Call over AIDS Row," August 21, 2006.

conventional wisdom that South Africa's state president since 1999, Thabo Mbeki, is behind the government's stark passivity and its aversion to the Geneva Consensus. Mbeki has expressed sympathy for the scientific views of scientists and laypersons who dissent from that consensus, such as Peter Duesberg, a professor of molecular and cell biology at the University of California, Berkeley; David Rasnick, a California-based biochemist; a set of Australian scientists; and peddlers of vitamin supplements and alternative therapies.[83] Because reputations and credentials carry political weight, it is important to point out that Duesberg has published many articles in leading scientific journals and has been supported by Kary Mullis, a somewhat eccentric scientist, but also a 1993 Nobel laureate—though not for his work on HIV. These individuals have either questioned the link between HIV and AIDS or challenged the efficacy of ARVs in suppressing the virus. Oftentimes, those challenging the Geneva Consensus cite these scientists alongside broader conspiracy theories, either of plots to smear or destroy certain subgroups (gays, blacks, Africans, etc.).[84] This group of dissidents has railed against the Geneva Consensus, and observers have argued that Mbeki's personal embrace of these views, alongside his tight control of the ruling party, is the fundamental explanation for the country's overall policy on AIDS.

There is little doubt that Mbeki has expressed sympathy for these heterodox views, and that he has used the veil of "open scientific debate" as justification for resisting the Geneva Consensus. Starting in late 1999, Mbeki began to publicly question the mainstream scientific wisdom about HIV and AIDS, and he emphasized the toxicity of antiretroviral drugs rather than their benefits for people living with HIV. No one would deny that these are powerful drugs with substantial side effects, but given clear scientific evidence that they dramatically improve and extend the lives of people with HIV, such talk was condemned by treatment activists in South Africa, by architects of the Geneva Consensus, and by leading scientists around the world. Mbeki's statements and questions about AIDS raised so much ire at the summer 2000 International AIDS Conference, held in Durban, South Africa, that in October 2000 he announced that he was "stepping out" of the AIDS debate. Nonetheless, Mbeki's health minister, Manto Tshabalala-Msimang, has perpetuated his heterodox ap-

---

[83] See Nattrass 2007, 22–33, for a clear summary of the denialist claims and their relationship to the broader scientific community.

[84] Sparks 2003, 289–90.

proach to HIV, advocating a nutritious diet and vitamins as primary remedies and expressing skepticism about antiretroviral drugs.[85] She too has been roundly criticized by AIDS activists and mocked for her dissident approach. Many observers blame South Africa's blazing epidemic and the government's failure to respond on the personal idiosyncrasies of Mbeki and his inner circle.

Indeed, scholarly analyses of AIDS policy have emphasized leadership variables, particularly in explaining the South African case. In a comparative analysis of the Ugandan and South African responses, "political leadership" is identified as one of four explanatory factors, most prominently comparing Mbeki and the far more aggressive Yoweri Museveni.[86] Nicoli Nattrass's study of the struggle to deliver antiretrovirals in South Africa concludes that the government's passive policies were rooted in an ideological commitment to "AIDS Denialism."[87] She identifies Mbeki's attachment to this idea as the root cause of the policy response, making the strong counterfactual claim, "If Mbeki had (seen and spoken with people using ARV's) . . . he would have come face to face with the AIDS epidemic and the power of ARV's to fight it. South Africa's history of AIDS policy may well have been very different."[88]

I do not reject this claim. If Mbeki had been persuaded by and promoted the Geneva Consensus, the history of his country's policies would certainly be different. But from a theoretical perspective, that conclusion is unsatisfying. While the expressed positions of Mbeki and his closest advisers were individual acts that had a proximate, negative influence on the speed and scope of the South African response, that response was not solely or even largely the product of Mbeki the person, autonomous from his political environment. Several factors support this claim: First, AIDS was largely neglected under the presidencies of two Nobel Peace Prize winners—Nelson Mandela and F. W. de Klerk.[89] Indeed, Mandela has said that he was advised against speaking out about AIDS because it was

---

[85] Almost no one doubts the positive effects of good nutrition for people who are HIV-positive, but this debate has centered around the importance of nutrition as a *substitute* for ARVs.

[86] Parkhurst and Lush 2004, 1916–18. In a similar manner, Kauffman 2004, 25–27, contrasts the South African case with the leadership of Museveni and President Abdou Diouf of Senegal.

[87] Nattrass 2007, 8.

[88] Nattrass 2007, 37.

[89] However, it would be wrong to assert that Mandela did nothing on AIDS. In 1995, for example, he urged provincial leaders to make condoms freely available to sexually ac-

a losing political issue. "I wanted to win and I didn't talk about Aids," Mandela recounted in an interview with the BBC.[90] Second, Mbeki before becoming president was a champion of HIV/AIDS prevention. Third, setting aside the issues of HIV/AIDS, Mbeki, the second president of postapartheid South Africa, was a respected leader who initially commanded broad respect in his own society[91] and on the international stage, where he was seen as a visionary leader in African integration.

Perhaps the most important challenge to the leadership thesis is the ANC's persistent popularity and the lack of widespread challenge to government policy. Only late in the second term of his presidency did Mbeki's popularity wane, largely because of dissatisfaction over economic inequality, jobs, and crime. In December 2007, he lost his bid to be reelected as president of the ANC. But the loss was to Jacob Zuma, a man who after being charged with raping an HIV-positive activist, explained during his trial that he took a shower afterward to reduce the risk of contracting the virus. While his ridiculous statements received enormous publicity in the news media, his political support was not undermined. Though Zuma has made other statements indicating a position on HIV/AIDS that is more in line with the Geneva Consensus, his election at the ANC's national congress at Polokwane reflects a persistent tolerance or even acceptance of heterodox views of HIV and AIDS among the party's leadership and its rank and file. If leaders are the impediments to aggressive AIDS policies in South Africa, what explains their ideas in the face of so much scientific evidence?

Leadership does not provide a compelling explanation for the Brazilian case. One important account indicates that government officials responded to pressures, rather than taking the lead on AIDS policy.[92] Most of the Brazilian presidents in power during the outbreak of the AIDS epidemic—Sarney, Collor, and Itamar Franco—were weak and unremarkable. Of the presidents who came to power during the recent democratic era, only Fernando Henrique Cardoso and Luiz Inácio Lula Da Silva ("Lula") can be described as strong leaders with broad popular support, but both presidencies postdate aggressive action on HIV/AIDS. Moreover, the lead actors in the Brazilian health ministry were hardly visionar-

---

tive young people. (Agence France-Presse, "Mandela Urges Greater AIDS Awareness," August 12, 1995).

[90] David Dimbleby, "No Peace for Workaholic Mandela," *BBC News*, March 2, 2003.

[91] Jacobs and Calland 2002.

[92] Berkman et al. 2005, 1166.

ies. Early in the epidemic, in the Ministry of Health some officials argued that AIDS did not satisfy the epidemiological criteria of "transcendence," "magnitude," and "vulnerability" necessary to warrant a response from public institutions. In 1985, INAMPS (Instituto Nacional de Assistência Médica da Previdência Social—the medical care division of the social security institute) argued that AIDS was a "public health problem," not a medical concern, and therefore an issue for the state health secretariats.[93] Although Brazil has become a world leader in AIDS, and impressive Brazilian public officials working in the field have emerged, I attribute more causal weight to broad sociopolitical inducements and constraints than to isolated individuals in government.

Federalism and Decentralization

Finally, it is useful to consider the implications of varying levels of political and administrative decentralization in the two countries. There is much greater policy autonomy at the subnational (*estado*) level in Brazil than in South Africa because of a deeper legacy of federalism and because of the single-party domination of the polity in South Africa (by the National Party until 1994, and by the African National Congress since). One could argue that decentralization and even political fragmentation facilitated the Brazilian response, whose origins lay in the early political entrepreneurship of activists and state-level public health officials from the southeastern states, but again, it would be very difficult to sustain the counterfactual claim that the South African national government's response would have been different with greater provincial autonomy. As in Brazil, the AIDS epidemic first hit South Africa's wealthiest cities, Cape Town and Johannesburg, and there has been space, albeit more limited, for more aggressive provincial action in the Western Cape and in KwaZulu-Natal—the provinces with the lowest and highest HIV prevalence, respectively. In South Africa, provinces have had significant, albeit concurrently shared responsibility for health since the mid-1990s, and we might expect in a country with a large and widespread epidemic that its national government would respond more effectively and decisively than a more fragmented state power such as Brazil.[94] Nonetheless, throughout

[93] As quoted in Teixeira 1997.
[94] Kohli 2004.

the history of the epidemic, there is clear evidence of rebukes and refusals from the South African national government. It is not that the provinces lacked information or aggressive actors to help push for a national policy. Particularly because provincial or national leaders were from the same party, there should have been clear information channels. The more problematic issue has been the resistance of the national government to an agenda that it viewed as untenable and undesirable from the perspective of the politics of intergroup competition. Especially interesting in the Brazilian case is that the national government has been so aggressive, even when the problem was so clearly concentrated in one region. To explain how the Brazilian epidemic became a national emergency meriting an expansive response, despite much lower HIV prevalence and more spatially concentrated infections, while the South African epidemic was treated with much less urgency, I must turn to boundary politics.

The Effect of Boundary Institutions

The point of the foregoing analyses was not to reject alternative accounts of AIDS policy in Brazil and South Africa. Scholars have marshaled evidence to demonstrate that the Brazilian federal government's approach to AIDS can be understood as a product of its preexisting public health infrastructure, a strong civil society that made demands on the government, and foreign pressure and support. Beyond these broader structural features, creative and dedicated individuals and activists, with the know-how to challenge, prod, and cooperate with bureaucrats, helped to drive a response. Moreover, scholars, journalists, and other observers have identified a "denialist" perspective among South African leaders, resulting in the country's more passive response.

But given the premise of my search for a broader theoretical model—for a nomothetic account that sheds light on a larger group of country cases—the comparative-historical analyses presented above reveal the limits of these other explanations.

A more promising alternative model (detailed in full in chapter 2) highlights the role of boundary institutions and their effect on AIDS policy formulation and implementation. This model helps to *explain* the denialism in South Africa, and why the presence of factors that drove the Brazilian response led to different outcomes in South Africa. Specifically, strong boundary institutions in South Africa derailed policymaking, while in Brazil permeable boundaries made possible strong national policies, even while the epidemic was relatively concentrated. Information about the spread of the virus, the perceived risk of infection, notions of shame and blame, and resulting approaches were all mediated by very different boundary institutions in the two countries.

Comparing Race Boundaries

First, it is necessary to be convinced that race boundaries in Brazil and South Africa are truly different, because amid phenotypical diversity in skin color in both countries one can find correlations with socioeconomic status and social discrimination. In one important comparative analysis of race-based prejudice around the world, Howard Winant writes, "Brazil is different. Of course, but not that different."[95] If the point were merely to highlight the near-universal discrimination experienced by people of color around the world, the point is certainly correct. But the concern here is with the strength of the formal and informal institutions that may consistently reinforce patterns of group difference, with the potential for an "us-them" dynamic.

Along these lines, the two countries are indeed profoundly different. Deliberate political actions during specific periods lay the foundation for the establishment of boundary institutions. Before the turn of the twentieth century, both countries experienced European immigration, the subjugation of people of color through legalized institutions, including chattel slavery, and sufficient miscegenation to produce a mixed population. Different political strategies and bargains to resolve political conflicts in the late nineteenth and early twentieth centuries produced different state policies and contrasting societal norms regarding the permeability and sociopolitical relevance of the color line.[96]

The history of South Africa, marked by institutionalized white supremacy for most of the twentieth century, created increasingly rigid categories of "white/European," "black/African," "Coloured," and "Indian." Eventually, the South African state would enforce policies of *apartheid* or apartness, banning sexual relations across the color bar, and categorizing the racial identity of individuals in official documents. The end of apartheid and the first truly inclusive national election in 1994

---

[95] Winant 2001, 241.

[96] For discussion of the historical origins and reproduction of these boundaries in these countries and in the United States, see Marx 1998; Skidmore 1995; Telles 2004.

marked an opportunity for creating a "nonracial South Africa," but centuries of separation, which reinforced economic, territorial, cultural, and linguistic distinctions, have meant that South Africans still experience their effects. In its attempts to redress racial injustice, the postapartheid state has collected almost all household and epidemiological data along racial lines, using the same four racial categories as the apartheid state. Strong preference policies (affirmative action) and official multilingualism[97] reinforce commonsense notions of group difference in society and polity. Official speeches and policies routinely identify race, and race continues to be a clear predictor of preferences and attitudes.[98] There is little doubt in South African society about how race groups are constituted and their respective sizes,[99] and census data report that the black population in South Africa is about 79 percent of the total, whites about 10 percent, Coloureds (mixed race) about 9 percent, and Indians about 2–3 percent. The end of apartheid government has witnessed some reduction in the strength of boundary institutions, but by any comparison with Brazil, or most other countries for that matter, these boundaries have remained strong.

In Brazil, following the abolition of slavery and the dawn of republican government in the last decades of the nineteenth century, the state embarked upon a radically different strategy. It began to promote "nonracialism" and a strategy of "whitening,"[100] which explicitly promoted sexual relations between people from different race groups. In the first half of the twentieth century, the sociologist Gilberto Freyre, whose ideas were centrally associated with the country's myth of a "racial democracy," argued that all Brazilians were *culturally* African, Amerindian, and European."[101] A long-standing policy of promoting Portuguese as a single language helped to unite people across the color bar, and across immigrant groups more generally. The 1967 and 1969 constitutions prohibited race distinc-

[97] In addition to race, language is also an ethnic boundary in South Africa, and the apartheid state tried to separate black/African groups into separate "national" groups. However, those formal boundaries were politically rejected by most blacks during the antiapartheid struggle in favor of a larger African identity. More recently, there is some evidence of the reassertion of those identities, especially Xhosa and Zulu identities, but these are far less institutionalized and politically important in South Africa.

[98] Gibson 2003.

[99] Jung 2000 does document some shifting of racial identities in South Africa, pointing out that they are indeed "social constructions," but there is little evidence of the type of wholesale shifting of racial classification within one's lifetime or across generations that is evident in Brazil.

[100] Skidmore 1995.

[101] As described by Fry 2000, 90.

tions and criminalized racial prejudice.[102] The Brazilian census of 1970 contained no questions about race or color, and the 1960 census data were never fully released,[103] suggesting that by the onset of the AIDS epidemic there would be little information about the size of different race groups in Brazil, let alone any agreement about relevant and meaningful categories. Historically, the IBGE (the government's central statistical and demographic agency) has avoided cross-tabulating color categories with socioeconomic variables and has not been forthcoming in its release of color-demarcated data.[104] Once outlawed, the gathering of racial identity along with health outcomes data is a recent phenomenon, and racial data are often gathered in an open-ended format, making it harder for potential political entrepreneurs to identify sharp racial differences.

As a result of these patterns, racial demographics are hard to pin down in Brazil. Open-ended survey questions that ask Brazilian citizens about their "color" often result in the reporting of dozens, and sometimes more than a hundred different responses,[105] epitomizing fluid boundaries. Different sources inside and outside Brazil report different categories and population size distributions (e.g., the Central Intelligence Agency's World Factbook reports the "black" population as 6.2 percent of the population, while the Minorities at Risk database reports the "Afro-Brazilian" population as 48.2 percent). In a fascinating recent study, in which researchers obtained samples of genetic markers that allowed them to trace locations of ancestral origin, they found that "in Brazil, at an individual level, color, as determined by physical evaluation, is a poor predictor of genomic African ancestry, estimated by molecular markers."[106] Brazilians are well aware of this history of mixing. And while "racial democracy"—a slogan generally intended to imply the irrelevance of race or color, particularly as contrasted with the American case—may be far from the Brazilian reality, cross-racial contact is widespread in practice and perception, and racial boundaries are clearly flexible, if not entirely permeable.[107]

Because of the obvious associations between skin color and life chances, there has long been enormous potential to invoke race in ordinary debates

---

[102] Htun 2004, 65.
[103] Nobles 2000a.
[104] Nobles 2000b, 1744.
[105] Turra and Venturi 1995.
[106] Parra et al. 2003, 177.
[107] Excellent reappraisals of race scholarship on Brazil are offered by Fry 2000; Telles 2004; and Owensby 2005.

over policy, but strong norms against such mobilization have weighed against framing social phenomena in racial terms in most political debates (as distinguished from scholarly discussions, which are increasingly concerned with the causes and consequences of race). For example, the title of a chapter of a study of Brazil from the Minorities at Risk project is "Poverty Without Protest."[108] Even prior to the onset of AIDS, many Brazilian analysts had identified statistical relationships between skin color, wealth, and status, but racial politics had been much less central and less conflictual than in South Africa, particularly because permeable boundaries impeded the formation of strong and recognizable groups.

The varied manifestation of racial boundaries can be observed in group-based attitudes and patterns of behavior in the two countries. As reported in table 4.6, there are striking differences in the negative attitudes expressed toward racial "others" in four waves of data from the World Values Survey. Comparable data for the two countries exist for the 1995–97 wave and 1999–2000 waves. In the most recent wave, eight times as many South Africans said that they did not want people of a different race as neighbors. Negative views toward people of a different race have worsened in South Africa since the 1995–97 "honeymoon period" of national reconciliation following the election of Nelson Mandela. In both countries, such statistics probably underestimate true national sentiments because people recognize it is not socially acceptable to express prejudice, but there is no reason to believe that underreporting accounts for such large differences between the countries.

Different social attitudes reinforce and are reinforced by national rates of interracial marriage. While less than 1 percent of white South Africans had nonwhite spouses according to the 1996 census, a full 23 percent of Brazilians reported being married to persons of a different color in 1991.[109] Such dramatic differences indicate that there is much greater real and perceived intimate contact across the racial line in Brazil than in South Africa.

It is also important to highlight the ways in which language and communication reinforce group boundaries in the two countries. South Africa's eleven languages are easily coded in racial terms. In their homes, whites generally speak English or Afrikaans or both; most Coloureds in the Western Cape speak Afrikaans; and black Africans speak Xhosa, Zulu, Ndebele, Venda, Sepedi, Southern Sotho, Tswana, Tsonga, Tswati, and

[108] Burke and Gurr 2000.
[109] Telles 2004, 176–77.

TABLE 4.6
Racial Boundaries in Brazil and South Africa

		South Africa	Brazil
Institutions	Official nondiscrimination	Not until 1994	Since 1891
	Race on census	Always, consistent	Mixed
	Reporting of race for health statistics	Always	Rarely
	Race-based labor preference policies	Always (in favor of blacks after 1994)	2004
	State policy on interracial sex (prior to 1980s)	Prohibited by immorality act	Encouraged ("whitening" strategy)
Practices	Self-reported rates of "intermarriage"	<1% (1996)	23% (1991)
	Flexibility of racial identities	Low: 4 categories	High: >100 categories. Census and ordinary usage are distinct.
Attitudes	Percentage saying they "would not like to have [someone of different race] as a neighbor"	17% (1981) $N = 1,529$	
			5% (1990) $N = 1,502$
		11% (1995–97) $N = 1,493$	3% (1995–97) $N = 1,494$
		24% (1999-2000) $N = 3,000$	3% (1999-2000) $N = 1,149$

Source: Inglehart et. al. 2004; Telles 2005.
Note: Stronger boundaries are shaded.

some other languages. English is the language of business and generally of government, and is widely understood by elites from all groups, but radio and television programs have sharply differentiated racial demographics, and newspapers are disproportionately read by whites. By contrast, in Brazil, linguistic homogenization (almost 100 percent of Brazilians speak Portuguese) means that a true national media can exist, and indeed, the leading television network, Sistema Globo de television, was in 1990 the world's fourth largest (after the three leading American networks), and enjoyed nightly audiences of 60–80 million people.[110] There is no significant "ethnic" press in the form of a large circulation newspaper that is read by groups identifiable in terms of race or skin color. The idea of a major "Moreno" newspaper would be nonsensical in Brazil.

Recently, however, against a long backdrop of flexibility and mixing, Brazilian boundary institutions are changing in potentially important ways. Owing to a host of factors, including increased international attention to questions of racial and ethnic disparities with a focus on Brazil, as well as long-standing inequalities in the Brazilian context, during the first years of the twenty-first century, the Brazilian government has ushered in the institution of affirmative action policies, both in educational institutions and in government ministries. These mark a radical departure, and if the general argument I propose about the impact of boundary institutions is correct, we should expect to observe some impact on the politics of AIDS. Although much of the discussion and elite pressures leading to such changes evolved during the 1990s, there was no broad-based social movement leading to such changes,[111] and the policies were largely elite-led initiatives. The policies have also met resistance from academics and political leaders, who while acknowledging color-based inequalities, have resisted an American-style codification of race categories. Moreover, it is important to keep in mind that such institutions have changed quite late in the epidemic, after a government AIDS response had already been well institutionalized.

Assessing the Impact of Boundaries on AIDS Politics and Policy

What is the evidence that leads to a conclusion that these differences in the strength of race boundaries mediated the effects of earlier-described

[110] Randall 1993, 628.
[111] Htun 2004.

pressures on policymaking, in turn leading to different political and policy responses to AIDS? State and societal actors in their discourses around the epidemic have used terms and language that suggest different frames of risk and responsibility; ideas about blame; and evidence of attempts to avoid shame from association with the virus. These varied patterns can be understood directly from the institution of race boundaries, and while most of the direct evidence is from the South African case, where boundaries were strong, the Brazilian case suggests a useful counterfactual of what *could have been*, had divisions around race been less sharply drawn.

My account is consistent with country studies of AIDS policy completed by other scholars, but by situating the two cases in a common theoretical framework we are able to isolate more clearly the effects of identity-based factors and to understand each country case as an example of a broader phenomenon. For example, several observers have linked the legacy of apartheid government to the spread of HIV in the country, as well as to the specific question considered here, of the weak South African government response.[112] And in the case of Brazil, scholars have highlighted the role of "solidarity" and unity in the mobilization around and eventual delivery of an aggressive policy.[113] These findings are consistent with a theory of boundary politics, but the latter goes deeper in its identification of the roots of potential conflict. Sharp institutional boundaries create an "us-them" dynamic that prompts competition and conflict over group esteem, whereas weak internal boundaries facilitate the framing of risk as a shared concern. If we can be convinced of this account as a richer explanation of the paired comparison, we will have a theoretical model that might "travel" to other places.

THE EFFECT OF STRONG BOUNDARIES IN SOUTH AFRICA

The most striking finding of the South African case is the degree to which HIV and AIDS have been racialized. For all the international rhetoric to the effect that AIDS knows no boundaries, in South Africa, ideas and discourses about risk of infection, who is to blame for this epidemic, and ideas about how to respond have been categorized in terms of race, rather than as issues surrounding a truly national problem. It is certainly true that since the early 1990s, a much greater proportion of South Afri-

---

[112] For example, Crewe 1992; Van der Vliet 2001; Grundligh 2001; Petros et al. 2006.
[113] For example, Berkman et al. 2005; Galvão 2000; Parker 1994b.

cans identifying as black have been HIV-positive than persons in other race categories, but this social "fact" is important and observable only because race boundaries were already so well institutionalized in the country at the start of the epidemic. Moreover, like in Brazil, the epidemic was initially concentrated among people with white skin.

Nonetheless, the South African AIDS epidemic has been consistently understood as being at least two epidemics—a "white" and a "black" one. In 1993, at an AIDS center located in Guguletu, a squatter camp just outside the center of cosmopolitan Cape Town, a cartoon summed up the conventional wisdom: A white figure saying, "It's the blacks," and a black one saying, "It's the white man's disease."[114]

Although over two hundred South Africans died of AIDS by 1990, the first diagnosed case of a black heterosexual was not until 1987, and this helped to fuel what would become one "sticky" idea about the disease as a white/gay one.[115] For example, a prominent Soweto-based physician, Nthato Motlana, recalled that when he told a patient that he ought to get tested for HIV, he responded, "That's white man's propaganda. . . . I'm not homosexual."[116] And indeed, through the early 1990s, AIDS was often reported in South Africa as a white, gay, and First World disease.[117] And even as epidemiological patterns have evolved, these early ideas continued to resonate. In one qualitative study of how groups in South Africa perceive the disease, the authors concluded, "Whites accuse Blacks, and Blacks accuse Whites, of having brought AIDS into South Africa." The study reported on the comments of one black man from the Eastern Cape who in 2002 said, "Europeans are infecting Black people, they are the ones that caused this epidemic. These women with whom we live [are infected], because many of them sleep with these Europeans."[118]

Given a history of conflict between these groups, blame has been framed in terms of conspiracies to harm the other. Even though the virus had been reported by the mid-1980s to be brought into the country in a

[114]Kitty Pilgrim, CNN Transcript 917–5, "AIDS Threatens to Decimate South Africa's Workforce," June 7, 1993.

[115]Fourie 2006, 59.

[116]Christopher Wren, "AIDS Rising Fast among Black South Africans," *New York Times*, September 27, 1990.

[117]Hila Bouzaglou, "Aids and the Media: A Love-Hate Relationship," *Mail and Guardian*, December 1, 2006.

[118]Petros et al. 2006, 71. NB: In the South African context, the term *European* is used here to reflect the white, European-descended groups in South Africa, not visitors from Europe.

variety of ways, including through flight attendants who had traveled overseas and through blood transfusions, the conflict over the apartheid system of government and race-based citizenship began to frame the discussion of the disease. In a 1987 interview, foreign minister R. F. Botha explained to a public audience that the "real" threat was from black challengers to the apartheid government: "AIDS gets into this country in ways you wouldn't even think of. . . . Terrorists cross our borders carrying a more dangerous bomb in their bodies than in their hands. They come from camps where AIDS is rife."[119]

As was true in the United States,[120] conspiracy theories have impeded many black leaders and organizations from taking the threat seriously or acting on it in the manner prescribed by the Geneva Consensus. Phillips points out that an important black magazine, *Drum*, reprinted in 1991 (without comment) an article from an African American journal entitled, "Is AIDS a Conspiracy against Blacks?" In the black community, the disease was nicknamed "Afrikaner Invention to Deprive us of Sex."[121] In 1994, the *Sowetan*, a newspaper read almost entirely by black South Africans, reported that apartheid-era police deliberately spread AIDS in the black community.[122] After 1994, newspapers carried additional reports of former government plots to infect the black population with AIDS. Such rumors reinforced racial myths as directly relevant for HIV/AIDS.

There is also substantial evidence of racially distinctive interpretations of the risk associated with HIV among the country's white population even before a substantial epidemic developed among the country's black population. For example, in 1988, inhabitants of a small white resort town argued against the desegregation of South African beaches, citing the risk of AIDS as a reason for barring a visiting black Canadian professor. A town spokesman told a South African newspaper reporter that while the beach was officially open to all races, blacks would need to use nearby bathroom facilities. "We are not prepared to share our toilets with blacks. . . . What if they have AIDS?"[123] Members of the Conservative

[119] Associated Press, "Botha: Terrorists Bring AIDS to South Africa," March 20, 1987.

[120] Cohen 1999.

[121] Phillips 2001, 15.

[122] Associated Press, "Newspaper Alleges Police Killed, Spread AIDS," December 2, 1994.

[123] Brendon Boyle, "AIDS Cited as Reason to Bar Blacks from South African Resort," UPI, January 10, 1988.

Party were warning against the integration of hospitals, arguing that this would increase the spread of HIV.

Science and politics are rarely far apart when it comes to a problem like AIDS. In 2002, researchers from the Medical Research Council—the South African government's official research organization, akin to the National Institutes of Health in the United States—presented a study at the International AIDS Conference entitled "Challenging Racial Stereotyping of AIDS in South Africa with Prevalence and Incidence of HIV in Pregnant Women."[124] According to the abstract, the study was motivated by the observation that "there is a perception in other race groups that HIV is a 'black' problem. It is thus important to determine the prevalence and incidence in all the various race groups so as to factually challenge racial stereotyping." The study reported on blood samples from Indian and Coloured women, and found HIV prevalence of 0.8 percent for Indian and 4.6 percent for Coloureds, and concluded, "HIV infection is not limited to any one race group. The HIV prevalence provides evidence to challenge the misconception that AIDS is a 'black' disease in South Africa." Even the most casual observer of AIDS in South Africa knew that estimated HIV prevalence for blacks was much higher, but researchers at an official government organization believed it was critical to provide concrete evidence of infections in other groups, suggesting that some may have thought they were largely immune.

Indeed, there has been quite a bit of controversy over the epidemiology of HIV and AIDS in South Africa. For example, estimates of white prevalence have varied widely. One study in 2000 estimated prevalence among South African whites at 2 percent.[125] Only two years later, a high-profile 2002 Nelson Mandela/Human Science Research Council survey—the first national household survey, which included an HIV test—reported that HIV prevalence among black adult South Africans was 18.4 percent and 6.2 percent among whites.[126] Many public health experts doubted the accuracy of the findings, particularly the high prevalence among whites, but were reluctant to speak out for fear of inflaming racial tensions. A subsequent 2005 survey presented significantly lower HIV prevalence es-

---

[124] A. Dilraj, S. S. Karim, and S. Pillay (Medical Research Council, Durban, South Africa), "Challenging Racial Stereotyping of AIDS in South Africa with Prevalence and Incidence of HIV in Pregnant Women," International AIDS Conference, 2002 July 7–12; 14 (abstract no. WePeC6104).

[125] Laurice Taitz, "SA Whites Have Record HIV Rates," *Sunday Times*, July 30, 2000.

[126] Shisana, Simbayi, and Human Sciences Research Council 2002, 8.

timates for whites (0.6 percent), and according to the study's authors, a relatively high refusal rate among whites might explain the large discrepancy between this number and the estimate from 2002.[127] Given the challenges of obtaining reliable data, it is not possible to state conclusively which figures are the most accurate, but several facts are striking: First, although reported estimates indicated that white South Africans have had higher prevalence than in most developed countries, and higher than in Brazil, in the context of social identity conflict with a proximate black group, there has been little evidence of panic among whites over AIDS. Moreover, it is clearly evident that for a wide variety of South African actors, there has been an enormous thirst for race-based information about the epidemic, and a preference to report on those findings that cast one's group as being less severely affected than other groups.

Reflecting the essentialization of race in the country, even the blood supply, separated from human bodies, was racialized owing to the HIV/AIDS epidemic. In fact, starting in 1993, the head of the South African national blood services (SANBS) proposed banning black donors because of the high rates of infection in that community. In response, the director of the South African Health and Social Services Organisation attacked the plan, relying on boundary-less logic: "AIDS has no barriers, racial or otherwise."[128] But soon thereafter, the SANBS would use race as a key factor in calculating the risk profile of donors; in 2004 this policy was finally eliminated after challenges from an employee brought to light that blood from black and Coloured donors was being disposed of.[129] The very idea of racialized blood and risk was created in the context of a high boundary environment, a process quite distinct from what would happen in Brazil.

CONFLICT OVER AIDS POLICY

Strong boundaries in South Africa laid the foundation for understanding the AIDS epidemic in terms of distinct racial groups, but when they combined with the stigma of the virus, blaming, shame avoidance, and political conflict ensued. South African governments, both before and

---

[127] Shisana et al. 2005.

[128] Agence France-Presse, "Black Blood Donors Should Be Banned: Transfusion Chief," November 14, 1993.

[129] Melanie Peters, "Blood of Black Donors Is Too Risky—SANBS," *Independent Online* (www.iol.co.za), December 4, 2004.

after the fall of apartheid, have contributed to these dynamics by reinforcing the idea of the epidemic as racially differentiated. Because the leaders of these governments have been associated with particular race groups, they have acted in ways that would be predictable from social identity theory, emphasizing messages and strategies that help to improve their own group's esteem or status relative to the other.

Just as apartheid was ending, it became clear that any government policy trying to control the epidemic would face racially based political sensitivities. Even if a white government were to have fully adopted the Geneva Consensus, its implementation would have been rejected by the black population as a mark of blaming and social stigmatization. Writing in 1990, just seven months after the historic unbanning of the ANC, a prominent white South African political commentator, R. W. Johnson, wrote,

> The indications are, however, that there is no time to waste and that all black organizations will have to lend their moral authority to the health and education campaigns which are urgently necessary to head off the epidemic. . . . It will be a thankless task—the black population will not take kindly to attempts to get it to change its sexual mores—and it is not quite what the ANC dreamt power would mean during its long years in exile. But, as in so much else, the movement has only to look at the situation elsewhere in Africa to see all too clearly what has to be avoided here at almost any cost.[130]

When over one hundred political and health groups met with the government and the ANC in 1992 to discuss a comprehensive plan, Mandela himself explained in an opening meeting, "The government does not have the credibility to convince the majority of black South Africans to change their sexual behavior."[131] Unlike other public health problems, for which even a politically challenged government might have been able to implement a purely technical response, the obvious threats to social status implied by a white government making explicit reference to the social behavior of blacks would be rejected in this strong boundary environment.

---

[130] Sapa-AP, "ANC 'Should Aid Anti-AIDS Drive,'" *Cape Times*, September 10, 1990.
[131] Tina Susman, "AIDS Sufferers Lost in the South African Politics," Associated Press, November 16, 2002.

All of this begged the question of whether, as the epidemic was increasingly being understood as predominantly "black" or "African," a government run and supported largely by blacks would do any better. That would make sense if the political mechanism driving the response to AIDS were merely one of resource allocation—that is, a game of ethnic groups competing for resources. But boundary institutions remained strong and could be expected to shape politics and policy given the theorized incentives to avoid shame of association with the stigmatized virus.

Indeed, Nelson Mandela, who in his capacity as former president has become a leading international advocate of the Geneva Consensus, was, in office from 1994 to 1999, rather passive in his approach to the growing epidemic. He has conceded that he said little about the epidemic during the election campaign, and has acknowledged that he did too little as president. His first major public speech on AIDS did not occur until 1997, and that speech took place in Switzerland at a meeting of the World Health Organization.[132] In fact, Mandela's government inherited what was generally thought to be an excellent blueprint for managing the AIDS epidemic in the NACOSA National AIDS Plan that had been drafted during the transition, but it was not implemented effectively.

More than any other major South African figure, Mandela himself espoused boundary-blurring ideals, promoting reconciliation and the idea of a "rainbow nation" during the transition and his presidency, and it would be surprising if he had engaged in much explicit race-based blaming. And indeed, I have found no evidence that he did. But Mandela's quiet on AIDS must be attributed at least in part to his perception that this was a politically losing proposition. He had been well briefed on the many dangers of the epidemic, particularly as African countries north of the Limpopo were already being ravaged. Insiders such as Chris Hani were writing and speaking about the dangers in the early 1990s.[133] But as the disease had already been highly politicized in racial terms, attention to it had the potential to inflame the very conflicts over race-based morality and culture that Mandela sought to avoid. Reflecting back on the time, a key antiapartheid figure and former vice chancellor of the University of Cape Town, Mamphela Ramphele, explained,

---

[132] Jon Jeter, "Free of Apartheid, Divided by Disease," *Washington Post*, July 6, 2000: 1.

[133] Van der Vliet 2001, 151.

Why did it take so long to have clarity infusing our policy responses? We have the depth of scientific know how and economic resources to have been a front-runner in comprehensive care and treatment to deal a mortal blow to the disease as Brazil did. But the scientists were largely white, male, urban based, and outside the policy making domain of government. Mistrust of the racist system that denied the majority of South Africans scientific literacy and proficiency, constrained evidence based policy-making.[134]

Even amid the political "honeymoon" period he inspired, members of Mandela's cabinet got caught up in identity-based competition and acted in contradiction to the Geneva Consensus, setting the stage for the AIDS policies of the Mbeki presidencies. As mentioned earlier, HIV/AIDS did not figure as prominently in legislative debates in the 1990s as one might have expected given the growing pace of the epidemic, but when it did, blame and shame-avoidance were evident. Take, for example, the following debate in the National Assembly on March 10, 1998.[135] The minister of health, Nkosazana Dlamini-Zuma, began by making quite universal appeals:

> Madame-Speaker, HIV/AIDS continues to be the most important public health concern in the country. No country in the world can claim to be totally free of the HIV infection. The Joint UN Programme on HIV/AIDS reported that by December 1997 30.6 million people worldwide were living with HIV/AIDS . . . South Africa is considered to have the fastest growing HIV epidemic in the world, with close to 50,000 people infected every month.

But then she went on to highlight the racial distinctiveness of the epidemic.

> Though HIV/AIDS knows no colour, race, or gender, it is, however, more common amongst the blacks, the poor and the poorer parts of our communities.

In response to the minister's speech, a representative from the Democratic Party, an almost entirely white opposition party, challenged past state-

---

[134] Mamphela Ramphele, HIV/AIDS: The Mirror in South Africa's Face," speech delivered at the 2005 South African AIDS Conference, June 7–10, 2005, Durban.
[135] Text from Hansard, *Debates of the National Assembly*, March 10, 1998.

ments and actions of the minister, revealing how difficult it was to build consensus around the epidemic:

> What the DP finds totally unacceptable is the malicious and false statement made by the hon the Minister in which she stated, and I quote: The DP hates ANC supporters. If they had it their way we would all die of AIDS. [Interjections.] She is a disgrace to the office she holds, and she deserves to be fired, unless she withdraws that remark. It is impossible for her to ask parties to participate in her programmes when she makes statements of that nature. While she is apologizing she should make it clear why she has not followed through with investigation into other AIDS research. . . . She should also make it clear why she stopped funding to various AIDS NGO's such as Nacosa and the AIDS Law Project.

In continuation of this debate, Dr. J. S. Gous of the National Party argued:

> The hon the Minister of Health has repeatedly accused the NP of knowingly spreading AIDS. She must clarify that statement, and I would like her to clarify it scientifically and not in loose political terms. Until she does that, how can I help her in her AIDS Campaign? I must have my own AIDS campaign. In fact, I am prepared to say that scientifically that is utter nonsense, because she herself said that AIDS was colour-blind. How the devil did the NP train the AIDS virus?

In a parliamentary system with an overwhelming ANC majority and tight party discipline, such debates have little direct implication for policies and practices, which are formulated at the national level by the minister of health, the president, and other cabinet and department heads. However, they reveal the politicizing and racializing of a viral epidemic, which weakened resolve to address the problem. While the health minister was making broad proclamations about the importance of the problem, she was also engaged in long-standing political conflicts over the virus that would reinforce its links to group-based conspiracies and myths, which in turn would set the stage for policies that were divorced from scientific best practice.

By the end of Mandela's presidency, Mbeki, health minister Zuma, and other government leaders would begin to rebuff civil society and international pressures to provide ARVs. One argument concerned toxicity and drug safety,[136] and another concerned affordability.[137] By the end of Mbeki's first year as president, his administration showed stark contempt for the Geneva Consensus and its architects.

Such challenges can be understood, at least in part, by recognizing Mbeki's desire to lift the standing of black Africans as autonomous and critical thinkers, and to address the racial stereotyping and myths he believed were being fueled by discourses on AIDS at home and abroad. These were noble goals, and consistent with his broader strategies of promoting an "African Renaissance." Nonetheless, the starkly oppositional quality of the rhetoric led Mbeki to accept untruths along with valid insights. For example, he was right to highlight the vulnerabilities associated with poverty, but he did not need to go so far as to question the link between HIV and AIDS. In challenging his critics, he wound up alienating those who sought to address the growing AIDS tragedy. In a now infamous speech at Fort Hare University in 2001 he ranted,

> Others who consider themselves to be our leaders take to the streets carrying their placards . . . convinced that we are but natural born, promiscuous carriers of germs, unique in the world, they proclaim that our continent is doomed to an inevitable mortal end because of our unconquerable devotion to the sin of lust.[138]

Echoing such sentiments, at an ANC meeting in 2002, a document justifying the heterodox stance toward AIDS was circulated by the leadership in the wake of the AIDS-related death of an ANC member, which some in Mbeki's circle claimed was due to the toxicity of ARVs. Parts of the document employed a sarcastic tone, which revealed clearly that race politics was central to the conflict over AIDS.

> Yes, we are sex-crazy! Yes, we are diseased! Yes, we spread the deadly HI virus through our uncontrolled heterosexual sex! In this regard, yes, we are different from the [United States] and Western Europe! Yes, we, the men, abuse women and the girl-child with gay abandon! Yes, among

---

[136] See Agence France-Press, "SAfrica-AIDS: Mbeki Stokes Row over Anti-AIDS Drug," October 29, 1999.

[137] Agence France-Presse, "SAfrica-AIDS-drug: South Africa Cannot Afford Anti-AIDS Drug AZT: Minister," November 16, 1999.

[138] Gumede 2005, 163.

us rape is endemic because of our culture! Yes, we do believe that sleeping with young virgins will cure us of Aids! Yes, as a result of all this, we are threatened with destruction by the HIV/Aids pandemic! Yes, what we need, and cannot afford because we are poor, are condoms and antiretroviral drugs! Help![139]

Such rhetoric extended beyond Mbeki. Other cabinet-level leaders have tried to convey a sense of having the problem "under control" and have challenged calls to action as a "white" hysteria, disconnected from reality. Health minister Tshabalala-Msimang referred to TAC leader Mark Heywood—also a progressive ANC loyalist—as a "white man" manipulating black people to pressure the government on AIDS.[140] Foreign defense minister Trevor Lekota responded to concerns about AIDS by saying, "All of this noise every day about HIV/Aids and so on, that suggest that this country is about to collapse as a result of HIV/Aids, is really unfounded. There is no alarm in this country."[141]

It is difficult to know to what extent fellow ANC members supported Mbeki's position because they fundamentally agreed with it, or because of a party structure that would discipline members for dissent.[142] For example, in 2001, despite recommendations by the KwaZulu-Natal provincial health department that nevirapine be supplied for PMTCT in all 112 municipal clinics, senior ANC members in the Durban Metropolitan Council voted against the measure. At the time, the Inkatha Freedom Party was the ruling party for that province, and according to one ANC member, "We can never embarrass the national government, which has adopted a wait and see approach."[143] Even Nelson Mandela was "rapped on the knuckles for speaking out of turn on HIV/AIDS" during the ANC's National Executive Committee meetings in March 2002.[144] Even if the tacit acceptance of the government's weak AIDS policy was rooted in loyalty, the motivations behind the policy require further explanation.

---

[139]Jaspreet Kindra, "Aids Drugs Killed Parks, Says ANC," *Mail and Guardian*, March 22, 2002.

[140]Friedman and Mottiar 2005, 525.

[141]"Lekota: No AIDS Alarm in SA," *Mail and Guardian*, October 8, 2003.

[142]Thanks to Patrick Heller for pushing me to consider the possibility that a "Leninist" party dynamic may have been at work here.

[143]"ANC in New HIV/Aids Denial," *Mail and Guardian*, December 7, 2001.

[144]Mangcu 2008, 55 and n. 11.

By identifying the prevalent denialism in the South African administration as the product of group conflict and the desire to elevate the esteem or social standing of one's group, we can begin to explain the nature of the actions that the government *did* take to address the mounting deaths and disease. The explanation makes sense of the government's eagerness to pursue "traditional" medical approaches to the epidemic, rooted in African culture, though such solutions were untested. Eventually, the health minister would become infamous for her emphasis on foods such as the "African potato," but initially a more pharmacological approach was taken. The government in 1997 (under the Mandela presidency) aggressively pursued a treatment developed by South Africans—Virodene—on the basis of little scientific evidence of its efficacy. Later, the biomedical community would routinely refer to this supposed invention as "snake oil." Virodene contained toxic industrial solvents, and the research to develop it circumvented established scientific norms. Although the scientists associated with Virodene were white, the strategic investment in the proposed solution and its discovery under the ANC leadership were expected to reflect well on the ANC and the prospects for advancement under black government.

Although Nattrass is reluctant to use race boundaries to explain Mbeki's denialism, her history of AIDS politics provides substantial evidence of blaming and shame-avoidance, and she concludes that "Mbeki was concerned about negative normative judgments embedded in the mainstream understanding of AIDS."[145] In a letter to Tony Leon, Mbeki highlighted his concern with the perception that "most black [African] men carry the HI virus [and that] rape is an endemic feature of African society," and argued that "hysterical estimates of the incidence of HIV in our country . . . coupled with the earlier wild and insulting claims about the African and Haitian origin of HIV powerfully reinforce those dangerous and firmly entrenched prejudices."[146]

Moreover, some of the evidence Nattrass presents demonstrates that racialized politics have framed resistance to the challenges posed by the TAC in its campaigns of civil disobedience. Nattrass also relates that Christine Qunta, a close associate of Mbeki, made a racialized attack on the TAC leadership in 2003:

It seems as if white male rage is the black man's (and woman's) burden . . . the poor people of this country are in the paradoxical situation of

---

[145] Nattrass 2007, 88.
[146] As quoted in Nattrass 2007, 116.

suddenly having acquired white male champions in parliament, at Afrikaans universities and on the streets. As to the cause of the poverty and their role in creating it, they assume black people's memories are short and their hearts big.[147]

BOUNDARY POLITICS IN SOCIETY

Beyond elites, boundary politics have played a critical role in South Africa. As highlighted earlier, prevailing ideas about the epidemic have included framings of racial blaming—that it is the "other" group's problem. But beyond that, there is evidence of denial of the existence of the problem, as well as conflict over how to address it, both of which can be linked to racial boundaries.

The inclination to deny the problem of AIDS among ordinary South Africans has been staggering. This phenomenon has both reinforced and has been reinforced by elite rhetoric and policy. In a 2006 article for the *New York Times Magazine*—where she had chronicled Brazil's model successes on AIDS five years earlier—Tina Rosenberg portrayed the startling extent to which ordinary and elite South Africans have denied the risks of infection, the reality of their own infections, and the extent of the problem in their country. Asked about the dozens of funerals every Saturday in the townships, family members avoided mentioning AIDS and responded, "It was asthma, or tuberculosis, or 'a long illness.'" A health care worker described a woman who tested HIV-positive but refused to take the nevirapine that might prevent HIV transmission, saying, "Oh, no, I'm not positive."[148]

In my visits to South Africa and in reading of texts, studies, and documents, I have found the same pervasive denialism. During the summer of 2003, I visited Mtubatuba—a rural community of about 100,000 in northern KwaZulu-Natal, which at the time was estimated to have an adult HIV prevalence of 40 percent. According to the researchers and health workers, no one talked about HIV or AIDS. We visited a woman who was clearly suffering greatly from AIDS-related illness, but she explained her discomfort in terms of a minor cold.

Such responses are not due to a lack of basic information. As early as 1998, there was near-universal awareness of the disease (96.7 percent of

[147] As quoted in Nattrass 2007, 116.
[148] Tina Rosenberg, "When a Pill Is Not Enough," *New York Times Magazine*, August 6, 2006.

those surveyed in the Demographic Health Survey said they had heard of AIDS), and in this case, the individual had been told of her status. Rather, South Africans have been living in an environment in which AIDS is highly stigmatized, and for a great many individuals, incentives to deny being afflicted or at risk are stronger than incentives to accept risks and take action.

My point is *not* that these are irrational responses. People have been harassed, discriminated against, beaten, and even killed for being HIV-positive. In 1998, a year prior to Mbeki's engagement with the AIDS dissidents, a thirty-six-year-old activist, Gugu Dlamini, publicly revealed that she was HIV-positive, and was subsequently beaten to death in Kwa-Mancinza, a town in eastern KwaZulu-Natal province. At the time, an estimated 20–30 percent of adults in the area were HIV-positive. Reports of HIV-positive women being beaten have persisted. In many other countries around the world, there is evidence of similar responses, which in turn have stymied potential HIV-positive activists from pursuing an aggressive AIDS policy. But particularly when compared with Brazil, the stigma and denial in South Africa have been extreme. At the very least, the racialized discourse on AIDS that I have described has reinforced the tendency to avoid a problem that might reflect badly on one's identity group.

Although infection levels among other racial groups in South Africa are indeed lower than among black Africans, according to most estimates, even these rates have been higher than the national average in Brazil for most of the history of the epidemic. Nonetheless, the downplaying of risk is evident across all groups in South Africa. White South Africans seem to feel insulated from the risk of infection to a much greater degree than their middle-class (and generally light-skinned) counterparts in Brazil, because they see AIDS as a strictly black problem. According to AIDS Law Project leaders, "There's a mistaken belief among many middle- to upper-income professionals, particularly whites, that they are not at risk," and "The fact that HIV has disproportionately affected poor, black, young women is an indication that many of them think it cannot affect them."[149] In my own informal conversations with dozens of white South Africans, most have described themselves as being insulated from an epidemic that affects at least one in five adults in their own country. In general, whites

---

[149]Tamar Kahn, "Denial, Ignorance Continue to Define SA's Response to HIV/Aids," *Business Day*, December 1, 2004.

have criticized the government's AIDS policies as part of a broader problem of bad policy, not because they perceive themselves to be at risk or in need of AIDS-related services.

When I toured a largely Coloured community in Cape Town in June 2003 and asked people if they were concerned about AIDS, a similar message was repeated. One woman in her thirties said, "Our religious leaders say we ought to have compassion with those afflicted by AIDS." When asked if prevention messages were being spread by community leaders, she said, "They say if we follow God, AIDS will not be a problem for our community."

With such prevalent denial across groups, it becomes less surprising that demand for government action has been relatively low. More than a decade after blacks took power in South Africa, suspicion about the nature of the disease (real or imagined; viral or social; indigenous or created in the West) and about who is most vulnerable has suppressed public support for aggressive policies. According to the Afrobarometer survey of a nationally representative sample in 1999, only 0.5 percent of South Africans believed that AIDS was one of the three "most important problems facing the country that government ought to address," suggesting that the vast majority did not feel threatened. In later surveys, that percentage has grown steadily, to 30 percent in 2004, but compare those concerned about job creation, which was mentioned by 77 percent of those interviewed.[150] In line with public sentiment, the finance minister mentioned HIV or AIDS twice in his 2004 speech, but mentioned employment six times, poverty six times, and growth twenty-two times.[151] While Mbeki and his health ministers may have been extreme in their denialism, it resonated with public attitudes in other parts of the state and in society. To be certain, there have been vocal critics of Mbeki's policies both inside and outside of government, but Mbeki's thinking on AIDS reflects the reality of politics in his country.

Even among those who have acknowledged the problem of AIDS—leaders and members of organizations defined in terms of their commitment to AIDS, boundary politics has impeded solidarity. This has occurred between two civil society organizations, the TAC and the National Association of People Living With AIDS (NAPWA). At its first congress

---

[150] Afrobarometer 2005.

[151] Trevor Manuel, Minister of Finance, Budget Speech, Pretoria, South Africa, February 18, 2004.

in 2001 (the organization was formed in 1994), the NAPWA resolved "to distance itself from the Treatment Action Campaign and all its activities."[152] Although TAC membership is largely black, many of its leaders and supporters are white, and this has driven racial conflict. One such conflict flared up at a meeting of the AIDS consortium—an organization that had been established to unite AIDS-related organizations to "address the needs of people infected affected by AIDS." In a March 30, 2004, letter, TAC leader Mark Heywood recounted the confrontation:

> Today I attended the AIDS Consortium General meeting that was the subject of attack by NAPWA leaders and members. Apart from their general unruly and threatening conduct it is necessary to report and condemn the racism that is being formented and encouraged by NAPWA's leadership. The very first comment by a NAPWA member during the meeting included a racist attack on a white member of the AIDS Consortium Executive, Chloe Hardy, who was told that "we are sick of white people sitting at the front of the meeting; it causes us pain," to applause from the NAPWA leaders.
>
> At the end of the meeting Thandoxolo Doro, the national organiser of NAPWA, confronted me aggressively and shouted in front of other people "we are sick of you fucking white racists taking advantage of black people and people with HIV/AIDS."[153]

It is notable that NAPWA has been much more sympathetic to the "dissident" or "denialist" approach, has had a much closer relationship with government, and has critiqued the TAC's promotion of the Geneva Consensus in a manner quite similar to Tshabalala-Msimang. Indeed, NAPWA has received substantial funding from the South African government, arguably to support a civil society organization that would counter the challenge posed by the TAC. (While the organization has served this role, it has also challenged the government on how it allocated social grants to people living with AIDS.) NAPWA's Doro in 2003 challenged TAC's focus on ARVs, arguing, "The TAC in so doing is disregarding the real issues of people living with HIV/Aids as experienced by Africans in rural villages, informal settlements and townships of South Africa," and offered

---

[152] Proceedings of the 1st NAPWA Congress, May 25–27, 2001, Crown Mines.
[153] Mark Heywood, "Condemn the Threats by NAPWA against AIDS Activists," Treatment Action Campaign newsletter, March 30, 2004.

a contrasting perspective, emphasizing nutrition and access to other treatment above antiretroviral drugs.[154]

WEAK BOUNDARIES AS THE BASIS FOR SOLIDARITY AROUND AIDS IN BRAZIL

With the racialization of the epidemic, patterns of blaming, shame avoidance, denial, and deep conflicts in South Africa having been highlighted, the Brazilian case emerges as remarkably distinctive. Even with much lower levels of HIV prevalence, AIDS came to be seen as a national emergency, and unified a wide range of actors to act aggressively. There is no evidence of the conflicts found in South Africa, and as I mentioned earlier, many observers have pointed to the remarkable Brazilian solidarity, driven by a combination of creative and well-networked civil society actors, the real fear of disease and dying, and the momentum of the broader democratization and sanitary movements.

But what is remarkable from the perspective of a comparison with South Africa is the absence of conflict, particularly in a country with enormous racial diversity, and where one might assume similar dynamics. Yet, given the preexisting Brazilian institutions, it was virtually impossible to think of the epidemic in terms of race. In fact, it is extremely rare to find epidemiological data with racial breakdowns in any government report, a practice that has been consistent with the country's more general approach to race. Until approximately 2003, the Brazilian Ministry of Health did not collect any statistics on HIV or AIDS cases by race.[155]

Even researchers looking for racial patterns in behavioral and political responses have come up against the legacy of mixing and weakly formed racial identification. For example, as part of a 1993 clinical study of AIDS-related behavior in Brazil conducted by the U.S.-based National Institute on Drug Abuse, researchers tried to capture the racial background of individuals. Follow-up interviews revealed that a full 12.5 percent of respondents had actually changed their racial self-identification within just a few months. The authors of a study on the project, recognizing some of the complexities of race relations in Brazil, ultimately concluded, "Race is of little use in Brazil as a construct for analysis."[156] A dif-

---

[154] "Aids Activists Take On One of Their Own," *Mail and Guardian*, March 11, 2003.

[155] Interviews with Ministry of Health officials at the Fifteenth International AIDS Conference, Bangkok, July 15, 2004.

[156] Surratt and Inciardi 1998.

ferent study investigating the role of ethnicity among registered AIDS patients in São Paulo found that data on ethnicity are "registered in a subjective and non-standardized manner," and not widely implemented in the disease surveillance system.[157] Even when outsiders have tried to isolate racial patterns in the Brazilian epidemic, existing institutions have constrained such interpretation. Formally and informally, Brazilians simply did not discuss AIDS for the first two decades of the epidemic as being white or black or any of the multiple categories used to describe skin color.

As contrasted with South Africans, Brazilians are more able to draw on shared symbols and events that cut across skin color, such as annual Carnival celebrations—a time when the government has undertaken massive annual condom distribution programs. I do not want to overstate the resonance of a strong sense of national identity in Brazil, but the government AIDS program has had no reason to fear that ethnic political leaders would engage in blaming or shame-avoidance because the program implied the "targeting" of one race group.

In virtually all societies, the deadly HIV epidemic initially elicited fear, and in this respect, Brazil was no different. But deeper battles about the ethnic or racial quality of the epidemic were absent, even though the epidemic has at times been concentrated more or less among groups with differentiable skin color and regional or cultural characteristics. As a result, long-standing myths of social mobility across racial lines, as well as high levels of social interaction, particularly in public spaces, meant that a lethal, sexually transmitted virus could easily be interpreted as affecting all of "us"—even when actual rates of infection were fairly low and geographically concentrated within a continental landmass.

When Brazilian AIDS NGOs in the late 1980s emphasized "solidarity" with those infected, and the ministry's media campaigns attempted to avoid stigmatizing portrayals of AIDS victims in favor of an approach based on solidarity,[158] there were no obvious political contradictions. Such an approach has a long history in Brazil, where state-sponsored public health policies have been closely linked to broader "whitening" strategies.[159] Brazilians with darker skin often tend to self-identify "whiter," and

[157] Jamal et al. 2002.

[158] Galvão 2000, 85; Teixeira 1997, 61.

[159] Stepan 1991. If indeed, a "weak boundary" environment is good for the provision of certain public goods, it is again worth asking to what extent the development of public health institutions created at earlier periods of the epidemic might be responsible for these contrasting approaches to AIDS (i.e., a path-dependent effect), as compared with a more direct effect between boundary institutions and AIDS policies. In any case, as discussed

to seek lighter-skinned mates. Thus, it is perfectly understandable that there would be no outcry or rejection on the part of a darker-skinned majority that the state was "wasting" resources on a disease that initially affected people with lighter skin. Instead, it was easy to promote a politics of empathy and shared risk. Apart from the near-universal apprehensions about foreigners in the early stages of the epidemic—and especially gay foreigners—there has not been significant evidence in Brazil of the "blame" politics that characterized AIDS discourse in South Africa. When comparing the 1995–97 wave of responses to the World Values Survey, one finds that while 44 percent of South Africans believed "someone with AIDS" was an undesirable neighbor, only 14 percent of Brazilians were so concerned. "Western" medicine and germ theories of disease have generally not been politicized along race lines.

Because the Brazilian epidemic was initially concentrated in the southeast Brazilian states of Rio de Janeiro and São Paulo, where state-level resources are significant, fears and action might have remained localized. However, local leaders pushed hard for a national response. Dr. Alvaro Matida, an epidemiologist running Rio de Janeiro's AIDS program, explained, "At a state level we're still doing far less than we should, but isolated measures are not going to have any impact. This is a national problem that must be faced nationally."[160] From the perspective of technocrats in the national government, the problem remained minor—Parker argues that early in the epidemic, "the level of official denial had become almost absolute"[161]—but the increasing popular and political pressure became too much to bear. In 1985, public health authorities said they were being pressured by a "collective neurosis," and Brazil's health minister Carlos Sant'Anna said that AIDS was not a "priority," particularly when compared with other ailments with much broader impact on Brazilian society. "But in the face of what he called the public's 'massive hypochondria,' the Government is developing a strategy to respond to the problem."[162]

---

earlier, the Brazilian public health system is a product of many factors, and available measures suggest more similarity with South Africa than difference. Thus, boundary institutions seem to have a more proximate, as opposed to path-dependent, effect.

[160] Alan Riding, "Brazil Called Lax in AIDS Treatment," *New York Times*, December 15, 1986, 11.

[161] Parker 1994b, 33.

[162] Alan Riding, "Fright Grips Brazil as AIDS Cases Suddenly Rise," *New York Times*, August 25, 1985, 4.

Such discourse is revealing because it predated the formation of leading activist movements such as the AIDS Prevention and Support Group (1985), the Brazilian Interdisciplinary AIDS Association (1986), and Grupo Pela Vidda (1989), which helped drive the AIDS agenda forward. While these groups did go on to work with subnational governments to pressure the national government to act in a manner "based on solidarity and inclusion rather than discrimination and exclusion,"[163] such strategies were themselves highly structured by the historical legacies of weak boundary institutions.

It is worthwhile to reflect critically on the emergence of "solidarity" around AIDS in Brazil, and to ask why it has not applied for many other social issues, such as the alleviation of poverty. Certainly one critical factor is contagion. That is, weak boundaries are important for perceptions of risk of infection, but have far fewer implications for conditions not transmitted through social contact. In this sense, solidarity may be only partially the product of positive collective action, as it was the result of the "collective neurosis" identified at the outset of the epidemic. From a cynical perspective, Brazilians may not have feared the "contagion" of poverty, unemployment, or poor education, but in a society where sexual and intimate contacts are much less sharply mediated by stable social boundaries, it was possible to imagine that AIDS could affect "all of us."

Evidence of solidarity in Brazil is notable because the country is not homogeneous, and the epidemic has not been confined to the wealthiest or whitest members of society. AIDS has affected a wide diversity of Brazilians, and in fact, there are important behaviors associated with Afro-Brazilian religious groups, specifically rituals of scarification, that have placed people at extremely high risk for infection. However, government (and NGO) efforts to address such behaviors have generally not been challenged on political lines. If boundary institutions had been stronger and race had been more politically important, the interaction of race, culture, and demands for sacrifice in the form of sexual and cultural restraint could easily have provoked conflict, as in South Africa. But in general, Brazil's government has not been understood as "white," and researchers have found little resistance to efforts to influence scarification, for example, by encouraging the use of disposable blades rather than a single knife.[164] As in much of Africa and

[163] Berkman et al. 2005, 1166.

[164] J. Galvao, M. Soares, and C. Leal, "AIDS and Afro-Brazilian Religions," International AIDS Conference, 1992 July 19–24, 8:D436, abstract no. PoD 5294, via www.aegis.com;

elsewhere in the developing world, many followers of Afro-Brazilian cults practice traditional medicine, and witchcraft is culturally central. While active partnerships between public authorities and Afro-Brazilian religious leaders have been rare,[165] the relationship has also not been conflictual.

EVIDENCE OF CHANGE IN BRAZIL?

Racial boundaries are changing in Brazil. There is evidence that this change is beginning to affect the dissemination of information about the epidemic as well as social and political understandings of risk, blame, and shame, much in the way the theory advanced in this book predicts. In 2005, just as the government was announcing declines in the spread of infection, it also highlighted racially differentiated trends in new infections. A government spokesperson pointed out that among new AIDS cases, the number of people declaring themselves to be black or brown rose among women from 35.6 percent in 2000 to 42.4 percent in 2004. Whereas the government AIDS program had historically said little on the subject of race, the spokesperson argued, "It's clear racism is an additional factor making people vulnerable. When a poor white and a poor black go into the public health system, the poor white gets treated better."[166] In a stunning turnaround for politics and policymaking, the government declared the theme for World AIDS Day 2005 to be "AIDS is Racism."[167] The government in 2004 launched an "Afroattitude" program in the context of ten public universities to study the links between racism and AIDS, which includes the provision of one-year scholarships to "quota" students, of Afro-Brazilian descent.[168]

It is too early to assess to what extent such patterns will affect support for the Brazilian AIDS program, which is already well institutionalized

---

L. Mott, "The Afro-Brazilian Religions and the Reduction of Risk of HIV-Infection," abstract from the International AIDS Conference 1998, abstract no. 106/14215, via www.aegis.com.

[165] Parker 2003.

[166] Andrew Hay, "Brazil Bucks AIDS Trend, but Blacks Are Hard-Hit," Reuters, November 30, 2005.

[167] Thanks also to Peter Fry, an anthropologist from the Federal University of Rio de Janeiro, who communicated to me via email about this development.

[168] "Primeira Mostra Afroatitude é destaque no VI Congresso de Prevenção," Notícias do Programa Nacional DST-AIDS, http://www.aids.gov.br/data/Pages/LUMISE77B47C8ITEMID48DB52145F574D88B55A9095168D0049PTBRIE.htm (consulted December 15, 2006).

and a source of great national pride. Moreover, the persistence of flexible approaches to racial identification have made the implementation of affirmative action policies extremely difficult in Brazil, and race consciousness in politics remains undeveloped in comparison to South Africa. Brazilians continue to debate the appropriateness of affirmative action, even as color-based inequality is apparent. But at the very least, the Brazilian state has moved toward a greater institutionalization of race boundaries, and we are also beginning to observe a higher level of information being disseminated along racial lines. Whether or not this will create conflict and act as a constraint on risk-pooling remains to be seen.

WEAK BOUNDARIES AND OTHER ASPECTS OF BRAZILIAN
"CULTURE": SEX AND SEXUALITY

Comparing Brazil to South Africa lets us generate a distinctive hypothesis about the origins of AIDS policy divergence, namely differences in the nature of the two countries' sexual cultures. One account contends that "sexuality and sexual expression are also an integral part of Brazilian culture and have facilitated the development of an effective response to the epidemic."[169] As the argument goes, "openness" about matters of sexuality has allowed a response to a problem that requires discussion of sexual practice. This is a plausible argument, for which South Africa (and India) provide support, as these countries are less open in public displays and discussions of sex and sexuality.

Nevertheless, these observations do not suggest to me that sexual openness is the basis for a broader understanding of variations in AIDS policies. First, I believe much of the difference in these sexual cultures can itself be explained by differences in race boundaries. In South Africa, separateness meant legislating *against* various sexual activities, especially sexual contact *across* the color bar. The legal treatment of sexual violence—rape—was mediated by the racial identity of perpetrator and victim.[170] By contrast, in Brazil norms and policies of mixing and "whitening" literally *encouraged* sexual activity between groups. Thus, at least to a degree, sexual culture is endogenous to boundary institutions.

[169] Berkman et al. 2005, 1168.
[170] See, for example, Scully 1995, who chronicles the example of a confessed rapist in the Cape Colony having his death sentence commuted when the judge found that the female victim was not white, as initially thought, but was identified as a "bastard coloured person."

Second, one could easily make the argument in the opposite direction. That is, in more sexually "repressive" environments, there might be greater acceptance of political messages advocating restrictions on sexual activities, through abstinence, partner reduction, or the use of condoms. It is not clear why a sexually permissive society would more readily accept such policies. (It does seem likely that the policies might be better implemented in such a society, but this is distinct from the question of policymaking.)

Third, when considering the denialist rhetoric of various actors in South Africa, there has been less vitriolic disagreement about sex per se than about which *groups* were responsible and at risk for sexual transmission of the virus. In attempting to build a model of AIDS policymaking a theory of sexual culture appears both more vague and less promising than one rooted in the dynamics of boundary politics. Nonetheless, in chapter 6, I do explore this theory a bit further, and find that it holds less explanatory power than one rooted in ethnic boundaries.

Conclusion

The comparative analysis of Brazilian and South African responses highlight the role of boundary institutions as a factor explaining cross-country differences in AIDS policies. The degree to which race has mattered in these countries more generally has also been associated with differences in the collection and dissemination of information about the AIDS epidemic, as well as public discourses of risk and blame, with important consequences for policymaking. Although Cohen's insights about the effects of race in the United States provided a starting point for understanding the dynamics of AIDS policymaking in South Africa, the mechanism of marginalization is insufficient to account for the persistence of weak AIDS policy under a black government. To be certain, most black South Africans are extremely poor, but they have always been a numerical majority, and since 1994 they have fully dominated the polity. Amid a shift from white power to black power, persistent conflict over AIDS has resulted in a weak response. Racial boundaries seem to have mattered more than who was in power. While Brazil's response to AIDS has been impressive, no "positive" factor in place appeared extraordinary relative to South Africa, or many other countries for that matter. That Brazil would respond aggressively was not a foregone conclusion. A politics of solidarity was possible in Brazil's multiethnic society because formal and informal institutions for politicizing racial difference were largely unavailable.

Boundary institutions are not likely to account for cross-country differences in AIDS policy into perpetuity. Over the long term, other factors such as international and domestic pressures associated with increased mortality and morbidity are likely to weigh heavily on policymakers, and convergence on the Geneva Consensus will be visible. Facing overwhelming infection and mortality rates, the South African government is finally becoming more aggressive. But the costs of delay are large. Average life expectancy was similar in the two countries in the 1980s, reaching sixty-six in Brazil and sixty-three in South Africa in 1992. Yet largely because of AIDS-related mortalities, that number dropped to forty-six in South Africa by 2003, while in Brazil life expectancy continued to climb, reaching sixty-nine in 2003.[171]

The legacies of South African apartheid and Brazilian "whitening" are still prominent in these societies, but change is afoot. In Brazil, social and political actors have begun to mobilize around race and racial identities. The overt racialization of politics is still in its infancy in Brazil, and the independent institutionalization of the Brazilian AIDS program will be less subject to political influence than was the case at the earlier stages of the epidemic, when the state's course of action was far more uncertain. In the chapters that follow, I consider the extent to which some of the dynamics that relate boundaries to AIDS politics and policy can help to explain patterns of policymaking in other countries around the world.

[171] World Bank 2005.

5 ↺ A Model-Testing Case Study of Strong Ethnic Boundaries and AIDS Policy in India

In this chapter, I explore the link between boundary politics and AIDS policymaking through a case study of India. While the previous chapter was largely a model-building analysis in the sense that much of the general argument was developed through an inductive, theory-driven, comparative analysis of Brazil and South Africa, this chapter presents a model-testing analysis. I selected a case that was broadly comparable with the other two, ethnically divided, and with a reputation for a weak response to AIDS. Beyond confirming these characterizations with in-depth research, the main point of the analysis is to investigate whether a plausible account of the hypothesized effects of ethnic boundaries can be developed using the theory I have presented.[1]

I carried out two types of research: First, I considered a wide range of sources, including government documents, international reports, news articles, secondary accounts, and interviews with government officials, activists, representatives from international organizations, health care workers, and analysts and scholars. With this largely qualitative database, I identified pressures that affected the development of AIDS policies, with a focus on the effects of ethnic boundaries. Second, I gathered state-level

---

[1] For discussion of the distinction between "model-building" and "model-testing" case studies, see Lieberman 2005.

statistics in order to estimate the relationship between the (highly varied) level of ethnic boundaries and AIDS policy at this consequential subnational level. The findings from this research persuaded me that indeed, ethnic boundaries have strongly affected the production of AIDS-related policies in India through the political dynamics described in chapter 2. To be certain, there are other reasons why India's response emerged as it did, but the strength and number of ethnic boundaries had a negative effect that has not been widely recognized—highlighting the value added of a theory-driven case study.

While this chapter focuses on India, the Brazil–South Africa comparison presented in the previous chapter (see table 5.1) provides a baseline for analysis. To be sure, India differs from the other two countries in notable ways, but for the purposes of analysis on this issue, it is perhaps the best third case for structured comparison. Like Brazil and South Africa, it has had one of the world's largest AIDS epidemics in terms of total numbers of people infected, attracting the attention of the architects of the Geneva Consensus. By 2006 adult HIV prevalence had not surpassed 1 percent according to most official estimates, but high concentrations of infections in certain areas have led to warnings about the possibilities for an explosive epidemic. India is a large, developing country, which mixes extreme poverty and inequality with pockets of bureaucratic capacity and world-class pharmaceutical manufacturing capacity. Its record with democratic rule is far longer than either South Africa's or Brazil's, dating back to independence in 1947. While all three countries are organized along federal lines, India's history of decentralized federalism is much longer, more like Brazil's. More generally, political power in India has tended to be fragmented in terms of the organization of social movements and political parties, again more like Brazil than like South Africa. And for the period of the 1980s and early 1990s, India's international relations have been more like Brazil's, quite distinct from the pariah South African state, and the World Bank became actively involved in HIV programs in India beginning in 1992.

Of course, India is a much poorer country than either Brazil or South Africa, and on average, poorer countries have responded less aggressively to AIDS. But even if we take into account per capita income and adult HIV prevalence, the Indian government has spent less and has been less aggressive on several measurable indicators than we would expect given the policies of other developing countries. Low levels of economic development have not been determinate in other countries, in part because of

TABLE 5.1
Comparing AIDS, Politics, and Policy in India, Brazil, and South Africa

	Brazil	South Africa	India
Peak estimated adult HIV prevalence	<1%	21%	<1%
Regional "leader" in estimated number of infections?	Yes (Latin Am. / carib)	Yes (Africa)	Yes (Asia)
World "leader" in estimated number of infections?	Yes In 1980s, #2	Yes Mid-1990s– present, #1 or #2	Yes Late 1990s– present, top 3
Political regime	Democracy (transition mid-1980s)	Democracy (transition early 1990s)	Democracy (since 1948)
Major World Bank loan for HIV/AIDS	Yes, early	No	Yes, early
GDP/capita (1990)	$3,090	$3,152	$315
Devolution of political/ administrative power	Significant	Moderate	Significant
Population size (1990)	Large (149 million)	Medium (35 million)	Mega (850 million)
Local pharmaceutical industry	Yes	Yes	Yes
Ethnic boundaries	Weak	Strong: divided society	Strong: divided society
AIDS Policy Response	Aggressive	Not aggressive	Not aggressive

Note: Shaded cells reflect qualitative similarities across countries.

the availability of foreign funding and the low cost of many policies. Moreover, India has enjoyed unprecedented levels of economic growth during the AIDS epidemic, and it has a well-trained and competent public administration. On a fairly systematic cross-national "Weberianness" scale, India ranked seventh out of thirty-five countries in the quality of its bureaucracy, while Brazil ranked fifteenth (South Africa was not included in the survey).[2] The World Health Organization ranked India ahead of Brazil on three of eight indicators of health system performance in 1997, ahead of South Africa on five of eight, and ahead of Uganda on seven of eight,[3] again showing that India had the capacity to implement stronger policies on AIDS. India's record cannot be attributed to a lack of administrative capacity.

If the question is why India's response to AIDS was more like South Africa's than Brazil's, a plausible answer is that India also has strong boundary institutions. It is an extremely divided society along ethnic lines. Although the theory of boundary politics is not strictly deterministic, it leads us to predict that boundaries will produce certain political dynamics, including the framing of fragmented, as opposed to pooled, risk, and blame and shame-avoidance strategies. Conflict, including resistance from those likely to benefit from action on AIDS, will constrain influences that might otherwise lead to an aggressive response. And indeed, that is what one observes in India. Boundaries reinforced tendencies to stigmatize AIDS carriers and sufferers, allowing the vast majority of elites and ordinary citizens to consider themselves insulated from risk of infection. Group competition induced blame and denial of shameful links to the epidemic. Together these forces undermined political support for an aggressive response during most of the epidemic.

There are at least four sets of ethnic boundaries in India: caste, religion, language, and "tribe." They often manifest themselves in ethno-regionalism, through India's ethno-federation; and in work, through the country's ethnic division of labor. Ethno-regionalism and the ethnic division of labor have figured prominently in the politics of HIV/AIDS. The rhetoric of social boundaries—references to otherness, us/them, and untouchability—with respect to people living with HIV/AIDS or at high risk for infection is virtually identical to historical manifestations of ethnic competition.

As compared with South Africa, the effects of ethnic dividedness have been more subtle in political discourse on AIDS. There has been less explicit linking of the virus to ethnic groups in journalistic, organizational, and government accounts, and national political leaders more rarely make charges about viral pathogenesis and conspiracy. Indeed, most observers do not emphasize the effect of ethnic politics on AIDS policymaking, and point to other dynamics as the foundations of conflict over AIDS: social

[2] Evans and Rausch 1999.
[3] WHO 2000, annex 1.

conservatism, the marginalization of commercial sex workers, or regional differences. Indeed, such terms more frequently capture the explicit discourse of AIDS politics. However, they are both endogenous to, and often coded language for, ethnic political competition. I discuss below why such categories are manifestations of ethnic boundaries, not separate (nonethnic) forms of social boundaries. Such issues are difficult to resolve definitively. (Are American references to "inner city youth" or "ghetto culture" innuendos of class or race? There is some vagueness.)

The remainder of the chapter presents findings from my investigation into the link between boundaries and AIDS policy in India. The next section describes the progression of the Indian AIDS epidemic, demonstrating that it has been a general health threat, comparable to that which Brazil has faced. The second section relates the national government's response. The third section describes the nature of ethnic boundaries in India and their structuring of the politics of the response. The fourth section shows that cross-state variation in boundaries predicts differences in state-level responses to the epidemic. I conclude with reflections on how this analysis relates to other theories of Indian underdevelopment.

India's AIDS Epidemic

Although its exact extent is uncertain, India's AIDS epidemic is clearly significant, and public health officials have long described the potential for widespread infection, sickness, and death. By the end of 2006, India—home to about 16 percent of the world's population—was thought to contain between 10 and 20 percent of the world's people living with HIV, with the largest or second largest number of infections. The lead disseminator of such information, UNAIDS, reported an adult HIV prevalence of approximately 0.9 percent.[4] However, in June 2007 a new study indicated that the number of HIV infections was probably far less than prior estimates. As mentioned in chapter 1, in its annual epidemic update released in December 2007, UNAIDS described a change to its procedures for estimating country-level epidemics, and this change had the biggest impact on estimates for India. Whereas prior estimates had been based largely on sentinel surveys of pregnant women and of certain high-risk groups, national samples revealed that prior extrapolations had

[4]UNAIDS 2006.

overestimated the infections of other groups. The revised figures for India reduced the estimate to 2.5 million, or 0.36 percent of adults in 2006,[5] implying that about 8 percent of the world's infected population resided in India, and putting it behind Nigeria and South Africa in number of infections.

India is an extremely populous country, and national prevalence has never been dramatically high—with the highest estimates rarely above 1 percent. Such rates would be the envy of almost every sub-Saharan African country. On the other hand, by comparison with the rest of the world, India has had a serious HIV/AIDS problem, one that was identified two decades ago and has caused enormous concern to public health officials and activists both domestic and international. If we think of all HIV-positive individuals as potential vectors of transmission, India's large population, living in proximity to many infected individuals, leads one to expect a response from that government that may not be suggested by prevalence or incidence statistics alone. From a global perspective, actions taken by the Indian government can affect the trajectory of the pandemic worldwide.

The size of estimates and the timing of their dissemination are important for the analysis presented here, because they capture a degree of the "objective danger" involved with the AIDS epidemic. My argument concerning the value of incorporating ethnic boundaries into the policymaking process is based on the idea that perceptions and discourses of risk are based on both objective and subjective factors, as well as political factors. Even with the revised estimates, the problem of AIDS in India is clearly significant. Yet analysis of the history of AIDS politics and policy up until the release of the new estimates ought to be approached from the perspective of what was known and reported at the time. Information on the number of infections reported at any given time is more important than the true number of infections.[6]

The first case of HIV was reported in Chennai (formerly Madras), in the southern state of Tamil Nadu in 1986, the same year that the first case was reported in the majority of developing countries. Maharashtra state, and particularly Mumbai (formerly Bombay), was ground zero for India's

---

[5] UNAIDS 2007, Epidemic Update, 21.

[6] As an analogy, we would expect there to be enormous support for a military defense program if credible news and government sources reported an imminent attack, irrespective of the "reality" of that probability.

epidemic—sometimes referred to as the "Gateway for HIV/AIDS," in reference to the Gateway to India monument at the base of the city's harbor. In 1996, almost half the country's AIDS cases were from Maharashtra,[7] with as many as 50 percent of commercial sex workers in Mumbai testing positive for HIV. Like San Francisco, Hollywood, New York, São Paulo, Rio de Janeiro, and Cape Town, Mumbai is an international hub, in which the multiplicity of contacts among people helped spread the epidemic.

International public health experts were aware of the threat early in the epidemic and made public pronouncements of disasters on the horizon. By 1990, HIV prevalence among particular (tested) subgroups (sex workers and attendees at clinics on sexually transmitted infections in Maharashtra; and injecting drug users in Manipur) was over 5 percent. In 1992, the director of the WHO's Global Program on AIDS, Michael Merson, warned that if India did not aggressively control its epidemic, "in the next three years . . . the prevalence of HIV infection in India could reach that in Africa."[8] By 1994, there was clear and widely reported evidence that the virus was spreading to the "general population" in several states.[9] At the Eleventh International AIDS Conference in July 1996—a point of dissemination of the Geneva Consensus—India was placed at the top of the list of threatened nations.[10] A country increasingly concerned with its place in the international political economy faced pressure to control the growth of this pandemic. One World Bank study projected that by 2033, without a change in policy, 17 percent of Indian deaths would be AIDS-related.[11] Analysts have referred to the Indian epidemic as part of the "next wave" or "second wave" of the pandemic, given rising new infections (e.g., the 2002 report of the National Intelligence Council, which identified India, along with Nigeria, Russia, Ethiopia, and China as next-wave countries.) In 2002, Microsoft chairman and philanthropist Bill Gates explained his foundation's commitment to spend significant resources on HIV/AIDS in India. While noting the country's political and economic advances in recent years, he warned, "Much of this progress will be threatened by AIDS. . . . The choice now is clear and stark: India can

[7] NACO 2005a.

[8] Bhupesh 1992.

[9] Esktrand, Garbus, and Marseille 2003, 21.

[10] John F. Burns, "The AIDS Highway: Denial and Taboo Blinding India to the Horror of Its AIDS Scourge," New York Times, September 22, 1996, 1.

[11] Over and World Bank 2004, 16.

either be the home of the world's largest and most devastating AIDS epidemic—or, with the support of the rest of the world, it can become the best example of how this virus can be defeated."[12]

According to government estimates, by 2002, the rate of increase in prevalence had slowed.[13] On the other hand, given weak surveillance and a long chain of assumptions in producing infection estimates, it is extraordinarily difficult to estimate year-to-year changes in infection levels. UNAIDS estimates have always been reported with a huge uncertainty interval—for example, that between 2.6 million and 5.4 million Indians were living with HIV/AIDS at the end of 2001[14]—so facts can be widely interpreted. My own inspection of the state-level trends at surveillance sites shows some sites going from a handful of infections to zero infections. While there may have been no HIV-positive individuals in the subsequent round of testing in certain areas, the pregnant mothers tested previously were either still living with HIV or had died of AIDS, and neither result is well reflected in the surveillance data.

Though India's epidemic has been regionally concentrated, it has not been isolated, and almost every one of the country's states and union territories has reported at least one case. Nonetheless, virtually every analysis of AIDS in India until the end of 2006 emphasized that six states were hard hit—four are located in southern India (Andhra Pradesh, Tamil Nadu, Maharashtra, Karnataka) and two in northeastern India (Manipur and Nagaland). Together these six states accounted for nearly 80 percent of all reported AIDS cases in the country by the end of 2005. A comprehensive study of HIV prevalence estimates from 2000 to 2004 reported drops in HIV prevalence in the southern region, concluding that behavior change had most likely contributed to a reduction in new infections.[15]

As of 2003, more than 85 percent of HIV transmissions were estimated to be through sexual contacts, but particularly in the northeast—near Burma, Laos, and Thailand, where much of the world's heroin is produced—transmission has occurred through sharing needles while in-

---

[12] Bill Gates, "Slowing the Spread of AIDS in India," New York Times, November 9, 2002.

[13] Figures from India's National AIDS Control Organization (NACO), http://www.nacoonline.org/facts_overview.htm (consulted October 31, 2005).

[14] Ekstrand, Garbus, and Marseille 2003, 6.

[15] Kumar et al. 2006. The study uses a measure of HIV prevalence in order to derive estimates of HIV incidence (new infections), which are extremely difficult to observe directly.

jecting drugs. For 2003, the government estimated that 2.4 percent of infections were from injecting drug users; 2.7 percent from perinatal transmission; 2.6 percent from blood products, and the remaining 6.8 percent from unidentified routes.[16] Between 15 and 35 percent of all the country's truck drivers were estimated to be infected with the virus.[17] Although the epidemic was initially concentrated in urban settings, by 2003, the rural-urban distribution of estimated infections reflected the broader population. In 2004, among pregnant women attending antenatal clinics in Mumbai, Pune, Sangli, Hyderabad, and Manipur, HIV prevalence ranged between 2.0 and 2.5 percent,[18] making a wave of pediatric AIDS cases likely.

A great many facts and figures can be marshaled to describe AIDS in India. Whether or not the facts in India up until the end of 2006 ought to have been understood as a "crisis," a "coming crisis," or something much less threatening is ultimately a question of how risk gets socially and politically constructed. But given high levels of mobility around the country, the widespread use of commercial sex workers, and the sharing of needles among injecting drug users, there is every reason to believe that the spread of HIV, without significant interventions, could have truly disastrous implications. The large country is connected by a vast system of highways (see figure 5.1), and the "Golden Quadrilateral" of highways connecting New Delhi, Calcutta, Chennai, and Mumbai as well as the long north-south and east-west roads provide a conduit for contagion across a rapidly growing economy.[19]

THE GOVERNMENT'S RESPONSE: WEAK AND DELAYED

For most of the two decades since the onset of the AIDS epidemic, the Indian government has been relatively passive in its adoption of the Geneva Consensus. To be certain, there is evidence of change toward a more elaborate response after 2004, but this has been quite late, progress has been slow, and human rights have not emerged as an important dimension. From the perspective of authors of the Geneva Consensus, the Indian response has been frustratingly thin. As late as 2003, UNAIDS director

---

[16] NACO 2004, 14.

[17] Ekstrand, Garbus, and Marseille 2003, 21.

[18] National AIDS Control Organization, http://www.nacoonline.org (consulted June 20, 2006).

[19] Amy Waldman, "India Accelerating, an Epidemic Spreads: On India's Roads, Cargo and a Deadly Passenger," New York Times, December 6, 2005.

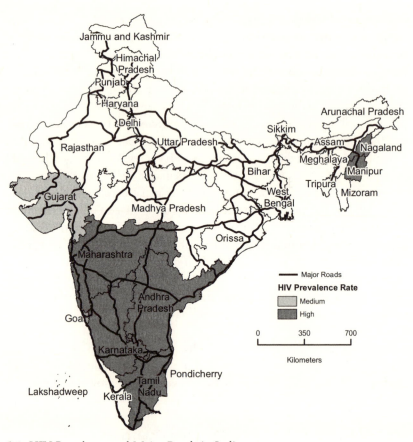

5.1. HIV Prevalence and Major Roads in India
Source: NACO 2004: 18; GFK Geomarketing.

Pieter Piot concluded, "At recent meetings in India, I heard great speeches, but as for action, zero."[20]

Whereas the Brazilian response, and eventually even the South African response to AIDS, addressed the entire population, through 2006 the Indian response was far more limited. According to the UNDP, the period from 1986 to 1992 was one in which the government's response could be characterized as a "denial of the threat of HIV"; from 1992 to 1997 as a "first acceleration of the program," but "limited" and "weak"; and the pe-

---

[20] M. Rosenblum, "Worldwide War on AIDS/HIV Still Coming Up Way Short," Associated Press, September 21, 2003 as cited on http://www.avert.org/aidsindia.htm (consulted February 15, 2005).

riod 1998 from 2001 as focused on "targeted interventions."[21] Since 2001, even the increased attention to AIDS has been almost entirely focused on certain groups and regions, not as a truly national project. In each of the four components of the Geneva Consensus, the Indian response appears much more like South Africa's than like Brazil's.

Bureaucratic Development

Budgetary outlays and administrative organization suggest that the Indian government has not made HIV/AIDS a priority. As in most countries, a shell of a bureaucratic response was developed early, created in 1987 with the National AIDS Control Program, followed in 1992 with the National AIDS Control Organization, (NACO) and the first of three "National AIDS Control Plans." NACO has remained the government agency in charge of AIDS and has enjoyed greater autonomy than any related structure in South Africa (but not more than in Brazil.)

However, such autonomy has meant little without sufficient government support. As late as 2005, NACO employed only nine senior officials, and fifteen full-time staff members—a bureaucracy charged with managing and coordinating one of the world's largest epidemics[22] with millions infected. While much of the response has been staffed by decentralized state AIDS control agencies, the thin national resources indicate that the problem was not being handled as a national one. One careful analysis of the development of the bureaucracy concluded that in 1997 "staffing at national and state levels reflected the low priority accorded to the epidemic"; most government officials assigned to AIDS held the responsibility as an additional charge and devoted little time to it.[23]

Expenditure has also been extremely low: Between 1992 and 1998, total cumulative government expenditure was $100 million, funded largely by external donors, especially through a World Bank loan.[24] The

---

[21] UNDP 2005.

[22] As described by Nafis Sadik, special adviser to UN secretary-general Kofi Annan and special envoy for HIV/AIDS in Asia and the Pacific. Reported in IANS/Navhind Times, October 13, 2005. In interviews, others described the NACO headcount as higher—forty-five to fifty—but this included part-time employees.

[23] Sethi 2002, 49–50.

[24] These expenditures account for virtually all of the government expenditure at the subnational level.

government of India spent only about $46 million of its own funds during the period 1999–2005, while NACO's entire budget for this period, including direct foreign assistance, was only about $315 million.[25] By 2005, total per capita government expenditure was still less than $0.10 (see table 5.2), including donor support. While this figure is up from $0.04 in 1996, it pales in comparison to the average of $0.41 among other developing countries,[26] let alone a country like Brazil. Even if we address India's "denominator problem"—that is, its very large population—and consider expenditures relative to the populations of the three largest high-prevalence states (Andhra Pradesh, Maharashtra, and Tamil Nadu), which in 2001 represented just under 23 percent of the country's entire population (see table 5.3), 1996 per capita expenditure was a mere $0.17, far below the mean expenditure for developing countries.

Moreover, as was often the case in South Africa, budgeted funds have often not been spent. In 1995, only 30 to 40 percent of the AIDS budget was disbursed, causing the World Bank to threaten cessation of funding.[27] As of 2001, despite having a sixth of the world's population, and an estimated one-tenth of all people infected with HIV, India had attracted only 1 percent of the global resources aimed at fighting HIV/AIDS.[28]

After 2001, global expenditure on HIV/AIDS began to accelerate rapidly as the international donor community focused more heavily on global AIDS, particularly around the UNGASS declaration of commitment, the launch of "Three-by-Five," and the start-up of the GFATM. The UK's development agency, DFID made commitments of $175 million for the period (2001–6); USAID committed $120million (2003–7); and the Gates Foundation $200 million (2003–7).[29] The Government of India made HIV/AIDS-related applications to the GFATM in rounds 2, 4, and 6, and received a maximum of $209 million in committed funds.[30]

Testing and surveillance initiatives have developed slowly. Between 1986 and 1992, surveillance activities were launched in fifty-five cities in

[25] See table 5.1. This does not include direct donor support to state-level projects or the very minor amount spent directly by state governments out of their own health budgets.

[26] Author calculations using data described in chapter 6.

[27] "India to be Asia's AIDS Capital: Study," Courier-Mail, October 11, 1995. See also Sethi 2002, 49–50.

[28] Angus Donald, "India Slow to Wake Up to Reality of Aids," Financial Times, June 2, 2001, 7.

[29] Ekstrand, Garbus, and Marseille 2003, 17.

[30] Government of India proposals to the GFATM.

TABLE 5.2
National Government Per Capita Expenditure on AIDS in India, 1999–2005

	1999–2000	2000–2001	2001–2002	2002–2003	2003–2004	2004–2005
Government of India	$0.004	$0.006	$0.006	$0.007	$0.006	$0.015
World Bank Credit	$0.024	$0.030	$0.034	$0.036	$0.034	$0.056
USAID		$0.000	$0.001	$0.003	$0.004	$0.006
DFID		$0.002	$0.005	$0.005	$0.006	$0.009
UNDP				< $0.001	< $0.001	$0.001
GFATM						$0.004
Total	$0.028	$0.037	$0.048	$0.052	$0.050	$0.091

Source: NACO 2005, 18.

Notes: Figures in $US per capita. Dollar amounts calculated using exchange rate of 45 rupees per dollar.

three states, but with little central guidance.[31] A regular, nationwide annual sentinel surveillance system began only in 1998, with 184 test sites in 1998, 455 in 2003,[32] and 750 in 2005.[33] Relative to the population, this is weak coverage, which has led to great uncertainties about the extent of the epidemic. In interviews I conducted with government officials at the national and local levels in New Delhi and Mumbai, as well as with private sector, domestic, and international NGOs, there was uniform agreement that surveillance methods were inadequate to gain an accurate picture of the epidemic.

Executive Leadership

When considering "softer" forms of government action, notably vocal leadership from the chief executive, India's record has also been weak until

[31] UNDP 2005.

[32] UNDP 2005.

[33] NACO, Ministry of Health and Family Welfare, Government of India, Progress Report on the Declaration of Commitment on HIV/AIDS, prepared for the United Nations General Assembly Special Session on HIV/AIDS, 2005, 6.

TABLE 5.3
India's Ethnic Demographics

State	Population (millions)	Language			Caste	Tribe	Religion			Religions fractionalization
		Mother tongue	% Speaking	ELF	Scheduled caste %	Scheduled tribe %	% Muslim	% Christian	% Sikh	
East										
Chhattisgarh	20.8									
Jharkhand	26.9									
Orissa	36.7	Oriya	81.8	.323	16.2	22.2	1.8	2.1	0.1	.102
West Bengal	80.2	Bengali	85.8	.251	23.6	5.6	23.6	0.6	0.1	.386
North										
Bihar	82.9	Hindi	33.5	.349	14.6	7.7	14.8	1.0	0.1	.299
Delhi	13.8	Hindi	80.5	.397	19.1	0.0	9.4	0.9	4.8	.288
Gujarat	50.6	Gujarati	91.5	.170	7.4	14.9	8.7	0.4	0.1	.191
Haryana	21.1	Hindi	88.9	.172	19.8	0.0	4.6	0.1	5.8	.199
Him. Pradesh	6.1	Pahari	41.9	.206	25.3	4.2	1.7	0.1	1.0	.080
Jammu and Kashmir	10.1			.693						

Madhya Pradesh	60.4	Hindi	56.0	.289	14.5	23.3	5.0	0.6	0.2	.136
Punjab	24.3	Punjabi	92.1	.258	28.3	0.0	1.2	1.1	63.0	.484
Rajasthan	56.5	Hindi	38.9	.189	17.3	12.4	8.0	0.1	1.5	.199
Uttar Pradesh	166.1	Hindi	82.1	.189	21.0	0.2	17.3	0.1	0.5	.303
Uttaranchal	8.5									
Northeast										
Arunachal Pradesh	1.1	Nepali	9.4		0.5	63.7	1.4	10.3	0.1	.590
Assam	26.6	Assamese	57.3	.999	7.4	12.8	28.4	3.3	0.1	.468
Manipur	2.4	Manipuri	60.4	.991	2.0	34.4	7.3	34.1	0.1	.545
Meghalaya	2.3	Khasi	37.8		0.5	85.5	3.5	64.6	0.1	.531
Mizoram	0.9	Lushai/Mizo	75.0		0.1	94.8	0.7	85.7	0.0	.256
Nagaland	2.0	Ao	14.0	.985		87.7	1.7	87.5	0.1	.224
Sikkim	0.5	Nepali	63.1	.509	5.9	22.4	0.9	3.3	0.1	.456
Tripura	3.2	Bengali	65.4	.515	16.4	31.0	7.1	1.7	0.0	.244

(continued)

Table 5.3 (continued)

State	Population (millions)	Language Mother tongue	Language % Speaking	Language ELF	Caste Scheduled caste %	Tribe Scheduled tribe %	Religion % Muslim	Religion % Christian	Religion % Sikh	Religion Religions fractionalization
South										
Andhra Pradesh	75.7	Telugu	84.8	.270	15.9	6.3	8.9	1.8	0.0	.198
Goa	1.3	Konkani	51.5		2.1	0.0	5.3	29.9	0.1	.489
Karnataka	52.7	Kannada	66.2	.549	16.4	4.3	11.6	1.9	0.0	.257
Kerala	31.8	Malayalam	96.6	.078	9.9	1.1	23.3	19.3	0.0	.580
Lakshadweep		Malayalam	84.5			93.2	94.3	1.2	0.0	.109
Maharashtra	96.8	Marathi	73.3	.448	11.1	9.3	9.7	1.1	0.2	.327
Pondicherry		Tamil	89.2		16.3	0.0	6.5	7.2	0.0	.248
Tamil Nadu	62.1	Tamil	86.7	.263	19.2	1.0	5.5	5.7	0.0	.207
India	1,027	Hindi	27.8		16.3	8.0	12.1	2.3	1.9	.312
Mean (states)	35.3		66.2	.413	13.2	23.6	11.6	13.5	2.9	.311
Median (state)	24.3		73.3	.306	15.9	9.3	7.1	1.8	0.1	.257

Source: State population from 2001 census; linguistic fractionalization (ELF) 1981, calculated by Wilkinson (2004); All other statistics from India Census 1991, via Datanet India 2006. Religious Fractionalization calculated by the author.

recently—when virtually every observer I met in India echoed reports in the media that there has been a noticeable change. For the first fifteen years after the virus was identified in India, government leaders made little public pronouncement about the growing scope of the problem or the risks of infection. But in 2001, Prime Minister Vajpayee made public pronouncements, addressing parliament and identifying HIV/AIDS as a serious health challenge.[34] In 2004, there was much more public discussion by India's leaders, including rare displays of bipartisan support across the Congress and Bharatiya Janata (BJP) parties. In 2005, after Congress's return to power, Prime Minister Manmohan Singh spoke on Independence Day, highlighting the success of the country in bringing certain diseases under control, but also saying, "AIDS is now becoming a major national problem and we need to tackle this on a war-footing. We need to have a mass movement to ensure that this disease is rapidly checked and its growth arrested."[35] In June 2005, Singh convened a National Council on AIDS, to lead a multisectoral response to the epidemic, embracing a more orthodox application of the Geneva Consensus. By this stage in the pandemic, however, such words and displays were remarkably late when compared with more aggressive governments elsewhere in the world. It is also worth highlighting that as of 2001, the international resources available for all countries for HIV/AIDS were escalating dramatically and international pressures for slow-moving governments accelerating.

Despite the emerging shift relative to the past, the Indian government has not acted on AIDS as a national priority. For example, in National (Union) budget speeches from 1998 through 2006, there was no mention of HIV or AIDS until 2004, and in that speech, just one paragraph mentioned AIDS. By contrast, in the same speech employment figured in seven paragraphs, health (not including HIV/AIDS) in nine paragraphs, and education in ten paragraphs. In 2005, there was again no mention of HIV or AIDS, and in 2006, the only mention was the proposal "to reduce the customs duty on 10 anti-AIDS [and fourteen anticancer] drugs to 5 per cent." By contrast, in the same year in Gambia, an African country with relatively low HIV prevalence, HIV figured prominently in three paragraphs of the budget speech, and in Zambia, a country with a widespread epidemic, HIV/AIDS figured in seven paragraphs. In its own ratings of political

[34] Ekstrand, Garbus, and Marseille 2003, 122.
[35] Indo Asian News Service, "AIDS Should Be Fought on 'War Footing,' Says PM," August 15, 2005.

"support" for the HIV/AIDS program in the country, the NACO rated the country at 2 (out of 10) in 2003.[36]

Partnering with NGOs and Civil Society

The Indian government has initiated greater involvement with civil society organizations only late in the epidemic—by the government's own accounting, since 2003.[37] This relationship reflects an odd tightrope the government must walk: although commercial sex work and homosexuality are both criminalized in India, commercial sex workers and MSMs are labeled "high-risk" groups. In order to effectively target such groups, NACO and state and municipal AIDS organizations have found it necessary to work with NGOs to avoid direct contact with illegals. Nonetheless, the government is hardly coordinated on this strategy, and police routinely harass and sometimes arrest members of NGOs who work with MSMs or intravenous drug users or who discuss sexual practices.

Prevention

If we were to create a mere checklist of government prevention policies developed and implemented, the Indian government would score fairly high, having done most of what is prescribed in the Geneva Consensus, albeit later than in countries we could describe as aggressive on AIDS. Information and education campaigns were initiated in the early 1990s, including the "University Talks AIDS" campaign, and beginning in 1994, street plays and performances were sponsored by the government.[38]

And yet with limited financial support and executive leadership, the reach and scope of these programs have been limited, and observers of government AIDS policies have highlighted a lack of deep commitment to these policies, and oftentimes inappropriate applications to the challenges of the Indian epidemic. For example, the head of one state AIDS control society explained in an interview, "There was very little commitment from various leaders to do something. Our political leaders would

---

[36] UNGASS Report 2005 (India), 51.
[37] UNGASS Report 2005 (India), 26.
[38] http://www.nacoonline.org/prog_iec.htm (consulted February 10, 2005).

talk too much of A and not B or C.[39] This didn't make sense for truckers or commercial sex workers." Under the BJP government, the minister of health, Sushma Swaraj, banned condom ads on television, an edict reversed in 2004.[40] It was only in 2000 that a feasibility study was executed for the use of AZT in the prevention of mother-to-child transmission, and by the end of 2005, less than 2 percent of HIV-positive pregnant women received antiretroviral prophylaxis.[41]

Treatment

Unlike Brazil, which began offering ARVs in 1996, India only began to provide them free of cost beginning in April 2004, on a rather limited basis in the six high-prevalence states of Tamil Nadu, Andhra Pradesh, Maharashtra, Karnataka, Manipur, and Nagaland and in the capital city of Delhi.[42] The World Bank estimated that as of 2002 11,700 people were receiving treatment in India, but it was largely unstructured, not conforming to NACO or WHO guidelines. At that time, in the absence of a government program, all costs were borne privately.[43] By the end of 2005, less than 5 percent of the people in need of ARV treatment were receiving it through public centers, and the government estimated that a similar number received treatment privately.[44]

There is a bitter irony to the fact that India was one of the countries furthest away from the Three by Five targets, because it is home to an extraordinary manufacturing base for drugs, which have been exported at low costs to African countries as well as to the Brazilian government for its heralded AIDS program. The WHO ranked India as having the second largest (after South Africa) "unmet need" for ARVs. While such rankings

---

[39] That is, emphasizing abstinence over being faithful or using condoms.

[40] In a January 2006 interview with Swaraj, she claimed that under her tenure the distribution of condoms doubled.

[41] UNAIDS 2006, annex 3, 555. Most South and Southeast Asian countries had similarly low coverage, with the exception of Thailand, for which estimates ranged from 31 to 83 percent.

[42] NACO 2004, 87.

[43] Over and World Bank 2004, 3.

[44] NACO, Ministry of Health and Family Welfare, Government of India, *Progress Report on the Declaration of Commitment on HIV/AIDS*, prepared for the United Nations General Assembly Special Session on HIV/AIDS, 2005, 12.

are in part simply reflections of the large size of HIV-positive populations, it is important to note that of the countries compared in this study, 2005 coverage in India of 4–9 percent is better only than five other countries. By contrast, in South Africa, coverage was estimated at 10–14 percent; in much more aggressive Thailand, more than 50 percent of those in need were being provided with ARV therapy.[45] Close to 100 percent of those in need received ARV therapy in Brazil.

Rights Orientation

India's approach to HIV/AIDS has also been notable for its inattention to human rights, despite its identity as the world's largest democracy, and among the most stable. Its policy has conflicted with the Geneva Consensus on rights in two key ways: the government maintained mandatory and coercive policies, and failed to offer protections against discrimination to individuals who were, or were suspected of being, HIV-positive. In practice, agents of the state—including health-care workers at public hospitals and clinics and police—have been brutally discriminatory in their treatment of those infected with HIV or suspected to be.

In fact, the first piece of AIDS-related legislation was the Goa Public Health Act Amendment of 1987 (Section 53.I.vii), which allowed local authorities to isolate people with HIV/AIDS. Subsequently, the Railway Board Administrative Notification of 1989 allowed the railways to deny passage to those infected. Despite international condemnation of such restrictive policies, neither piece of legislation was rescinded until 1996.

To be sure, some actions did follow the Geneva Consensus on rights, including a 1992 administrative notification from the Ministry of Health and Family Welfare to all state governments directing them to ensure nondiscriminatory access to treatment and care for people who were HIV-positive. In May 1997, a Mumbai High Court judgment held that employers could not base employment decisions on HIV status of employees.[46] Nonetheless, there have continued to be widespread reports of discrimination by government and public sector employees. Between 1998 and 2002 the Supreme Court actually banned HIV-positive people from getting married. According to the "Civil Society" response to the UNGASS sur-

---

[45] WHO 2005.
[46] Information about the details of these acts are from UNDP 2005.

vey filed in 2005 by NACO, the country has neither laws nor regulations that protect people with HIV/AIDS from discrimination, nor specific protections for those thought to be particularly vulnerable to HIV.

At the end of 2005, a draft HIV/AIDS bill had been completed by an active NGO, the Lawyers Collective, in conjunction with the government. It is ultimately a detailed endorsement of the Geneva Consensus, especially on the matter of rights. While it is likely that this bill will ultimately be passed, it was still awaiting legislative attention in February 2008. In a democracy almost six decades old, this is a slow pace at which to extend rights to a group suffering from massive discrimination.

EXPLANATION: THE ROLE OF BOUNDARY POLITICS

Given domestic and international resources and the country's sizable AIDS epidemic, why was the Indian government's initial response so lackluster? If we compare possible drivers of policy responses in India to those in Brazil and South Africa (see table 5.1), it appears plausible that what drove non-aggressive responses in South Africa and India were ethnic boundaries stronger than Brazil's. But additional evidence is needed to support the link from cause to effect, especially because it has been rare for Indian policymakers or for other analysts to discuss AIDS in terms of ethnic politics.[47]

I detail the connection between India's ethnic boundaries and its weak AIDS policy in a series of steps. First, I describe four different types of ethnic difference in India. Second, I show that these categories are recognizable in mappings of the AIDS epidemic, even when the labels are not used explicitly, and I highlight the role this information plays in discussions of risk and ethnically defined dynamics of blame and shame-avoidance. Finally, I identify examples of political leaders using strategies of denial in order to avoid ethnic sensitivities to this stigmatized concern.

Ethnic Boundaries

Ethnic categories are routinely deployed in Indian politics and society, though unlike Brazil and South Africa, no significant settler group remains

---

[47] More generally, it is rare for Indian policymakers to use explicit ethnic discourse concerning policy issues, so this is not unique to AIDS.

in the country, and "race" is not a label applied to any of its ethnic categories. Instead, caste, religious, tribal, and language groups are the primary sources of ethnic division and boundaries.[48] In all three countries, the juxtaposition of culturally diverse groups has raised the question of what constitutes "the nation" and to what degree different groups should be formally and explicitly recognized for cultural, socioeconomic, and political differences. As in South Africa, most efforts at "nation building" have promoted a sometimes tenuous "unity through diversity," a far cry from Brazilian nation building, which achieved linguistic homogenization and helped to blur internal race and religious boundaries. For a period following the onset of Indian independence, a "secular" Indian nationalism gained political traction, but by the time the AIDS epidemic unfolded in the 1980s, strong boundary politics—understood as "communalism"—were evident across India,[49] though manifest in different ways in different places.[50] While in independent India there are no analogues to the institutionalized white supremacy in South Africa, other deep-seated institutions have had similar effects on politics and society in the sense that ethnic identity has become a primary basis for social and political organization.

Across each of the four cleavages, there is enormous demographic diversity (see table 5.3) and evidence of institutionalized boundaries within and across Indian states.

LANGUAGE

Language is an important marker of culture and ethnic identity in India, and the linguistic diversity highlights its ethnic diversity. Approximately 325 languages are spoken in India, with at least seventeen mother tongues spoken by over one million people in 1991.[51] More Indians claim Hindi as their mother tongue than any other language (approximately 233 million, or 28 percent of the population according to the 1991 census), and at independence many imagined it would become the national

---

[48] With the exception being that some "lower-caste" groups have referred to themselves as "India's blacks" as part of a larger campaign of political solidarity with oppressed ethnic groups in other parts of the world.

[49] A surge in communal politics began in the mid-1980s (Kohli 1990a).

[50] See, for example, both Varshney 2002 and Wilkinson 2004, for analyses of patterns of Hindu-Muslim violence, at the town and state levels.

[51] According to the 1991 census and the Anthropological Survey of India, via Datanet India 2006.

language. However, many other language groups resented the imposition of the language, and it became an official language of the country and of only a few states, all in the north.[52] Instead, a federal constitution was created that afforded autonomy to diverse linguistic communities, deepening a trend toward linguistic autonomy in place prior to independence,[53] and often language demands and resulting reorganizations in the decades following reinforced the centrality of language as a sociopolitical identity.[54] The "Hindi heartland" encompasses the four most populous states of Uttar Pradesh, Bihar, Rajasthan, and Madhya Pradesh, as well as the state of Haryana and Delhi. By contrast, distinctive Dravidian and other languages are spoken in several southern states—the basis for a recognized "north-south" language cleavage[55]—and only a small minority speak Hindi; and in the northeast, a variety of other languages are spoken.

Several language groups have mobilized ethno-nationalist movements. Notably, Nagaland and Manipur were the sites of violence in the 1950s (and violence continues in Nagaland) and the Minorities at Risk project identifies "Nagas" and scheduled tribes in the northeast more generally as being "at risk" minorities.[56] Similarly in the 1950s, Tamil nationalists insisted that Tamils were a separate racial and cultural group, descended from a Dravidian society indigenous to southern India prior to the arrival of "northern Aryans."[57] In the 1960s in Maharashtra state, the Shiv Sena advanced a "sons of the soil" platform, focused on "Maratha-centric" politics.[58] And the regional Telugu Desam party became important in Andhra in the mid-1980s.[59] In each case, political leaders have used the territorial concentration of certain groups to mobilize a politics of cultural difference from the rest of the nation.

CASTE AND "UNTOUCHABILITY"

A second set of relevant ethnic boundaries have circumscribed caste identities. Although caste politics in India (and South Asian and Hindu

---

[52] Brass 1994, 158–62.
[53] Dasgupta 2001, 52.
[54] Brass 1994, 169–74.
[55] Windmiller 1954, 292.
[56] MAR 2005, analytic summaries of "at-risk" groups in India.
[57] Kohli 1998, 18.
[58] Katzenstein, Kothari, and Mehta 2001, 219.
[59] Brass 1994, 89.

societies more generally) can appear highly distinctive from other ethnic divides because of the historical and religious underpinnings of this system of social stratification, from an analytic perspective, this divide is the most similar of the four central Indian cleavages to the racial cleavage identified in South Africa and Brazil (and the United States, for that matter). All of these are instances of what Donald Horowitz calls "ranked" categories because of the close correspondence between identity and socioeconomic position/occupation.[60]

Historically, India's caste system stratified groups by specifying families as members of a *varna* (broad, ranked groupings) and a *jati* (more specific and localized subgroup). To be certain, the organization and meanings of these groups shifted over time, and there has been much scholarly debate about their place in Hindu texts and in the context of imperial rule.[61] And yet several properties of the caste system are relevant for the theory of boundary politics: the designation of a group of "caste-less" or "untouchable"[62] people around whom extraordinarily strong boundaries have been placed; and the rules (made illegal in modern India but widely practiced nonetheless) of enforcing endogamy and even limited physical contact reinforced by myths of "pollution" from lower castes. Indeed, caste institutions prohibit not merely sexual contact, but other forms of direct and even indirect contact (such as food handling) across the "caste bar," and violations of this boundary are addressed with visible, violent, and sometimes murderous consequences.

The caste system was a target of reform by many leaders of the independence movement, notably Mohandas Gandhi, and the Indian constitutional architect Dr. B. R. Ambedkar, and much Indian legislation has targeted the injustices of the caste system. Nonetheless, caste boundaries remain strongly institutionalized formally and informally, and caste-

---

[60] Horowitz 1985, 24–32.

[61] See Bayly 1999.

[62] A note on terminology: Discussion and analysis of ethnic labels always carries certain problems. Labels used by some groups are often deemed offensive by others; labels change; and the norms of acceptability often vary across both time and space. For the group once known as "untouchables," Mohatma Gandhi used the term *Harijans,* or "children of God," which has been largely rejected as paternalistic. More recently, members of this group have referred to themselves more affirmatively as *Dalits,* and by the government and in much official parlance as "Scheduled castes." I make reference to the label I deem most associated with the social and political context being discussed. When I use the term "untouchable," I do so in quotations to remind the reader of its distasteful connotations, but also to highlight what I find—that the negative attitudes about this group are similarly directed at those with HIV/AIDS. As documented in news reports, the term "untouchable" is still widely used.

based violence and discrimination continue. Much of the postindependence period in India has been characterized by political initiatives and conflicts reminiscent of American-style affirmative action and South African black economic empowerment. Disadvantaged castes were identified through specific schedules that determined equity-enhancing/preferential treatment, and in the 1991 census, approximately 16 percent of the Indian population identified as members of scheduled castes. To address grievances concerning inequalities generated from the past, the Indian state has detailed provisions including job and educational reservations, as well as seats in the national (Lok Sobha) and state legislative assemblies.[63] In the independence era, the groups that are commonly referred to as "backward" castes have mobilized to demand greater power and resources, and have often determined political support blocks and political parties. In 1980, the government's Mandal commission sought to rectify social inequalities associated with a large number of caste categories; the Bahujan Samaj Party was formed in 1984, claiming to represent lower-caste interests;[64] both of these developments have almost certainly increased the political salience of caste during the AIDS pandemic. Members of these previously disadvantaged groups have enjoyed material and other successes owing to such policies and political mobilization, but as in other polities, preferential policies have increased, not eliminated, the salience of such group identities.[65] The policies and the parties make distinctions based on ascription, not on one's place in the economic order or mode of production, and so they reinforce *ethnic* boundaries.

In national surveys on types of people that individuals would "not like to have as a neighbor," 36 percent of Indians identified someone of a different race (in the survey translated as "someone of a different caste"), a higher share than in any other country in the 1995–97 World Values Survey. Perhaps even more compelling, a full 53 percent of Indians surveyed in 2004 said they "somewhat agreed" or "fully agreed" that there ought to be a ban on intercaste marriages, while only 35 percent disagreed.[66] Given the near-universal bias toward the underreporting of such sentiments, these findings are stunning evidence of the wide recognition and support for strong ethnic boundaries in India.

[63] Brass 1994, 95.
[64] See, for example, Chandra 2004.
[65] Brass 1994; Weiner 2001.
[66] Palshikar 2004, 5429.

While caste-based endogamy may be eroding as a social institution, it still remains firmly rooted as a normative ideal. In a 2004 study of elites in the capital city of Delhi,[67] when asked about the importance of factors in selecting mates for marriage, 93 percent of those between the ages of forty-seven and sixty-two said religion was important, 78 percent said caste, and 96 percent said virginity, while only 15 percent said that love was important. By contrast, among the younger cohort, 50 percent said religion was important; 27 percent said caste, and 78 percent said virginity, while 73 percent said that love was important. There is a clear generational difference; the older cohort, presumably the one that has most influenced AIDS policy, attaches strong importance to the maintenance of social boundaries.[68] Confirming the findings, a 1997 national survey found that 72 percent said they would not allow their son or daughter to marry someone from another caste.[69] Again, given norms against overt "casteism," the data show the strength of these boundaries.

When I have asked scholars, political leaders, and professionals about the role of caste and identity in Indian society and politics, several have claimed that caste is an institution alive "only in the rural areas." Undoubtedly, urban and rural areas differ in the degree and openness of caste prejudice. But caste continues to play a role in sex and marriage beyond rural areas. One can find clear traces of concern for caste among literate, Internet-savvy, urban Indians: for example, the popular Internet "matrimonial" service Shaadi—similar to an American-style dating service, but with the explicit goal of finding spouses—asks individuals to list complexion, ethnicity, and caste as key parts of one's profile.[70] While Indians from cosmopolitan centers and the news media report that "love marriages" are on the rise, Shaadi's request for such information highlights its value among a "modern" elite. In my informal discussions with relatively young university

---

[67] In the Mathur and Parameswaran 2004 study, 181 Asian Indian Hindu men and women living in New Delhi participated. This sample included forty-six men and forty-five women who had older teenage children and children in their early adulthood. All of the participants in this group were between the ages of forty-six and sixty-two. The sample also included forty-five male and forty-five female youths between the ages of eigtheen and twenty-six. All of the participants belonged to the upper middle social classes and lived in an urban setting. The vast majority of the participants had graduated from college, and the youths who did not already have a bachelor's degree were working toward one.

[68] Mathur and Parameswaran 2004, 168.

[69] *India Today International*, August 18, 1997, 34, as cited in Weiner 2001, 195.

[70] See http://www.shaadi.com/.

graduates, they conceded that most people still know their caste identities, and tend to wind up with mates and friends from their own group.

RELIGION

Religious identities are often a social and political fault-line in Indian politics, and in recent years, riots, lynchings, temple-burnings, and inflammatory language have occurred across this divide. Four major religious identities and groupings—a large Hindu majority of approximately 80 percent; a Muslim minority of approximately 13 percent; and small Christian and Sikh minorities of approximately 2 percent each—drive additional boundary-making (table 5.3 reports the size of the religious minorities, and the remainder in all states is virtually all Hindu.). In modern history, the violent separation of a Muslim Pakistan from India epitomizes this religious divide, while ongoing violence has occurred at the town and state levels. Reinforcing religion as a basis of identity in relation to the state, separate civil codes were established for Hindus and Muslims.[71] Separate marriages acts—the 1955 Hindu Marriage Act; and the 1939 Dissolution of Muslim Marriages Act—recognize families in quite distinctive ways under the law, and with no obvious provision for "mixed" marriages. According to the 2004 National Election Survey, 56 percent of Indians somewhat or fully agreed that there ought to be a ban on interreligious marriages; and 54 percent agreed that there ought to be a ban on conversions. Only 35 percent and 37 percent disagreed with those propositions.[72]

In recent decades, overtly "ethnic" political parties have gained political support—with a Hindu Nationalist party (BJP) winning enough electoral support to lead the government from 1996 to 2004. Other organizations, such as the Rashtriya Swayamsevak Sangh (RSS) and more locally based parties, such as Shiv Sena in Maharashtra state, have reinforced the political salience of ethnic identity as attached to religion, as leaders have used Muslim outsiders as an ever-present source of scapegoating. In recent years, there have been increasing reports of violence against Sikhs and also Christians.[73] Particularly since the nineteenth century, Christian mission-

[71] Brass 1994, 14.

[72] Palshikar 2004, 5429.

[73] See, for example, Human Rights Watch, "Politics by Other Means: Attacks against Christians in India," October 1999, vol. 11, no. 6, http://www.hrw.org/reports/1999/

aries have been linked with the West, and there have been violent reprisals when Dalits have converted to Christianity.

TRIBE INDIGENOUS GROUPS

Finally, India is home to indigenous groups, who together with members of lower-caste groups were collectively understood as the "depressed classes" prior to Indian independence. These *adivasis* (original inhabitants) are spread across the central, northeast, and southern regions of the country.[74] There exist several hundred of these "tribal" groups in the country, who in some places have minimal political identity, and in others have organized collectively, and sometimes violently. In 2000, the state of Jharkhand was created out of Bihar owing to the demands and challenges of indigenous organizations. Historically, indigenous people in India have suffered from social and economic discrimination, and the Indian constitution also defines "scheduled tribes," with economic, educational, and political reservations to address past injustices and persistent inequalities. This group represented 8 percent of the total population in the 1991 census, but represents more than 90 percent of the population in some Indian states.

Implications: Framing the Epidemic in Terms of Differentiated Risk

Thus, by almost any comparative metric, India is an ethnically diverse society in which formal and informal institutions reinforce a strong sense of ethnic difference. The theory of boundary politics predicts that where ethnic boundaries are strong, the epidemic is more likely to be framed along ethnic lines. The collective mapping of the epidemic is likely to coincide with ethnic maps of the country.

Indeed, this proves to be true in India, though the epidemic has been discussed in terms that are less explicitly ethnic than in South Africa. For example, one does not find in India the same extent of government-released infection data reported explicitly along the lines of caste, language, or religion, and only some information about risks and infection among scheduled tribes. In fact, widespread awareness of the often explo-

---

indiachr/ (consulted January 19, 2007). After the 1984 assassination of Indira Gandhi by her two Sikh guards, there was a wave of anti-Sikh violence.

[74] MAR 2005: analytic summaries of "at risk" groups in India.

sive tensions over those categories constrains the state and other public institutions from releasing data about the incidence of social problems according to these categories. Nonetheless, reports and surveys commissioned and released by the Indian government concerning questions of vulnerability provide clear pictures that ethnic boundaries are relevant predictors of risk. For example, the three rounds of the National Family Health Survey released by the government identify indicators of knowledge and risk-related behavior in terms of caste, religion, region, and tribal status. Among surveyed men, 34.8 percent of those identified as scheduled castes and 23.3 percent of identified as scheduled tribes reported that they used a condom during their last "higher-risk" sexual intercourse,[75] as compared with 50.4 percent of men who were not from those groups or from "other backward" groups.[76] Moreover, other "information brokers" in Indian society have drawn explicit links between ethnic categories and HIV transmission. One study concluded simply, "Indigenous People of India are more prone to HIV/AIDS."[77]

Almost all dissemination of information about AIDS in India has emphasized "unevenness" in the epidemic—concentrated in particular states and regions, and in three "high-risk groups": sex workers, truckers, and IV drug users. The shaded regions depicting HIV prevalence in figure 5.1 are based on a typical "official" map of the epidemic, released by the NACO,[78] which highlights distinctions across space and occupation/risk group: six states were declared to be "high prevalence" because the epidemic became so generalized that more than 1 percent of pregnant women in antenatal clinics tested HIV-positive; in "medium-prevalence states" fewer than 1 percent of pregnant women tested positive, but more than 5 percent of "high-risk" groups were estimated to be HIV-positive; and in the remaining "low-prevalence states," even among high-risk groups HIV prevalence is less than 5 percent, and among pregnant women, HIV prevalence is much lower than 1 percent. In particular, the conclusion that the four southern and two northeastern states are "high prevalence" is consistently reiterated, and such an understanding has

---

[75] Defined as sexual intercourse with a partner who was neither a spouse nor who lived with the respondent.

[76] IIPS and Macro International 2007, 347.

[77] R. Nainakwal and M. Nainakwal, "Indigenous People of India Are More Prone to HIV/AIDS, Evidence from NFHS-I & NFHS-II," abstract presented at the International AIDS Conference, Toronto, August 13–18, 2006.

[78] "Adult HIV Prevalence—2003," from NACO 2004, 18.

been self-reinforcing because testing and surveillance as well as policy have been targeted in particular states, and at sites focused on these very groups (pregnant women and high-risk groups such as commercial sex workers, truckers, and IV drug users).

Both space (states and regions) and occupation are categories with important ethnic connotations in India. In discussions of the epidemiology of HIV and AIDS, mention of "high-prevalence states" is so common that an outside observer could easily take for granted the deeper meaning of these geographic entities as neutral facts of the Indian landscape. We cannot lose sight of the deeper ethnic implications of statehood in the Indian context. If we consider the maps depicted in figures 5.1 and 5.2 together, what becomes clear is that no state in the (shaded) "Hindi heartland"—widely understood as the "core" of India—has been designated as "high prevalence," despite that region's relatively much lower levels of human development. By contrast, all six "high prevalence" states have languages other than Hindi as their official language, other languages are the mother tongue of most inhabitants, and only small minorities report Hindi as their mother tongue.[79] The northeast is home to the highest concentration of scheduled tribes (STs), and it is only in the northeastern states that STs comprise more than 30 percent of the population. Finally, these states are religiously distinctive. Although Christians comprise only 2.9 percent of the national population, Christians are in the majority in Nagaland and one-third of the population in Manipur. In the southern states, Christians are fairly small minorities, but still larger than in the northern states, and they are recognized for being relatively literate, economically privileged, and more culturally tied to the West.

In short, despite the mobility afforded by the transportation links in the country, much Indian political discourse indicates a perception that the Hindi heartland is "immune" to the risk of HIV/AIDS relative to the ethnically distinctive regions where the problem is rife, and for which blame-related information is consistently disseminated. For example, in the northeast the primary mode of HIV transmission is IV drug use, a "vice" that is widely understood in ethno-regional terms. Indian newspapers routinely report on drug use in the northeast, and even the UN Office on

[79]While in some of these states, such as Maharashtra, Hindi is widely understood, the ethnolinguistic identity is distinct, as more than 73 percent of residents claim Marathi as their mother tongue and Marathi is compulsory in state schools. Because my argument is about social identity, not about the possibilities for communication across boundaries, the degree to which Hindi is spoken or understood does not imply weaker boundaries.

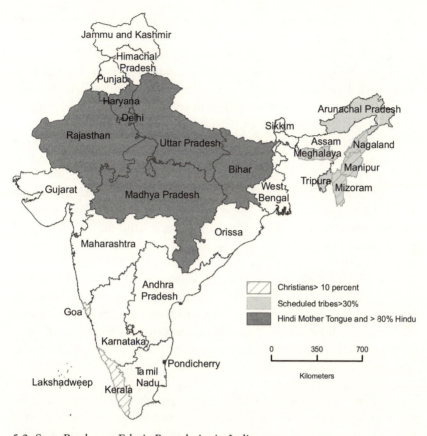

5.2. State Borders as Ethnic Boundaries in India
Source: Table 5.3.

Drugs and Crime has helped to reinforce perceptions of the cultural connection to this behavior, identifying a "tribal population" and "large concentrations of members of the Christian faith" in the region.[80] People in the northeastern states are thought to be more culturally similar to neighboring countries such as Burma, and as a result, consistent reports of high levels of IV drug use in the northeast reinforce this sense of cultural difference.[81] The NACO's own report on a "Tribal Strategy and Implementation

[80] http://www.unodc.org/india/ind_e41.html (consulted January 18, 2007).
[81] See, for example, Patricia Mukhim, "Killing Them Softly," *Telegraph India*, July 26, 2005.

Plan," states, "The Northeast region of the country, especially the states of Manipur, Nagaland and Mizoram have predominantly tribal populations, and high HIV prevalence, fueled by high injected drug use."[82]

For the four southern states, the main mode of transmission has been heterosexual contact, and here as well, ethnic and cultural stereotypes have fueled the idea that HIV infection could be bounded within those states. Sexual behavior is often discussed in terms of states and regions in India, with strong ethnic connotations. For example, an article in the national newspaper, the *Hindu*, reported about the state of Andhra Pradesh in its section on "Southern States," "Promiscuity in State Highest, Says Survey."[83] Similarly, the country director of UNAIDS told me of what he had learned during his stay in the country: "There is much greater promiscuity in the south than in the north." In interviews and more casual conversations with political actors and analysts, individuals provided unprompted explanations of differences in sexual norms in strictly regional terms, attempting to explain away the concentration of (high prevalence) states in the south of the country in cultural terms. In fact, the third National Family Health Survey shows no such regional differences, at least in reported numbers of sexual partners. Nonetheless, the hegemonic perception that the southern states are less socially conservative than the Hindi heartland provides a powerful basis for an ethnic mapping of the epidemic.

Thus, the consistent reporting of HIV prevalence in these six states, provides signals to national political leaders, and in turn to interested citizens, that the epidemic is concentrated among ethnic minorities—"outsiders" from the perspective of the Hindi heartland—constituted in multiple and sometimes overlapping ways. As late as 2005, health minister Anbumani Ramadoss said that "there was no national HIV epidemic in India, but that there are 'sub-national' epidemics in six of the nation's 28 states."[84] This is a revealing political framing for a national leader who could have emphasized the general or "pooled" threat of an infectious disease, but instead chose to highlight boundaries. From this perspective, the Hindi heartland, which contains the largest block of voters and legis-

---

[82] Government of India n.d.

[83] "Promiscuity in State Highest, Says Survey," in "Southern States—Andhra Pradesh" section, *The Hindu*, August 14, 2003.

[84] T. V. Pamda, "Experts Dispute Indian Claims of Huge Drop in HIV Cases," SciDev. net, May 31, 2005, http://www.scidev.net/news/index.cfm?fuseaction=printarticle&itemid =2125&language=1.

lative seats of any region, can perceive itself to be "ethnically" insulated from widespread HIV infection, as the "subnational" epidemics are all outside this region (see figure 5.2). This can be contrasted with Brazil, where although the epidemic was also regionally concentrated, particularly in the early years, it was far less common to use such regional mappings, which in turn allowed AIDS to be imagined as a national epidemic.

In a country with one of the world's largest epidemics, what is striking is the extent to which public and political discourse on AIDS has made it "somebody else's" problem. In "heartland" states such as Uttar Pradesh (UP)—the country's most populous—there is less urgency about the risks of a national epidemic, because the nature of state monitoring and politics have constructed the epidemic as regional. When people have tested positive for the virus in locales of UP, the illness is known in many parts of the state as *Bambaiwallah bimari*, or, "Mumbai's Sickness,"[85] suggesting once again the important tendency to look for blame, rather than to mobilize the threat of contagion as shared. AIDS experts highlighted to me their fears of an explosion of AIDS in places like UP and Bihar, where there has been little surveillance or willingness to believe that the epidemic could take root in their communities.

Beyond the highly bounded identification of the epidemic in terms of space (states and regions), the collection and dissemination of information about infection in India has overwhelmingly focused on occupational "groups"—commercial sex workers (CSWs), and truck drivers. Indeed, such groups have been identified in contexts around the world as vectors of HIV transmission because of their mobility and multiple sexual partners. Nonetheless, in the context of an ethnically divided society, in which there is often a cultural division of labor,[86] these high-risk groups can take on ethnic connotations.

Commercial sex work and truck driving also to a significant degree are occupations that map onto an ethnic division of labor in India. In the crudest terms, both are associated with "low caste" men and women or with particular language and ST groups. There is a long and well-recognized history of women from particular caste origins (usually lower, but not always)

[85] Abhijit Das, "Wake up Call for HIV/AIDS in UP," *India Together*, August 5, 2005, http://www.indiatogether.org/2005/aug/hlt-uphivaids.htm (consulted January 31, 2006). See also Anne-Christine d'Adesky, "India's Generics Play a High-Stakes Game," American Foundation for AIDS Research, June 2002, http://www.aegis.com/pubs/amfar/2002/AM020601.html (consulted January 19, 2007).

[86] Hechter 1978.

being forced into prostitution, caused by both economic and cultural pressures felt by certain ethnic identities. Though scheduled castes and scheduled tribes together comprised only 22.2 percent of the population of Andhra Pradesh (and 24.3 percent of the Indian population) in 1991, a study found that 51.8 percent of that state's street-based female sex workers came from these groups. "Other backward castes" accounted for an additional 36.1 percent of street-based sex workers, for a total of 87.9 percent.[87] These figures are not merely correlates of socioeconomic status, but the outcome of institutionalized practices, whereby caste groups in certain locations maintain commercial sex work as a "cultural" practice.

For example, well entrenched in many parts of India, particularly southern India, is the "Devadasi" system, in which young women of low caste are "married off" to gods and goddesses, and expected to have multiple sexual partners in their lifetimes, and to "collect alms," practices that eventually are realized as commercial sex work. According to some accounts, the system was invented by an upper-caste ruling elite to have access to lower-caste women.[88] The institution is prevalent in Maharashtra state, initially ground zero for the AIDS epidemic, and one of the high-prevalence states, along with Karnataka and Andhra Pradesh, where the Devadasi system is also important. The government, while claiming to be acting to eradicate the system, may actually reinforce it, by providing pensions after the age of forty to women who have engaged in such practice.[89] According to one scholarly analysis of the Devadasis in Karnataka, "Since the advent of HIV/AIDS they have been identified as central players in a complex of contagion as both the cause of, and cure for, disease spread."[90]

Other caste groups in other localities—for example, Bedias (mostly from Rajasthan)—are often understood to promote prostitution as a basis for female livelihood from a young age: "The Bedias are regarded as a 'warrior' caste, which initially took to prostitution, hunting and illicit brewing after suffering a series of military defeats in earlier times. It is said that to a member of the warrior caste, robbery or prostitution is preferable

---

[87] Dandona et al. 2006, 4. The study comprised 6,648 confidential interviews with sex workers in thirteen districts.

[88] Shaikh Azizur Rahman, "Caste Away," *South China Morning Post,* October 23, 2007.

[89] Based on interviews with Professor Sadhana Zadbuke, an activist working in Kolhapur, as reported in Neil Pate, "State Govt under Fire over Devdasi System," *Times of India,* December 11, 2001.

[90] Orchard 2007, 2380.

to manual labour."[91] Again, it is important to recognize here that it is caste boundaries, and not merely being at the bottom of a socioeconomic ladder, that affect the likelihood of entering into commercial sex work.

Beyond caste, commercial sex work is associated with particular ethno-linguistic identities. For example, in Maharashtra state, individuals indicated that the commercial sex trade was populated largely by "Bengalis," and girls trafficked from "Nepal"—often a coded reference for people with Mongoloid features, who are from the northeastern states. In Goa, one AIDS researcher hypothesized that the bulldozing of a red-light district might have been inspired by the government's "anti-migrant ideology," because "most CSW's had migrated from other states—e.g., Karnataka and Andhara Pradesh."[92] Amid such perceptions, the prospects for solidarity around social problems, especially ones like HIV, are constrained.

Although I have not found as much evidence directly linking truck drivers to particular castes, trucking is an occupation accorded relatively low status in Indian society, and media accounts routinely identify truck drivers as members of lower castes.[93] In one study conducted in Chennai, of three hundred truckers identified for a survey at locations frequented by such drivers, 41 percent were from "lower" castes, 53 percent from "middle castes," and only 7 percent from "upper castes."[94] Almost by definition, truckers appear in the Indian context as people from "somewhere else." In fact, commercial sex work and trucking are understood in India as markers of migrancy—people from other states and sometimes other countries. Given the strong link between space and ethnic identity in the Indian ethno-federation, these jobs are doubly understood as occupied by ethnic outsiders.

A striking indication of the commonsense notion that almost all groups in society perceive themselves to be safe from infection can be found in a public service announcement from the Heroes Project—an organization largely dedicated to media campaigns about the AIDS epidemic, funded largely by foreign luminaries such as the American actor Richard Gere and American foundations. One commercial, produced by a local media organization, portrays three men, contextualized to represent three different

[91] Sudeshna Banerjee, "Reform Slow for Bedia Sex Workers, Say Experts," Inter Press Service, August 22, 2002.

[92] Shahmanesh and Wayal 2004, 1298.

[93] See for example, the reference to a trucker as a "Dalit," in "Lovers End Life over Caste Hurdle," *The Telegraph*, May 31, 2005.

[94] Bryan, Fisher, and Benziger 2001, 1416.

class identities—upper, middle, and lower—each of whom is asked about HIV/AIDS. The upper-class man responds, "HIV/AIDS?—no, that is a problem among the lower and middle classes." Each of the other men likewise identifies the classes of which he is not a member. As in South Africa, all groups emphasize that the virus exists among others. When I asked the executive director of the Heroes Project what "class" meant in India, she described the caste system—highlighting both the role of *varna* and of *jati*, though I had not given her any indication of interest in these links. The exchange confirmed that indeed, when Indians describe the class basis of the epidemic, they have in mind the less mutable and tradition-bound notion of caste. The executive director explained the standard mind-set of the Indian population: "People think, 'They deserve it. . . . Normal people like us don't believe it will happen to us. It is them.'"

To be clear, I am not attempting to prove that HIV is in fact disproportionately concentrated among particular castes, religions, language groups, or scheduled tribes. This may be true, but we lack the epidemiological data required to draw such conclusions. My point is simply that Indians and outsiders involved in AIDS-related work, as well as those who work with ethnic minorities, are routinely making these connections, and when it comes to politics, generalized perceptions are far more determinative of policy preferences and policy-related behavior. The nature of surveillance and both official and casual discussion of the epidemic provide readily accessible mental maps about the ethnic distribution of the epidemic.

Conflict over, and Resistance to, Aggressive Policies

According to the theory of boundary politics, when the epidemic is framed in ethnically fragmented terms, it should map onto preexisting ethnic conflicts, leading some groups to make accusations of blame, emphasizing moral deficiencies of "infected" groups as the basis for their illness. Strong boundaries will also lead other groups to avoid being associated with the virus to escape shame and reputational costs, even if those groups may stand to benefit from action on the epidemic. Indeed, such discourses of blame and shame-avoidance have been evident throughout the history of the AIDS epidemic in India. If the politics of AIDS in Brazil are remarkable for "social solidarity," the Indian case has been virtually the opposite.

Stigma and discrimination have been global properties of the AIDS epidemic, but such sentiment has been extreme in India. For example, in the 1990 World Values Survey, a staggering 91.6 percent of Indians indicated they would not like to have someone with AIDS as a neighbor, making it the least accepting of all countries surveyed. By the 1995–97 survey, the figure had dropped to 60 percent, but this was still far above average. Looking more closely at reported manifestations of such stigmatization and prejudice, I have found examples of negative references to people with HIV in connection to additional ethnic identities; as well as negative references in which the manner of social interaction was patterned on preexisting conflicts, especially in terms of caste relations, and the metaphor of "untouchability."

Even in academic research produced in India one can find disparaging references to ethnic groups, identifying them in terms of blame and risk for HIV infection. For example, an abstract from the 2006 International AIDS Conference explains:

Most of the sex seller Women in Rajasthan are from nomadic tribes. The Bediyas, the Kanzars, the Bheels, the Gadia Lohars, the Rajnats are main among them. . . . Since neither they had got no land for cultivation nor any job to do, the women of these communities adopted prostitution. The increasing number of the clients of these tribal prostitutes is alarming, especially the category of truck drivers, tourists and middle class crazy youth. During a survey conducted by GBS (Gram Bharati Samiti) 2 facts have come out—absolute illiteracy and ignorance about the knowledge of HIV infection as well as use of condom among them.[95]

Researchers have initiated studies of HIV prevalence, knowledge, and risk-related behaviors among STs. One such study, conducted with 113 respondents in a "Migrant Tribal Slum Community" in the state of Orissa concluded:

In this migrant tribal community, the majority of women are sexually active at an early age. . . . A considerable prevalence of pre- and extramarital sex among married and unmarried respondents is reported, in addition to unsafe sexual practices including not using condoms.

[95] K. Jain. "Tribal Sex Seller Women & HIV/AIDS Infection in India," abstract from the International AIDS Conference, 1994, August 7–12, abstract number PD0126.

Knowledge of using condoms and of the prevention, cure and cause of HIV is very poor. *A low risk perception and negative attitude towards AIDS are also reported.*[96]

Of note is the extent to which those infected with HIV/AIDS have been described as the country's "new untouchables."[97] This is a label that persists (at least in the English-language press read by elites and policymakers), and it also seems to reflect the treatment of those who are "discovered" to be infected. The same insulating strategies used to maintain social distance between castes are used with those thought to be infected with HIV. Reporting on the plight of individuals afflicted with HIV/AIDS, the *Times of India* featured a woman from Ahmedabad, who said that she and her husband—both HIV-positive—were called "untouchables" by his family as they were thrown out of the house. A different patient also reported being treated like "an untouchable."[98] In her reporting on AIDS in southern India, Anne-Christine D'Adesky found that "a number of HIV-positive female sex workers I met identified themselves as 'untouchables,'"[99] though it is not clear whether this identity was recognized at birth, acquired through sex work, or through HIV status. Clearly, this stigmatized label was the product of the country's strong ethnic boundaries, and its use in the country's political discourse links the ethnic group to the epidemic.

When the head of Kerala's state AIDS agency went to New Delhi for the first-ever national forum on the disease in 2000, he said a local politician who saw HIV-positive activists serving themselves lunch from a buffet refused to eat the same food.[100] It is worth noting that even in Kerala, with the highest rates of literacy in the country, and with the greatest awareness of HIV/AIDS, discrimination is still widespread; schoolchildren have been denied admission because of their HIV status. Moreover, CSWs and truckers are often treated in a manner that smacks of (illegal) caste discrimination. For example, in the small town of Nippani, which lies on the border of Maharasthra-Karnataka in western India, town offi-

[96] Mishra et al. 2008, abstract; emphasis added.

[97] John F. Burns, "A Wretched New Class of Infected Untouchables," *New York Times*, September 22, 1996, 10.

[98] Prathima Nandakumar and Radha Sharma, "Society's New Untouchables," *Times of India*, February 9, 2004.

[99] D'Adesky 2004, 46.

[100] Joanna Slater, "In India, Stigma of AIDS Curbs Control of HIV," *Wall Street Journal*, June 2, 2001.

cials told prostitutes who wished to organize and to meet that they should "use a side road formerly reserved for untouchables."[101] In a study of AIDS-related stigma, researchers found that hospital staff in Bangalore routinely identified truck drivers and sex workers

> as the major sources of HIV transmission in their city or state, labeling them as "bad" men or women with "dirty" habits, who were "not satisfied with what they have at home." The poor, the slum-dwellers, and the illiterate were commonly believed to be "AIDS infected" in larger proportions than the rest of the population. The migrant population from neighbouring states was targeted even more frequently.[102]

Consistent with the theory of boundary politics, ethnic "blaming" is not always associated with the most socioeconomically depressed ethnic groups. For example, in Chochi, a village inhabited almost entirely by members of the Jat caste, a relatively prominent group, the confirmed AIDS-related death of a single individual in April 1997 led to the ostracization of the entire village by surrounding villages, including prohibitions against trading and marriages. A village headman from Chochi said that he "was shocked by local newspaper reports that described Chochi as an 'AIDS village,' implying also that its inhabitants are somehow promiscuous."[103] During the national elections in 1998, in that same village just sixty-five kilometers from the national capital, and traditionally frequented by campaigners, national government leaders refused to come to the town to eat or to stay in the house of the village headman. Such behaviors were readily understood as familiar displays of caste superiority and concerns about "pollution"[104]—a remarkable turn for a group often in caste conflict with Dalits in the region.

In a toolkit developed by international and local NGOs working to address the stigma of HIV/AIDS, a training module entitled "Sex, Moral-

---

[101] According to an NGO leader, as reported in Meena Menon, "Small Town's Sex Workers Put Up Big Fight," Inter Press Service, March 5, 2002. See also UNESCO 2002.

[102] Bharat, Aggleton, and Tyrer 2001, 50–51.

[103] Ranjit Devraj, "HIV Creates New Untouchables in India," Inter Press Service, July 8, 1997.

[104] Ranjit Devraj, "Election Fever Bypasses 'HIV Village,'" Inter Press Service, March 1, 1998.

ity, Shame and Blame"[105] provided "occupational cards" to get people to lay bare their assumptions and prejudices. People were asked to identify the person in a picture and to answer questions: "How would you or the community judge this person (high blame, low blame or no blame)? Why?"; "What risk does this person have of getting HIV (high risk, low risk or no risk)? Why?"

Among the sample answers were "Occupation: Sweeper"; "Blame: High"; "Risk: High." (Why?) "Dalit—no respect. Cleans toilets—dirty; HIV Risk: High. Sex with many partners." Another example: "Occupation: Barber"; "Blame: High." (Why?) "Low caste—Low respect; seen as dirty profession. Cleans toilets—dirty"; "HIV Risk: Low. However, uses same knife for everyone so could help to spread HIV."

In a message to facilitators, the authors of the toolkit wrote, "Double stigma: Some groups of people are already stigmatized for coming from a certain caste, e.g., sweepers, fishermen, rickshaw pullers, agricultural laborers. These groups face double stigma if they are assumed to be promiscuous."

Beyond the underestimation of risks by those presumed to be less directly affected by the virus, the theory of boundary politics predicts that under the conditions of ethnic conflict, groups will reject being targeted in AIDS campaigns. Such responses are indeed understandable in societies where groups are aware of the pain associated with group-based discrimination, but they have the effect of stalling aggressive AIDS policy. As discussed earlier, this had been the case in the United States,[106] and also in South Africa. The notion that AIDS policy might be weak because the most vulnerable groups are politically weak simply does not hold here. In fact, as mentioned earlier, there are ample caste-based parties and other organizations representing such groups, and if politics were merely the raw pursuit of welfare-enhancing goods, absent concerns about status or reputation, one would predict the appearance of advocates for AIDS-related policies and resources that would benefit their groups. But just the opposite has been the case: these organizations have been mostly silent on the problem of AIDS, and when groups have been targeted by outsiders, they have rejected those initiatives to avoid the stigma of being associated with the virus.

---

[105] Kidd, Ross, Sue Clay, and Chipo Chiiya, *Understanding and Challenging HIV Stigma: Toolkit for Action*, International HIV/AIDS Alliance, Academy for Educational Development, International Center for Research on Women, 2007, module C4, 107.

[106] As described by Cohen 1999.

While such linking of caste politics to AIDS politics and policy has been rare in analyses of the Indian case, it is not fully exceptional. For example, one scholar observed that "caste continues to play a role in how the state crafts certain public policy decisions. Caste is still an identifying characteristic among communities within civil society, as well. With such a system in place, those with HIV neatly fill a role that was reserved for people once also believed to be sick, unclean, and beyond redemption. These societal shackles inhibit people with HIV from mobilizing and place limitations on how they express themselves."[107] A different analyst arrived at a similar conclusion: "Vulnerable groups: women, lower castes, and marginal populations—are so afraid of the consequences of raising the AIDS issue that they will not take measures to protect themselves lest they are accused of immorality or of spreading the virus themselves."[108] One development organization that estimated Devadasis had an HIV prevalence of 9 percent in rural Belgaum (in Karnataka) decided to retreat from a plan to target Devadasi women "after learning that people in the area were already accusing them of spreading AIDS." Representatives of the organization were concerned that the program "would only brand them further as outcasts."[109] While the organization would adopt a more "inclusive" approach to HIV education, the episode revealed the challenges of addressing the epidemic in a context with strong social boundaries: The existence of boundaries induces policy activists to target groups, but for stigmatized problems, members of those groups actively resist such targeting.

Throughout India, leaders representing ethnic groups have complained that news of the epidemic has been inflated with respect to their own group. For example, *Dalit Voice*, a Bangalore-based journal advocating Dalit interests, has posted on its website an article, "Debate on AIDS: A White Man's Conspiracy to Finish Blacks?" The article begins with the line, "AIDS is the greatest myth of our times,"[110] and the website hosts other articles supporting the "dissident" perspective on AIDS. In the February 16–28, 2005 edition, the journal commented, "Our fears that the AIDS disease being a White Western racist conspiracy against Blacks and India's Black Untouchables are shared by a large number of peoples all

---

[107] Krishnan 2003, 814.

[108] Mitra 2004, 61.

[109] Margaret Dadian, "Women's Forum: Inclusive Prevention Efforts Fight Stigma in Rural India," Family Health International 2008.

[110] http://www.dalitvoice.org/Templates/august2004/article3.htm (consulted January 18, 2007).

over the world."[111] More moderate Dalit organizations have simply been silent on the issue despite the easy claims they could make, that they are disproportionately vulnerable to the epidemic.

Indeed, strong ethnic boundaries are also associated with a moral conservatism, as social identity theory predicts members of groups will attempt to demonstrate their moral standing. Such dynamics can be observed in Dalit politics, with important implications for HIV/AIDS. For example, in December 2005, two militant Dalit organizations, the Dalit Panthers of India and the Pattali Makkal Katchi protested against statements made by a famous actress, Kushboo, in a Tamil magazine, in which she "made a plea for safe sex and against placing a cultural premium on women's virginity at the time of marriage."[112] Ironically, even as North Indians often claim higher levels of sexual promiscuity in the south, these Tamil nationalist organizations, led by Dalits, would present Kushboo "to the Tamil public as a north Indian woman whose actions and ideas are alien to the so-called Tamil notions of sexual morality."[113] By rejecting safe sex messages as part of an identity-based political campaign, these organizations created disincentives for policymakers to be more aggressive on AIDS.

Because of the obvious ethnic boundaries in India, many AIDS-related actors assumed that ethnic targeting would be an efficient and culturally sensitive strategy, but in practice, it exacerbated social identity competition. In 2001, for example, UNICEF created an uproar by sponsoring a report on "Caste-Based Prostitution in Madhya Pradesh." The explicit linking of an ethnic identity to a social practice that could reinforce stigmatization generated strong reactions. The Bedia community "demanded withdrawal of the report as one which tended to make its members the object of suspicion and exacerbated caste discrimination." AIDS workers were harassed for highlighting sexual practices in the community that led to higher risk of contracting HIV.[114]

Similarly, in Uttar Pradesh in 2000 four AIDS activists were jailed for their publication of a Macarthur Foundation–funded study on the risk factors and behaviors associated with increasing HIV prevalence. Mobs attacked the NGO Sahyog, which produced the report making references to

---

[111] http://www.dalitvoice.org/Templates/feb_a2005/reports.htm (consulted January 18, 2007).

[112] Anandhi 2005, 4876.

[113] Anandhi 2005, 4876.

[114] Ranjit Devraj, "Anger Grows at UNICEF-Funded HIV/AIDS Study," Inter Press Service, May 28, 2001.

polyandrous practices, for "the portrayal of the inhabitants of the region as promiscuous and prone to high-risk behaviour."[115] Indeed, what is particularly relevant is the degree to which shame and blame emerged as more important to the local community than the fear of widespread infection. Given the experience of the Chochi village described above, it is understandable that a town might want not to be recognized as a home to people infected with the virus that causes AIDS.

In a society as ethnically divided as India, in which group esteem is highly sensitive to insults to the moral "value" of particular groups, attempts to deliver standardized AIDS prevention messages easily give offense. In UP, HIV/AIDS campaigns sponsored by UNICEF with the state AIDS control society were perceived as insensitive, and local civil society organizations convinced these organizations to halt their campaigns.[116] Meanwhile, AIDS workers from NGOs have been arrested in Lucknow and other parts of UP by local police for "obscene" materials and for "promoting homosexual culture." It is extraordinarily difficult for any authority to penetrate the Hindi heartland with policies that might put a spotlight on "risky" behaviors or even susceptibility to HIV and AIDS.

Many committed AIDS activists within India and abroad have recognized such conflicts over AIDS, and have tried to identify unifying campaigns. A strategy used around the world to generate consensus on HIV/AIDS has been to bring in publicly appealing figures as spokespersons. But in India no major public figure with HIV has stepped forward as a "face" for HIV/AIDS. Film stars—revered in India to a degree almost without parallel—have begun to speak out about the problem of HIV/AIDS, but there has often been an adverse response on the part of the public, who view such individuals as role models, who ought not to be speaking of HIV/AIDS. Indeed, many Indians have reiterated the idea that the country needs a Rock Hudson to support the idea that AIDS can affect everyone. Richard Gere, the well-known American film star, has long been involved with Indian culture and society and has tried to promote AIDS awareness through his own efforts and through media initiatives, including partnerships with the Kaiser Foundation and MTV Networks. And yet the receptivity of Indian film stars to such campaigns has been decidedly mixed. The Gates Foundation provided over $250 million of funding to produce AIDS-

---

[115] Kumar 2000; see also Sudeshna Banerjee, "Hill Women Caught between Poverty, Risk of HIV/AIDS," Inter Press Service, July 18, 2002.

[116] Abhijit Das, "Wake Up Call for HIV/AIDS in UP," *India Together*, August 5, 2005, http://www.indiatogether.org/2005/aug/hlt-uphivaids.htm (consulted January 31, 2006).

related films over a five-year period, but the acclaimed director Mira Nair said in January 2007 that she was unable to attract A-list Bollywood actors for the project: "Lots of actors don't want to be associated with the virus."[117] I have no data that would allow me to infer the degree to which such celebrity resistance has been based on ethnic calculation. But their resistance clearly reveals a general *absence* of solidarity around AIDS of the type that has been evident in Brazil and in many other countries.

Policymakers: Minimizing and Externalizing the Problem

So far, I have argued that the relatively weak policy response to AIDS can be understood from the relatively weak demand, caused at least in part, by the dynamics of ethnic boundary politics. But we can also look at the supply side, from the policymakers themselves. The evidence presented above suggests why being aggressive on AIDS might hurt rather than help politicians. Groups that might think of themselves as low risk see little need to spend resources on AIDS because they believe themselves to be insulated; while those labeled high risk often resist being targeted. I believe that Indian political leaders have treaded lightly on AIDS because this calculation has been obvious to them. It is not simply the case, as some have argued for other public goods, that particularistic and patronage policies have crowded out these policies.

It is never easy to know exactly which drives any policymaker. They themselves may not know, or they may be reluctant to say their calculations publicly. For the most part, when contemporary politicians are interviewed by a Western investigator, virtually all say that AIDS is extremely important, and the rest point to the prevalence of other more pressing problems in the country as reasons for inaction. They are not likely to openly concede reluctance to advance AIDS policy because of fear of a backlash among constituents. Nonetheless, there is evidence that high-level political leaders have reinforced the sense of insulation from risk of infection throughout the epidemic, and this demands explanation, given unprecedented offers of external assistance. This has not been merely a case of doing little for a big problem, but a case of leaders actively countering the idea that a problem exists. Why would they be so adamant?

[117] Reuters, "Bollywood Plots AIDS Message Despite Stars' Apathy," January 22, 2007.

When faced with evidence about growing infections, Indian leaders have revealed commonsense views about the integrity and importance of boundaries that distinguish social groups from one another. Those in government have tried to avoid the minefield of ethnic challenges to potentially stigmatizing AIDS policy. By contrast, foreign leaders who have been less politically sensitive to these ethnic constituencies have walked into the minefields. I do not claim that all examples of Indian "denialism" can be attributed to the effect of internal boundary politics on risk perception and status conflict, but they certainly emerge as important.

From the onset of the epidemic, Indian leaders emphasized the foreignness of the virus. Just as many North Americans came to see HIV/AIDS as a black/African/Haitian disease, and as many Africans initially viewed it as a "white" or European disease, images of a Western and African epidemic have been used to suggest an insulation from risk for Indians. Again, while there has been an almost universal tendency to understand the HIV/AIDS epidemic, at least initially, as a foreign epidemic, Indian policymakers and political leaders have gone to extremes to further this idea.

For example, in 1988, A. S. Paintal, the government's chief medical research official. announced as a strategy that Indians should avoid having sexual relations with foreigners.[118] According to Dr. Gheeta Bhave, who in 1990 was heading the country's small AIDS surveillance unit,

> AIDS is still seen here as a disease of the poor, the illiterate, the prostitutes and the deviants. The bureaucrats still don't think this is their disease. It is not a problem of the ministries or their politicians or their bureaucrats. . . . We get samples from the so-called five-star hospitals all the time, and many are positive . . . so it has definitely already reached the ruling-class level of our society. But even then, it's all just pushed under the rug. In India, nobody accepts openly that this promiscuous sex is going on. Of course it is going on, but no one will talk about it. So for them, it doesn't exist. And neither does AIDS.[119]

Throughout the 1990s, many Indian politicians and other opinion makers did not allocate significant resources to AIDS, and in particular,

---

[118] Sanjoy Hazarika, "To Fight AIDS, Indian Urges Ban on Sex with Foreigners," *New York Times*, June 15, 1988.

[119] Mark Fineman, "Superstition, Poverty May Bring AIDS Crisis in India," *Los Angeles Times*, May 28, 1990.

nationalists have been "reluctant to acknowledge that India could become the focus of a disease linked to sexual practices and drug use."[120]

While it is not surprising that such sentiments existed early in the epidemic, it is more shocking how notions of foreignness have persisted quite late in the epidemic. In 2001, Dr A. N. Malviya, of the respected All-India Institute of Medical Science, said that India was unlikely to follow the African model because Indians were of "a higher moral order."[121] Responding to my questions in an interview in January 2006, Deepak Gupta, Additional Secretary in the Ministry of Health, explained, "AIDS is still seen as an African disease."

In addition to comparisons made with Brazil, it is also useful here to highlight contrasts with Thailand—a case that was far more like Brazil, as a society with much weaker internal ethnic boundaries, and also produced one of the world's most aggressive responses. Initially, most popular and official interpretations of HIV in Thailand emphasized that it was a "foreign" disease. However, as early as 1987, a prison guard named Cha-on Suesem, who had been infected with HIV, spoke out in media outlets about the nature of the disease, and became a symbol that this could happen to "anyone." Moreover, the revelation that large numbers of CSWs were infected became a social fact that was recognized as potentially affecting Thai men throughout the country. In turn, the government adopted the most aggressive response in Asia.[122] The contrast with India is stark, because Thailand reveals that in the *absence* of strong ethnic boundaries, even quite limited information about the infection of certain occupational groups could be interpreted as nationally threatening, and warrant a response on that scale.

While the Indian response has never been characterized with the same consternation as the "denialist" stance of South African leaders, architects of the Geneva Consensus have expressed frustration with both countries. The executive director of the GFATM, Richard Feachem, said in 2003, "There is a fairly widespread view among educated people and opinion leaders in India that HIV-AIDS is primarily an African problem and that Hindu and Muslim culture will protect India from the most serious consequences of the virus. . . . There has been a resort to the mythology of

---

[120] John F. Burns, "The AIDS Highway: Denial and Taboos Blinding India to the Horror of Its AIDS Scourge," *New York Times*, September 22, 1996, 1.

[121] Angus Donald, "India Slow to Wake Up to Reality of Aids," *Financial Times*, June 2, 2001, 7.

[122] This account draws from AIDSCAP 1996.

cultural immunity—it can't happen to us because we're different. . . . I found on my visit a persistent tendency to minimize the current scale of the epidemic and the potential future growth."[123] In 2006, Richard Holbrooke, former U.S. Ambassador to the UN and current head of the Global Business Coalition on HIV/AIDS, has said of the country's political and business leaders, "The Indians will tell you over and over again that what happened in Africa can't happen in India. And that's just bull."[124]

As in South Africa, Indian political leaders have rejected the attempts of such international actors to press them on AIDS. Sanjay Nirupam, a member of the Hindu nationalist Shiv Sena party in Mumbai, said in 2004, "One always hears about AIDS and how it's this big problem. But I have personally never come across anyone with AIDS or seen anyone dying due to AIDS-related illnesses. I think it's just hype."[125]

Of particular relevance for the theory being discussed here, in 2001 India's health minister, C. P. Thakur, challenged external estimates by highlighting the role of boundaries for understanding the AIDS epidemic. "In the Indian context it is difficult to estimate the exact prevalence of HIV because of the varied cultural characteristics, traditions and values with special reference to sex-related risk behaviours."[126] In other words, rather than trying to imagine the AIDS epidemic as a single national phenomenon, it was for him natural to think about separate subgroups, whose behaviors and ramifications would be rather insulated from one another. This was a switch from a strategy denying the existence of a problem for all Indians, but in the face of mounting reports of widespread infection, this comment tacitly acknowledged the preferred view that AIDS is a boundary-sensitive phenomenon, and that a national strategy might not be possible.

The claim that India's slow response to AIDS is due to the prevalence of more pressing problems seems to wither in the face of the repudiation of foreigners for attempting to provide resources on AIDS. For example, former U.S. president Bill Clinton, whose foundation is a major supporter of AIDS initiatives around the world, was accused by Hindu nationalist leaders of promoting the interests of multinational corporations when speaking

[123] John Lancaster, "Indian Leaders Accused of Downplaying HIV," *San Francisco Chronicle*, June 13, 2003.

[124] Bruce Einhorn, "AIDS in India: A Case of Denial," *Business Week*, February 1, 2006.

[125] Sanjoy Majumder, "Ignorance Hinders India's HIV/AIDS Campaign," You and AIDS, http://www.youandaids.org/Features/India2August2004.asp (consulted November 10, 2006).

[126] Ranjit Devraj, "Anger Grows at UNICEF-funded HIV/AIDS Study," Inter Press Service, May 28, 2001.

out about HIV/AIDS in India.[127] Similarly, Richard Feachem and Bill Gates have been strongly criticized—again mostly by Hindu nationalists—for their efforts to address HIV/AIDS in India. In 2002, health minister Shatrughan Sinha accused Gates, who was providing a $100 million donation, of spreading "fear" and "false propaganda."[128]

Feachem also found himself in hot water when he stated at a Paris conference that he expected the epidemic to grow faster among Hindus than among Muslims because of the custom of male circumcision in the latter group (there are strong scientific findings showing that circumcision reduces rates of transmission). BJP's Singhal commented angrily, "This is obnoxious. Has there been any study done on the spread of HIV/AIDS in the different religious communities in India? Anyway we are not going to tolerate such remarks made against Hindus." Other pro-Hindu organizations responded in turn, resolving to demonstrate outside the offices of UNAIDS until "Feachem came to India and apologized publicly and unconditionally to all Hindus."[129] All of this was ironic given that there has been almost no public discourse on Hindu-Muslim disparities in HIV prevalence. But the episode did highlight the social identity conflicts that can erupt on the basis of little in the way of objective disparities.

Explaining Policy Variation across Indian States

Beyond the national story, in which India is a case of strong ethnic boundaries and weak AIDS policy, we can test additional implications of the theory by analyzing within-country variation on these factors. While state governments in India and the respective state AIDS control societies are largely dependent on the center for resources and administrative direction, they also enjoy some autonomy in the execution of the government's AIDS plans. More generally, health is a responsibility of state governments under the Indian constitution. As the director of the National AIDS Control Program described to me, more entrepreneurial states can

[127] "Clinton Creating AIDS Panic: Govindacharya," Press Trust of India, June 1, 2005.

[128] Ranjit Devraj, "Important Partnership, but Regarded with Suspicion Because of Foreigners, India Looks Askance at Bill Gates' HIV/AIDS Grant," Inter Press Service, November 11, 2002.

[129] Ranjit Devraj, "HIV/AIDS Campaigns Turning Communal, Say Hindu Leaders," Inter Press Service, May 19, 2005.

do more and can be more expansive in their implementation of the Geneva Consensus, while truly reluctant states can drag their feet on hiring staff and implementing policy. The possibility for such within-country variation in policy invites further investigation. While it is true that all states in India exist in a nationwide sociopolitical environment characterized by strong boundaries, there are differences in the extent to which the ethnic cleavages have been mobilized in the different states. By using measures of ethnic demographics, and interethnic attitudes and conflicts from the 1980s and 1990s, we can estimate the effects of ethnic boundaries on AIDS policies. In particular, I consider the effects of caste boundaries, which are politically relevant at more localized levels of politics and government in India, and which have already been shown to be relevant in the framing of the risks associated with HIV/AIDS.

To carry out this analysis, I compiled a cross-sectional, state-level statistical dataset of social and economic variables as well as AIDS policy indicators, which I joined to the ethnic demographic data presented in table 5.3. In addition to measures of the size of the scheduled caste population in each state, I drew upon survey-based attitudinal data on interethnic contact. The 2004 Indian National Election Study surveyed 27,189 citizens, stratified across states, and asked questions about ethnic boundaries.[130] Of particular interest, it asked people to respond to the statement: "Marriage of boys and girls from *different castes* should be banned." Nationally, 48.6 percent of respondents "fully" or "somewhat" agreed with the statement, which is a striking finding of the extent to which Indians favor endogamy. As shown in figure 5.3, there is substantial variation across Indian states—for example, ranging from a low of 20.2 percent of citizens agreeing with the statement about caste boundaries in Arunachal Pradesh to a high of 69 and 70 percent in Rajastahn and Gujarat, respectively.[131]

In order to estimate the effect of these ethnic variables on government AIDS policy, I considered four measures of AIDS policy (see table 5.4): per capita expenditure on AIDS by state for the period 2000–2004, the number of PMTCT and VCT sites per million people created under the

---

[130] Centre for the Study of Developing Societies, National Election Study (India) 2004.

[131] Using data from the 1995 World Values Survey, it is possible to calculate the share of the state population indicating that they would not like someone from a different caste as a neighbor for fourteen states. These statistics are correlated with the NES data at $r = .53$. Gujarat scored much higher in terms of anticaste sentiment on the later survey, Andhra lower.

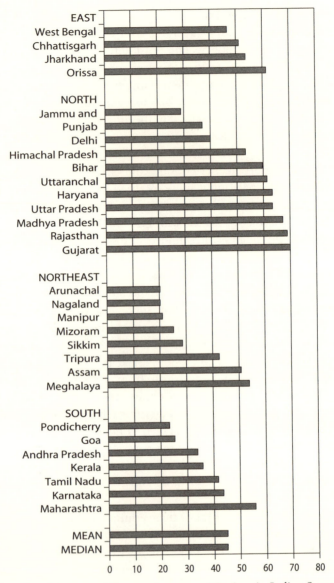

5.3. State-Level Support of Bans on Intercaste Marriage in Indian States
Source: Survey data from India 2004 National Election Study (N = 27,189); percentage of respondents saying "Fully Agree," or "Somewhat Agree"; stratified random sampling was carried out at the state level with samples sufficiently large to make cross-state comparisons. Further details on the sampling strategies employed are available at http://www.ceri-sciencespo.com/archive/sept04/methodo.pdf.

TABLE 5.4
AIDS-Related and Social Indicators in Indian States

	HIV prevalence 2000 (%)	GDP per capita 2000–2001	Female literacy 2001 (%)	AIDS expenditures per capita 2000–2004	PMTCT centers / million people 2005	VCT centers / million people 2005	% aware AIDS is sexually transmitted 2002
East							
Chhattisgarh			42.40			0.77	
Jharkhand			39.38			0.45	
Orissa	0.11	$189.93	50.97	$0.07	0.08	0.54	61.5
West Bengal	0.25	$357.16	60.22	$0.13	0.12	0.34	50.6
North							
Bihar	0.05	$113.51	33.57	$0.05	0.07	0.76	37.5
Delhi	0.36	$863.64	75.00	$0.23	0.73	1.89	85.0
Gujarat	0.32	$427.29	58.60	$0.14	0.20	0.75	52.0
Haryana	0.23	$527.60	56.31	$0.10	0.09	0.95	76.2
Himachal Pradesh		$420.44	68.08	$0.36		1.97	87.7

(continued)

TABLE 5.4 (continued)

	HIV prevalence 2000 (%)	GDP per capita 2000–2001	Female literacy 2001 (%)	AIDS expenditures per capita 2000–2004	PMTCT centers/ million people 2005	VCT centers/ million people 2005	% aware AIDS is sexually transmitted 2002
Jammu and Kashmir	0.09	$275.53	41.82	$0.09		1.09	77.8
Madhya Pradesh	0.25	$240.07	50.28	$0.06	0.03	0.61	51.3
Punjab	0.12	$556.62	63.55	$0.08	0.25	0.70	88.1
Rajasthan	0.12	$266.18	44.34	$0.04	0.11	0.57	57.1
Uttar Pradesh	0.05	$216.02	42.98	$0.06	0.00	0.47	44.8
Uttaranchal			60.26		0.12	1.89	
Northeast							
Arunachal Pradesh	0.23	$324.16	44.24	$0.85	0.00	9.17	69.6
Assam	0.14	$226.62	56.03	$0.15	0.11	0.86	63.2
Manipur	2.27		59.70	$1.64	4.19	9.21	88.8
Meghalaya	0.21	$291.42	60.41	$0.22	0.00	0.43	
Mizoram	0.41		86.13	$2.22	0.00	10.10	
Nagaland	0.48		61.92	$1.76	4.52	21.12	

Sikkim	0.16	$345.56	61.46	$1.41	1.85	5.56	68.9
Tripura	0.22	$318.84	65.41	$0.22	0.00	0.31	
South							
Andhra Pradesh	1.22	$363.84	51.17	$0.21	1.28	2.71	85.1
Goa	1.00	$1,002.33	75.51	$0.55	0.74	2.98	91.3
Karnataka	0.86	$400.91	57.45	$0.15	1.12	2.33	78.0
Kerala	0.28	$467.69	87.86	$0.17	0.16	1.26	97.7
Lakshadweep	0.53						
Maharashtra	0.96	$492.87	67.51	$0.14	0.75	1.30	78.9
Pondicherry	0.32						
Tamil Nadu	0.78	$441.98	64.55	$0.27	2.67	0.90	73.3
Mean	0.46	$396.97	58.18	$0.44	0.77	2.83	71.11
Median	0.26	$357.16	59.70	$0.16	0.12	0.95	74.75

Source: NACO and Government of India via Datanet India 2006.
Note: $US, based on 45 rupees per dollar

NACP through December 2005,[132] and a measure of awareness of AIDS—the percentage of people in each state responding affirmatively to a question on a 2002 survey that AIDS can be transmitted through sexual conduct.[133]

First, I estimated the effects of ethnic boundaries on AIDS expenditures using ordinary least squares (OLS) regression, and the results are reported in table 5.5.[134] I began with a "baseline" model (1), estimating simply the effect of HIV prevalence in 2000 (logged) and the state's level of female literacy as a proxy for level of development. This latter measure has the benefit of capturing existing levels of social development, with better data coverage, and is less strongly correlated with HIV prevalence than per capita income. On average, states with higher levels of female literacy and those with higher prevalence tended to spend more on AIDS policy, as we would expect, but only the estimate of the latter was statistically significant.[135]

The estimates presented in columns 2–5 describe the further impact of forms of ethnic *diversity*. The results are mixed: A higher share of scheduled castes is associated with *lower* levels of AIDS expenditure, while higher levels of linguistic diversity and larger numbers of STs (and these two variables are themselves highly correlated ($r = .83$; $p = .000$) are both associated with *higher* levels of AIDS expenditure. Thus, ethnic diversity per se is not a good predictor of AIDS policies at the state level in India.

However, as presented in column 6, I estimated a model that includes caste *boundaries*—a cleavage of great importance for state-level politics, and also of high salience for HIV/AIDS, and the results indicate solid support for the hypothesis that the strength of ethnic boundaries has a negative effect on the aggressiveness of state-government policies: The larger the share of the population opposing cross-ethnic marriages, the lower the government's expenditure on HIV/AIDS. This result holds up

---

[132] State expenditures under the National AIDS Control Program, released by NACO. Infrastructure data is as of December 2005, a response to Rajya Sabha Unstarred Question No. 2023 dated March 10, 2006, all from Datanet India 2006.

[133] Datanet India 2006.

[134] For the statistical analyses presented in this chapter and in the next, I attempt to follow Achen's (2002) "Rule of Three," by presenting at least one model estimate that contains simply my central explanatory variable and no more than two other regressors.

[135] Similar results are obtained using per capita income. However, the coefficient estimate for HIV prevalence is no longer statistically significant, almost certainly because of high multicollinearity with per capita income, and the loss of cases because of missing data.

TABLE 5.5
OLS Estimates of the Effect of Ethnic Boundaries on AIDS Expenditures in Indian States (2000–2004)

	Dependent variable is logged per capita AIDS expenditure								
	(1)	(2)	(3)	(4)	(5)	(6)	(7)	(8)	(9)
Female literacy	2.483	1.820	1.727	2.600	1.953	0.697	0.679	0.680	0.664
	(1.87)	(1.32)	(1.36)	(1.57)	(1.87)	(1.25)	(0.90)	(0.84)	(0.91)
HIV prev - ln	0.496*	0.335*	0.518***	0.245	0.484*	0.0622	0.0712	0.0507	0.0791
	(0.25)	(0.17)	(0.18)	(0.19)	(0.24)	(0.18)	(0.13)	(0.13)	(0.13)
Scheduled castes/population		−7.999***					−5.808***	−5.376***	−5.930***
		(1.94)					(1.35)	(1.82)	(1.37)
Scheduled tribes/population			2.313***					0.492	
			(0.52)					(0.51)	
Ethnolinguistic fractionalization (ELF)				2.360***					
				(0.62)					

(continued)

TABLE 5.5 (continued)

	Dependent variable is logged per capita AIDS expenditure								
Religious fractionalization					1.987 (1.42)			-1.446 (0.86)	
% favor ban on intercaste marriage						-5.733*** (1.04)	-4.200*** (0.83)	-4.958*** (0.95)	-4.140*** (0.84)
% votes for top two parties									0.691 (0.75)
Constant	-0.125 (2.22)	0.258 (1.57)	-0.0660 (1.61)	-2.807 (1.87)	-0.536 (2.19)	0.978 (1.44)	1.041 (1.05)	1.602 (1.05)	0.627 (1.15)
Observations	24	23	24	20	24	24	23	23	23
R^2	0.35	0.66	0.67	0.66	0.40	0.74	0.86	0.89	0.87

Note: Standard errors in parentheses.
$*p < .1$ $**p < .05$ $***p < .01$

when we control for the size of the scheduled caste population (column 7). When I replace the other measures of ethnic diversity back into the model (column 8), these variables no longer have a substantively or statistically significant relationship with the outcome.

To further check the robustness of the results, I considered the structure of party competition as a potentially important alternative political explanation of state-level variation in the production of public goods in India. One important study found that two-party competition was associated with higher levels of public goods provision across Indian states, arguing that the dynamics of such competition required that parties garner support from many different groups.[136] Using the vote share of the top two parties in elections for state assemblies as of February 2002[137] as a measure of party competition, as reported in column 9 in table 5.5, I confirmed that this relationship is also positively associated with AIDS expenditures, but with relatively large standard errors.

Table 5.6 presents estimates of the effects of ethnic boundaries on the four different AIDS policies using seemingly unrelated regression (SUR),[138] and further confirms that levels of support for bans on intercaste marriage are consistently strong predictors of lower levels of aggressive AIDS policy even though the effects of the other control variables vary across each of the regressions. As one would predict, for example, AIDS awareness is higher in states with higher levels of female literacy; and HIV prevalence is generally associated with more aggressive policies. Most important, the ethnic boundaries variable proves to be the most consistent predictor of AIDS policies.

There is no getting past the fact that these statistical estimates are based on a relatively small number of cases—I am ultimately constrained by the number of Indian states and the fact that time-varying data are not available, but the subnational analysis provides a nicely controlled comparison. Visual inspection of the cases relative to the regression line reveals that no particular outliers are driving the findings. And perhaps most important, the statistical findings resonate with some "thicker" knowledge concerning differences across states, rounding out a convincing case that they are an accurate reflection of the Indian reality.

[136]Chhibber and Nooruddin 2004.

[137]I use Wilkinson's (2004, 143) data, and expand the number of observations from fifteen to twenty-two states by following his procedures and counting the two top party vote shares from the Indian Election Commission Reports available at www.eci.gov.in.

[138]This technique is used to increase the efficiency of the parameter estimates, as I have a system of four equations, using the same independent variables to estimate related dependent variables, which implies that the errors are almost certainly correlated.

TABLE 5.6
SUR Estimates of the Effect of Caste Boundaries on AIDS Policies in Indian States (2000–2005)

	Expenditures/ capita (logged)	VCT centers/ million (logged)	PMTCT centers/ million (logged)	AIDS awareness (% surveyed)
Female literacy	-0.201 (1.32)	-1.629 (1.20)	-2.168 (1.49)	62.82*** (19.2)
HIV prevalence - ln	0.212 (0.17)	0.274* (0.15)	0.860*** (0.19)	5.056** (2.43)
% favor ban on intercaste marriage	**-4.563*** (1.16)**	**-3.759*** (1.06)**	**-4.239*** (1.31)**	**-30.84* (17.0)**
% votes for top two parties	0.994 (0.94)	0.650 (0.85)	1.239 (1.06)	-5.256 (13.7)
Constant	1.037 (1.48)	4.113*** (1.34)	6.315*** (1.66)	81.03*** (21.5)
Observations	18	18	18	18
Pseudo R^2	0.70	0.65	0.80	0.76

Note: Seemingly Unrelated Regression (SUR). Standard errors in parentheses.
* $p < .1$ ** $p < .05$ *** $p < .01$

For example, West Bengal and Tamil Nadu are two of the larger states, and in recent decades, both have been characterized by some of the lowest levels of interethnic conflict.[139] It would surely be an overstatement to claim that these states have been immune to internal ethnic political competition, but during the years when the AIDS epidemic was accelerating in India, West Bengal was notable for the strength of organized labor and Communist Party leadership, which trumped communal divisions, and a collective Tamil identity helped to lessen the political salience of cultural differences in the state. As the theory presented here would predict, these states have also been much stronger in responding to AIDS than other states of similar size, wealth, and epidemic spread. Beyond the reported expenditure levels by the state AIDS control society, the two states are consistently extolled by people inside and outside of India.

First, there is the well-known Sonagachi project, which has successfully mobilized commercial sex workers in Kolkata (formerly Calcutta) in the state of West Bengal.[140] In that city in 1992, Dr. Smarajit Jana initiated a pathbreaking program to work with prostitutes in the Sonagachi district. Although many consider Sonagachi a nongovernment organization, it is important to point out that Jana was deployed to the project by the All India Institute of Hygiene and Public Health, part of the Indian government's Ministry of Health, which has continued to support the project in partnership with local NGOs, foreign funders, and a "collaborative committee" or union of the sex workers themselves.[141] Virtually all accounts of the project have highlighted the remarkable collective organization of the prostitutes, who have managed to enforce the use of condoms and more generally to campaign for the rights of commercial sex workers. Other

[139] On West Bengal, and an historical explanation for the weakness of caste boundaries in that state, see Kohli 1990b, 375, 395–403; on Tamil Nadu, see Kohli 1998, 18–20; and Singh 2008.

[140] Kohli's (1987) comparative analysis of West Bengal, Karnataka, and Uttar Pradesh found the highest level of redistributive policy in West Bengal, owing to the coherency of its well-institutionalized social democratic Communist Party. Drèze and Sen (1995, 195) similarly identify achievements in West Bengal for social issues as the result of "effective organization of disadvantaged groups under the leadership of the 'left front' parties." While these arguments are distinctive, they are not contradictory to mine in the sense that social democratic/leftist parties can be agents for reducing the salience of ethnic boundaries, and I claim that this is the mechanism through which it was possible for political leaders to act more aggressively on AIDS.

[141] Paroma Basu, "Giving AIDS the Red Light," *Village Voice*, September 18, 2002; Celia W. Dugger, "Fighting Back in India: Calcutta's Prostitutes Lead the Fight on AIDS," *New York Times*, January 4, 1999, A1.

projects have been inspired by the success of this one, including the establishment in 2001 of a city counseling center in downtown Kolkata.[142]

A second important example of aggressive action on AIDS is the overall response of the Tamil Nadu State AIDS Control Society, particularly in the capital city of Chennai.[143] The very idea for state AIDS control societies was pioneered in that state, where committed physicians and activists, such as Sunithi Solomon, who diagnosed the first AIDS case in the country and founded the NGO, YRG Cares, acted to circumvent the red tape of the Indian national bureaucracy. Almost everyone familiar with India will point to the exceptional willingness of leaders in that state to be aggressive in rolling out prevention programs. The development of the state AIDS control societies allowed that state, and eventually others, to partner more directly with international organizations and funding agencies such as the World Bank and the Gates Foundation. It was the first state to introduce AIDS education in high schools, the first to set up an information hotline; and its prevention programs target the general population, not just high-risk groups. It has even trained barbers to spread HIV prevention messages.[144] Those familiar with attitudes about AIDS in India say that AIDS awareness campaigns have paid off in Tamil Nadu, and stigma and discrimination have been on the decline.

Manipur is a small state in the northeast, with the highest HIV prevalence in the country, but also low internal ethnic boundaries even amid high levels of ethnic heterogeneity. On survey questions on intercaste and interreligious marriage, respondents from that state supported bans less than did respondents from all other states in India. According to the theory of boundary politics, we would predict among the highest levels of political support and AIDS policy response, and again, that is what we find. In 2002, the *Times of India* reported, "Politicians in Manipur have a new constituency. HIV-infected and AIDS patients and high risk groups like drug users and sex workers. And every political party has put HIV/AIDs awareness and control on their 'priority lists' and in their manifestos."[145]

---

[142] Basu, "Giving AIDS the Red Light."

[143] Amy Waldman, "As AIDS Spreads, India Is Still Struggling for a Workable Strategy," *New York Times*, November 8, 2007, 7.

[144] Soma Basu, "In Tamil Nadu, Women Lead the War against HIV," Inter Press Service, October 13, 2005; Miriam Jordan, "India Enlists Barbers in the War on AIDS," *Wall Street Journal*, September 25, 1996.

[145] Sujay Gupta, "HIV/AIDS High on Agenda on Manipur Parties," *Times of India*, February 8, 2002.

More generally, high-risk groups have been highly stigmatized in Indian politics, but in Manipur's much more permeable boundary environment, these groups, including the ethnic groups thought to be at high risk, have been actively courted as legitimate constituents. Such groups have less to fear from blaming and shaming, and as a result, have been more willing to mobilize in civil society and in cooperation with political parties. In turn, Manipur is ranked first or second on every state-level policy indicator. To be certain, a degree of this aggressiveness is surely due to the relatively high prevalence, but the political dynamics are consistent with the theory.

These three cases can be favorably contrasted with the AIDS programs in most other large cities and states in India, but notably with Maharashtra state and its capital, Mumbai, which are similarly economically developed, with large commercial sex industries (like Kolkata), and relatively large epidemics (like Tamil Nadu). Government responses in Mumbai have been slow and uneven, meeting resistance along the way. Although this appears to be changing, along with increased efforts on the part of the national government, the record of AIDS politics and policymaking in this municipality and state has been characterized by blaming and shaming. The results of the contrasting policies are quite remarkable: while only about 5 percent of tested female sex workers in Kolkata were HIV-positive in 1999, more than 50 percent were HIV-positive in Mumbai. According to NACO, that figure dipped just below 50 percent only in 2004.

While many observers have argued that the explanation for the aggressiveness of certain key states was the presence of outstanding public health entrepreneurs such as Jana and Solomon, it is important to point out that experienced physicians and civic and business leaders also reside in the wealthy city of Mumbai. However, Mumbai and Maharashtra have been racked by interethnic conflict throughout the AIDS epidemic. Not only have anticaste sentiments been higher in Maharashtra, but Hindu-Muslim riots have been more prevalent. In Maharashtra, the nationalist Shiv Sena party, created in the 1960s in Maharashtra state as a "sons of the soil" party, and focused on "Maharashtrian-centric" politics,[146] has been very strong. It has promoted a *Hindutva* (Hindu supremacist) ideology, which asserts that India is a Hindu society, and other religions, particularly Christianity, are foreign to the country. Leaders of Shiv Sena and related political organizations have actively railed against films and campaigns with open displays of

[146] Katzenstein, Kothari, and Mehta 2001, 219.

sexuality.[147] High levels of labor migrancy into Mumbai have fueled ideas that the social problems of the city, especially commercial sex work and AIDS, are caused by outsiders. Although Mumbai is a truly international hub, its politics have not been "cosmopolitan," and progress on AIDS policy has been stifled by claims and charges of morality in a fierce boundary politics. Political leaders have been prone to the denialist, blame-and-shame politics that have characterized Indian AIDS politics and policymaking more generally.

In fact, when the national education ministry along with NACO tried to introduce in 2007 a new adolescent sex education program for fifteen- to seventeen-year-olds, motivated in large part by the growing AIDS epidemic, the states with the highest internal caste boundaries pushed back and banned the curriculum. Specifically, the heads of the Gujarat, Madhya Pradesh, Maharashtra, Karnataka, and Rajasthan governments all suspended the program. Reminiscent of Thabo Mbeki's search for a nativist solution to the growing problem, Madhya's chief minister, Shivraj Singh Chouhan, wrote to the education minister that rather than sex education, "the younger generation should be taught about yoga, Indian culture and its values."[148]

CONCLUSIONS AND ALTERNATIVE EXPLANATIONS

In this model-testing case study, I set out to apply a general argument to the otherwise unordered details of the history of India's AIDS epidemic and of the government's response. Rather than simply rehashing the narratives of AIDS politics and policy as told by involved actors and analysts, I tried to assess how well the facts fit within the relevant predictions from the model. By investigating a case study where few had described the politics of AIDS and the resulting policy passivity in terms of ethnic conflict or ethnic boundaries, I set up a challenging test for the theory of boundary politics. Through this approach, important facts and relationships were unearthed, highlighting the deep ways in which ethnic politics has contributed to denialism and resistance to action on AIDS. I have marshaled

---

[147] Sudha Ramachandran, "Lesbian Film Fires Up Hindu Hardliners," *Asia Times*, June 19, 2004.

[148] Amelia Gentleman, "Sex Education Curriculum Angers Indian Conservatives," *International Herald Tribune*, May 24, 2007.

evidence to demonstrate that in India, AIDS has been linked to ethnic groups—in terms of language/region, religion, and caste—and that these links have shaped understandings of risk of infection. Even with threats of widespread disease and death, and available international assistance, the politics of AIDS have mapped onto preexisting patterns of ethnic conflict, generating blame and shame-avoidance politics, rather than a mass demand for governmental response. If we return to the assumption that government leaders try to avoid making unpopular demands or policies, it becomes more understandable that the Geneva Consensus would not be advanced, and would often be resisted by political leaders in India.

By analyzing variation in government responses across states, I found additional evidence that the general theory of boundary politics provides real and novel insights into the patterns of responses to AIDS in India. Differences in the responses of state governments could be predicted by the strength of ethnic boundaries within those states after controlling for HIV prevalence and per capita income.

The political and policy outcomes resemble those of South Africa much more than Brazil. To be certain, there have been Indians who have fought aggressively against AIDS, including dedicated physicians (such as Sunithi Soloman from Tamil Nadu) and interested civil servants (such as Sujatha Rao, who would eventually lead NACO). They deserve at least some of the credit for advancing AIDS policy. The existing AIDS policy framework is nonnegligible, and in some parts of the country seems to be making an impact on knowledge, behavior, rates of infection, and the well-being of people who are HIV-positive. My point has been simply to show that less has been done than might have been were the country's ethnic boundaries weaker and more permeable.

My argument and the findings presented herein are related to, but quite distinct from, others that have been published about the cultural and ethnic origins of India's AIDS policy, and of weak social policy in India more generally. Those inclined to accept Baldwin's hypothesis, that government responses to AIDS are likely to be highly conditioned by earlier responses to public health problems, will find evidence that supports that theory. The condition of leprosy, for example, was highly stigmatized in India and remains incompletely addressed to this day. Yet before we accept a patterned determinism to policy responses, we must question the sources of those other responses. Studies have showed that caste divisions mediated the understanding of the Indian leprosy epidemic. Although members of lower castes were worst affected, they were the ones who faced the greatest stigmatization from co-ethnics.[149] It is plausible that similar dynamics structured the policy response I have described here for HIV/AIDS.

Other prominent arguments have focused on the role of Indian culture. For example, Myron Weiner's classic *The Child and the State in India* identified the "belief systems" of the state bureaucracy and the middle class as the central barriers to equitable development in the country. Specifically, he argued that middle-class Indians with the power to effect change believed that "excessive" education would disrupt the social order, which was characterized by sharply differentiated economic strata.[150] Since AIDS affects citizens from both upper and lower economic strata, that argument simply does not apply. AIDS policies are not purely redistributive social policies, and yet representatives from all economic strata in India seem to have been lukewarm or openly hostile to aggressive AIDS policy. As an important nuance in Indian politics, I note that marginalized actors, such as lower-caste groups, will reject a policy intended to improve their long-term welfare because it undermines socially based competition across groups.

A slightly different argument relates India's deep social cleavages to the underprovision of public goods via an electoral logic. For example, one study points out that Indian politicians have long made promises of targeted goods to individual citizens or to interest groups, particularly as organized along social cleavages, as a way of shoring up electoral support.[151] While this may help to explain why aggressive AIDS policies might get crowded out by other policies, it does not explain the often active opposition to action on AIDS. If stigma and social identity competition were not playing a role, we might have seen politicians making promises of AIDS funding to villages, cities, and even individuals affected by the epidemic. Only in a few states where ethnic boundaries were weak did I find evidence of politicians speaking of AIDS as "our" problem.

Of course, some might simply conclude that in general, the lackluster response to AIDS is unsurprising and unworthy of serious investigation because most things "don't work well" in India when it comes to social and health policy. While such pessimism can be understandable when

---

[149] Krishnatray and Melkote (1998, 332) summarize several studies supporting these conclusions.

[150] Weiner 1991, 5.

[151] Keefer and Khemani 2004.

considering a country with India's poverty and inequality, the general conclusion is unwarranted. Pockets of extraordinary responsiveness exist in both the Indian state and society, for responding to AIDS as well other problems and challenges. Even if weak policy responses are the norm, they still demand explanation, particularly when external pressures for action are heavily applied.

Perhaps the most promising attempt to understand the relationship between the identity basis of policy and implementation across Indian states is Singh's study investigating the extent to which "subnationalism" leads to higher levels of social development.[152] She stresses the flip side of the phenomenon I have taken up here, namely the positive effects of mobilizing a collective subnational identity as the basis for generating public goods, particularly around education and health care more generally. By contrast, my research has highlighted the intensification of resistance to goods and policies associated with a stigmatized condition when internal divides are strong. Although subnationalism and ethnic boundaries are surely related and negatively correlated, they are conceptually distinct: for example, strong subnationalism does not necessarily exist in a polity with weak ethnic boundaries.

The problem of AIDS in India also speaks to theories about the relationship between democracy and development. As in Brazil and South Africa, AIDS policymaking in India has emerged in the context of democracy, and one of the most powerful conclusions articulated by Nobel laureate economist Amartya Sen is that democracy can be a critical force for averting developmental disasters. His research demonstrated that a relatively open chain of communication has helped to avert possible famines. "A government that has to face criticism from opposition parties and free newspapers, and that has to seek reelection cannot afford to neglect famines, since famines are conspicuous miseries which can be easily brought into the arena of public discussion."[153] On the other hand, as Sen and coauthor Jean Drèze point out, "The reach of public criticism can be less effective when the deprivations are less extreme, more complex to analyze, and less easy to remedy."[154] AIDS is clearly a problem that can be so characterized, and democracy turns out to be an insufficient condition for an aggressive AIDS policy.

[152] Singh 2008.
[153] Drèze and Sen 1995, 87.
[154] Drèze and Sen 1995, 87–88.

Arguments about the importance of civil society for mobilizing a robust policy response to AIDS similarly appear to fall away in the Indian context. Scholars have noted that India is sometimes described as the "NGO capital of the world."[155] There exist a great many AIDS-related NGOs as well. But as in South Africa, the mere existence of such NGOs has not been sufficient to galvanize popular opinion and to convince political leaders that the Geneva Consensus would do more to win political support than to lose it. Varshney has pointed out that in India, civil society organizations vary in the degree to which they are organized along interethnic lines.[156] The data presented in this chapter are not sufficiently fine-grained to assess the effects of such variation on political attitudes about AIDS. Future research could test the hypothesis that perceptions of risk go up and inclinations toward shaming and blaming go down when individuals and communities are characterized by dense networks of interethnic ties.

Although the comparison with Brazil and South Africa has provided useful opportunities for analytic control, important questions remain about generalizability and the role of alternative explanations. For example, to what extent does the argument apply only to democracies? How much of an effect does level of development have on a government's responsiveness? In the next chapter, I consider these questions by taking a much broader comparative perspective, simultaneously analyzing the relationship between ethnic boundaries and AIDS policy across several dozen countries.

[155] Katzenstein, Kothari, and Mehta 2001, 248.
[156] Varshney 2002.

6 ❧ Ethnic Boundaries and AIDS Policies around the World

In the two previous chapters, I described the impact of ethnic boundaries on the politics of AIDS policymaking in three key countries. I found that strong caste and ethno-regional lines in India, and strong racial lines in South Africa, were sources of conflict, and ultimately of national government passivity on AIDS policy. By contrast, in Brazil, much greater ethnic tolerance and norms of mixing in combination with a legacy of institutional prohibitions against ethnic classification meant that race and ethnicity played almost no role in the politicization of HIV/AIDS for most of the history of the epidemic. It was possible for AIDS activists to drive forward perhaps the most aggressive AIDS policy rollout in the entire developing world, without serious divisions involving group-based blame or shame. The idea that the risks of infection were shared across society was not seriously challenged by any social or political actors; and when there has been denial or blame, it has not been expressed in ethnic- or race-group competition. Thus, in these three large democracies, all of which faced epidemics, variation in the strength of internal boundaries played an important role in shaping government responses.

And yet important questions remain that are characteristic of the nature of the analyses presented. First, each of the countries comes from a different world region, begging questions about comparability, given differing regional epidemics and external influences. To what extent do ethnic boundaries predict variations in responses across countries throughout the developing world, and how strong is the effect relative to other factors, particularly those used as analytic controls in the prior chapters, such as regime type, per capita income, and infection (objective threat) level? Are there other factors that could account for cross-country variation in the three cases that might predict broader patterns of AIDS policy, such as more general norms concerning sex and sexuality?

To address these questions, I subjected the central hypotheses and alterative hypotheses to broader cross-country statistical analyses across a much larger group of developing countries. Ultimately, I find strong evidence that ethnic boundaries constrain policy aggressiveness. Such analyses provide a powerful complement to comparative case studies.

As will become clear in the pages that follow, I have tried to use multiple indicators and analyses in order to make sure that no particular finding was simply an idiosyncratic artifact of any single measurement or estimation procedure. Like many social science concepts, "ethnic boundaries" and "policy aggressiveness" are large-scale phenomena that are difficult to measure. I have pushed on available data in a number of different ways in order to see how well the argument applies to subgroups of my universe of cases, and while there are some differences, I am struck by the consistency of the effects. Several factors in addition to ethnic boundaries clearly have affected the aggressiveness of AIDS policies, and ethnic boundaries do not *determine* AIDS policies. But on average, ethnic boundaries have mattered a great deal.

I begin by describing the data collected for the analysis, before turning to a discussion of the statistical results, within which I highlight additional qualitative evidence for many countries in the dataset.

THE DATA

The analysis considers the record of AIDS policymaking from the mid-1990s until the end of 2006 for countries with per capita GDP of less than $8,000 in 1995—below Korea, Barbados, and Mauritius in world rankings. There is a qualitative difference between the developed and developing countries in available resources, financing flows in the international order, and overall levels of public service provision, such that the dynamics of policymaking are not well analyzed in a common framework. Ironically, relevant and comparable cross-country data are more widely available for the developing countries because of their coordination by the architects of the Geneva Consensus. Moreover, micro-states—defined as countries with a population less than 500,000—are absent from the analyses because of limited data. Further, I limit the analyses to those countries located in Asia, Africa, and Latin America/Caribbean—the regional homes of the three countries analyzed in the case studies. As for the East European/Central Asian countries and Middle Eastern countries that would fall into the low- or middle-income group, the onset of the epidemic was generally later, the main modes of transmission have been somewhat different (primarily IV drug use), and there is a scarcity of time-varying AIDS-related data. It is worth noting, however, that when I have included the available data from these regions in the analyses, the results remain largely unchanged.[1]

Ethnic Boundaries

While ethnic tensions can be quite palpable in societies, the task of identifying appropriate quantitative indicators remains a great challenge for scholars carrying out related empirical research. Attempts have been made to develop quantitative measures of the extent of ethnic diversity and conflict, and each is marked by advantages and disadvantages.[2]

---

[1] See Lieberman 2007 for statistical results that include these additional cases. There is also qualitative evidence suggesting that the dynamic holds in countries in other world regions. For example, in the case of Estonia, despite one of the most acute HIV/AIDS problems in Europe, and a generally strong and effective state, the government has been notoriously slow to respond to AIDS. According to one account, "The epidemic has . . . forced Estonia to confront the divide between its own people and the country's Russian-speaking minority, a population that grew out of the Soviet Union's desire to Russify Estonia." Initially, AIDS was most prevalent among Russian-speakers, but even as it spread more widely among Estonians, denial persisted. The director of the country's AIDS program explained, "It is difficult to change the way of thinking of the community because when the epidemic started, everyone was talking about how it was a problem of homosexual men, then Russian-speaking, unemployed, IV drug users. They thought this problem does not concern us" (Lizette Alvarez, "HIV Surge Catches Tradition-Bound Estonia Off Guard," *New York Times*, February 15, 2004).

[2] Uncertainty about codings can leave some to ask whether there is really something "there" in the notion of ethnic competition, dividedness, or boundaries. Chandra 2006, for example, highlights reasons to be skeptical about our ability to be analytically precise in distinguishing "ethnic" phenomena from other types. My response to such concerns is that while it is true that reasonable observers could disagree about what counts as ethnic and what strong boundaries might look like, for the most part, these constructs are observable

In the case study chapters, I was able to elaborate upon a fairly wide range of evidence about the histories of Brazil, South Africa, and India, drawing upon my own firsthand knowledge of those countries, survey data, extensive secondary literatures, and other documented evidence of ethnic boundaries. Moreover, those three cases are fairly extreme and paradigmatic, which make them easier to characterize. But the task of extending this analysis to several dozen other countries—establishing exactly how to measure the strength of ethnic boundaries and levels of fractionalization—is more difficult, though obviously essential to estimate their effects on AIDS policy outcomes.

The ultimate challenge is to identify how we would know a country with strong and multiple ethnic boundaries if we saw one. In theory, the number of ethnic boundaries (ethnic diversity/fractionalization) and the strength of ethnic boundaries (institutionalization) are separable dimensions, but clearly interrelated. Any observation of ethnic diversity implies some degree of institutionalization and vice versa. Ultimately, as discussed in chapter 2, my theory is concerned with the combination of the two dimensions, and in considering possible measurement strategies, including attitudinal surveys, demographic approaches, and institutional measures, I highlight the extent to which they pick up one or the other dimension to a greater extent. All of the variables have been scaled from 0 to 1.

SURVEY/ATTITUDINAL APPROACH

Asking people their views about ethnic "others" is one important strategy for assessing the *strength* of ethnic boundaries, and I have reported the results of such efforts in the preceding case study chapters. Unfortunately, no standardized, cross-cultural surveys exist that ask comparable questions in a majority of the countries considered in my analyses. However, the World Values Survey, discussed in chapters 4 and 5, was fielded in sixteen of the countries,[3] and it asked a question about groups that people would

---

at the macro-level, and we can distinguish countries in which such divides are clear and salient from those in which they are not using the definitions of ethnicity specified in chapter 2. Indeed, any complex analytic construct, whether it be democracy, development, class, or revolution, is likely to clearly distinguish a host of phenomena and outcomes from one another, while leaving a potentially gray middle ground, which must be sorted out through more careful review and definitional clarification.

[3] Argentina, Bangladesh, Brazil, Chile, China, Colombia, Dominican Republic, Ghana, India, Mexico, Nigeria, Peru, Philippines, South Africa, Uruguay, Venezuela.

"not like to have as neighbors," providing a battery of possible responses. One option was "someone of a different race group," which was translated into locally relevant groups. For example, in India it was "someone of a different caste." I created a variable, which I label "*antirace*," calculated as the percentage of those surveyed for each country responding that they would *not* like to have someone of a different race group as a neighbor. During the waves of the survey completed between 1990 and 2000, individual countries were surveyed as few as one and as many as three times, and I used the statistic with the highest share of respondents expressing such sentiments given the bias toward underreporting on such questions. While this is a useful measure, questions about the validity of measurement remain, in the sense that it is not clear that respondents were always referring to people who would be understood as a different race group *in their own country*.[4] The measure also says nothing about levels of fractionalization. But most scores appear reasonable in the sense that they sort extreme countries as we might expect: classically ethnically divided countries such as India, Nigeria, and South Africa had among the highest numbers of respondents identifying racial others as unwelcome neighbors (all above 20 percent) while countries with weaker boundaries such as Colombia, Argentina, and Brazil had the lowest numbers of respondents (all below 5 percent).

DEMOGRAPHIC AND CULTURAL/POLITICAL RELEVANCE APPROACHES

A second set of measures of ethnic boundaries includes those that take a more demographic approach. A great deal of social science scholarship investigating the effects of ethnicity on development has focused on the concept of diversity as the basis for conflict, using measures of the relative size of ethnic groups in a society to capture "homogeneity" and "heterogeneity." Specifically, scholars have used a Herfindahl index—calculated as 1 minus the sum of the squared percentage share of each group—to provide a summary measure of the extent of ethnic diversity. The resulting statistic, ranging from 0 to 1, is typically interpreted as the likelihood that any two randomly selected individuals from the country would be from different ethnic groups. Not only do such indicators provide much better

[4] For example, on the third wave of the China World Values Survey, 23 percent responded that they would not want someone of a different race group as a neighbor, and I surmise that respondents interpreted this question as referring to foreigners.

cross-country coverage, but they do not suffer from normative biases associated with survey/attitudinal indicators. These indicators tend to do a worse job of picking up the degree of institutionalization of boundaries, but they do a better job of picking up the *number* of boundaries in a society, which is why they are understood to be measures of ethnic *fractionalization*. Such data are important for estimating a model that highlights the dynamic of group competition over a condition that may be perceived as affecting only certain groups.

Several widely used measures capture diversity in this manner: First is the Ethnolinguistic Fractionalization (ELF) index,[5] and I use Roeder's most inclusive approach to ethnicity, treating linguistic, racial, and other groups (i.e., settler vs. indigenous) as ethnic groups, based on data from the 1964 *Atlas Narodov Mira*, and several additional sources.[6] Because religion is identified as a possible basis for ethnic conflict, I also consider a separate religious fractionalization index (Relig).[7] The use of such fractionalization indicators in studies of ethnic politics has been criticized because they do not capture social or political salience and do not fully reflect the constructed nature of such identities or groups.[8] In particular, the existence of a great many religious groups in a society often indicates tolerance as much as ethnic division.[9] Just as we cannot infer class consciousness directly from income inequality, a purely demographic understanding of ethnic diversity is also limited as a basis for ethnic consciousness. Because these measures are widely used in the literature, and because they almost certainly capture *some* of the phenomenon under investigation, they are considered in my analysis, but with caution.

Fortunately, two available indicators combine a measure of ethnic diversity with greater attention to salience and the institutionalization of boundaries, and these provide better estimates of the strength of ethnic boundaries as developed in this book. James Fearon's cultural fractionalization[10] index (Cdiv) was developed in a manner similar to the above-mentioned fractionalization indices, but with greater attention to social significance based on coding rules and subjective judgments about whether or not people with identifiably common ethnic traits are recognized by

[5] Used in the seminal Easterly and Levine 1997 article.
[6] Roeder 2001.
[7] Alesina et al. 2003.
[8] Laitin and Posner 2001.
[9] Alesina et al. 2003, 175.
[10] Fearon 2003.

themselves and others as "groups."[11] Groups are further weighted according to degree of cultural division or dissimilarity using taxonomies of primary languages.[12] Thus, when groups' languages are structurally different, the overall fractionalization score increases relative to a country with the same number and size of groups, but in which languages are mutually comprehensible. This certainly captures an important aspect of boundaries. The approach puts a high premium on language as a basis for ethnic differentiation, and while linguistic difference is neither necessary nor sufficient for ethnic mobilization, it is an extraordinarily important form of ethnic boundary.[13] It is relevant for the theory considered here in the sense that we might expect language to pose a relevant barrier for marriage or sexual contact and for communicating ideas about risk. The greater the distance between the languages of people from two different groups, the greater the degree to which people might imagine the boundaries between them.

Daniel Posner's "politically relevant ethnic group fractionalization index" (which he labels as PREG), currently available only for countries in sub-Saharan Africa, is also essentially the calculation of a Herfindahl-based fractionalization score, using the relative size of ethnic groups, but including only those groups with some political salience. As he points out, for his study of macroeconomic policies he identifies politically relevant groups for that policy area, suggesting that other sets of groups might be relevant for other policies. Nonetheless, I consider this index for AIDS policy under the assumption that the groups identified are those that are generally relevant and the index provides an indicator of the distribution of salient ethnic boundaries that is causally prior to the onset of AIDS, which is one of the key strengths of the research design. If no ethnic groups are identified as politically salient, or if there is only a single group, then the ethnic landscape is characterized as equivalent to that of an ethnically homogeneous society (PREG = 0).

Both Cdiv and PREG are more sensitive to variations in diversity than they are to salience, but overall they do a better job than ELF and Relig of

---

[11] Fearon 2003, 202–3 explains that he sought out sources that indicate "groupness," or "mobilized" groups.

[12] See Fearon 2003, 220 fn. 23, 24 for the specific algorithm used to compute cultural fractionalization.

[13] See, for example, Smith 1989, 343, and Laitin 1998. While Laitin's (1992) investigation of state construction in Africa highlights the prevalence of multilingualism in those countries, that very fact reflects the inability of contemporary states to authoritatively shape a single national identity.

capturing my construct of "strength and number of ethnic boundaries." Of all of the demographic indicators considered, cultural fractionalization combines the widest geographic coverage, with the most deliberate attention to likely social and political salience.

INSTITUTIONAL APPROACH

A third approach is to consider the formal and informal institutions that divide ethnic groups—in other words, a more direct measure of the strength of ethnic boundaries themselves. The challenge here is to identify what counts as evidence. Among the key observables of ethnic boundaries would be the use of ethnic-based preference policies, the use of ethnic labels in political discourse, reports of violence widely understood as conflicts between ethnic groups, and the existence and prevalence of political parties and other organizations that make explicit ethnic claims, or that are widely understood to represent particular ethnic groups. While such a direct approach is desirable, one must recognize threats to the reliability of the measure, in that a highly varied and eclectic information base must be considered in order to score countries. Again, such concerns are also problematic for other macro-level variables such as democracy, development, or state capacity, which are used to characterize units with a fair degree of internal heterogeneity.

One effort to create an index of "institutional ethnic conflict" for the period 1990-6 has been carried out by Tatu Vanhanen,[14] who uses a 0–100 scale, creating eight anchoring cutpoints for levels of conflict, ranging from 0, "No significant ethnic organizations; no significant ethnic inequality in political representation," to 100, "The share of ethnic parties 90–100 percent; all significant organizations are ethnic by nature; practically all interest conflict between groups takes place along ethnic lines." Vanhanen's measure also captures the highest degree of demonstrated institutional ethnic conflict for the period, and was based on single- and multicountry books, articles, and international encyclopedias and databases. I have divided the Vanhanen measure by 100 to maintain a consistent scale.

ETHNIC BOUNDARY INDEX

Finally, I have developed an ethnic boundary index (country scores are reported in appendix table 6.A1), which addresses some of the shortcom-

[14]Vanhanen 1999.

ings identified in the measures already described, and develops an indicator that is most closely aligned to my theoretical specification of the construct. The ethnic boundary index is sensitive to both the level of institutionalization and the number of ethnic boundaries in a given country. Unlike the fractionalization scores, it is more sensitive to variation in institutionalization and less sensitive to variations in demographic diversity.

For each of the eighty-five countries, I considered relevant data on the nature of ethnic politics, including the country-level fractionalization scores (described above), MAR data on group histories, CIA World Factbook data on group sizes, State Department country studies; U.S. Library of Congress country studies; and Polity Country Reports; as well as additional scholarly articles, books, and book chapters on related subjects of ethnic, race, or national politics. When source material was still thin, I conducted Internet searches on related search terms on Lexis-Nexis and Google to unearth other potentially relevant news articles or reports.

Using these sources, I classified countries in terms of the institutionalization of boundaries and the number of boundaries (as summarized in table 6.1). Institutionalization refers to the degree to which ethnic categories formally and informally structure social and political interactions in the polity. I identified six types or levels of institutionalization:

None: countries in which there was no evidence that ethnic distinctions had substantial relevance in political life at the national level.

Low: countries in which ethnic differences were evident, and where people were often categorized in terms of such differences, but where there was little consistency in the use of such labels, and individuals had substantial leeway in how they identified themselves from day to day. In such cases, there was no evidence of substantial political mobilization of ethnic groups or there may have been a strong legacy of nation-building or cultural homogenization.

Concentrated: countries in which ethnic boundaries were more sharply defined and consistently used, but only within a single, geographically concentrated area, such that for the rest of the country, ethnic distinctions would not appear well institutionalized. This would include cases with small secessionist movements in a peripheral area.

Mixed/contradictory: countries in which there was evidence of counter-vailing pressures or contradictory evidence about the strength of ethnic boundaries. In such cases, the strong legacy of effective nation-building programs, including linguistic homogenization, stood

TABLE 6.1
Framework for Classifying Ethnic Boundary Index Scores

Institutionalization	Fragmentation		
	None/very low (homogeneous)	Some (diverse)	Extreme (highly diverse)
None	0	0	0
Low	0	.25	.25
Concentrated	0	.25	.25
Mixed/Contradictory	0	.5	.5
Moderately Strong	0	.75	.75
Very Strong	0	.75	1

alongside the perpetuation of mobilized ethnic-based claims, or periodic outbreaks of ethnic violence. Some political parties might be identifiable as "ethnic-based," but few would describe the larger party system as an ethnic one.

Moderately strong: countries in which there was evidence of substantial ethnic-based violence, party mobilization, repeated categorization, or repeated public discourse indicating the centrality of ethnic labels in determining equity and resource allocation, but in which available evidence also highlighted some ambiguity, fluidity, and the waxing and waning salience of specific ethnic categories.

Very strong: countries in which ethnic identities were clearly central, with almost no moderating caveats. Substantial evidence could be marshaled to describe the relevant ethnic categories and the strength of the boundaries that divided groups from one another.

In terms of the number or fragmentation of ethnic boundaries, I developed three categories: *None*, for largely homogeneous countries, for which there was no evidence of a single ethnic minority comprising more than 5 percent of the population (except in the case of countries where all groups were less than 5 percent, which were considered highly fragmented); *Some*, for all other cases in which there was at least one ethnic minority greater than 5 percent, but where the maximum fractionalization score was less than .7; and *Extreme*, for those cases where the maximum fractionalization score was .7 or greater.

I identify five conceptually meaningful distinctions based on the combination of these two dimensions, which are relevant for the theory identified in chapter 2.

0—Extremely weak or nonexistent ethnic boundaries: If a country was classified as being homogeneous, or having "no institutionalization" of boundaries, it received an index score of 0. Even if one could identify substantial ethnic diversity, the absence of substantial social or political salience rendered it equivalent to a homogeneous country.

.25—Mostly weak or permeable ethnic boundaries: If a country had low or concentrated levels of ethnic institutionalization, it received an index score of .25, as long as there was one substantial ethnic minority. For this category, ethnic boundaries exist, but they rarely divide people into clear "us-them" juxtapositions.

.50—Intermediate levels of ethnic boundaries: Countries characterized by mixed evidence about level of institutionalization received an index score of .50, as long as there was one substantial ethnic minority.

.75—Mostly strong or multiple ethnic boundaries: Countries were classified in this category when the level of institutionalization was "strong"; or when institutionalization was "very strong," but the level of fragmentation was not "extreme." In these cases, ethnic boundaries could be expected to be consistently, highly relevant, but either because of a single large majority in the country, or some mitigating circumstances, there might be substantial sets of issues where this was not the case.

1—Extremely strong and multiple ethnic boundaries: Countries were so classified when there was evidence of "very strong" institutionalization and "extreme" fragmentation of groups. In such countries, there is always a good chance that any issue, political event, or mobilization will take on an ethnic character.

Obviously, such an index retains a degree of subjectivity, but theoretically and empirically it does a somewhat better job of sorting countries with greater attention to social and political salience and to the configurations that are most likely to map onto the politics of AIDS as highlighted in earlier chapters. Because the index is sensitive to the size and number of groups only for countries with reasonably high levels of institutionalization, it avoids the "mis-scoring" of countries that are highly diverse, but where ethnicity has little or no relevance in politics. The index is not a simple multiplicative interaction of the two dimensions, as the number of boundaries or level of fragmentation only matters when the boundaries themselves are salient.

COMPARING THE MEASURES: DISTRIBUTIONS AND RELATIONSHIPS

Figure 6.1 depicts the distribution of the various measures for the three world regions and for the entire sample considered in the analysis with a series of histograms (except for the antirace variable, for which there are too few cases to make meaningful comparisons across the subgroups). In any given histogram, a greater skew to the right (more tall bars on the right side of the graph) implies that there are relatively more cases with more and stronger ethnic boundaries within that group. Consistently, the African countries emerge as the most ethnically heterogeneous subsample and the one with the strongest boundaries. Alternatively, the Latin American countries, on average, are least divided by ethnic boundaries. Nonetheless, there is substantial variation within all three regions, which allows for the testing of the effects of ethnic boundaries and related variables on outcomes of interest.

In table 6.2, I report the correlations between the ethnic indicators included in the analysis. The indicators measure slightly different aspects of the ethnic concept under investigation, so we should not be surprised that the relationships between these variables display some variability. While it is true that the ethnic boundary index I created is strongly correlated with the cultural (Cdiv) and politically relevant ethnic group (PREG) fractionalization indexes, this is not terribly surprising since those data played a role in how I classified cases, and I cannot use those statistical relationships as an independent test of the validity of the measurement. More reassuring is that my ethnic boundary index is strongly correlated with Vanhanen's scale of institutionalized ethnic conflict at $r = .77$. Also of interest, despite only sixteen observations, the survey-based measure of "antirace" is fairly well correlated with all of the indicators that capture the strength of ethnic boundaries (at levels above .5).

It is notable in table 6.2 that religious fractionalization has the weakest relationship with the other indicators. Religious diversity tends to be more cross-cutting, in the sense that in a country, there may be a diversity of religious affiliations among people who speak the same language, and a shared religion among those who speak different languages. While there are cases in which religious difference is clearly associated with strong ethnic boundaries (e.g., Nigeria, India), religious diversity is not a good proxy for the larger concept. We should not expect this variable to have effects on AIDS policies similar to the other indicators.

AIDS Policies

Although the concept of AIDS policy aggressiveness is fairly straightforward, the task of developing a suitable metric for cross-country comparison is not, and again, I use a series of indicators for the analysis. It is important to recall that because this investigation is concerned with the determinants of policies—and not with the implementation or impact of such policies on actual behavior, the spread of infection, or health and well-being—I avoid conflating the outcomes that may be produced by the policy with the policies themselves. One might assume that government actions are so closely connected to AIDS-related outcomes—including knowledge and behaviors that lead to new infections or the care and treatment of those infected—that we could use changes in prevalence and incidence as proxies for government action.[15] However, this would be a faulty strategy because social, cultural, economic, and international influences surely influence patterns of HIV transmission, in addition to government responses. Ultimately, my theory and analysis speak to questions about why governments do or do not respond, not to the efficacy of particular policies.

For that reason, I attempt to use more direct measures of government policy, prior to impact. This choice has important consequences for how we classify and interpret cases, because it causes me to score certain countries such as Botswana as highly aggressive, even while estimated adult prevalence remains among the highest in the world. Indeed, one could say that Botswana's government has been unsuccessful in lowering the high prevalence and even the incidence of HIV infections, but it has outspent all other African countries on a per capita basis, and HIV/AIDS has long been included as a line item in the national budget. The government developed unprecedented international partnerships with the Gates Foundation, Merck pharmaceuticals, and Harvard University to provide ARVs to HIV-positive citizens, and President Festus Mogae (1998–2008) was outspoken

[15]Price-Smith, Tauber and Bhat 2004.

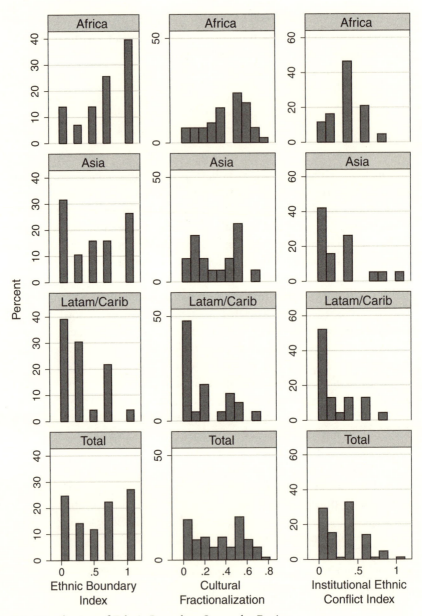

6.1. Distribution of Ethnic Boundary Scores, by Region

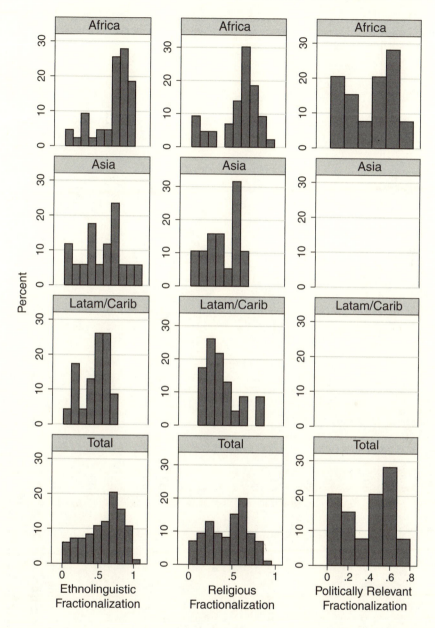

TABLE 6.2
Bivariate Associations of Measures of Ethnic Boundaries

	Ethnic Boundary index	Institutional ethnic conflict	Cdiv	PREG	ELF	Relig	Antirace
Ethnic Boundary Index	1.00						
	85						
Institutional ethnic conflict index	.77	1.00					
	.00						
	85	85					
Cultural fractionalization (Cdiv)	.69	.61	1.00				
	.00	.00					
	83	83	83				
Politically relevant ethnic group (PREG) fractionalization	.72	.38	.52	1.00			
	.00	.02	.00				
	39	39	39	39			
Ethnolinguistic fractionalization (ELF)	.62	.43	.68	.56	1.00		
	.00	.00	.00	.00			
	83	83	81	39	83		
Religious fractionalization (Relig)	0.38	.33	.17	.36	.34	1.00	
	0.00	.00	.13	.02	.00		
	85	85	83	39	83	85	
Percent not wanting other race group as neighbor (antirace)	.61	.50	.67		.28	.20	1.00
	.01	.05	.00		.28	.45	
	16	16	16	3	16	16	16

Note: Pearson's *r*; *p*-values; *N* observations reported.

on HIV/AIDS. The fact that prevalence is high may indicate as much about the fact that citizens in that country are staying alive despite their sero-status as it does about the diffusion of knowledge and behavior change associated with a reduction in new infections.

To measure AIDS policy aggressiveness across countries, I compiled data on government expenditure on AIDS, AIDS policy coverage, and a summary measure of AIDS policy aggressiveness, and I report descriptive statistics for all of these measures in table 6.3.

EXPENDITURE

I consider two forms of AIDS-related expenditures: those from government revenue accounts, and those from donors. The donor expenditures described here are limited only to those funds that in some way flow through and have been reported by governments themselves. Government use of its own scarce and limited financial resources is obviously a strong indicator of priority. And while levels of donor expenditure might seem to be completely "donor-driven," donors face inducements and constraints on aid in terms of the behavior of recipient countries. Again, in the case of Botswana, donors indicated to me in interviews that their focus on that country was strongly influenced by the perception that the government would be an eager partner. By contrast, particularly early in the epidemic, many government leaders in developing countries rejected financial assistance on HIV/AIDS as they denied there was a significant problem within their borders. In any case, the relationship between domestic politics and donor-provided expenditure is an empirical question I consider in the analysis. Expenditures include all moneys spent on AIDS-specific prevention and treatment programs.

Most of the expenditure data are from UNAIDS reports,[16] and from SIDALAC studies,[17] but I have also gathered additional expenditure data from government documents and secondary sources, including submissions to the GFATM (which required that CCMs report this information) in order to gather as many observations as possible. All data are analyzed as log values on a per capita basis using official $US exchange rates. While

[16]Ernberg et al. 1999; UNAIDS 2006.
[17]SIDALAC is the regional AIDS initiative for Latin America and the Caribbean, a multiorganization partnership implemented by the Mexican Health Foundation. Reports were accessed from http://www.sidalac.org.mx/.

TABLE 6.3
Descriptive Statistics of AIDS Policy Aggressiveness Indicators

Description	Mean	Minimum	Median	Maximum	Countries	Year start	Year end	N	SD
Government expenditures per capita $US	1.7	0.00009	0.19	93	71	1995	2005	313	6.6
Donor expenditures per capita $US	1.3	0.00039	0.24	55	63	1995	2005	153	6.2
Mentions of HIV/AIDS in the budget speech	5.4	0	2	35	21	1995	2006	87	8.9
Antiretroviral drug therapy coverage	29%	0%	21%	100%	82	2005	2005	82	26%
PMTCT coverage	14%	0%	5.5%	100%	68	2003	2005	68	20%
AIDS Policy Index	61	35	61	82	50	2003	2003	50	12

one can raise valid concerns about the possibilities of different countries classifying expenditures in different ways, including whether expenditures were actual or budgeted, it is not clear that there should be any systematic bias in a particular direction. Moreover, the availability of national AIDS account frameworks and the role of international actors provides some basis for confidence in the comparability of findings, and UNAIDS has published much of these data as a metric for measuring country progress in responding to the pandemic.[18] Moreover, countries with extremely strong reputations for having been aggressive on HIV/AIDS in general report high levels of expenditures, and vice versa, suggesting that we can have some confidence in the measurement validity[19] of the indicators.

While actual expenditures are revealing about government commitment, there are limitations. What happens if a government is aggressive and efficient in delivering HIV prevention and treatment services, such that it manages to lower overall costs? Unfortunately, this would indicate under our budgetary analyses a decrease in aggressiveness. Alternatively, what about when a relatively wealthy government allocates a substantial portion of money, but with little true political support such that the program languishes? Again, budgetary/expenditure data alone might overscore such countries as being aggressive.

In order to check for these problems, while also tapping into more symbolic aspects of government aggressiveness, I employ a slightly different measure of budgetary priorities: the word content of budget speeches. That is, I sought out as many budget speeches as was reasonably possible for countries in the dataset, for all available years after 1994, counted the number of times the words *HIV* or *AIDS* (and their equivalents, such as *SIDA*) were mentioned in the text of the speech, and reported that total. This also corrects for the inherently challenging issue of unit equivalence across countries of different size. Regardless of the population or size of the economy, we can compare central government aggressiveness in terms of the discourse of the chief financial officers of the government. If they discuss HIV/AIDS, we can be fairly confident about the government's general commitment to the problem. The word counts were strongly correlated with per capita government expenditure on AIDS for the country-years in which both measures were available ($r = .66$; $N = 37$), further suggesting that expenditures are a good measure of policy aggressiveness.

---

[18] UNAIDS 2006.
[19] Adcock and Collier 2001.

As described in earlier chapters, the advent of specialized drug therapies designed to mitigate the effects of HIV initially marked a milestone, but one that was available almost exclusively to wealthy individuals or individuals living in wealthy countries. As part of the Three by Five initiative and the MDGs, the United Nations began to collect data on the numbers of people on ARVs, as well as the number of people in need. The ratio of those two factors is generally reported as the degree of coverage—with 100 percent signifying that everyone in need is receiving ARVs in a given country. I consider the data from the end of 2005, which was the target date for the Three by Five campaign.

A second policy measure that has been championed in the Geneva Consensus is the provision of antiretroviral prophylaxis to prevent the vertical transmission of HIV from mother to child during childbirth. UNAIDS provides two types of data: results from a coverage survey, and data reported by governments. For the years in which both figures are available, the correlation is $r = .73$, which is strong, but does highlight a fair degree of discrepancy in the measurements given that they are attempting to capture the exact same outcome, and UNAIDS officials familiar with the data informed me that they were concerned about its reliability. I therefore interpret results of the analysis with a degree of caution. I have calculated the average of available data for the years 2003 and 2005 as a single measure, which helps to limit the amount of missing data.

While other policies, such as condom marketing and distribution, are of vital importance in the overall Geneva Consensus, not only do we lack good quality data with wide coverage, but these policies are extremely difficult to compare across large groups of countries. Because condoms play an important role in other policies, including family planning and control of other sexually transmitted infections, one must control for the other determinants of condom use and policies, including preexisting birth control policies and norms, for which data are not readily available. As these considerations became intractable, I opted not to use such data in the analysis.

Finally, I considered a summary measure that attempts to capture a broader portrait of government aggressiveness on AIDS with a fuller array of information. Several of the Geneva Consensus architects, including

UNAIDS, USAID, the WHO, and the Policy Project of the Futures Group, developed an elite survey instrument—the AIDS Program Effort Index (API)—to measure national "effort." Their 2003 survey thoughtfully combines "yes/no" questions on 167 items, combined with subjective evaluations scores on each of ten components of the overall index. The final score, averaged between both "objective" and "subjective" measures and scaled to 100, provides a reasonable indicator of policy effort. On average, sixteen respondents were interviewed for each country. They were "not meant to be a representative sample but were carefully selected for their professional and in-depth knowledge."[20] The method and questionnaire appear sensible, and the scores for the country cases plausibly distinguish levels of aggressiveness. Although Uganda—the country much heralded for its action on HIV/AIDS—does score in the top quartile of African countries rated by the API, its score of 77 out of 100 places it behind Burkina Faso (82), Rwanda, Malawi, Botswana, and Senegal, which cuts somewhat against the conventional wisdom of its being the model case. Nonetheless, the classification of this group of countries as "high" on aggressiveness makes sense in light of other studies and reports. The bigger problem with this measure, however, is the incomplete nature of the data in terms of country coverage: there is a strong bias toward countries with AIDS epidemics (in my dataset, the mean HIV prevalence of included countries was 6.6 percent, compared with a prevalence of 1.8 percent for countries not included). As a result, several countries that have been extremely aggressive and successful in combating AIDS were left out of the analysis, including notable cases such as Cuba.

Control Variables/Alternative Explanations

As discussed in chapter 2, there are quite plausible rival or complementary explanations for why AIDS policies vary across countries, and these

---

[20] UNAIDS, USAID, and Policy Project 2003, 5. The first attempt to implement the API was much less successful. The survey asked in-country respondents to evaluate program effort on one hundred items on a 0–5 scale, but the authors of the study found that "respondents in different countries used different frames of reference in rating the items. As a result, it was difficult to compare scores across countries" (UNAIDS, USAID, and Policy Project 2003, 4). Many of the resulting scores from that index had no relationship to the realities of government aggressiveness.

require further investigation. It is important to control for both the relative size of the threat and capacity to act on the problem, which I have attempted to do through estimates of HIV prevalence and GDP/capita. In order to avoid potential endogeneity, I lag these variables.[21]

I also include regional dummy variables, which capture important regional differences in the size of the threat, as well as differences in the regional administration and influences of international organizations. Admittedly, it is difficult to interpret the specific, substantive effects of such dummy variables, but we cannot ignore the clearly regional context in which states operate.

I test for the effects of factors associated with leading alternative explanations as discussed in chapter 2, many of which appear in other cross-country statistical analyses of AIDS policies,[22] and in other studies of AIDS policy, health policy, and human development.[23] These include regime type as measured by the Polity index,[24] the degree of freedom in the form of civil liberties and for the press;[25] levels of urbanization; public

---

[21] In the case of adult prevalence, I use the estimate from the prior five-year period, and for GDP/capita, I use a five-year average, lagged three years. None of the estimates are particularly sensitive to the specifics of these choices, and I made choices in order to minimize case exclusion based on missing data. Over the long term, there are good reasons to believe that the aggressiveness and relative success of AIDS policies would affect both per capita income and HIV prevalence, but for the period considered in the analyses, there have been no clear and consistent effects, and particularly given the lagged model specification, biased estimates produced by endogenous relationships should be quite minimal.

[22] Exceptions include Bor 2007; and Nattrass 2006.

[23] E.g., Filmer and Pritchett 1999; McGuire 2006, Gerring, Thacker, and Alfaro 2006; Boone and Batsell 2001; De Waal 2006; Patterson 2006.

[24] I use the Polity 2 score from the Polity IV dataset of Marshall and Jaggers 2006, which are calculated as the basis of two ratings—a "democracy" score ranging from 0 (least democratic) to 10 (most democratic), and an "autocracy" score ranging from 0 (least autocratic) to 10 (most autocratic). The index is calculated by subtracting the autocracy score from the democracy score. For years of foreign domination, the score is considered missing; for years of transition, the score is an average of the years prior and subsequent to the transition; and for years of incoherent "interregnum," the score is 0.

[25] These scores are based on ratings developed by the Freedom House Organization. Civil liberties are judged for countries on a yearly basis from 1 (most free) to 7 (least free), in terms of the overall degree to which a country comes closest to ensuring the freedoms expressed in a civil liberties checklist, including freedom of expression, assembly, association, education, and religion; and where citizens enjoy free economic activity and the government strives for equality of opportunity. Press Freedoms are rated from 0 (most free) to 100 (least free) based on several component scores that aim to establish the degree to which information is centrally controlled by the government. For fuller descriptions of the methodology and data, see www.freedomhouse.org.

health spending;[26] and overall state capacity and government effectiveness.[27] I also consider variables for which I do not have time-varying data, including the Catholic population share, the Muslim population share, and dummy variables for countries with British colonial legacies, French colonial legacies, and federal governments.[28] In order to estimate a model of donor-funded AIDS expenditures, I control for overseas development assistance/GDP, excluding AIDS expenditures.[29]

In general, when there are multiple measures associated with a particular analytic construct—for example, regime type—I report the analyses for which the strongest effects of these control variables are evident. I do not include any two control variables correlated at .70 or greater. Descriptive statistics of these variables are reported in table 6.4.

ANALYSIS AND DISCUSSION: ESTIMATES OF THE EFFECT
OF BOUNDARIES ON AIDS POLICY

Having described the data, I can turn to the central analytic question: do countries with stronger ethnic boundaries wind up being less aggressive on AIDS than we would otherwise expect given other country characteristics, such as the size of the country's epidemic and its level of development? Given the research design, the estimation of the effects of ethnic politics on government AIDS policy turns out to be much more straightforward than the analysis of other outcomes in prior econometric research. For example, in the cases of economic growth, infant mortality, democratic development, school provision, or general health care expenditures,

[26] Urbanization is the percentage of the population living in "urban areas," and public health expenditure is measured as share of GDP. Both from the World Bank 2005.

[27] I use the Kaufman, Kraay, and Mastruzzi 2005 "government effectiveness" index, which is based on a metaanalysis of surveys, and combines responses on the quality of public service provision, the quality of the bureaucracy, the competence of civil servants, the independence of the civil service from political pressures, and the credibility of the government's commitment to policies.

[28] All of these data were gathered from Teorell, Holmberg, and Rothstein 2008, which is a compendium of country-level data on governance and related social, economic, and political variables. The federalism variable is originally from Treisman 2007; the colonial legacy variables are from Teorell and Hadenius 2005; and the religious population share data are from La Porta et al. 1999.

[29] In order to reduce the deletion of cases owing to missing data, I take the average of all years of valid ODA data from the prior five years.

TABLE 6.4
Descriptive Statistics of Political, Social, Economic, and HIV Prevalence Variables

	Mean	Minimum	Maximum	N	SD
GDP/capita $US	1,329	57	8,213	1,129	1,626
Government effectiveness rating	−0.46	−2.6	1.4	336	0.63
% living in urban areas	41	5.7	93	1,190	21
Polity 2 scores	1.9	−10	10	1,098	6.2
Freedom House, civil liberties	4.2	1	7	1,186	1.5
Freedom House, press freedom	53	11	100	932	21
Overseas Dev. Assistance (ODA)[a]	9.5	−0.21	99	1,102	12
Public health expenditures/GDP	2.7	0.33	9.7	508	1.5
GINI coefficient	47	30	74	64	9.5
% Catholic 1980	34.4	0	96.6	85	35.81
% Muslim 1980	19.1	0	99.8	85	29.55
Federal	0.09	0	1	85	0.29
British colonial legacy	.34	0	1	85	0.48
French colonial legacy	.24	0	1	85	0.43
HIV prevalence 1988	1.2	0.05	15	78	2.3
HIV prevalence 1993	3.6	0.05	30	78	6.3
HIV prevalence 1998	4.6	0.05	30	78	7.1
HIV prevalence 2003	5.2	0.05	30	79	8.0
HIV prevalence 2003[b]	4.9	0.10	39	78	8.0

[a] ODA: Less observed assistance targeted for HIV/AIDS
[b] WHO 2005. All other HIV prevalence data are mid-points of range estimates from UNAIDS/WHO 2004.

it is extremely difficult to parse out the direction of causality—not merely in relation to ethnic diversity, but also with respect to any explanatory variables that are plausibly affected by the outcomes under investigation, because we lack information about how those variables were related during earlier periods. In this study, because the measures of ethnic boundaries are based on observations and patterns of demographic and political development that largely preceded the onset of the AIDS pandemic, we can be certain that the latter is not causing the former. Moreover, I find no statistical relationship between estimates of (1988) HIV prevalence and the ethnic indicators, so we can safely conclude that there are not even problems of selection bias in terms of the countries facing the most significant AIDS epidemics.[30]

Over the longer term, AIDS-related illness and death and AIDS policies will almost surely affect both ethnic demographics and ethnic boundaries across countries. Because my ethnic boundary indicators are not time varying, I cannot estimate the effects of HIV prevalence or AIDS policy as a feedback, but it is extremely unlikely that AIDS-related illness or mortality had any substantive effects on relevant ethnic variables for the period under analysis. While I cannot completely exclude this possibility, particularly in the 1980s and early 1990s, AIDS policies in most developing countries were so minimal that it is unlikely they would have had much of an impact on our results even if we could estimate those effects. In any case, when the statistical analyses are restricted to just the earlier periods in the dataset, allowing us to isolate most conceivable feedback effects, the estimates are basically unchanged.

In table 6.5, I present regression estimates of the two types of expenditures,[31] and of the budget speech data. Because the error terms are serially

---

[30] Because of missing data, the countries of Somalia, Comoros, Bhutan, North Korea, Djibouti, Sierra Leone, Guinea Bissau, are absent from the analyses, even though they meet the criteria for inclusion in this set of countries. These countries are all extremely poor, with very low HIV prevalence, and thus their inclusion in the analyses would not likely have changed the results substantially.

[31] While studies point to government expenditure as a general indicator of policy aggressiveness, there have been very few systematic empirical analyses of the determinants of government HIV/AIDS spending, particularly looking across a large group of countries. The World Bank report, *Confronting AIDS*, carried out preliminary analysis of expenditure patterns across countries, but reported on statistical analyses using just two explanatory variables: per capita income and adult prevalence. That study found that both national and donor funding tended to increase with higher prevalence, but that government spending increased with per capita income, while donors favored lower-income countries. World Bank 1999, chap. 5.

TABLE 6.5
The Effect of Ethnic Boundaries on AIDS Expenditures and Budget Speeches (1995–2006)

	(1) Government AIDS Expenditures (Per cap $US–ln)	(2) Government AIDS Expenditures (Per cap $US–ln)	(3) Government AIDS Expenditures (Per cap $US–ln)	(4) Donor AIDS Expenditures (Per cap $US–ln)	(5) Government AIDS Expenditures (Per cap $US – ln) (with model 4 residuals)	(6) Budget Speech HIV/AIDS word count
Ethnic boundaries (Cdiv)	-1.877***	-2.291***	-2.243***	-2.692***	-2.221***	-2.094***
	(0.71)	(0.67)	(0.66)	(0.89)	(0.64)	(0.39)
HIV prev – ln	0.603***	0.285	0.349**	0.671***	0.360**	0.389**
	(0.091)	(0.19)	(0.15)	(0.14)	(0.15)	(0.15)
GDP/capita – ln	1.059***	0.649***	0.664***	0.319	0.654***	0.186**
	(0.13)	(0.20)	(0.18)	(0.34)	(0.18)	(0.077)
year	0.212***	0.277***	0.278***	0.146**	0.281***	0.0399
	(0.039)	(0.068)	(0.047)	(0.056)	(0.045)	(0.045)
Polity 2 scores		0.00553	0.0250	-0.0265	0.0245	-0.0180
		(0.034)	(0.034)	(0.034)	(0.032)	(0.012)
Government Effectiveness		0.734**	0.895***	1.174**	0.910***	
		(0.30)	(0.32)	(0.49)	(0.30)	
% Catholic		-0.00483				
		(0.0100)				

% Muslim	−0.00362 (0.011)			
Federal	−0.103 (0.54)			
Public health expenditures	−0.195 (0.23)			
British colony	0.171 (0.57)			
French colony	−0.596 (0.58)			
Africa	2.123*** (0.79)	1.629** (0.68)	−0.611 (0.58)	1.573** (0.67)
Latin Am. / Carib.	1.873** (0.86)	1.252** (0.59)	−0.942 (0.65)	1.252** (0.54)
Overseas development assistance			0.619*** (0.17)	
Donor Effort				0.370** (0.15)

(continued)

TABLE 6.5 (continued)

	(1) Government AIDS Expenditures (Per cap $US–ln)	(2) Government AIDS Expenditures (Per cap $US–ln)	(3) Government AIDS Expenditures (Per cap $US–ln)	(4) Donor AIDS Expenditures (Per cap $US–ln)	(5) Government AIDS Expenditures (Per cap $US – ln) (with model 4 residuals)	(6) Budget Speech HIV/AIDS word count
Constant	−431.9***	−559.8***	−562.3***	−293.8**	−568.8***	−79.11
	(77.1)	(137)	(93.0)	(112)	(89.0)	(89.1)
Countries	71	69	70	62	70	21
Observations	298	254	290	134	290	78
R^2	0.57	0.64	0.62	0.59	0.64	

Models 1–5: OLS; model 6: Poisson Regression; Robust cluster (country) standard errors reported in parentheses

*** $p<0.01$, ** $p<0.05$, * $p<0.1$

correlated for countries with repeated observations across years, I estimated the statistical relationships using robust-cluster estimates of the standard errors, clustering around each country unit.[32] This is the best strategy given the data and model specification because it requires few assumptions about the nature of the error term: it provides valid estimates even in the presence of within-unit clusters (countries), but assumes that errors are not correlated across clusters. In order to control for the effects of simultaneous influences across all countries, I include a "year" variable in the analyses.[33]

Columns 1–3 present estimates of spending from government sources. Column 1 is an extremely parsimonious model; column 2 is a kitchen-sink model that includes all of the leading control variables; and column 3 is a "trimmed" model. Column 4 presents estimates of donor-sourced expenditures; and in column 5, I reestimate the model from column 3, while including the residuals from column 4, which can be interpreted as "excess donor effort," beyond what is explainable from the shared regressors and the inclusion of total overseas development assistance (less AIDS-related assistance). In column 6, I present Poisson regression estimates of the number of times HIV or AIDS appear in budget speeches.

Most striking for the analysis, the impact of the cultural diversity (Cdiv) indicator of ethnic boundaries is negative and statistically significant at the .01 level for all six models, even after controlling for per capita income and several of the variables that other scholars had concluded were already negatively influenced by ethnic fractionalization. Although I do not bore the reader here with the dozens and dozens of alternative model

---

[32]This is an estimation strategy Bradley et al. 2003 employ for an analogous problem of analyzing an unbalanced panel with few observations over time. The most prominent studies of the effects of ethnic fractionalization, including Easterly and Levine 1997; Posner 2004; and Alesina et al. 2003, use seemingly unrelated regression or ordinary least squares with robust standard errors, clustered by countries, which allow them to gain additional analytic leverage from multiple observations, despite the fact that the central explanatory variable is largely invariant within countries for the time periods considered.

[33]There is no unanimous consensus on the best practice for estimating time-series cross-sectional data under these conditions, however, and the results presented are robust to quite a large number of estimation procedures, restrictions and expansions of the universe of cases included, and the inclusion and exclusion of other analytic controls. For example, similar estimates are generated when using Feasible Generalized Least Squares and time-series cross-sectional regression with random effects, and when using the original country-year data or data averaged over five-year periods. Fixed effects models are inappropriate because the explanatory variable is time invariant for the periods considered, and the central goal of the analysis is to account for cross-country variation, not changes over time. The relationship between ethnic boundaries and AIDS policy appears to be consistently negative and strong.

specifications, these are rather robust results in the sense that I consistently find a fairly large, negative effect, within conventional bounds of statistical significance. Even when I remove Brazil, South Africa, and India, generating a truly independent "test" of the model from the qualitative case study chapters, the statistical results are almost identical.

To be certain, other factors matter as well. As predicted, HIV prevalence has a positive and statistically significant effect almost across the board. Given that these are estimates of logged values, the implication is that the magnitude of the effects of HIV prevalence will diminish with increasing levels. While this might seem to be merely a statistical artifact, it probably reflects the realities—at low levels, an increase of a percentage point in adult prevalence will appear dramatic to citizens, policymakers, and donors, but at higher levels, it generally takes much larger shifts in reported infections or income to garner anyone's attention. Per capita income has a positive and statistically significant effect on government expenditure. Not surprisingly, the estimate is smaller and not statistically significant in the model of donor expenditures. In fact, we might have expected a negative coefficient under the assumption that donors would want to target resources at poorer countries all else being equal.

In order to translate these results into more substantively meaningful terms, it is useful to calculate the expected values of the outcome variable given varying levels of particular explanatory variables. That is, we can try to use the statistical estimates to make claims about what would have happened under alternative conditions. I used the Clarify macro,[34] which produces 1,000 simulated observations generated from the regression estimates presented in model 5 from table 6.5, in order to calculate such expected values. For each of the main theoretical explanatory variables, I calculated the expected value by first setting that variable at its tenth-percentile value and then at its ninetieth percentile, all the while holding the other variables at their means. The difference between these two expected values can be interpreted as a counterfactual analysis: taking the "average" country and observing the effects of an isolated shift on a single variable. Those values are presented in rank order in figure 6.2, and we see that after HIV prevalence and per capita income, which are obviously extremely important determinants of government action, the cultural fractionalization index has a sizable effect on the outcome, more so than a government's general effectiveness, its regime type, or "excess" donor effort.

[34] King, Tomz, and Wittenberg 2000.

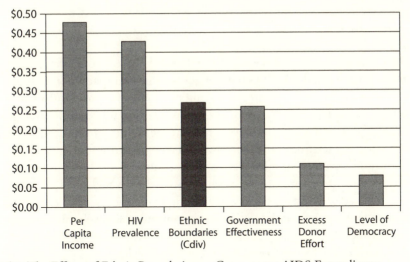

6.2. The Effects of Ethnic Boundaries on Government AIDS Expenditures ($US per capita)

Source: Simulated parameters calculated with Clarify software based on model 5 in table 6.4. Statistics are the difference between expected value given the tenth percentile for the indicated variable, and the ninetieth percentile, setting all other parameters set to their means.

Moreover, these may be conservative estimates of the effect of cultural fractionalization since they do not take into account either the indirect effects on level of development or the effects on donor expenditure.

In table 6.6, I report estimates of the effects of ethnic boundaries on ARV and PMTCT coverage as well as the AIDS Program Effort Index. Because I do not have time-varying policy data, I do not require time-varying prevalence data, and I use the more precise HIV point-estimate data available for 2003. Again, the estimated effects of cultural fractionalization are negative for all three policies, as predicted, though not statistically significant in the case of PMTCT, which as described earlier, is almost certainly our most unreliable measure.[35] These findings support the conclusion that increasingly strong ethnic boundaries constrain the realization of the Geneva Consensus at the country level.

[35] For the analysis of the API score, I have removed the sharply outlying case of Lesotho. That country's extremely low score is at odds with other information about the Lesotho response, which suggests that at the very least, it has sustained a moderate, if not somewhat aggressive response.

Alternative Explanations

As discussed above, and as evident in tables 6.5 and 6.6, other factors certainly have influenced AIDS policies across time and space. For example, countries that have been rated as having more effective governments have tended to be more aggressive on AIDS. While it is true that on average, more democratic countries have tended to be more aggressive, much of the statistical relationship washes away when we control for per capita income and government effectiveness. I do confirm prior findings that increased press freedoms are positively associated with higher API scores,[36] but the size of standard errors increases dramatically for estimates of the other AIDS policy variables, beyond conventional levels of statistical significance.

Many other factors seem not to matter much, including degree of trade openness, federalism, the share of the population that is Catholic or Muslim, the extent to which a country spends a great deal on public health, or levels of foreign direct investment in a country. Dummy variables for colonial legacies also had no substantively or statistically significant effects. Indeed, there are isolated statistical models where one or more of these variables can be found to have some statistically significant relationship, but this is highly sensitive to the specification of the model. The same is true for other structural variables such as measures of income inequality.[37] When I tried to replace the measure of GDP/capita with other highly correlated measures of a country's level of development, such as levels of literacy, female literacy, or urbanization, the overall fit of the statistical models deteriorated.

In estimating diffusion effects, the fact that regional dummy variables tend to be statistically significant could be interpreted as evidence that such mechanisms are at play, and to be certain, there are regional forums and coordinating bodies for AIDS policy. On the other hand, regional similarities may have as much to do with the shared threat of AIDS

---

[36] Which Bor 2007 finds in a host of other specifications.

[37] In an investigation of the effects of income inequality, Nattrass 2006 also found no statistical relationship with ARV coverage. Bor 2007 finds that the GINI index measure of income inequality has a negative and statistically significant effect on the "political support" component of the API. However, that finding is based on imputed data, and using available data, I find no relationship with any of the outcome variables presented in this article.

TABLE 6.6
The Effect of Ethnic Boundaries on AIDS Policies

Coefficient	(1) ARV drug treatment coverage 2005 (ln)	(2) PMTCT coverage 2003–5 (ln)	(3) AIDS Policy Index 2003
Ethnic boundaries	**–0.861***	**–0.554**	**–15.31****
(Cdiv)	(0.50)	(0.96)	(7.35)
HIV prev – ln	0.0102	0.259	1.180
	(0.095)	(0.18)	(1.13)
GDP/capita – ln	0.307**	0.846***	–2.809
	(0.14)	(0.29)	(1.85)
Press freedom	–0.00448	–0.0109	–0.194**
	(0.0065)	(0.012)	(0.089)
Government	0.293	–0.347	9.318***
effectiveness	(0.27)	(0.52)	(3.44)
Africa	0.519	0.309	4.909
	(0.42)	(0.78)	(4.53)
Latin Am. / Carib.	0.856**	–0.197	–6.521
	(0.40)	(0.75)	(5.58)
Constant	–3.506***	–3.637*	97.88***
	(1.10)	(2.16)	(14.7)
Observations	72	59	47
R^2	0.50	0.32	0.49

Note: Ordinary least squares estimates; standard errors in parentheses. In model 3, the extreme outlying case of Lesotho is removed from the analysis.
    *** $p<0.01$,   ** $p<0.05$,   *$p<0.1$

within regions—which differs in intensity across regions—and the high degree of within-region variability in response, especially across neighboring countries, suggests a limit to propositions that policy learning is diffused across state borders or through culturally similar networks. As discussed in chapter 3, most policy diffusion takes place at the global level through the broadcasting of the Geneva Consensus, and this can be observed through changes over time—a claim that is consistent with the consistently positive and statistically significant estimates of the effect of the year variable. However, this dynamic does not help to account for cross-sectional variation, which is the focus of the investigation.

Comparing the Effects of Alternative Measures of Ethnic Boundaries, across Regions

Virtually all of the analysis presented above has been conducted using the cultural fractionalization indicator, which, based on its properties of combining attention to ethnic salience with wide geographic coverage, was well suited for estimating the effects of interest. I did not want to present the initial results with the indicator I created (the ethnic boundary index) in order to avoid concern that I "cooked the books" in support of my favored hypothesis. But my motivation for constructing an alternative measure of ethnic boundaries was that I could create an even better fit with the analytic construct by adjusting the calibration of the indicator. At the very least, one would like to know how sensitive the results are to choice of indicators and approaches to the measurement of ethnic division. And to what extent are the effects consistent across world regions? Table 6.7 compares the effects of the six different summary measures of ethnic boundaries on government expenditures and on ARV coverage for the full sample and for subsamples of each region. Of course, as we whittle down to regional samples, the number of observations becomes extremely small (to as few as eleven cases), and we must expect that standard errors will go up, making it less likely we will identify relationships that fall within conventional ranges of statistical significance. Nevertheless, the coefficient estimates still describe the direction and magnitude of the relationships in these subsamples, and I complement these findings with discussion of specific cases in each region.

The most consistent effects were indeed from the ethnic boundary index, and in general, the standard errors were lower for estimates of indicators that were more attuned to social and political salience—including the ethnic boundary index, the institutional ethnic conflict index, and the Cdiv and PREG indicators.

In the case of religious fractionalization, none of the negative estimates of expenditure were statistically significant, and one estimate (in the Latin

TABLE 6.7
The Effects of Alternative Measures of Ethnic Boundaries, by World Region

	Dependent variable: government expenditures[a]			
	Total	Africa	Lat.Am./ Carib.	Asia
Ethnic boundary index	−1.31***	−2.39***	−0.38	−0.16
standard error	0.43	0.56	1.00	0.76
countries; obs.	72; 303	35; 147	23; 87	14; 69
Institutional ethnic conflict index	−1.24**	−2.00	−0.12	−0.70
standard error	0.58	1.29	1.30	0.86
countries; obs.	72; 303	35; 147	23; 87	14; 69
Cultural fractionaliza- tion (Cdiv)	−1.88***	−3.45***	−0.64	−0.02
standard error	0.71	1.14	1.43	1.23
countries; obs.	71; 298	35; 147	23; 87	13; 64
Politically relevant ethnic group fraction- alization (PREG)		−2.20**		
standard error		0.97		
countries; obs.		35; 147		
Religious fractional- ization (relig)	−0.89	−1.45	2.04	−1.70
standard error	0.89	2.04	1.36	1.85
countries; obs.	72; 303	35; 147	23; 87	14; 69
Ethnolinguistic frac- tionalization (ELF)	−0.99	−2.26**	−0.57	0.23
standard error	0.88	1.02	1.47	1.57
countries; obs.	70; 292	35; 147	23; 87	12; 58
	Dependent variable: ARV coverage (2005)[b]			
Ethnic boundary index	−0.72***	−0.53	−0.25	−1.33
standard error	0.26	0.41	0.26	0.79
countries; obs.	74	38	23	13

(continued)

TABLE 6.7 (*continued*)

	Total	Africa	Lat.Am./ Carib.	Asia
			Dependent variable: ARV coverage (2005)[b]	
Institutional ethnic conflict index	−0.89**	−1.13	0.14	−2.31
standard error	0.45	0.78	0.37	1.33
countries; obs.	74	38	23	13
Cultural Fractionalization (Cdiv)	−0.87*	−1.04	0.14	−3.09
standard error	0.46	0.74	0.41	1.80
countries; obs.	73	38	23	12
Politically relevant ethnic group fractionalization (PREG)		−0.89		
standard error		0.72		
countries; obs.		35		
Religious Fractionalization (relig)	−0.37	−0.31	0.11	1.13
standard error	0.51	0.84	0.48	2.14
countries; obs.	74	38	23	13
Ethnolinguistic Fractionalization (ELF)	−0.70	−0.94	0.06	−0.68
standard error	0.42	0.72	0.44	1.49
countries; obs.	72	38	23	11

[a] *Cells report parameter estimates for the indicated ethnic indicator, using the specification from model 1 from table 6.4 cluster–robust standard errors.*

[b] *Cells report parameter estimates for the indicated ethnic indicator, using trimmed specification from model 1 from table 6.5 (other regressors are HIV prevalence and GDP/capita).*

America/Caribbean subsample) was positive.[38] On the other hand, the estimate of the effects of religious fractionalization on ARV coverage for the African subsample was negative and statistically significant, suggesting at

[38] Prior research on the effects of ethnic fractionalization on public goods provision also found that religious diversity sometimes had a positive, rather than a negative, effect, and the authors concluded that religious diversity may better reflect a tolerant society than a divided one (Alesina et al. 2003, 158).

the very least that the impact of religious diversity per se on AIDS policy remains somewhat ambiguous.

When we compare the two sets of estimates of the two policy measures, there is a generally weaker fit between measures of ethnic boundaries and ARV coverage. One reason for this may be that there are fewer observations, which generates larger standard errors. But more substantively, the process of gaining access to antiretrovirals in the developing countries has been a more recent phenomenon, owing to a wide range of international efforts and partnerships, and treatment coverage certainly reflects less about government policymaking than does government spending. In Latin America, ethnic boundaries seem to have had almost no impact on treatment coverage, though it is still worth pointing out that as the region where ethnic boundaries have mattered least, treatment coverage has been higher on average.

Nonetheless, the portrait that emerges from dozens of model specifications and analyses is that the existence of multiple ethnic boundaries, particularly those with relatively strong social and political salience, has impeded government action on AIDS. To further support those claims, I consider each of the three world regions in a bit more depth, identifying additional trace evidence for select countries on the relationship between ethnic boundaries and the politics of this stigmatized social problem.

SUB-SAHARAN AFRICA

The effects of ethnic boundaries are most consistent in the African subsample, which is not surprising given the fact that the epidemic has been most severe in Africa, and the cross-country variation in ethnic diversity and salience is the widest, allowing for the strongest tests of the core hypothesis. If the ELF measure picks up ethnic diversity, this factor on its own has a substantial negative effect across the African countries,[39] but the effects of ethnicity on AIDS policies have been particularly strong when formal and informal institutions—ethnic boundaries—have rendered those identities socially and politically meaningful. The finding of systematic political influences on AIDS policy in Africa stands in contrast to what other scholars have previously found—that the African state has

[39] It is worth noting that the correlation between cultural fractionalization and ELF is much higher in the African subsample than in the Latin American and Caribbean subsample.

been largely immune to the politics of AIDS,[40] and relatedly, that the central variable was political leadership. In Africa, Patterson finds conflicting support for the hypothesis that regime type or the strength of civil society strongly affects policy responses, and both De Waal and Bor similarly find little difference between democracies and autocracies, though Bor finds a significant effect for press freedom in analyses of the AIDS Political Support Index.[41] I obtain similar results in analyses of the overall AIDS Policy Index, but not in analyses of other AIDS policy indicators. The fact that I find such striking effects for ethnic boundaries cuts against De Waal's argument that African governments have been largely unresponsive to political concerns about AIDS. On the contrary, ethnic political competition—a standard axis for conflict over public policy—has mediated demands for, and in turn the supply of, AIDS policies across countries.

Beyond the analysis of AIDS policies reported in table 6.7, for the African subsample I was also able to estimate the effects of ethnic boundaries on popular attitudes about AIDS policy. The Afrobarometer survey project asked citizens in several African countries if they thought that "the government should devote many more resources to combating HIV/AIDS, even if this means that less money is spent on things like education." In table 6.8, I report the effects of PREG on the percentage of citizens agreeing with this statement, and I find a very strong, negative relationship across the fourteen countries for which we have data. This does not necessarily indicate that decision-makers respond to citizens' demands, because it is equally plausible that such sentiments are the result of weak mobilization of opinion by political and government leaders. However, this analysis does support a key implication of the theory—that strong boundaries are associated with lower demand for aggressive policy, holding other factors constant. The association between the measures of ethnic dividedness and levels of citizens' urgency on AIDS increases the plausibility of the claim that government policy is structured by the discourses of risk and intergroup competition mechanisms described in chapter 2.

The intra-African results also highlight a fact that is sometimes ignored when thinking about Africa in comparative perspective: there is a great deal of variability in the ethnic dimension of African countries, and in the quality of policymaking.

---

[40] De Waal 2006.

[41] A component of the larger AIDS Policy Index, which considers subjective evaluations of overall political support for AIDS policy by high-level leaders.

TABLE 6.8
The Effect of Ethnic Boundaries on Citizen Attitudes toward AIDS Policy in African Countries

Dependent Variable: Percentage agreeing with the statement, "The government should devote many more resources to combating HIV/AIDS, even if this means that less money is spent on things like education."	
Politically relevant ethnic group fractionalization (PREG)	**−20.33**** (7.06)
HIV prevalence − ln	2.922 (1.73)
GDP/capita - ln	−3.844* (1.91)
Constant	69.95*** (11.9)
Observations	14
R^z	0.51

Source: Afrobarometer 2005.
Note: Standard errors in parentheses.
*** *p<0.01,*   ** *p<0.05,*   * *p<0.1*

Several West African countries are notable for the fact that they are linguistically and ethnically diverse, but for the most part, ethnicity is not salient in political life, and ethnic boundaries are considered far weaker and more permeable than in many other countries on the continent. In Senegal and the Gambia, for example, the informal institution of "joking cousins" or "joking kinship" has long existed as a tie across ethnic groups. This institution is in many ways exactly the opposite of the Indian institution of caste, especially the "caste-less" category of untouchability, in that it encourages friendships and close relationship across ethnic groups. Such institutions are understood to have mitigated the potential for interethnic conflict, and this is reflected in Posner's index, where the fractionalization scores are substantially lower for these cases relative to the demographic indices.

In turn, Senegal is notable for one of the earliest, most deliberate, and most steadfast responses to AIDS on the continent. Burkina Faso is a similar case. Although dozens of languages are spoken in Burkina and there is enormous potential to politicize ethnicity, most observers have recognized that ethnic identities are not an important basis for political organization in that country, and state institutions do not use them as important instruments of governing. Burkina is exceptional because despite the country's low level of development, it has mobilized an aggressive AIDS policy, scoring quite high on virtually all of the indicators of AIDS policy. This does not imply that the original impetus for such policy came from domestic leaders or even from civil society groups, as foreign involvement has been heavy in both of these countries. National government leaders did not resist such efforts at least in part because they did not face interethnic conflict and political backlash.

The cases of Botswana and Swaziland are also notable. They have consistently spent more on AIDS on a per capita basis than South Africa and Namibia, even when we adjust for their higher infection levels. Central government attention to AIDS has also been more intense: The words *HIV* and *AIDS* also appear much more frequently (as much as eight times more frequently) in the budget speeches of Swaziland and Botswana, which suggests that those governments are putting their mouths where their money is. Botswana boasts the most comprehensive treatment program on the African continent, and one of the world's leading AIDS researchers has observed of Swaziland, "In some ways, the state response has been quite path breaking."[42] Swaziland largely imagines itself as ethnically homogeneous ("Swazi"), and Botswana has relentlessly pursued strong nation-building strategies since independence. The government has consistently acted to minimize the salience of subnational ethnic identities, and in both cases the PREG score is 0. Again, in both cases, there has still been a great deal of stigma attached to HIV and AIDS during most of the epidemic, and foreign actors have played an influential role, but I do not see the same levels of political derailment that were evident in South Africa, and chronicled in chapter 4.

More like South Africa is Namibia, a country in which the state historically imposed strong ethnic boundaries, and ethnic divides have been socially and politically meaningful during the AIDS pandemic. In line with the theory, HIV prevalence has been reported to be significantly higher in the Ovambo region, producing the hypothesized sense of insulation

---

[42] Whiteside 2005, 121. Nevertheless, few would hold up the Swazi response as a model, in large part owing to the whims of the Swazi king. Patterson 2006 nicely details some of the contradictions associated with the politics of the Swazi response.

among other groups. Non-Ovambos have been reported to say: "It is an Ovambo disease, it is not our culture."[43] When members of the pastoral Himba group were confronted with the prospect of a growing epidemic, many responded to AIDS workers that "AIDS is not a disease of (our) tribe," and that it is "considered the disease of those who have been in contact with the Ovambo."[44] In turn, Namibia's president, Sam Nujoma, engaged in the same "denialist" approaches to the epidemic that Mbeki has been blamed for in South Africa. In 2001, he said that HIV-AIDS was created by the Americans as part of a biological warfare program during the Vietnam War.[45] While recently both the South African and the Namibian governments have introduced plans and taken actions that suggest greater attention to the problem of HIV/AIDS, based on objective comparisons the more ethnically homogeneous countries in the region have acted more aggressively, unhindered by group-based conflicts. In particular, government expenditure and rhetoric have been weak in Namibia relative to Botswana and Swaziland, though in the case of providing access to ARV treatment, Namibia has been more aggressive.

The deleterious effects of ethnic boundaries on AIDS policy are also evident in Nigeria, an ethnically heterogeneous and divided country according to virtually any metric (at or above the seventy-fifth percentile among African countries for the measures used in this study). The country is divided by religious identity, roughly as Muslims in the north and Christians in the South,[46] and by linguistic and more localized ethnic identities. Figure 6.3 depicts the location of some of the major socially and politically relevant language groups, as well as those states that are under Sharia. The country has also faced an AIDS epidemic, but with national prevalence lower than in southern Africa (Nigeria's HIV prevalence was estimated to be 3.9 percent in 2005). As shown in figure 6.4, estimated infection levels vary widely across Nigerian states.[47] Notably, HIV

[43] Philippe Bernes-Lasserre. "Africa-AIDS: Some African Communities Remain in AIDS Denial," Agence France-Presse, November 30, 2002.

[44] "NAMIBIA: HIV/AIDS Brings Change in Himba Communities," *Irin*, April 11, 2006.

[45] "President Accuses Americans of Creating HIV-AIDS," *The Namibian*, April 9, 2001.

[46] Lewis 1994.

[47] According to a WHO official I interviewed at the International AIDS Conference, Toronto, August 2006, it is extremely difficult to obtain reliable subnational estimates of HIV infections across countries because state/provincial leaders either refuse to release the data or will not agree to its being published and disseminated.

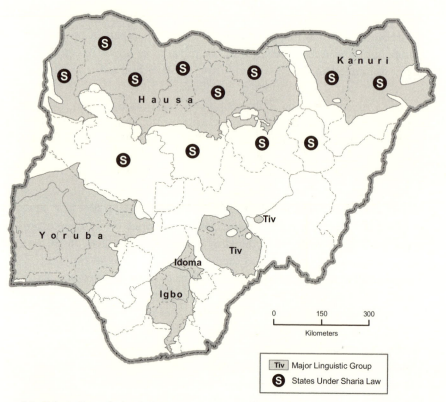

6.3. Ethnic Boundaries in Nigeria.
Source: Ethnologue data from Global Mapping International; BBC 2002.

prevalence is much lower in the northern states, a "social fact" that cuts squarely across the religious divide in the country. Among the political narratives highlighted in news reports is one in which northern/Muslim leaders dismiss proposed HIV prevention programs as a "Western" invention that would encourage promiscuity, often making reference to Christian organizations with international links.[48] Moreover, certain ethnolinguistic areas are identifiable as HIV "hot spots," including Benue state (populated mainly and recognizably by Tiv and Idoma), and this has created additional tensions. Leaders of the Idoma ethnic group have argued

[48]"Northern Islamic Clergy Condemn AIDS Seminar," *Irin*, January 9, 2001.

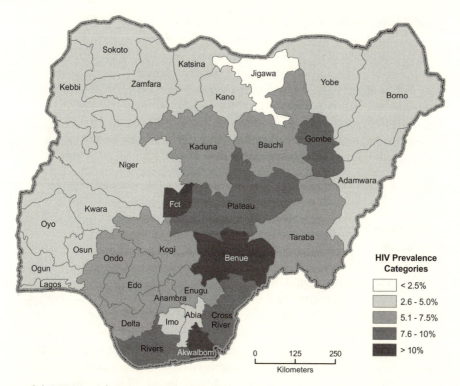

6.4. HIV Prevalence in Nigerian States
Source: National Intelligence Council 2002.

that the refusal of the federal government to address the AIDS crisis is part of a deliberate plot to "destroy them."[49]

Given the consistently tense and often violent nature of ethnic and religious conflict in Nigeria, and the relative ease with which political leaders can infuse it with ideas about HIV risk and transmission, centrally mandated policies concerning HIV/AIDS are likely to have ethnic-based consequences, potentially infuriating to multiple groups. Not only are

[49] Abel Orih in Yola, "Idoma Allege Plot to Destroy Them," http://www.thisdayonline. com/archive/2002/10/30/20021030dia02.html (consulted November 7, 2005). The prevalence of such political discourse was confirmed in informal discussions between the author and AIDS researchers and employees of international organizations and NGOs from Nigeria during the 2006 International AIDS conference in Toronto, August 13–18.

there likely to be conflicts about using government expenditures for a problem that may affect groups unevenly, but there are likely to be conflicts over the accuracy of the data, and what they signify about the moral standing of ethnic groups in a larger national debate. Thus, it is not be surprising that Nigeria's government expenditures on HIV/AIDS are extremely low ($0.05 per capita in 2003, or just one-tenth of median African AIDS expenditure for 1999–2004). Among the factors cited as constraining a national government response in a Family Health International assessment were "low perception of risk among policymakers and the general population" and "conservative social values, and regional religious and cultural differences."[50] To be certain, as the statistical models highlighted, several factors affect spending outcomes, but the Nigerian case does highlight the role ethnic competition can play in derailing a response.

There is evidence that such macro-level political dynamics resonate at the individual level. One critical ethnographic study of perceptions of risk in Nigeria among young, Christian, Igbo-speaking migrants in Kano and Aba found that perceptions of risk are not "personalized," and the author concludes that "risk [of being infected with HIV] is projected onto variously constructed 'others' in a process that intertwines biological infection, sexual immorality and religious identity."[51] Similar findings were obtained from a study based on 96 in-depth interviews with Maasai migrants in Tanzania, where the author ultimately concluded, "The majority of respondents construct risk at the group level—location and ethnicity—and not at the individual level."[52]

Ethnically divided Kenya also reveals how perceptions of risk are mobilized in terms of ethnic identities. Like Nigeria, regions in Kenya are associated with particular ethnic groups, and HIV prevalence varies by region. Members of certain ethnic groups (especially Luo and Meru/Embu) are more likely to report "risky" sexual behavior,[53] and they reside in areas with higher reported prevalence. Many Kenyan nationals have related to me that indeed, Luo are thought to be more promiscuous, and that AIDS has traditionally been though to be "their" problem.[54] According to a Nairobi-based

[50] TvT Associates 2002, 3.

[51] Smith 2004, 434.

[52] Coast 2006, 1007.

[53] Based on data from the 1998 Kenyan Demographic and Health Survey, as analyzed in Akwara, Madise, and Hinde 2003, 402.

[54] See also Hyden and Lanegran 1993, 59, who argue that Kenyan president Daniel Arap Moi's inattention to AIDS relative to Uganda's president Museveni was due to the fact that his Kalenjin group was not the group primarily affected.

medical professional, who highlighted the cultural practices that put Luo in Nyanza province at greater risk, "If you look at the Luo community as a whole . . . it has been observed that they tend to have a relatively higher HIV prevalence."[55] In turn, as predicted by the theory, these types of boundary politics have had an adverse effect on government responsiveness. An assessment by the British International Aid agency in 2001 found that "Kenya has been notoriously slow to admit to its HIV/AIDS problem, to see it without an ethnic focus and to demonstrate high-level political commitment."[56] While the Kenyan government has acted more aggressively more recently, the first-order response appears to be in line with what is predicted by the theoretical model put forth in chapter 2.

Because the model presented in this book is a probabilistic one, and ethnic homogeneity or harmony is neither necessary nor sufficient for high levels of spending, no single case can be used to prove or to disprove the core hypothesis. Nonetheless, the notable case of Uganda—a flagship case for aggressively responding to HIV/AIDS—is also ethnically diverse with a long history of ethnic-based conflict. Uganda was the first country to have a serious and major outbreak, and its early, extremely high rates of infection proved to be more important in driving a response, perhaps along with certain other exceptional features.[57] In that case, a "great man" explanation of policymaking in the form of President Yoweri Museveni, who has repeatedly and skillfully garnered high levels of foreign economic support, may be the answer, but this explanation provides few generalizable insights. Although Museveni has publicly proclaimed his efforts to "stamp out" ethnicity through a "no-party" democracy, careful observers of Ugandan politics have emphasized that ethnic boundaries remain important. Seen in this light, the case does not support the theory, and it certainly indicates that even in the context of ethnic fractionalization, aggressive policy responses are possible, even if less likely.

Beyond the more general political exceptionalism of Uganda, it is also important to note the exceptional nature of that country's AIDS epidemic. It was the first country in the world to report extremely high rates of AIDS deaths and infections, and was the first to break the barrier of a 10 percent estimated HIV prevalence. The onset of the Ugandan

---

[55] "Cultural Traditions Fuel the Spread of HIV/AIDS," *Irin*, November 30, 2005.

[56] As reported by Human Rights Watch, 2001, vol. 13, no. 4. "Kenya, in the Shadow Of Death: HIV/AIDS and Children's Rights in Kenya," http://www.hrw.org/reports/2001/kenya/kenya0701.PDF (consulted June 17, 2008).

[57] Van de Walle 2001 similarly points to Uganda as an exceptional case in its adoption of macroeconomic reform policies.

pandemic took place in the (southwestern) Rakai district, and as the Ugandan epidemic spread early, and in the midst of widespread violence and civil unrest in the country,[58] illness and death fell upon many ethnic groups quite quickly, making it less likely that any single group might be able to feel insulated. The same was not true for other Great Lakes countries such as Kenya and Tanzania, where particular groups were identified as uniquely infected early in the epidemic.[59] Thus, while the Ugandan case does not lend great support to the theory, some of these exceptional circumstances do show why it is not a strong piece of contradictory evidence.

LATIN AMERICA AND THE CARIBBEAN

The effects of boundary politics are less pronounced in the statistical estimates reported in table 6.7 for the Latin America and Caribbean subsample than for the African subsample. Nonetheless, the estimated effects of ethnic boundaries are consistently negative. It is true, as Alesina et al. point out,[60] that a measure of ethnic fractionalization based on language will not detect much of the ethnic diversity in Latin America, where large numbers of indigenous, African-descended, and European-descended people can be recognized as distinct ethnic or racial groups. On the other hand, linguistic conformity reflects the product of much stronger nation-building legacies within the region, which have mitigated ethnic claims in the political arena (even if ethnic- and race-based socioeconomic inequalities remain severe). The cultural fractionalization and ethnic salience measures reflect more about the deliberate "whitening"[61] and *mestizaje*[62] strategies—the social and political constructions of "mixed" nations—that characterize much of Latin America, albeit to varying degrees across countries.

While the Brazilian case, discussed in chapter 4, is perhaps the best known of the region's most aggressive responses to AIDS, it is not unique. For example, Cuba reacted aggressively to AIDS, albeit certain strategies, such as a quarantine, contradicted the Geneva Consensus on a rights-oriented approach. By most quantitative measures and reasonable assessments of policy records, Argentina, Costa Rica, and Uruguay have also

---

[58] Barnett and Whiteside 2002, 131–36.
[59] Hyden and Lanegran 1993; author interviews with country nationals.
[60] Alesina et al. 2003.
[61] Stepan 1991; Skidmore 1995.
[62] Martinez-Echazabal 1998.

been aggressive on AIDS, both in their prevention policies and in their near universal provision of free ARV drug treatment (Costa Rica was the first country in Central America to offer treatment). One could identify features in each of these countries that seem to explain its aggressive response—such as Cuba's well-developed health care system, Costa Rica's long history of democratic rule, or Uruguay's relatively advanced social development. However, the characteristic that unites these countries is that none has strong ethnic boundaries that divide groups from one another. In none of these countries is AIDS understood as a white, black, indigenous, or other group disease. Thus, actors interested in promoting an aggressive response were able to do their jobs.

The island of Hispaniola provides solid evidence of contrasting approaches to AIDS that can be explained with the theory of boundary politics. The Dominican Republic (DR) is much wealthier than its island neighbor, Haiti. Nonetheless, the latter's response to AIDS has been much more aggressive, while the DR's response has been lambasted by critics, who point to "government disinterest and outright obstructionism."[63] The Dominican Republic is ethnically divided between people of European and "mixed" descent on the one hand, and the approximately 10–15 percent of the population that is "Haitian," on the other. Haitians have long experienced strong and active discrimination in the DR,[64] and the problem of AIDS is concentrated in the *bateyes*—shantytowns originally built to house migrant sugarcane workers—which are largely Haitians.[65] Strong anti-Haitian sentiments exist in the DR, and AIDS is often understood as a problem of Haitians, not of the country more generally. In turn, spending and treatment coverage are among the lowest in the Latin American and Caribbean region. By contrast, in Haiti, ARV coverage has been better and the overall response to AIDS has been much stronger than in the DR. It is true that Haiti has received a great deal of Western attention and intervention, notably the spectacular efforts of Paul Farmer's organization, Partners In Health. But there has been no ethnic conflict over AIDS in Haiti—a highly homogeneous country—that might have derailed the response. In Haiti AIDS has been viewed as "our problem," whereas in the DR it has been "their problem," and the government responses have followed suit.

[63] Cohen 2006, 473.
[64] See, for example, the group summary for Haitian blacks in the Dominican Republic in the MAR database (2005).
[65] Cohen 2006, 473.

More like the Dominican Republic, other countries with the strongest boundaries in the region including Trinidad and Tobago, Bolivia, and Ecuador, have not responded to AIDS in a particularly aggressive manner relative to other countries in the region.

ASIA

It is most difficult to estimate the effects of ethnic boundaries in Asia, because eleven of the nineteen countries considered have not experienced AIDS epidemics. And yet, even in this region, there is some important support for, and little direct contradiction of, the central implications of the theory. Among the developing countries of Asia, Thailand stands out as a "model" response. Faced with a growing AIDS epidemic, the government implemented an aggressive campaign to promote condom use, and it has been the site of key scientific trials, including the "Thai Short Course" for prevention of mother-to-child transmission. Although it is an ethnically diverse country, ethnic boundaries are weak, and a history of strong nation-building and the promotion of Thai as a national language[66] are reminiscent of Brazil and Senegal, not India and South Africa. Vietnam and Cambodia have been lauded for their aggressive responses to AIDS, and both are relatively homogeneous ethnically; small ethnic minorities are fairly dispersed and do not figure prominently in national politics.

China is of great interest to policymakers and has been heavily criticized for aspects of its response to AIDS, which, however, is not disproportionate given the size of its epidemic and its level of economic development. Because it is an ethnically homogeneous country, we would expect its response to be relatively more aggressive than that of other countries with similarly sized epidemics and resources, and in fact, this is largely the case.

More ethnically divided Asian countries, including India, Pakistan, Myanmar, Sri Lanka, and Fiji, have all responded less aggressively to AIDS.

---

[66] According to Thomson 1993, 67, Thais have maintained a strong sense of national identity, and this interpretation has long been cultivated and maintained in popular culture, religious activities, and politics. The intrusion of an alien group into Thai society was not necessarily considered a threat, and the group was increasingly incorporated into the social, political, and economic life of the country. According to Smalley 1994, Thailand has maintained relative stability despite its eighty languages, particularly through the state's imposition of Thai as the undisputed *national* language.

Other Dimensions of Boundaries and (In)tolerance

Ultimately, my research has tried to investigate the effects of *ethnic* boundaries. The argument does not, however, foreclose the possibility that other boundaries, particularly those within which groups could imagine themselves as endogamous and with minimal intimate contact, might matter in a similar manner.

Indeed, since the inception of the epidemic, AIDS has been associated with homosexuals, even as the number of heterosexual transmissions worldwide has risen to be orders of magnitude greater than through homosexual transmissions. Moreover, as discussed in earlier chapters, because so much of the response to HIV and AIDS involves discussion of sex and sexuality, observers have conjectured that what really explains cross-country differences in policy responses is the degree to which a society is sexually "open." The prevalence of sexual imagery and open cross-dressing in major Brazilian cultural events, including Carnival, has led many to conclude that such tolerant or liberal attitudes laid the foundation for an aggressive response to HIV and AIDS. Indeed, by comparison, both India and South Africa have seemingly far more repressed sexual cultures, and are arguably less tolerant toward homosexuals, leaving us to wonder if either of these two other variables might be similarly good predictors of government policy responses.

Analogous cross-country data are not available to measure either the size of groups according to sexual orientation, or the institutionalization of sexual boundaries. However, the World Values Survey does provide some opportunities for cross-country comparisons for a limited number of countries. In addition to the "antirace" variable described earlier in the chapter, I was able to construct an almost identical variable based on attitudes toward homosexuals, which I label "antigay," measured as the share of the surveyed sample saying they would not like to have a homosexual as a neighbor. For "sexual freedom," I used the survey question, "If someone said that individuals should have the chance to enjoy complete sexual freedom without being restricted, would you tend to agree or disagree?" I created a three-point index, ranging from 0 to 2 based on the possible answers, "Tend to disagree," "Neither/It depends," and "Tend to agree," and calculated the average for each country, such that higher scores reflect higher levels of sexual tolerance. Indeed, Brazil scores highest among the fifteen countries in my dataset, confirming the characterizations of other observers highlighted in chapter 4.

As reported in table 6.9, I present trimmed models of government AIDS expenditures, which allow us to compare the effects of the antirace, antigay, and sexual freedom variables, while controlling for per capita income, HIV prevalence, and year; and in models 4–6, I repeat this analysis without per capita income, which is so highly correlated with the "tolerance" measures that it is difficult to estimate the independent effect of the latter with so few cases.

All of the estimates are consistent with expectations in the sense that the governments of countries with more strongly negative views of other race groups and of gays spend less on AIDS, and those with higher levels of sexual tolerance spend more. Nonetheless, at least for this relatively small sample, the effects of antirace appear to be far stronger than for the other two variables. When we remove GDP/capita from the regression model, both antirace and antigay become statistically significant, but the size of the antirace coefficient is about twice as large. While the data on sexual freedom are consistent with the characterization of Brazil, when viewed in broader comparative perspective, this variable is a very noisy predictor of the other cases.

Much more research is required to estimate the influence of sexual boundaries more precisely, and it would not be surprising if their effects were strong in more restricted domains of time, space, and issue. In trying to explain patterns of variation in government response to HIV/AIDS, however, ethnic politics has proved far more prominent as a cleavage in polities around the world, and one that varies in its degree of institutionalization. These analyses support my conclusion that ethnic boundaries have an autonomous and powerful effect on policymaking, and it is not merely some *other* form of tolerance or cultural attitude that is driving the results, both in the case studies and for the larger sample.

Conclusion

This chapter has demonstrated that ethnic boundaries have had a consistently strong and negative effect on the aggressiveness of AIDS policy in the developing countries. Most of the countries that have been extremely aggressive on AIDS, including Brazil, Senegal, Thailand, Botswana, Cuba, Burkina Faso, Costa Rica, Argentina, and Uruguay, are characterized by the *absence* of formal or informal institutions that divide their societies

TABLE 6.9
The Effect of Nonethnic Boundaries on AIDS Policies

	Dependent variable: government expenditures on AIDS/capita (ln)					
	1	*2*	*3*	*4*	*5*	*6*
Antirace	−2.668			−11.44***		
	(2.29)			(3.20)		
Antigay		−0.465			−5.822***	
		(1.17)			(1.59)	
Sexual freedom			0.163			1.951
			(0.79)			(2.05)
HIV prev – ln	0.741***	0.756***	0.748***	0.706*	0.876**	0.763*
	(0.13)	(0.16)	(0.17)	(0.35)	(0.33)	(0.40)
GDP/capita – ln	1.582***	1.650***	1.702***			
	(0.20)	(0.23)	(0.23)			
Year	0.174**	0.177**	0.176**	0.264**	0.251*	0.301**
	(0.071)	(0.075)	(0.078)	(0.12)	(0.12)	(0.13)
Constant	−360.2**	−366.4**	−365.9**	−526.5**	−500.3*	−605.1**
	(142)	(148)	(155)	(234)	(241)	(269)
Countries	15	15	15	15	15	15
Observations	69	69	69	69	69	69
R^2	0.84	0.84	0.84	0.55	0.58	0.40

Robust cluster standard errors in parentheses.
*** $p<0.01$,   ** $p<0.05$,   * $p<0.1$

into many separate groups. Most of the countries that have been slow or limited in their responses, even in the face of epidemics, are characterized by strong internal boundaries, including South Africa, India, Nigeria, Ethiopia, Congo, Myanmar, Chad, Niger, Sudan, and Central African Republic. While such findings are consistent with other published research on the relationship between ethnic diversity and the provision of public goods, the empirical tests presented here are far stronger because we can be confident that most of the patterns of ethnic politics were independent of the outcomes under analysis. To be sure, ethnic politics did not determine these outcomes, and the larger history I have presented shows that

AIDS policy has largely been externally driven. However, ethnic boundaries have constrained that impetus in important ways. This finding suggests that more aggressive AIDS policies are more likely in countries with weaker ethnic boundaries, a proposition that raises important normative concerns, which I discuss in the concluding chapter.

6.A1
Ethnic Boundary Index Country Scores (1985–95)

0: Extremely weak or non-existent ethnic boundaries	.25: Mostly weak or permeable ethnic boundaries	.5: Intermediate levels of ethnic boundaries	.75: Mostly strong and/or multiple ethnic boundaries	1: Extremely strong and multiple ethnic boundaries
Argentina	Brazil	Bhutan	Angola	Cameroon
Bangladesh	Colombia	Guinea Bissau	Benin	Central African Republic
Botswana	Gabon	Indonesia	Bolivia	Chad
Burkina Faso	Gambia	Lao PDR	Burundi	Congo
Cambodia	Honduras	Madagascar	Dominican Republic	Congo, DR
Chile	Nicaragua	Mali	Ecuador	Cote d'Ivoire
China	Panama	Mexico	Ghana	Djibouti
Comoros	Peru	Mozambique	Guatemala	Ethiopia
Costa Rica	Philippines	Somalia	Malawi	Fiji
Cuba	Senegal	Tanzania	Mauritania	Guinea
El Salvador	Thailand		Myanmar	Guyana
Eritrea	Venezuela		Nepal	India
Haiti			Rwanda	Kenya
Jamaica			Sierra Leone	Liberia
Korea, North			Sri Lanka	Malaysia
Lesotho			Trinidad and Tobago	Namibia
Mongolia			Uganda	Niger
Paraguay			Zambia	Nigeria
Swaziland			Zimbabwe	Pakistan
Uruguay				Papua New Guinea
Vietnam				South Africa
				Sudan
				Togo

7 ❧ Conclusion: Ethnic Boundaries or Cosmopolitanism?

Analyses of data and evidence concerning the history of AIDS and AIDS policy in the developing countries reveal that where strong ethnic boundaries were in place, governments were far less aggressive in their responses to the epidemic. While unprecedented external pressures have weighed on governments throughout the world, especially on high-prevalence countries in Africa, Asia, Latin America and the Caribbean, the adoption of the "Geneva Consensus" was strongly conditioned by the quality of ethnic politics in those countries. Substantial evidence shows that citizens and elites behaved in ways predicted by social identity theory: they attempted to disassociate themselves from a condition that might besmirch their group's reputation or esteem. In ethnically divided societies, discourses of risk were more likely to focus on particular ethnic groups than on the society at large, reducing the potential base of support for aggressive policies. The net effects were substantial in terms of expenditure levels, prevention and treatment coverage, and the timing of certain policies. Although more recent years have witnessed increasing convergence and coordination across countries in their actions on AIDS, lost time has cost lives and magnified the epidemic.

It is difficult to assess the validity of political models of policymaking because multiple pressures and motivations are almost always at work. Actors cannot be relied upon to describe what motivates their behavior because they want to cast themselves in the most favorable light, and also because they do not describe their actions in ways that highlight counter-factual conditions. Indeed, most policymakers, government leaders, and AIDS activists would not tell the story I have detailed in the previous chapters, because their perspectives are rarely explicitly comparative and historical. As an alternative, I have relied upon multiple social scientific methods and analytic strategies to estimate the effects of hypothesized pressures on policymaking. A comparative analysis of Brazil and South Africa highlighted the political problems that unfolded when understand-ings of the epidemic got caught up in racial politics. Although South Af-rica has characteristics that many analysts believe helped to drive an ag-gressive policy on AIDS in Brazil, a different political and policy outcome ensued. A case study of India supported these claims: the linking of re-gional and occupational identities to ethnic boundaries created a political dynamic more similar to that found in South Africa than in Brazil, help-ing to account for India's relatively weak response to AIDS. And across Indian states, variation in antiethnic sentiments similarly predicted much of the variance in state responses. Taking the proposition to a dataset in-cluding several dozen low- and middle-income countries, I obtained simi-lar results. For several different measures of policy aggressiveness, and of citizens' preferences for aggressive AIDS policies, indicators of ethnic di-videdness were consistently negative predictors of the outcome.

My findings resonate with prior scholarship demonstrating a strong negative relationship between ethnic fractionalization and the provision of public goods, but the study of the effects of ethnicity in the context of a strong exogenous shock—the onset of AIDS—advances us a great deal in supporting the claim that ethnic boundaries have a *causal* effect on the outcome. In the years to come, if the AIDS epidemic continues its path of human devastation, it will certainly re-shape the demography of many countries, and is likely to affect ethnic boundaries as well, but not neces-sarily in predictable ways. AIDS may help to reinforce existing boundaries in places where AIDS-related illness and death are associated with certain groups and where political leaders mobilize such differences; but it may also help to blur boundaries in places where the burden of disease is distrib-uted more equally and where political entrepreneurs successfully mobilize the slogan from the opening of this book: "AIDS knows no boundaries." Nevertheless, for the earlier period of the epidemic considered in this book—its first quarter-century—the investigation comes as close to a large-scale, macro-historical natural experiment, as we find in social science research. This is a powerful aid in drawing conclusions because, contrary to much observational analysis, we can feel confident that we have not improperly inferred the direction of causality.

To be certain, not all countries fit the pattern perfectly—the central propositions are only probabilistic, not deterministic—but the consistency of the accounts across these investigations reveals that a powerful dynamic is at work. Across a wide diversity of countries, varying in world region, level of economic development, regime type, and other factors, the politics of AIDS policymaking has been shaped by nationally distinctive institutions. While we cannot always be sure, *ex ante*, which institutions will matter for which policy problems, for an epidemic such as HIV/AIDS, with its potential to be understood as a "selective" bad or danger, and which engenders metaphors of blood, sexuality, sanitation, and morality, ethnic institutions appear remarkably powerful.

Institutions are more than constraints on purposive, instrumental, rational actors. Rather, institutions shape the very preferences that guide the politics of policymaking. They affect the dissemination and interpretation of information, making certain policies and practices appear valuable, as public goods, or repugnant, as public bads. Boundary institutions, in particular, can shape the very nature of political competition by reinforcing the salience of groups as social realities. Given a near universal proclivity toward social competition, such institutions can impede political consensus on key policies and actions.

While the analysis of boundary institutions took center stage in the analysis, other factors influenced policymaking in predictable ways: Governments and donors have been affected by the size of epidemics in countries and regions, and richer countries have tended to respond more aggressively. But none of these factors had a deterministic influence on policy: some countries responded aggressively before a major epidemic developed, and several poor countries carried out aggressive policies. The absence of absolute constraints on responsiveness ought to be a source of optimism when we consider the possibilities for responsive governance institutions in the developing world. Two countries highlighted in this book for their lackluster responses—South Africa and India—have taken steps toward more comprehensive AIDS plans in recent years. Of particular note is that as the virus has continued to spread and its stigma has declined, the potential political cost of being aggressive on AIDS has also decreased.

While by definition, the politics and processes of policymaking differ, in democracies and authoritarian regimes, aggressiveness on policy does not appear to differ systematically by regime type. Democracy is intrinsically desirable for human freedom, and it is useful to think of democracy as one aspect of development. But we ought not to believe that democracies are programmed to solve complex social problems efficiently and effectively. Democracies offer freer flows of information and opportunities to express dissatisfaction with nonresponsive governments. On the other hand, information does not always lead to demand for public policies and public goods, particularly for problems that are initially limited in scope. Moreover, the free spread of certain information may impede action. Thus, there are aggressive and nonaggressive responses both in democratically governed countries and in those governed by authoritarian regimes.

Implications

Have we learned lessons that could be applied to the AIDS pandemic and other large-scale social problems? Because this is not a book about HIV pathogenesis, or the effects of treatment options, I cannot conclude with a call for specific prevention or treatment policies. Most of the prescriptions in the Geneva Consensus are still appropriate, though some ideas are more appropriate to particular contexts, and universally effective ones are yet to be identified. Nonetheless, as I pointed out in chapter 3, action on the AIDS pandemic provides a promising message for efforts in public health and beyond. As this book is being completed, millions infected with HIV are receiving treatment and enjoying longer, healthier lives; countless infections have been averted; and persons once shunned for their HIV status are being treated with dignity. These developments are occurring not just in the rich, but in poor countries around the world. Could more be done? Absolutely. Should other human needs receive greater attention? Without doubt. But in the face of an extraordinarily complex, global pandemic, actors around the world have coordinated policies to reverse its progression. One can only imagine what the pandemic would be in the absence of such efforts.

If we appreciate the profound, if incomplete and uneven, social transformations associated with the epidemic, it makes sense to reflect on the sources of authority in an era of globalization, in which power often appears diffuse. At the broadest level, domestic political institutions still matter a great deal. In a world of national states, national governments remain important in addressing major problems, and the understanding of those problems is mediated by the political process. Donors of financial and technical resources often conclude that their efforts are most effective where national governments mobilize and implement policy.[1] Even in countries characterized by state weakness, government actions have substantive implications for people's lives. In an increasingly interconnected world, governments that lack financial and technical capacity, but desire to act, may find possibilities for action through partnerships.

Yet if governments are to lead, the proper political incentives must be in place. Whether the task is delivery of water, malaria control, tuberculosis, or education, there are no technical quick fixes. People in every society must interpret the circumstances before them and make choices. Governments are not likely to lead if they fear a backlash. Persons or organizations that offer aid or respond to pleas for assistance are naive if they assume that political considerations will not matter.

The central political consideration I have highlighted is ethnic political competition. However, it is a misinterpretation of the findings of this book to conclude that ethnic *diversity* is the problem. That is not what I have argued, nor what I have found in my research. While more homogeneous countries tend to respond more aggressively, ethnic homogeneity is itself often a sociopolitical construction, as in Botswana, where different choices made less than a half-century ago might have led to very different internal boundaries. Moreover, many ethnically *heterogeneous* countries such as Brazil, Cuba, Senegal, and Burkina Faso have largely avoided the institutionalization of ethnic boundaries for most of their modern histories. Rather than merely "technical" role models for the best policies, these countries are surprising political models, at least in their institutions of ethnic tolerance.

Thus, a key implication is that efforts to mitigate ethnic division may induce more responsible and beneficial provision of public goods. This argument resonates with two recent works of moral philosophy: one by Nobel laureate and economist Amartya Sen and the other by the noted

---

[1] As Tom Kenyon, chief deputy coordinator of PEPFAR commented in June 2007, "We get the best results in countries where the host government assumes the leadership for the response. . . . We want to be led by the host country" (Julie Steenhuysen, "AIDS Efforts Found to Work Best When Nations Take the Lead," Reuters, June 13, 2007).

philosopher Kwame Anthony Appiah. Sen's *Illusion of Destiny* and Appiah's *Cosmopolitanism* draw on the authors' own multiple affiliations, and highlight the dangers of reifying ethnic cleavages and identities in social and political life. They argue for more flexible identities that transcend multiple groups, and ultimately call for recognition of global citizenship as one of many sets of identities, loyalties, and obligations. According to Appiah, two ideas undergird the notion of cosmopolitanism:

> One is the idea that we have obligations to others, obligations that stretch beyond those to whom we are related by the ties of kith and kind, or even the more formal ties of a shared citizenship. The other is that we take seriously the value not just of human life but of particular human lives, which means taking an interest in the practices and beliefs that lend them significance. People are different, the cosmopolitan knows, and there is much to learn from differences.[2]

It is important to note, however, that neither Sen nor Appiah calls for the erasure of national or more localized identities, but point to the need for flexibility and the possibility for shared citizenship across boundaries.[3] In a related manner, Robert Putnam observes that while countries are becoming more diverse, and while confirming in his own research that such diversity initially impedes social solidarity and the provision of public goods, he concludes that the best strategy for diversifying societies "is to create a new, broader sense of 'we.'"[4]

The cosmopolitan perspective of Sen and Appiah, like Putnam's call for broadening of identity, is at odds with a quite different strand of normative theory, which Walker describes as "culturalism."[5] The luminary of this perspective is the Canadian scholar Will Kymlicka, but it is also embodied in the works of Joseph Raz, Vernon van Dyke, Michael Seymour, and others, all of whom respond to the existence of ethnic diversity with calls for greater ethnic autonomy and official recognition. From this perspective, people are fundamentally tied to ethnic groups and communities, and they require opportunities to express such identities in order

---

[2] Appiah 2006, xv.

[3] By contrast, Martha Nussbaum advocates a more extreme form of "global citizenship," in which national patriotisms are abandoned for allegiance "to the worldwide community of human beings (Nussbaum and Cohen 1996, 4).

[4] Putnam 2007, 131.

[5] Walker 1997.

to live free and autonomous lives. Like cosmopolitanism, culturalism is concerned with the challenge of organizing diverse societies in ways that recognize liberty, autonomy, and equality. Neither perspective calls for homogenization or the trampling of cultural difference—in fact, both embrace cultural diversity as a fundamental source of human wealth. However, they arrive at starkly different conclusions about how governments and societies ought to address ethnic diversity in order to achieve those goals. Culturalism seeks to strengthen ethnic boundaries in order to protect cultures and identities. It advocates greater recognition of and autonomy for ethnic political leaders, culturally distinctive education strategies, and ethnically delineated rights. By contrast, cosmopolitanism charges against a static or strongly institutionalized recognition of any one group or set of groups, allowing for a greater ebb and flow of identities and affiliations, including affiliations that transcend the national state. Rather than seeking to "preserve" particular groups, cosmopolitanism assumes that cultures and identities will cross-pollinate and gain exposure to one another, leading to the forging of new identities.

Because my work is essentially positive, not normative, I have not directly engaged debates about the intrinsic ethical implications of these alternative approaches, and I recognize that both positions make valid points. Questions about the desirability of "melting pot" or "mosaic" approaches to ethnic pluralism remain lively sources of debate among scholars, citizens, and political elites. Nonetheless, my research does weigh in on this debate in terms of the implications for development. I find that the cosmopolitan approach is more likely to produce the public goods and public policies that are beneficial for equitable development and for preventing certain types of devastation. Indeed, the motto that "AIDS knows no boundaries" reflects an intuition that risk pooling across groups is an effective strategy for building solidarity. Similar implications can be drawn from other research highlighting the negative effects of ethnic fractionalization on the provision of public goods and development more generally. As political leaders at various levels of governance contemplate strategies for addressing increasing cultural pluralism, social and economic inequalities, and their overlap, they need to take into account the trade-offs of emphasizing or de-emphasizing particular ethnic identities.

Of course, the boundary institutions described in this book are not simply willed into or out of existence by any single political leader. They are often themselves the product of long political struggles, and they are manifest in different ways in different places. These institutions are also sticky, in the sense that the discontinuation of an institution—for example, the elimination of ethnic counting in the Nigerian census—is not likely to have an immediate effect on the collective consciousness, and may have the effect of reinforcing boundaries. Moreover, there is no single recipe for the weak boundary institutions that promote cosmopolitanism. In Brazil and Cuba, state policies of nonracialism and racial mixture were part of a more general Latin American pattern of promoting a mixed, mestizo, or *mestizaje* identity. In Senegal and other countries in West Africa, informal institutions have developed that mitigated ethnic tensions. Specifically, the informally institutionalized practice of "joking cousins" or "joking kinship," with specific rituals for promoting interethnic ties, has minimized tensions between ethnic groups and political mobilization along ethnic lines. In the state of West Bengal in India, a strong labor movement and political party organization diminished the importance of ethnic affiliations. These are by no means ideal societies, nor have they stamped out ethnic prejudice or even ethnic violence. What they have done is to reduce the mobilization of ethnic distinctions in the political arena. In each of these places, deliberate institution-building helped minimize the salience of ethnic boundaries, promoting a form of cosmopolitanism.

One might imagine that international institutions charged with promoting development and helping governments to provide public goods and resources would embrace a cosmopolitan approach to identity—if they were to embrace any approach at all. And yet, in recent years, much of the international development community has taken the opposite approach. The World Bank, the Inter-American Development Bank, and the Ford Foundation, just to name a few, have embraced culturalism in projects and initiatives. I don't want to overstate this orientation, but all have pursued projects that gather and disseminate information about ethnic minorities, or promote civil society institutions organized along ethnic lines. In countries where ethnic boundaries were already strong and well institutionalized, this approach might have been unavoidable, but it has occurred even where ethnic boundaries were generally weak.

Such initiatives have been well intentioned: the developing world—in fact, the entire world—is characterized by enormous socioeconomic disparities that are highly correlated with ethnic identities. The logic is that the best way to address such inequality is to spotlight it wherever possible. In 2001, the United Nations hosted an international conference on racism, which has inspired projects aimed at identifying and measuring ethnic disparities. International organizations have formed an Inter-Agency

Consultation on Race, and in a 2007 report, Edward Telles, a leading sociologist of Latin American race relations, argued that governments and other organizations ought to collect *more* data along ethnic and racial lines. On behalf of the organization, he critiqued the Millennium Development Goals for being silent on the issue of racial and ethnic inequalities.[6] Organizations such as the Ford Foundation have been providing resources to ethnic groups to develop organized leadership.[7] The 2004 edition of the UNDP's influential *Human Development Report* highlighted the critical importance of cultural identities for the politics of development and, having consulted figures such as Sen as well as Kymlicka, recommended a mix of cultural protections, and flexibility in the development of more cosmopolitan identities. Ultimately, however, the report recommends "multicultural policies that explicitly recognize cultural differences," including greater explicit recognition of multiple languages, cultures, and cultural rights,[8] arguing that the alternative is "cultural exclusion." As possible multicultural policies it recommends asymmetric federalism and executive power sharing; affirmative action programs; and separate, publicly funded schools for particular cultural/ethnic groups.

As might be predicted, general attention to ethnic political and socioeconomic disparities has given rise to more focused concerns about the ethnic correlates of health provision and health outcomes, particularly in developing countries. *The Lancet*, a leading scientific journal of public health, ran a series of articles in 2006 highlighting the challenges of indigenous health on a global scale, even while demonstrating how difficult it is to create a workable definition of the category "indigenous." In 2005, a newly established permanent secretariat for indigenous peoples (United Nations Permanent Forum on Indigenous Issues) called on all "relevant actors" to establish programs and budgets to address indigenous health issues, including HIV/AIDS.[9] The United Nations' cultural institution—UNESCO—partnered with UNAIDS to develop a program, "A Cultural Approach to HIV/AIDS Prevention and Care," stating that indigenous

---

[6] Telles 2007, 1.

[7] For example, for the period 2007–8, the foundation's grants database reports $151,000 to the Organization for Ethnic Community Development in Honduras, for "education and training to develop leadership capacity within the Afro-descendent populations of Honduras, Guatemala and Nicaragua." From http://www.fordfoundation.org/grants/database/detail?105174 (consulted January 9, 2008).

[8] UNDP 2004, 37, 47.

[9] Stephens et al. 2006, 2024.

people "have distinct cultures and cultural beliefs that often differ from the dominant society and thus the existing prevention programs do not address these populations in appropriate ways."[10]

"Ethnodevelopment" approaches are increasingly prevalent in the major international development organizations. In 1993, the World Bank launched its Indigenous Peoples Development Initiative, and the authors of an internal report on this first project in Ecuador highlight a strategic approach emphasizing ethnic autonomy: "This vision builds on the positive qualities of indigenous cultures and societies—such as their sense of ethnic identity, close attachment to ancestral land, and capacity to mobilize labor, capital and other resources for shared goals—to promote local employment and growth."[11] A related World Bank research paper identifies "lessons and opportunities that should be taken by the Bank to assist indigenous peoples to improve their lives while maintaining and strengthening their cultures."[12] The Inter-American Development Bank highlights ethnodevelopment as a strategy and maintains a vast database on ethnically targeted legislation in Latin America.[13]

Such initiatives are understandable in the sense that they are motivated by a desire to redress *very real* problems of discrimination, poverty, and inequality along ethnic lines. And of course, a degree of cultural sensitivity—at the bare minimum communicating in languages people can understand—is necessary for any policy to be effective. Yet these initiatives reveal a belief that the most viable strategy for addressing problems of inequality and discrimination and for improving human welfare is to focus on ethnic boundaries. Any targeted ethnodevelopment strategy requires at the bare minimum official definitions of ethnic group membership, recognition of ethnic leaders, and the collection of data along ethnic lines. It also involves discussion of policy options in terms of ethnic groups.

By contrast, my research, and that of others, suggests that such inequalities are not always best solved through explicit attention to ethnic data and the ethnicization of political institutions. The explicit identification of groups and potentially stigmatizing disparities may have negative

[10] "Indigenous Peoples and a Cultural Approach to HIV/AIDS Prevention and Care," November 21, 2003, www.unesco.org/aids (consulted November 30, 2007).

[11] Van Nieuwkoop and Uquillas 2000, 3.

[12] Partridge, Uquillas, and Johns 1996.

[13] Available at http://www.iadb.org/sds/ind/ley/leyn/datamap.cfm?lang=EN. Thanks to Sarah Chartock for identifying this. Her doctoral dissertation seeks to explore the determinants of cross-country variation in such policies across Latin American countries.

consequences for members of those groups and for societies. By making these categories "official" in the context of scientific reports and government documents, and by demanding that people select identities in health care settings, authorities propagate the "illusion of identity as destiny." The politics of public policymaking is strongly affected by the degree to which constituents conceive of their destinies as shared, with interconnected risks and opportunities, and boundary-making is a bulwark against such a collective consciousness. The effects of recognizing ethnic claims almost inevitably include a chasm between groups. When institutions emphasize boundaries, a collective consciousness becomes less possible. If risks, costs, and benefits are understood as separable across ethnic groups, political leaders will find it almost impossible to advance policies that favor equitable redistribution and to provide universalistic policies.

Moreover, the increased reification of ethnic categories by states and governance authorities more generally is likely to induce ethnically differentiated medical treatment, even if it is not warranted. In a study of the effects of such practice in the United States, scholars lament that "state-sanctioned but ill-defined categories of race have entered medical research and practice with the admirable intent of ensuring full racial and gender inclusion in clinical trials, but with unanticipated consequences for health outcomes."[14] Bioethicists have raised questions about the appropriateness of prescribing certain drugs only to particular racial or ethnic groups—such as BiDil for African Americans in the United States—when social and political factors play such a strong role in determining the rules of membership.[15] Indeed, the medicalization of ethnicity is likely to reify myths of ethnic essentialism, even as physicians remain skeptical of the validity of the very categories they are forced to use. In turn, ordinary citizens would have every reason to believe that such categories were rooted in biological, rather than more mutable social and political, foundations.

To date, global governance leaders have not been sufficiently attuned to social scientific findings about the political dynamics of policymaking, and instead have sometimes inflamed certain tensions and conflicts by making choices to gather and to disseminate ethnically differentiated data in a way that is likely to weaken rather than strengthen political support. Richard Feachem's predictions of different transmission rates for Hindus and Muslims (discussed in chapter 5) are an example, even if his remarks

[14] Braun et al. 2007.
[15] For example, Sandra Soo-Jin Lee labels this "racial profiling in biomedicine" (Braun et al. 2007).

were technically correct. Global governance architects spend too much time looking for leaders and leadership without realizing that their strategies could be more politically viable for any leader. Leadership on policy is more likely to emerge when the political costs of advancing it are diminished. In these ways, global governance policymakers and leaders need to become more politically savvy.

When it comes to the provision of public policies and public goods that can improve human development, the effects of boundaries are double-edged. On the one hand, political boundaries are necessary for administrative control, and for tailoring policies and services to the needs of communities. Even for the provision of "global" public goods, more localized authorities are needed to monitor and to implement most policies. At each level of government, political authorities attempt to gain loyalties and cooperation by highlighting the shared identity of people within the jurisdiction of the polity. And yet when a political administration encompasses multiple and competing ethnic identities, it may be extremely difficult to mobilize the notion of shared risks and rewards that are necessary to induce cooperation and compliance. Citizens and political leaders may challenge characterizations of social problems and the proposed solutions if they perceive threats to their status and well-being. Such responses are not founded on vanity or irrationality. Members of ethnic groups understandably try to resist association with conditions that lead to discrimination that causes economic, physical, and psychological stress. The problem, of course, is that denying the problem of an infectious disease has problematic long-term consequences. A more fundamental solution to such a dynamic demands greater political attention to the connections between groups, the shifting of identities, and the permeability of boundaries. Cosmopolitanism or global citizenship may be one such strategy.

FUTURE RESEARCH

The evidence and analyses presented in this book suggest frontiers for future research of the type that may simultaneously answer deep theoretical questions about social and political life and inform policy debates and strategies. Tragically, I anticipate no retreat in the need for careful social research on AIDS to complement ongoing biomedical research. At this point, virtually every serious observer would predict that AIDS will remain central to the social, economic, and political future of much of the developing world, especially sub-Saharan Africa, for many years to come. There is no conclusion in sight for the global AIDS pandemic.

While extraordinary efforts are being made to provide treatment, to expand care and support, and to spread messages of prevention, the pace of new infections continues to grow. This is not the case everywhere—some countries and localities have turned the tide on AIDS—but even where progress has been solid, there can be relapses, as in the United States. Racial politics continue to shadow the prospects for an effective response. In a 2007 report documenting the spread of HIV in the southern United States, two clinicians explained,

> There are fewer black physicians who provide AIDS care than are needed, and white doctors may either lack cultural sensitivity or be otherwise in an unfavorable position to win the trust of black patients, given the legacy of segregation. . . . A prevalent myth is that HIV was developed by the U.S. government for the purpose of racial genocide. All of these barriers may, individually or collectively, lead to delayed uptake of optimal care or affect HIV treatment adherence and outcome.[16]

In a related manner, this work has focused on policies, but more research is needed on the question of *implementation*. What factors help to translate national policy into effective actions? Just as policymaking is not a purely technocratic affair, neither is implementation. The use and misuse of funds and the technical efforts employed by bureaucrats depend upon local pressures and politics. We ought to assume that policies and expenditures are important but highly incomplete aspects of a response. Ultimately, we need to understand how and why citizens do or do not comply with government policies, especially in the area of behavioral change.

And beyond governments, more careful analytic attention must be paid to nonstate actors, including transnational and local NGOs, as well as private enterprises. The prominence of these organizations has been clear to any observer of the AIDS pandemic for many years, but more systematic social scientific analysis is required to understand their role in people's lives and the social and political factors that drive variations in organizational responsiveness across time, space, and policy areas. One finding of the statistical analyses in chapter 6 was that donor spending seemed not to

[16] Qian and Vermund 2007, 25.

crowd out government spending, but to be positively associated with it. It is necessary to investigate similar questions about NGOs: do they reinforce, replace, or crowd out state authority in particular domains?

Beyond concerns about determinants of AIDS policy responses specifically, important questions about the effect of AIDS on the state and state capacity more generally need to be addressed. A clear problem is that many of the civil servants employed as teachers, tax collectors, inspectors, and health care workers have been incapacitated by AIDS-related illnesses. On the other hand, while discussions of the potential ravages of this epidemic are well known, there also exist interesting opportunities for development, opened by the collective efforts engendered in crisis. As I sat in the parliamentary gardens in Kampala, Uganda, during the summer of 2005, a representative from the Rakai district told me of the phenomenal transformations wrought on his community by AIDS. At first, during the 1980s, there was a great deal of pain and suffering, as people fell ill and died from an ailment known as "Slim disease." But eventually, because of the new relationships forged through citizens working together with government to combat this shared threat, local governance became more effective. Improvements in social services and social welfare became a source of pride. Salvaged out of misery and death sometimes is a hopeful rebuilding—a story not unfamiliar to students of war, conflict, and disease. Scholars will need to parse out these effects in order to fully appreciate the nature of the changes wrought by this disease.

What are the effects of so much attention to this single disease? Well-informed observers have commented that international attention to the AIDS pandemic has been hallowing out state capacities in basic areas of public service such as sanitation removal, clean water, and public health by luring away professionals with higher pay. One expert echoed the sentiment of many when he wrote, "The real-world needs of Africans struggling to survive should not continue to be subsumed by the favorite causes du jour of well-meaning yet often uninformed Western donors."[17] Indeed, one plausible conclusion is that the focus on single diseases is creating unbalanced public health systems. Another distinctive possibility, however, is that the focus on a single disease may lay the foundation for other capacities, as was the case in Rakai district, and as Tilly reported for state-building following the buildup of war-making apparatuses. Untangling the effects of

[17] David Halperin, "Op-Ed: Putting a Plague in Perspective," *New York Times*, January 1, 2008.

disease-specific crises and responses, as distinguished from general health challenges and responses, would help us to understand the political processes of building state capacity and to inform donors and other governance authorities.

More generally, the propositions developed here ought to be considered in the context of other public health problems and other policy problems. Central to the theory advanced in chapter 2 is that the social problem to be addressed was associated with risk and social stigma. To what extent do these dynamics characterize other problems, and how well does the theory explain patterns of variation in policymaking? Is there something unique about AIDS, or might other policies hit similar political chords?

Finally, we require further investigation of how policies and strategies can promote cosmopolitan approaches to ethnic diversity. Many donors seem to have been persuaded that solutions to inequality in ethnically diverse societies must target ethnic groups. It is certainly *possible* that these are the best solutions, but that conclusion is based on intuition and the opinions of ethnic elites, who have incentives to promote it. Social scientists ought to explore alternative institutional arrangements and their effects on social boundaries and development more generally. Harsh policies of cultural assimilation are correctly rejected, but the opposite extreme, that of reinforcing cultural boundaries, is likely harmful to social solidarity. In a world with so much mixing across and within countries, the prospects for cosmopolitanism appear strong. Successful development will require careful appreciation of how institutions affect interests and identities, so that these social forces can be harnessed for human development.

REFERENCES

MULTICOUNTRY DOCUMENTS

All various years; comparable country reports considered for all available countries.
Country Proposals to the Global Fund for AIDS, TB, and Malaria.
Ministries of Finance. Budget Speeches.
Country Progress Reports on Declaration of Commitment on HIV, for the UNGASS 2006.
Centers for Disease Control (CDC)/Global AIDS Program (GAP)/USAID. Country Reports.
International AIDS Society. Abstracts from International AIDS Conferences available from www.aegis.com.
UNAIDS. Country Profiles.
UNAIDS. Country Epidemiological Fact Sheets.
UNDP. Country reports and country profiles
World Health Organization. Treatment Scale-Up Country Summary Profiles.
SIDALAC Country-level and Multi-Country HIV/AIDS Expenditure Data/ (VIH/SIDA) Cuentas Nacionales en VIH/SIDA. Mexico City, Mexico.

ARTICLES, BOOKS, BOOK CHAPTERS, REPORTS, DATABASES

Periodicals and news service reports are cited in the footnotes.
Achen, Christopher H. 2002. "Toward a New Political Methodology: Micro-foundations and ART." *Annual Review of Political Science* 5: 423–50.
Adcock, Robert, and David Collier. 2001. "Measurement Validity: A Shared Standard for Qualitative and Quantitative Research." *American Political Science Review* 95 (3): 529–47.
Afrobarometer. 2005. "AIDS and Public Opinion in South Africa." Afrobarometer Briefing Paper No. 14, August.
Aggleton, Peter, Richard G. Parker, and Mirima Maluwa. 2003. *Stigma, Discrimination, and HIV/AIDS in Latin America and the Caribbean*. Washington, D.C.: Inter-American Development Bank.
AIDS Control and Prevention Project (AIDSCAP). 1996. "The Evolution of HIV/AIDS Policy in Thailand 1984–1994." Family Health International, Working Paper no. 5.
Akerlof, George A., and Rachel E. Kranton. 2000. "Economics and Identity." *Quarterly Journal of Economics* 115 (3): 715–53.

Akwara, Priscilla A., Nyovani Janet Madise, and Andrew Hinde. 2003. "Perception of Risk of HIV/AIDS and Sexual Behavior in Kenya." *Journal of Biosocial Science* 35 (3): 385–411.

Alesina, Alberto, Reza Baqir, and William Easterly. 1999. "Public Goods and Ethnic Divisions." *Quarterly Journal of Economics* 114 (4): 1243–84.

Alesina, Alberto, Arnaud Devleeschauwer, William Easterly, Sergio Kurlat, and Romain Wacziarg. 2003. "Fractionalization." *Journal of Economic Growth* 8 (2): 155–94.

Alesina, Alberto, and Edward L. Glaeser. 2004. *Fighting Poverty in the US and Europe: A World of Difference.* Oxford: Oxford University Press.

Allport, Gordon W. 1954. *The Nature of Prejudice.* Cambridge, Mass.: Addison-Wesley.

Altman, Dennis. 1999. "Globalization, Political Economy, and HIV/AIDS." *Theory and Society* 28: 559–84.

Anandhi, S. 2005. "Sex and Sensibility in Tamil Politics." *Economic and Political Weekly*, November 19, 4876–77.

Appiah, Anthony. 2006. *Cosmopolitanism: Ethics in a World of Strangers.* New York: W. W. Norton.

Ashforth, Adam. 2002. "An Epidemic of Witchcraft? The Implications of AIDS for the Post-apartheid State." *Journal of African Studies* 61 (1): 121–52.

Ballard, John. 1992. "Australia: Participation and Innovation in a Federal System." In *AIDS in the Industrialized Democracies: Passions, Politics, and Policies*, ed. David L. Kirp and Ronald Bayer. New Brunswick, N.J.: Rutgers University Press.

Baldwin, Peter. 1999. *Contagion and the State in Europe, 1830–1930.* Cambridge: Cambridge University Press.

———. 2005. *Disease and Democracy: The Industrialized World Faces AIDS.* Berkeley and Los Angeles: University of California Press; New York: Milbank Memorial Fund.

Barnett, Tony, and Alan W. Whiteside. 2002. *AIDS in the Twenty-first Century: Disease and Globalization.* New York: Palgrave Macmillian.

Barry, John M. 2004. *The Great Influenza: The Epic Story of the Deadliest Plague in History.* New York: Viking.

Barth, Frederik. 1969. *Ethnic Groups and Boundaries.* Boston: Little, Brown.

Bates, Robert H. 1974. "Ethnic Competition and Modernization in Contemporary Africa." *Comparative Political Studies* 6: 457–84.

Bates, Robert H., Avner Greif, Margaret Levi, Jean-Laurent Rosenthal, and Barry R. Weingast. 1998. *Analytic Narratives.* Princeton, N.J.: Princeton University Press.

Bayer, Ronald. 1991. *Private Acts, Social Consequences: AIDS and the Politics of Public Health.* New Brunswick, N.J.: Rutgers University Press.

Bayer, Ronald, and David L. Kirp. 1992. "The United States: At the Center of the Storm." In *AIDS in the Industrialized Democracies: Passions, Politics, and*

Policies, ed. David L. Kirp and Ronald Bayer. New Brunswick, N.J.: Rutgers University Press.

Bayly, Susan. 1999. *Caste, Society and Politics in India from the Eighteenth Century to the Modern Age*. Vol. 4.3 of *The New Cambridge History of India*. Cambridge: Cambridge University Press.

BBC. 2002. "Nigeria Sharia Architect Defends Law." March 21. http://news.bbc .co.uk/2/hi/africa/1885052.stm#map (consulted May 1, 2006).

Behrman, Greg. 2004. *The Invisible People: How the U.S. Has Slept through the Global AIDS Pandemic, the Greatest Humanitarian Catastrophe of Our Time*. New York: Free Press.

Beigbeder, Yves. 2007. "HIV/AIDS and Global Regimes: WTO and the Pharmaceutical Industry." In *AIDS and Governance*, ed. Nana K. Poku, Alan W. Whiteside, and Bjorg Sandkjaer. Burlington, Vt.: Ashgate.

Bennett, Colin J. 1991. "What Is Policy Convergence and What Causes It?" *British Journal of Political Science* 21 (2): 215–33.

Berkman, Alan, Jonathan Garcia, Miguel Muñoz-Laboy, Vera Paiva, and Richard G. Parker. 2005. "A Critical Analysis of the Brazilian Response to HIV/AIDS: Lessons Learned for Controlling and Mitigating the Epidemic in Developing Countries." *American Journal of Public Health* 95 (7): 1162–72.

Bharat, Shalini, with Peter Aggleton and Paul Tyrer. 2001. "India: HIV and AIDS-Related Discrimination, Stigmatization, and Denial." Joint United Nations Programme on HIV/AIDS, August.

Bhupesh, Mangla. 1992. "India: Disquiet about AIDS Control." *Lancet* 340: 1533–35.

Braun, Lundy, Anne Fausto-Sterling, Duana Fullwiley, Evelynn M. Hammonds, Alondra Nelson, William Quivers, Susan M. Reverby, and Alexandra Shields. 2007. "Racial Categories in Medical Practice: How Useful Are They?" *PLoS Medicine* 9 (e271).

Biehl, João. 2004. "The Activist State: Global Pharmaceuticals, AIDS, and Citizenship in Brazil." *Social Text* 22 (3): 105–32.

Bisin, Alberto, and Thierry Verdier. 2000. "'Beyond the Melting Pot': Cultural Transmission, Marriage, and the Evolution of Ethnic and Religious Traits." *Quarterly Journal of Economics* 115 (3): 955–88.

Boone, Catherine. 2003. *Political Topographies of the African State: Territorial Authority and Institutional Choice*. Cambridge: Cambridge University Press.

Boone, Catherine, and Jake Batsell. 2001. "Politics and AIDS in Africa: Research Agendas in Political Science and International Relations." *Africa Today* 48: 3–33.

Bor, Jacob. 2007. "The Political Economy of AIDS Leadership in Developing Countries: An Exploratory Analysis." *Social Science and Medicine* 64: 1585–99.

Bradley, David, Evelyne Huber, Stephanie Mollerr, François Nielsen, and John D. Stephens. 2003. "Distribution and Redistribution in Postindustrial Democracies." *World Politics* 55 (2): 193–228.

Brady, Henry E., and David Collier, eds. 2004. *Rethinking Social Inquiry: Diverse Tools, Shared Standards*. Lanham, Md.: Rowman and Littlefield.

Brass, Paul R. 1994. *The Politics of India since Independence*. 2nd ed. Vol. 4.1 of *The New Cambridge History of India*. Cambridge: Cambridge University Press.

Brewer, Marilynn. 1999. "The Psychology of Prejudice: Ingroup Love or Outgroup Hate?" *Journal of Social Issues* 55 (3): 429–44.

Brooke, James. 1993. "In Deception and Denial an Epidemic Looms." *New York Times*, January 25, 1993, A6.

Brown, Jonathan C., Didem Ayvalikli, and Nadeem Mohammad. 2004. *Turning Bureaucrats into Warriors: Preparing and Implementing Multi-sector HIV-AIDS Programs in Africa*. Washington, DC: World Bank.

Brown, Rupert. 2000. "Social Identity Theory: Past Achievements, Current Problems and Future Challenges." *European Journal of Social Psychology* 30: 745–78.

Brubaker, Rogers. 2004. *Ethnicity without Groups*. Cambridge: Harvard University Press.

Bryan, Angela D., Jeffrey D. Fisher, and T. Joseph Benziger. 2001. "Determinants of HIV Risk among Indian Truck Drivers." *Social Science and Medicine* 53 (11): 1413–26.

Bulatao, Rodolfo A., and John A. Ross. 2002. "Rating Maternal and Neonatal Health Services in Developing Countries." *Bulletin of the World Health Organization* 80: 721–27.

Burke, Pamela L., and Ted R. Gurr. 2000. "Afro-Brazilians: Poverty without Protest." In *Peoples versus States: Minorities at Risk in the New Century*, ed. Ted R. Gurr. Washington, D.C.: United States Institute of Peace Press.

Busby, Joshua William. 2007. "Bono Made Jesse Helms Cry: Jubilee 2000, Debt Relief, and Moral Action in International Politics." *International Studies Quarterly* 51 (2): 247–75.

Cardoso, Fernando Henrique, and Enzo Faletto. 1979. *Dependency and Development in Latin America*. Berkeley and Los Angeles: University of California Press.

Central Intelligence Agency. 2006. *CIA World Factbook*. https://www.cia.gov/library/publications/the-world-factbook/index.html.

Centre for the Study of Developing Societies. 2004. "National Election Study (India) 2004." Delhi.

Chandra, Kanchan. 2004. *Why Ethnic Parties Succeed: Patronage and Ethnic Headcounts in India*. Cambridge: Cambridge University Press.

———. 2006. "What Is Ethnicity and Does It Matter?" *Annual Review of Political Science* 9: 397–424.

Cheibub, José Antonio. 1998. "Political Regimes and the Extractive Capacity of Governments: Taxation in Democracies and Dictatorships." *World Politics* 50: 349–76.

Cheru, Fantu. 2002. "Debt, Adjustment and the Politics of Effective Response to HIV/AIDS in Africa." *Third World Quarterly* 23 (2): 299–313.

Chhibber, Pradeep, and Irfan Nooruddin. 2004. "Do Party Systems Count? The Number of Parties and Government Performance in Indian States." *Comparative Political Studies* 37 (2): 152–87.

Coast, Ernestina. 2006. "Local Understandings of, and Responses to, HIV: Rural-Urban Migrants in Tanzania." *Social Science and Medicine* 63 (4): 1000–1010.

Cohen, Cathy J. 1999. *The Boundaries of Blackness: AIDS and the Breakdown of Black Politics.* Chicago: University of Chicago Press.

Cohen, Jon. 2006. "Dominican Republic: A Sour Taste on the Sugar Plantations." *Science* 313: 473–75.

Collier, Ruth Berins, and David Collier. 1991. *Shaping the Political Arena.* Princeton, N.J.: Princeton University Press.

Committee for the Evaluation of the President's Emergency Plan for AIDS Relief (PEPFAR). 2007. *PEPFAR Implementation: Progress and Promise.* Ed. Jaime Sepulveda, Charles Carpenter, James Curran, William Holzemer, Helen Smits, Kimberly Scott, and Michele Orza. Institute of Medicine, National Academy of Sciences, March 30.

Crepaz, Markus M. L. 1998. "Inclusion versus Exclusion: Political Institutions and Welfare Expenditures." *Comparative Politics* 31 (1): 61–80.

Crewe, Mary. 1992. *AIDS in South Africa: The Myth and the Reality.* London: Penguin .

D'Adesky, Anne-Christine. 2004. *Moving Mountains: The Race to Treat Global AIDS.* London: Verso.

Dandona, Rakhi, Lalit Dandona, G. Anil Kumar, Juan-Pablo Gutierrez, Sam McPherson, Fiona Samuels, and Stefano Bertozzi. 2006. "Demography and Sex Work: Characteristics of Female Sex Workers in India." *BMC International Health and Human Rights* 6 (5): 1–10.

Dasgupta, Jyotirindra. 2001. "India's Federal Design and Multicultural National Construction." In *The Success of India's Democracy,* ed. Atul Kohli. Cambridge: Cambridge University Press.

Datanet India. 2006. Indiastat.com. *www.indiastat.com.*

Davies, Christie. 1982. "Ethnic Jokes, Moral Values and Social Boundaries." *British Journal of Sociology* 33 (3): 383–403.

De Waal, Alex. 2003. "How Will HIV/AIDS Transform African Governance?" *African Affairs* 102: 1–23.

———. 2006. *AIDS and Power: Why There Is No Political Crisis—Yet.* London: Zed Books; Cape Town: David Philip.

Department of Blood Safety and Clinical Technology and the World Health Organization. 1999. *Report of the Meeting of Experts in Blood Transfusion Services.* Geneva: WHO.

Diamond, Jared M. 1999. *Guns, Germs, and Steel: The Fates of Human Societies.* New York: W. W. Norton.

Dobbin, Frank, Beth Simmons, and Geoffrey Garrett. 2007. "The Global Diffusion of Public Policies: Social Construction, Coercion, Competition, or Learning?" *Annual Review of Sociology* 33: 449–72.

Douglas, Mary. 1992. *Risk and Blame: Essays in Cultural Theory.* London: Routledge.

Drèze, Jean, and Amartya Kumar Sen. 1995. *India: Economic Development and Social Opportunity.* Oxford: Oxford University Press.

Drezner, Daniel W. 2001. "Globalization and Policy Convergence." *International Studies Review* 3: 63–78.

Duffy, Patrick, and Theonest K. Mutabingwa. 2005. "Rolling Back a Malaria Epidemic in South Africa." *PLoS Medicine* 2 (1): 1076–77.

Easterly, William, and Ross Levine. 1997. "Africa's Growth Tragedy: Policies and Ethnic Divisions." *Quarterly Journal of Economics* 112 (4): 1203–50.

Ekeh, Peter. 1975. "Colonialism and the Two Publics in Africa: A Theoretical Statement." *Comparative Studies in Society and History* 17 (1): 91–112.

Ekstrand, Maria, Lisa Garbus, and Elliot Marseille. 2003. "HIV/AIDS in India." AIDS Policy Research Center, University of California, San Francisco.

Epstein, Helen. 2005. "God and the Fight against AIDS." *New York Review of Books*, April 28.

————. 2007. *The Invisible Cure: Africa, the West, and the Fight against AIDS.* New York: Farrar, Straus and Giroux.

Ernberg, Gunilla, Marjorie Opuni, Bernhard Schwartländer, Neff Walker, Daniel Tarantola, and Mary Pat Kieffer. 1999. "Level and Flow of National and International Resources for the Response to HIV/AIDS, 1996–1997." UNAIDS Secretariat and François-Xavier Bagnoud Center for Health and Human Rights, Harvard School of Public Health. http://data.unaids.org/Publications/IRC-pub01/JC213-Level-Flow_en.pdf (consulted May 26, 2008).

Evans, Peter. 1985. "Transnational Linkages and the Economic Role of the State: An Analysis of Developing and Industrialized Nations in the Post–World War II Period." In *Bringing the State Back In*, ed. Peter Evans, Dietrich Rueschemeyer and Theda Skocpol. Cambridge: Cambridge University Press.

Evans, Peter, and James Rausch. 1999. "Bureaucracy and Growth: A Cross-National Analysis of the Effects of 'Weberian' State Structures on Economic Growth." *American Sociological Review* 64 (5): 748–65.

Farmer, Paul. 1992. *AIDS and Accusation: Haiti and the Geography of Blame.* Berkeley and Los Angeles: University of California Press.

————. 2003. *Pathologies of Power: Health, Human Rights, and the New War on the Poor.* Berkeley and Los Angeles: University of California Press.

Fearon, James. 2003. "Ethnic Structure and Cultural Diversity by Country." *Journal of Economic Growth* 8 (2): 195–222.

Feldman, Eric A., and Ronald Bayer. 1999. *Blood Feuds: AIDS, Blood, and the Politics of Medical Disaster.* New York: Oxford University Press.

Fidler, David P. 2001. "The Globalization of Public Health: The First 100 Years of International Health Diplomacy." *Bulletin of the World Health Organization* 79 (9): 842–49.

———. 2002. "A Globalized Theory of Public Health Law." *Journal of Law, Medicine and Ethics* 30 (2): 150.

———. 2003. "Disease and Globalized Anarchy: Theoretical Perspectives on the Pursuit of Global Health." *Social Theory and Health* 1 (1): 21.

Finnemore, Martha. 1996. *National Interests in International Society.* Ithaca, N.Y.: Cornell University Press.

Fleet, Julian, and N'Daw Béchir. 2006. "Trade Intellectual Property and Access to Affordable HIV Medicines." In *The HIV Pandemic: Local and Global Implications,* ed. Eduard J. Beck, Nicholas Mays, and Alan W. Whiteside. Oxford: Oxford University Press.

Folayan, Morenike. 2004. "HIV/AIDS: The Nigerian Response." In *The Political Economy of AIDS in Africa,* ed. Nana K. Poku and Alan W. Whiteside. Burlington, Vt.: Ashgate.

Fourie, Pieter. 2006. *The Political Management of HIV and AIDS in South Africa: One Burden Too Many?* New York: Palgrave Macmillan.

Friedman, Steven, and Shauna Mottiar. 2005. "A Rewarding Engagement? The Treatment Action Campaign and the Politics of HIV/AIDS." *Politics and Society* 33 (4): 511–65.

Fry, Peter. 2000. "Politics, Nationality, and the Meanings of 'Race' in Brazil." *Daedalus* 129 (2): 83–118.

Galvão, Jane. 2000. *AIDS No Brasil: A Agenda de Construção de uma Epidemia.* São Paulo: ABIA / Editora 34.

Garbus, Lisa. 2003. "HIV/AIDS in South Africa." Country AIDS Policy Analysis Project, AIDS Policy Research Center, University of California, San Francisco, October. http://hivinsite.ucsf.edu/pdf/countries/ari-sf.pdf (consulted May 26, 2008).

Garcia-Abreu, Anabela, Isabel Noguer, and Karen Cowgill. 2003. *HIV/AIDS in Latin American Countries: The Challenges Ahead.* Washington, D.C.: World Bank.

Gauri, Varun, Chris Beyrer, and Denise Vaillancourt. 2004. "Brazil's Response to AIDS: Policy and Politics, 1983–2004." Unpublished manuscript.

———. 2007. "From Human Rights Principles to Public Health Practice: HIV/AIDS in Brazil." In *Public Health and Human Rights: Evidence-Based Approaches,* ed. Chris Beyrer and H. F. Pizer. Baltimore: Johns Hopkins University Press.

Gauri, Varun, and Peyvand Khaleghian. 2002. "Immunization in Developing Countries: Its Political and Institutional Determinants." *World Development* 30: 2109–32.

Gauri, Varun, and Evan S. Lieberman. 2006. "Boundary Politics and Government Responses to HIV/AIDS in Brazil and South Africa." *Studies in Comparative International Development* 41 (3): 47–73.

Gensini, G. F., M. H. Yacoub, and A. A. Conti. 2004. "The Concept of Quarantine in History: From Plague to SARS." *Journal of Infection* 49 (4): 257–61.

George, Alexander L., and Andrew Bennett. 2005. *Case Studies and Theory Development in the Social Sciences.* Cambridge: MIT Press.

Gerring, John. 2004. "What Is a Case Study and What Is It Good For?" *American Political Science Review* 98 (2): 341–54.

———. 2006. *Case Study Research: Principles and Practices.* Cambridge: Cambridge University Press.

Gerring, John, Strom C. Thacker, and Rodrigo Alfaro. 2006. "Democracy and Human Development." Unpublished manuscript, Boston University.

Gershenkron, Alexander. 1962. *Economic Backwardness in Historical Perspective.* Cambridge: Harvard University Press.

Ghobarah, Hazem Adam, Paul Huth, and Bruce Russett. 2004. "The Post-war Public Health Effects of Civil Conflict." *Social Science and Medicine* 59 (4): 869–84.

Gibson, James L. 2003. "The Legacy of Apartheid." *Comparative Political Studies* 36 (7): 772–800.

Gibson, James L., and Marc Morjé Howard. 2007. "Russian Anti-Semitism and the Scapegoating of Jews." *British Journal of Political Science* 37 (2): 193–223.

Gilens, Martin. 1995. "Racial Attitudes and Opposition to Welfare." *Journal of Politics* 57 (4): 994–1014.

Gilmore, Norbert, and Margaret A. Somerville. 1994. "Stigmatization, Scapegoating and Discrimination in Sexually Transmitted Diseases: Overcoming 'Them' and 'Us.'" *Social Science and Medicine* 39 (9): 1339–58.

Gourevitch, Peter. 1978. "The Second Image Reversed: The International Sources of Domestic Politics." *International Organization* 32 (4): 881–912.

———. 1986. *Politics in Hard Times: Comparative Responses to International Economic Crises.* Ithaca, N.Y.: Cornell University Press.

Government of India, NACP III: Tribal Strategy and Implementation Plan. n.d. Available from http://www.nacoonline.org/tribalstrategyNACP.pdf (consulted January 17, 2007).

Grundligh, Louis. 2001. "Government Responses to HIV/AIDS in South Africa as Reported in the Media, 1983–1994." *South African Historical Journal* 45: 124–53.

Gruskin, Sofia, Aart Hendriks, and Katarina Tomasevski. 1996. "Human Rights and Responses to HIV/AIDS." In *AIDS in the World II: Global Dimensions, Social Roots, and Responses*, ed. Jonathan M. Mann and Daniel Tarantola. Oxford: Oxford University Press.

Gumede, William M. 2005. *Thabo Mbeki and the Battle for the Soul of the ANC.* Cape Town: Zebra Press.

Hamilton, Robin. 1991. *Social and Economic Update* 14 (May). Special issue on AIDS. Johannesburg: South African Institute of Race Relations.

Hardin, Russell. 1995. *One for All: The Logic of Group Conflict.* Princeton, N.J.: Princeton University Press.

Harris, Paul G., and Patricia D. Siplon. 2007. *The Global Politics of AIDS.* Boulder, Colo.: Lynne Rienner.

Headley, Jamila, and Patricia Siplon. 2006. "Roadblocks on the Road to Treatment: Lessons from Barbados and Brazil." *Perspectives on Politics* 4 (4): 655–61.

Hechter, Michael. 1978. "Group Formation and the Cultural Division of Labor." *American Journal of Sociology* 84 (2): 293–318.

———. 2000. *Containing Nationalism.* New York: Oxford University Press.

Heller, Patrick. 2001. "The Politics of Democratic Decentralization in Kerala, South Africa, and Porto Alegre." *Politics and Society* 29 (1): 131–63.

Herbert, Daniel, and Richard G. Parker. 1993. *Sexuality, Politics, and AIDS in Brazil: In Another World?* London: Falmer Press.

Horowitz, Donald. 1985. *Ethnic Groups in Conflict.* Berkeley and Los Angeles: University of California Press.

Htun, Mala. 2004. "From 'Racial Democracy' to Affirmative Action: Changing State Policy in Brazil." *Latin American Research Review* 39 (1): 60–88.

Huddy, Leonie. 2001. "From Social to Political Identity: A Critical Examination of Social Identity Theory." *Political Psychology* 22 (1): 127–56.

Huntington, Samuel P. 1991. *The Third Wave: Democratization in the Late Twentieth Century.* Norman: University of Oklahoma Press.

Hyden, Goran, and Kim Lanegran. 1993. "AIDS, Policy, and Politics: East Africa in Comparative Perspective." *Policy Studies Review* 12 (1–2): 46–65.

Iliffe, John. 2006. *The African AIDS Epidemic: A History.* Athens: Ohio University Press; Oxford: James Currey; Cape Town: Double Storey.

Inglehart, Ronald, and Christian Welzel. 2005. *Modernization, Cultural Change, and Democracy: The Human Development Sequence.* New York: Cambridge University Press.

Inglehart, Ronald, et al. 2004. World Values Surveys and European Values Surveys, 1981–84, 1990–93, 1995–97, 2000–2001. Computer file. ICPSR version. Institute for Social Research, Ann Arbor, Mich., producer. Interuniversity Consortium for Political and Social Research, Ann Arbor, Mich., distributor.

International Institute for Population Sciences (IIPS), and Macro International. 2007. *National Family Health Survey (NFHS-3) 2005–6, India.* Mumbai: IIPS.

Jacobs, Sean, and Richard Calland, eds. 2002. *Thabo Mbeki's World: The Politics and Ideology of the South African President.* Pietermaritzburg, South Africa: University of Natal; London: Zed Books.

Jamal, L. F., S. Romera, N. J. Santos, S. M. Bueno, A. L. Monteiro, C. M. Nascimento, N. M. Rodrigues, and E. A. Ruiz. 2002. "Ethnicity in HIV/AIDS Patients of the Sao Paulo State STD/AIDS Referral and Training Center." Paper presented to the International AIDS Conference, July 7–12, Barcelona.

Joseph, Richard A. 1987. *Democracy and Prebendal Politics in Nigeria: The Rise and Fall of the Second Republic.* Cambridge: Cambridge University Press.

Jung, Courtney. 2000. *Then I Was Black.* New Haven: Yale University Press.

Kasfir, Nelson. 1979. "Explaining Ethnic Political Participation." *World Politics* 31 (3): 365–88.

Kates, Jennifer. 2005. "Financing the Response to HIV/AIDS in Low and Middle Income Countries: Funding for HIV/AIDS from the G7 and the European Commission." Henry J. Kaiser Family Foundation, July.

Kates, Jennifer, and Eric Lief. 2006. "International Assistance for HIV/AIDS in the Developing World: Taking Stock of the G8, Other Donor Governments and the European Commission." Henry J. Kaiser Family Foundation.

Katzenstein, Mary Fainsod, Smitu Kothari, and Uday Mehta. 2001. "Social Movement Politics in India: Institutions, Interests, and Identities." In *The Success of India's Democracy*, ed. Atul Kohli. Cambridge: Cambridge University Press.

Kauffman, Kyle Dean. 2004. "Why Is South Africa the HIV Capital of the World? An Institutional Analysis of the Spread of a Virus." In *AIDS and South Africa: The Social Expression of a Pandemic*, ed. Kyle D. Kauffman and David L. Lindauer. New York: Palgrave Macmillan.

Kaufman, Daniel, Aart Kraay, and Massimo Mastruzzi. 2005. "Governance Matters IV: Governance Indicators 1996–2004." World Bank, Washington, D.C.

Kaufman, Robert. 2003. "Latin America in the Global Economy: Macroeconomic Policy, Social Welfare, and Political Democracy." In *States, Markets, and Just Growth: Development in the Twenty-First Century*, ed. Atul Kohli, Chung-in Moon, and George Sorensen. New York: United Nations University Press.

Keck, Margaret E., and Kathryn Sikkink. 1998. *Activists beyond Borders: Advocacy Networks in International Politics.* Ithaca, N.Y.: Cornell University Press.

Keefer, Philip, and Stuti Khemani. 2004. "Why Do the Poor Receive Poor Services?" *Economic and Political Weekly*, February 28, 935–43.

Keohane, Robert O. 1984. *After Hegemony: Cooperation and Discord in the World Political Economy.* Princeton: Princeton University Press.

———. 2002. "Global Governance and Democratic Accountability." Milibrand Lectures, London School of Economics.

Keohane, Robert O., and Joseph S. Nye Jr. 2000a. "The Club Model of Multilateral Cooperation and the World Trade Organization: Problems of Democratic

Legitimacy." In *Efficiency, Equity, and Legitimacy: The Multilateral Trading System at the Millennium*, ed. Roger B. Porter, Pierre Sauve, Arvind Subramanian, and Americo Beviglia Zampetti. Cambridge, Mass.: Center for Business and Government, Harvard University; Washington, D.C.: Brookings Institution Press.

———. 2000b. "Introduction." In *Governance in a Globalizing World*, ed. Joseph S. Nye Jr. and John D. Donahue. Cambridge, Mass.: Visions of Governance for the 21st Century; Washington, D.C.: Brookings Institution Press.

Kickbusch, Ilona. 2003. "Global Health Governance: Some Theoretical Considerations in the New Political Space." In *Health Impacts of Globalization: Towards Global Governance*, ed. Kelley Lee. New York: Palgrave Macmillan.

King, Gary, Michael Tomz, and Jason Wittenberg. 2000. "Making the Most of Statistical Analyses: Improving Interpretation and Presentation." *American Journal of Political Science* 44 (2): 341–55.

Knight, Jack. 2002. "Informal Institutions and the Microfoundations of Politics." Prepared for the conference Informal Institutions and Politics in the Developing World, Weatherhead Center for International Affairs, Harvard University, April 5–6.

Kohler, Hans-Peter, Jere R. Behrman, and Susan C. Watkins. 2007. "Social Networks and HIV/AIDS Risk Perceptions." *Demography* 44 (1): 1–33.

Kohli, Atul. 1987. *The State and Poverty in India: The Politics of Reform*. Cambridge: Cambridge University Press.

———. 1990a. *Democracy and Discontent: India's Growing Crisis of Governability*. Cambridge: Cambridge University Press.

———. 1990b. "From Elite Activism to Democratic Consolidation: The Rise of Reform Communism in West Bengal." In *Dominance and State Power in Modern India*, ed. Francine R. Frankel and M. S. A. Rao. Delhi: Oxford University Press.

———. 1998. "Can Democracies Accommodate Ethnic Nationalism?" In *Community Conflicts and the State in India*, ed. Amrita Basu and Atul Kohli. Delhi: Oxford University Press.

———. 2004. *State-Directed Development: Political Power and Industrialization in the Global Periphery*. Cambridge: Cambridge University Press.

Krishna, Anirudh. 2003. "What Is Happening to Caste? A View from Some North Indian Villages." *Journal of Asian Studies* 62 (4): 1171–83.

Krishnan, Jayanth K. 2003. "The Rights of the New Untouchables: A Constitutional Analysis of HIV Jurisprudence in India." *Human Rights Quarterly* 25: 791–819.

Krishnatray, Pradeep K., and Srinivas R. Melkote. 1998. "Public Communication Campaigns in the Destigmatization of Leprosy: A Comparative Analysis of DIffusion and Participatry Approaches. A Case Study in Gwailor, India." *Journal of Health Communication* 3 (4): 327–44.

Kumar, Rajesh, Prabhat Jha, Paul Arora, Prern Mony, Prakash Bhatia, Peggy Millson, Neeraj Dhinga, Madhulekha Bhattacharya, Robert S. Remis, and Nico Nagelkerke. 2006. "Trends in HIV-1 in Young Adults in South Africa from 2000 to 2004: A Prevalence Study." *Lancet* 367: 1164–72.

Kumar, Sanjay. 2000. "Protests in India after Arrests of HIV/AIDS Activists." *Lancet* 355:1896.

Laitin, David D. 1986. *Hegemony and Culture: Politics and Religious Change among the Yoruba*. Chicago: University of Chicago Press.

———. 1992. *Language Repertoires and State Construction in Africa*. Cambridge: Cambridge University Press.

———. 1998. *Identity in Formation: The Russian-Speaking Populations in the Near Abroad*. Ithaca, N.Y.: Cornell University Press.

Laitin, David D., and Daniel Posner. 2001. "The Implications of Constructivism for Constructing Ethnic Fractionalization Indices." *APSA-CP* 12 (1): 13–17.

Lamont, Michèle, and Virág Molnár. 2002. "The Study of Boundaries in the Social Sciences." *Annual Review of Sociology* 28: 167–95.

La Porta, Rafael, Florencio López-de-Silanes, Andrei Shleifer, and Robert Vishny. 1999. "The Quality of Government." *Journal of Law, Economics and Organization* 15 (1): 222–79.

Levi, Guido Carlos, and Marco Antonio A. Vitória. 2002. "Fighting against AIDS: The Brazilian Experience." *AIDS* 16: 2373–83.

Levi, Margaret. 1988. *Of Rule and Revenue*. Berkeley and Los Angeles: University of California Press.

———. 1997. *Consent, Dissent, and Patriotism*. Cambridge: Cambridge University Press.

Levine, Ruth, and What Works Working Group. 2004. *Millions Saved: Proven Successes in Global Health*. Washington, D.C.: Center for Global Development.

Lewis, Peter. 1994. "Endgame in Nigeria? The Politics of a Failed Democratic Transition." *African Affairs* 93 (372): 323–40.

Lieberman, Evan S. 2003. *Race and Regionalism in the Politics of Taxation in Brazil and South Africa*. Cambridge: Cambridge University Press.

———. 2005. "Nested Analysis as a Mixed-Method Strategy for Comparative Research." *American Political Science Review* 99 (3): 435–52.

———. 2007. "Ethnic Politics, Risk, and Policy-Making: A Cross-National Statistical Analysis of Government Responses to HIV/AIDS." *Comparative Political Studies* 40 (12): 1407–32.

Lieberman, Evan S., and Prerna Singh. 2006. "An Institutional Approach to the Study of Ethnic Dividedness." Unpublished manuscript, Princeton University.

Lieberman, Robert C. 1998. *Shifting the Color Line: Race and the American Welfare State*. Cambridge: Harvard University Press.

Mahoney, James. 1999. "Nominal, Ordinal, and Narrative Appraisal in Macro-causal Analysis." *American Journal of Sociology* 104 (4): 1154–96.

Mallaby, Sebastian. 2004. *The World's Banker: A Story of Failed States, Financial Crises, and the Wealth and Poverty of Nations*. New York: Penguin.

Mangcu, Xolela. 2008. *To the Brink: The State of Democracy in South Africa*. Scottsville, South Africa: University of Kwazulu-Natal Press.

Mann, Jonathan M., and Daniel Tarantola, eds. 1996. *AIDS in the World II: Global Dimensions, Social Roots, and Responses*. Oxford: Oxford University Press.

Mann, Jonathan M., Daniel Tarantola, and Thomas W. Netter. 1992. *AIDS in the World: The Global Aids Policy Coalition*. Cambridge: Harvard University Press.

Marmor, Theodore, and Evan S. Lieberman. 2004. "Tobacco Control in Comparative Perspective: Eight Nations in Search of an Explanation." In *Unfiltered: Conflicts over Tobacco Policy and Health*, ed. Eric A. Feldman and Ronald Bayer. Cambridge: Harvard University Press.

Marshall, Monty G., and Keith Jaggers. 2006. Polity IV Dataset. Center for International Development and Conflict Management, University of Maryland.

Martinez-Echazabal, Lourdes. 1998. "Mestizaje and the Discourse of National/Cultural Identity in Latin America, 1845–1959." *Latin American Perspectives* 25 (3): 21–42.

Marx, Anthony. 1998. *Making Race and Nation*. Cambridge: Cambridge University Press.

Mathur, Smita, and Gowri Parameswaran. 2004. "Intergenerational Attitudinal Differences about Consumption and Identity among the Hindu Elite in New Delhi, India." *Journal of Intercultural Studies* 25 (2): 161–73.

McGuire, James. 2006. "Basic Health Care Provision and Under-5 Mortality: A Cross-National Study of Developing Countries." *World Development* 34: 405–25.

McNeill, William H. 1998. *Plagues and Peoples*. New York: Anchor.

Mello, Jeffrey A. 1999. "Ethics in Employment Law: The Americans with Disabilities Act and the Employee with HIV." *Journal of Business Ethics* 20 (1): 67.

Merson, Michael H. 2006. "The HIV-AIDS Pandemic at 25: The Global Response." *New England Journal of Medicine* 354: 2414–17.

Merson, Michael H., Robert E. Black, and Anne Mills. 2006. *International Public Health: Diseases, Programs, Systems, and Policies*. 2nd ed. Sudbury, Mass.: Jones and Bartlett.

Michalopoulos, Stelios. 2007. "Ethnolinguistic Diversity: Origins and Implications." Unpublished manuscript, Brown University.

Migdal, Joel S. 1994. "The State in Society: An Approach to Struggles for Domination." In *State Power and Social Forces: Domination and Transformation in the Third World*, ed. Joel S. Migdal, Atul Kohli, and Vivienne Shue. Cambridge: Cambridge University Press.

——. 2001. *State in Society: Studying How States and Societies Transform and Constitute One Another*. Cambridge: Cambridge University Press.

——. 2004. *Boundaries and Belonging: States and Societies in the Struggle to Shape Identities and Local Practices*. Cambridge: Cambridge University Press.

Miguel, Edward. 2004. "Tribe or Nation? Nation Building and Public Goods in Kenya versus Tanzania." *World Politics* 56: 327–62.

Minorities at Risk Project (MAR). 2005–7. Center for International Development and Conflict Management, University of Maryland. http://www.cidcm.umd.edu/mar/ (consulted various dates).

Mishra, Suchismita, Basanta Kumar Swain, and Bontha Veerraju Babu. 2008. "Sexual Risk Behaviour, Knowledge and Attitude Related to HIV Transmission: A Study among a Migrant Tribal Group Living in the Slums of Bhubaneswar City, Orissa, India." *Journal of Public Health*, forthcoming.

Mishra, Vinod, Simona Bignami, Robert Greener, Martin Vaessen, Rathavuth Hong, Peter Ghys, Ties Boerma, Ari Van Assche, and Shane Khan. 2007. "A Study of the Association of HIV Infection with Wealth in Sub-Saharan Africa." DHS Working Paper, 2007 No. 31.

Mitra, Pramit. 2004. "India's HIV/AIDS Crisis: A Moment of Truth." *SAIS Review* 24 (2): 55–67.

Nathanson, Constance A. 1996. "Disease Prevention as Social Change: Toward a Theory of Public Health." *Population and Development Review* 22 (4): 609–37.

National AIDS Control Organisation (NACO), India. 2004. *Annual Report 2002–2003–2003–2004 (up to 31 July 2004)*.

——. 2005a. NACO: Programs. http://www.nacoonline.org/prog_policy.htm (consulted February 10, 2005).

——. 2005b. *Progress Report on the Declaration of Commitment on HIV/AIDS 2005*.

National Intelligence Council. 2002. "The Next Wave of HIV/AIDS: Nigeria, Ethiopia, Russia, India, and China." ICA 2002-04D, September.

Nattrass, Nicoli. 2004. *The Moral Economy of AIDS in South Africa*. Cambridge: Cambridge University Press.

——. 2006. "What Determines Cross-Country Access to Antiretroviral Treatment?" *Development Policy Review* 24 (3): 321–37.

——. 2007. *Mortal Combat: AIDS Denialism and the Struggle for Antiretrovirals in South Africa*. Scottsville, South Africa: University of KwaZulu-Natal Press.

Ngwena, Charles. 1998. "Legal Responses to AIDS: South Africa." In *Legal Responses to AIDS in Comparative Perspective*, ed. Stanislaw Frankowski. The Hague: Kluwer Law International.

Niall, P., A. S. Johnson, and Juergen Mueller. 2002. "Updating the Accounts: Global Mortality of the 1918–20 'Spanish' Influenza Pandemic." *Bulletin of the History of Medicine* 76: 105–15.

Nobles, Melissa. 2000a. *Shades of Citizenship: Race and the Census in Modern Politics*. Stanford, Calif.: Stanford University Press.

———. 2000b. "History Counts: A Comparative Analysis of Racial/Color Categorization in US and Brazilian Censuses." *American Journal of Public Health* 90 (11): 1738–45.

Nussbaum, Martha C., and Joshua Cohen. 1996. *For Love of Country: Debating the Limits of Patriotism*. Boston: Beacon Press.

Nye, Joseph S., and John D. Donahue, eds. 2000. *Governance in a Globalizing World*. Cambridge, Mass.: Visions of Governance for the 21st Century; Washington, D.C.: Brookings Institution Press.

O'Donnell, Guillermo. 1994. "The State, Democratization, and Some Conceptual Problems (a Latin American View with Glances at Some Post-Communist Countries)." In *Latin American Political Economy in the Age of Neoliberal Reform: Theoretical and Comparative Perspectives for the 1990s*, ed. William C. Smith, Carlos H. Acuña, and Eduardo A. Gamarra. Coral Gables, Fla.: North-South Center, University of Miami; New Brunswick N.J.: Transaction Publishers.

Office of Development Studies. 2002. "Profiling the Provision Status of Global Public Goods." ODS Staff Paper, United Nations Development Programme, December.

Okie, Susan. 2006. "Fighting HIV—Lessons from Brazil." *New England Journal of Medicine* 354: 1977–81.

Orchard, Treena Rae. 2007. "Girl, Woman, Lover, Mother: Towards a New Understanding of Child Prostitution among Young Devadasis in Rural Karnataka, India." *Social Science and Medicine* 64 (12): 2379–90.

Organisation for Economic Co-operation and Development (OECD). 2005. *Development Cooperation Report*. www.oecd.org/dac/stats/dac/dcrannex (consulted January 4, 2007).

Ostergard, Robert. 2002. "Politics in the Hot Zone: AIDS and National Security in Africa." *Third World Quarterly* 23 (2): 333–51.

Over, A. Mead, and World Bank. 2004. *HIV/AIDS Treatment and Prevention in India: Modeling the Costs and Consequences*. Washington, D.C.: World Bank.

Owensby, Brian. 2005. "Toward a History of Brazil's 'Cordial Racism': Race beyond Liberalism." *Comparative Studies in Society and History* 47 (2): 318–47.

Palshikar, Suhas. 2004. "Majoritarian Middle Ground?" *Economic and Political Weekly*, December 18–24, 5426–30.

Parker, Richard G. 1994a. *A AIDS no Brasil, 1982–1992*. Coleção História social da AIDS, no. 2. Rio de Janeiro: ABIA: IMS-UERJ: Relume Dumará.

———. 1994b. "Public Policy, Political Activism, and AIDS in Brazil." In *Global AIDS Policy*, ed. Douglas A. Feldman. London: Bergin and Garvey.

———. 2003. "Building the Foundations for the Response to HIV/AIDS in Brazil: The Development of HIV/AIDS Policy, 1982–1996." *Divulgação em Saúde para Debate* 27: 143–83.

Parkhurst, Justin O., and Louisiana Lush. 2004. "The Political Environment of HIV: Lessons from a Comparison of Uganda and South Africa." *Social Science and Medicine* 59: 1913–24.

Parra, Flavia C., Roberto C. Amado, Jose R. Lambertucci, Jorge Rocha, Carlos M. Antunes, and Sérgio D. J. Pena. 2003. "Color and Genomic Ancestry in Brazilians." *Proceedings of the National Academy of Science of the United States* 100 (1): 177–82.

Partridge, William L., and Jorge E. Uquillas, with Kathryn Johns. 1996. "Including the Excluded: Ethnodevelopment in Latin America." Paper presented to the Annual World Bank Conference on Development in Latin America and the Caribbean, Bogotá, Colombia, June 30–July 2.

Patterson, Amy S. 2006. *The Politics of AIDS in Africa.* Boulder, Colo.: Lynne Rienner.

Petersen, Roger Dale. 2002. *Understanding Ethnic Violence: Fear, Hatred, and Resentment in Twentieth-Century Eastern Europe.* Cambridge: Cambridge University Press.

Petricciani, John C., et al., eds. 1987. *AIDS: The Safety of Blood and Blood Products.* New York: Published on behalf of the World Health Organization by Wiley.

Petros, George, Collins O. Airhihenbuwa, Leickness Simbayi, Shandir Ramlagan, and Brandon Brown. 2006. "HIV/AIDS and 'Othering' in South Africa: The Blame Goes On." *Culture, Health and Sexuality* 8 (1): 67–77.

Phillips, Howard. 2001. "AIDS in the Context of South Africa's Epidemic History: Some Preliminary Thoughts." *South African Historical Journal* 45: 11–26.

Pierson, Paul. 1995. "Fragmented Welfare States: Federal Institutions and the Development of Social Policy." *Governance* 8 (4): 449–78.

Poole, Stafford. 1999. "The Politics of Limpieza de Sangre: Juan de Ovando and His Circle in the Reign of Philip II." *The Americas* 55 (3): 359–89.

Pop-Eleches, Grigore. Forthcoming. *From Economic Crisis to Reforms: IMF Programs in Latin America and Eastern Europe.* Cambridge: Cambridge University Press.

Posner, Daniel. 2004. "Measuring Ethnic Fractionalization in Africa." *American Journal of Political Science* 48 (4): 849–63.

———. 2005. *Institutions and Ethnic Politics in Africa.* New York: Cambridge University Press.

Price, Robert. 1997. "Race and Reconciliation in the New South Africa." *Politics and Society* 25 (2): 149–78.

Price-Smith, Andrew T. 2002. *The Health of Nations: Infectious Disease, Environmental Change, and Their Effects on National Security and Development.* Cambridge: MIT Press.

Price-Smith, Andrew, Steven Tauber, and Anand Bhat. 2004. "State Capacity and HIV Incidence." *Seton Hall Journal of Diplomacy and International Relations* 5 (2): 149–60.

Przeworski, Adam, et al. 2000. *Democracy and Development: Political Institutions and Material Well-Being in the World, 1950–1990*. Cambridge: Cambridge University Press.

Putnam, Robert. 2007. "E Pluribus Unum: Diversity and Community in the Twenty-first Century. The 2006 Johan Skytte Prize Lecture." *Scandinavian Political Studies* 30 (2): 137–74.

Qian, Han-Zhu, and Sten H. Vermund. 2007. "The Continuing Spread of HIV/AIDS in the Southern U.S." *Touch Briefings* 2: 24–25.

Randall, Vicky. 1993. "The Media and Democratisation in the Third World." *Third World Quarterly* 14 (3): 625–46.

Rayside, David M., and Evert A. Lindquist. 1992. "Canada: Community Activism, Federalism, and the New Politics of Disease." In *AIDS in the Industrialized Democracies: Passions, Politics, and Policies*, ed. David L. Kirp and Ronald Bayer. New Brunswick, N.J.: Rutgers University Press.

Risse-Kappen, Thomas, Steve C. Ropp, and Kathryn Sikkink. 1999. *The Power of Human Rights: International Norms and Domestic Change*. Cambridge: Cambridge University Press.

Roeder, Philip G. 2001. "Ethnolinguistic Fractionalization (ELF) Indices, 1961 and 1985." February 16. http//:weber.ucsd.edu\~proeder\elf.htm (consulted May 27, 2008).

Rosenberg, Tina. 2001. "Look at Brazil." *New York Times Magazine*, January 28.

Sabatier, Renée, et al. 1988. *Blaming Others: Prejudice, Race, and Worldwide AIDS*. Ed. Jon Tinker. London: Panos.

Sandbrook, Richard. 1989. *The Politics of Africa's Economic Stagnation*. Cambridge: Cambridge University Press.

Schneider, Helen. 2002. "On the Fault-line: The Politics of AIDS Policy in Contemporary South Africa." *African Studies* 61 (1): 145–67.

Schneider, Helen, and Joanne Stein. 2001. "Implementing AIDS Policy in Post-Apartheid South Africa." *Social Science and Medicine* 52: 723–31.

Scully, Pamela. 1995. "Rape, Race, and Colonial Culture: The Sexual Politics of Identity in the Nineteenth-Century Cape Colony, South Africa." *American Historical Review* 100 (2): 335–59.

Secretary-General, United Nations General Assembly. 2006. "Declaration of Commitment on HIV/AIDS: Five Years Later." March 24.

Seidman, Gay. 1994. *Manufacturing Militance: Workers' Movements in Brazil and South Africa, 1970–85*. Berkeley and Los Angeles: University of California Press.

Sen, Amartya Kumar. 1999. *Development as Freedom*. New York: Knopf.

———. 2001. "Democracy as a Universal Value." In *The Global Divergence of Democracies*, ed. L. Diamond and M. F. Plattner. Baltimore: Johns Hopkins University Press.

———. 2006. *Identity and Violence: The Illusion of Destiny*. New York: Norton.

Sethi, Geeta. 2002. "AIDS in India: The Government's Response." In *Living with the AIDS Virus: The Epidemic and the Response in India*, ed. Samiran Panda, Anindya Chatterjee, and Abu S. Abdul-Quader. Thousand Oaks, Calif.: Sage.

Shadlen, Kenneth C. 2007. "The Political Economy of AIDS Treatment: Intellectual Property and the Transformation of Generic Supply." *International Studies Quarterly* 51 (3): 559–81.

Shahmanesh, Maryam, and Sonali Wayal. 2004. "Targeting Commercial Sex-Workers in Goa, India: Time for a Strategic Rethink?" *Lancet* 364: 1297–99.

Shilts, Randy. 2000. *And the Band Played On: Politics, People, and the AIDS Epidemic*. New York: St. Martin's Press.

Shisana, Olive, Thomas Rehle, Leickness Simbayi, Warren Parker, et al. 2005. *South African National HIV Prevalence, HIV Incidence, Behavior and Communication Survey 2005*. Cape Town: Human Sciences Research Council Press.

Shisana, Olive, Leickness Simbayi, and Human Sciences Research Council. 2002. *Nelson Mandela/HSRC study of HIV/AIDS: South African National HIV Prevalence, Behavioural Risks and Mass Media: Household Survey 2002*. Cape Town: Human Sciences Research Council.

Simmons, Beth, and Zachary Elkins. 2004. "The Globalization of Liberalization: Policy Diffusion in the International Political Economy." *American Political Science Review* 98 (1): 171–89.

Singh, Prerna. 2008. "Subnationalism and Social Development: A Comparative Analysis of Indian States." Unpublished manuscript, Princeton University.

Siplon, Patricia. 2005. "AIDS and Patriarchy: Ideological Obstacles to Effective Policy Making." In *The African State and the AIDS Crisis*, ed. Amy S. Patterson. Burlington, Vt.: Ashgate.

Skidmore, Thomas E. 1995. *Black into White: Race and Nationality in Brazilian Thought*. Durham, N.C.: Duke University Press.

Slaughter, Anne-Marie. 2004. *A New World Order*. Princeton, N.J.: Princeton University Press.

Slovic, Paul. 1999. "Trust, Emotion, Sex, Politics, and Science: Surveying the Risk-Assessment Battlefield." *Risk Analysis* 19 (4): 689–701.

Slovic, Paul, Melissa L. Finucane, Ellen Peters, and Donald MacGregor. 2004. "Risk as Analysis and Risk as Feelings: Some Thoughts about Affect, Reason, Risk, and Rationality." *Risk Analysis* 24 (2): 311–22.

Smalley, William Allen. 1994. *Linguistic Diversity and National Unity: Language Ecology in Thailand*. Chicago: University of Chicago Press.

Smith, Anthony D. 1989. "The Origins of Nations." *Ethnic and Racial Studies* 12 (3): 340–67.

Smith, Daniel Jordan. 2004. "Youth, Sin and Sex in Nigeria: Christianity and AIDS-Related Beliefs and Behaviour among Rural-Urban Migrants." *Culture, Health and Sexuality* 6 (5): 425–37.

Smith, Raymond A. 1998. *Encyclopedia of AIDS: A Social, Political, Cultural, and Scientific Record of the HIV Epidemic*. Chicago: Fitzroy Dearborn.

Smith, Raymond A., and Patricia D. Siplon. 2006. *Drugs into Bodies: Global AIDS Treatment Activism*. Westport, Conn.: Praeger.

Sontag, Susan. 2001. *Illness as Metaphor* and *AIDS and Its Metaphors*. New York: Farrar, Straus and Giroux.

South Africa. Parliament. Various years. Debates of the National Assembly (Hansard).

Sparks, Allister Haddon. 2003. *Beyond the Miracle: Inside the New South Africa*. London: Profile Books.

Stallings, Barbara. 1992. "International Influence on Economic Policy: Debt, Stabilization, and Structural Reform." In *The Politics of Economic Adjustment: International Constraints, Distributive Conflicts, and the State*, ed. Stephan Haggard and Robert R. Kaufman. Princeton, N.J.: Princeton University Press.

Steinmo, Sven, Kathleen Thelen, and Frank Longstreth, eds. 1995. *Structuring Politics: Historical Institutionalism in Comparative Analysis*. New York: Cambridge University Press.

Stepan, Nancy. 1991. *The Hour of Eugenics: Race, Gender, and Nation in Latin America*. Ithaca, N.Y.: Cornell University Press.

Stephens, Carolyn, John Porter, Clive Nettleton, and Ruth Willis. 2006. "Disappearing, Displaced, and Undervalued: A Call to Action for Indigenous Health Worldwide." *Lancet* 367: 2019–28.

Stiglitz, Joseph E. 2002. *Globalization and Its Discontents*. New York: W. W. Norton.

Strange, Susan. 1996. *The Retreat of the State: The Diffusion of Power in the World Economy*. Cambridge: Cambridge University Press.

Sunstein, Cass R., and Edna Ullmann-Margalit. 2001. "Solidarity Goods." *Journal of Political Philosophy* 9 (2): 129–49.

Surratt, H. L., and J. A. Inciardi. 1998. "Unraveling the Concept of Race in Brazil: Issues for the Rio de Janeiro Cooperative Agreement Site." *Journal of Psychoactive Drugs* 30 (3): 255–60.

Tajfel, Henri, and John C. Turner. 1986. "The Social Identity Theory of Intergroup Behavior." In *Psychology of Intergroup Relations*, 2nd ed., ed. Stephen Worchel and William G. Austin. Chicago : Nelson-Hall.

Taylor, Allyn L. 2002. "Global Governance, International Health Law and WHO: Looking towards the Future." *Bulletin of the World Health Organization* 80 (12). http://www.scielosp.org/scielo.php?script=sci_arttext&pid=S0042-96862002001200013 (consulted May 27, 2008).

Teixeira, Paulo Roberto. 1997. "Políticas Públicas in AIDS." In *Políticas, Instituições, e AIDS: Enfrentando a Epidemia no Brasil*, ed. Richard G. Parker. Rio de Janeiro: ABIA.

Telles, Edward Eric. 2004. *Race in Another America: The Significance of Skin Color in Brazil*. Princeton, N.J.: Princeton University Press.

———. 2007. "Incorporating Race and Ethnicity into the UN Millennium Development Goals." Race Report, Inter-American Dialogue, January.

Teorell, Jan, and Axel Hadenius. 2005. "Determinants of Democratization: Taking Stock of the Large-N Evidence." Department of Government, Uppsala University.

Teorell, Jan, Sören Holmberg, and Bo Rothstein. 2008. The Quality of Government Dataset. Version January 7. Quality of Government Institute, Göteborg University. http://www.qog.pol.gu.se.

Thomson, Curtis. 1993. "Political Identity among Chinese in Thailand." *Geographical Review* 83 (4): 67.

Tilly, Charles, ed. 1975. *The Formation of National States in Western Europe*. Princeton, N.J.: Princeton University Press.

———. 1992. *Coercion, Capital, and European States, AD 990–1992*. Malden, Mass.: Blackwell.

———. 2005. *Identities, Boundaries, and Social Ties*. Boulder, Colo.: Paradigm.

Treisman, Daniel. 2007. "What Have We Learned about the Causes of Corruption from Ten Years of Cross-National Empirical Research?" *Annual Review of Political Science* 10: 211–44.

Tuohy, Carolyn J. 1999. *Accidental Logics: The Dynamics of Change in the Health Care Arena in the United States, Britain, and Canada*. New York: Oxford University Press.

Turra, Cleusa, and Gustavo Venturi, eds. 1995. *Racismo Cordial*. São Paulo: Editora Ática.

TvT Associates. 2002. "HIV/AIDS in Nigeria: A USAID Brief." USAID, July.

UNAIDS. 2004. *Report on the Global AIDS Epidemic: Executive Summary*. Geneva: UNAIDS.

———. 2005. "AIDS in Africa: Three Scenarios to 2025." Geneva: UNAIDS.

———. 2006. *2006 Report on the Global Aids Epidemic*. Geneva: UNAIDS.

UNAIDS, USAID, and Policy Project (Futures Group International). 2003. The Level of Effort in the National Response to HIV/AIDS: The AIDS Program Effort Index (API) 2003 Round.

UNAIDS and WHO. 2004. "A Global View of HIV Infection." UNAIDS/WHO, Geneva.

———. 2007. "2007 AIDS Epidemic Update." UNAIDS, Geneva.

United Nations Development Program (UNDP). 2004. *Human Development Report 2004: Cultural Liberty in Today's Diverse World*. New York: UNDP.

———. 2005. "You and AIDS: India at a Glance." http://www.youandaids.org/Asia%20Pacific%20at%20a%20Glance/India/index.asp (consulted October 5, 2005).

UNESCO. 2002. "A Cultural Approach to HIV/AIDS Prevention and Care: Towards a Handbook for India." In *Studies and Reports Special Series*. Paris: UNESCO, Division of Cultural Studies.

Valenzuela, J. Samuel, and Arturo Valenzuela. 1978. "Modernization and Dependency: Alternative Perspectives in the Study of Latin American Underdevelopment." *Comparative Politics* 10: 535–57.

Van der Vliet, Virginia. 2001. "AIDS: Losing 'The New Struggle'?" *Daedalus* 130 (1): 151–84.

———. 2004. "South Africa Divided against AIDS: A Crisis of Leadership." In *AIDS and South Africa: The Social Expression of a Pandemic*, ed. Kyle D. Kauffman and David L. Lindauer. New York: Palgrave Macmillan.

Van de Walle, Nicolas. 2001. *African Economies and the Politics of Permanent Crisis, 1979–1999*. Cambridge: Cambridge University Press.

Vanhanen, Tatu. 1999. "Domestic Ethnic Conflict and Ethnic Nepotism: A Comparative Analysis." *Journal of Peace Research* 36 (1): 55–73.

Van Nieuwkoop, Martien, and Jorge E. Uquillas. 2000. "Defining Ethnodevelopment in Operational Terms: Lessons from the Ecuador Indigenous and Afro-Ecuadorean Peoples Development Project." Latin America and Caribbean Region Sustainable Development Working Paper. World Bank, Washington, D.C.

Van Praag, Eric, Karl L. Dehne, and Venkatraman Chandra-Mouli. 2006. "The UN Response to the HIV Pandemic." In *The HIV Pandemic: Local and Global Implications*, ed. Eduard J. Beck and Lynn-Marie Holland. Oxford: Oxford University Press.

Varshney, Ashutosh. 2002. *Ethnic Conflict and Civic Life*. New Haven: Yale University Press.

———. 2003. "Nationalism, Ethnic Conflict, and Rationality." *Perspectives on Politics* 1 (1): 85–99.

Walker, Brian. 1997. "Plural Cultures, Contested Territories: A Critique of Kymlicka." *Canadian Journal of Political Science* 30 (2): 211–34.

Wallerstein, Immanuel. 1974. "The Rise and Future Demise of the World Capitalist System: Concepts for Comparative Analysis." *Comparative Studies in Society and History* 16: 387–415.

Walt, Gill. 2006. "Global Cooperation in International Public Health." In *International Public Health: Diseases, Programs, Systems, and Policies*, 2nd ed., ed. Michael H. Merson, Robert E. Black, and Anne Mills. Sudbury, Mass.: Jones and Bartlett.

Weber, Max. 1968. *Economy and Society: An Outline of Interpretive Sociology*. Ed. Guenther Roth and Claus Wittich. Trans Ephraim Fischoff et al. 3 vols. New York: Bedminster Press.

Weindling, Paul. 1993. "The Politics of International Co-Ordination to Combat Sexually Transmitted Diseases, 1900–1980s." In *AIDS and Contemporary*

History, ed. Virginia Berridge and Philip Strong. Cambridge: Cambridge University Press.

Weiner, Myron. 1991. *The Child and the State in India: Child Labor and Education Policy in Comparative Perspective*. Princeton, N.J.: Princeton University Press.

———. 2001. "The Struggle for Equality: Caste in Indian Politics." In *The Success of India's Democracy*, ed. Atul Kohli. Cambridge: Cambridge University Press.

Weingast, Barry. 2002. "Rational-Choice Institutionalism." In *Political Science: The State of the Discipline*, ed. Ira Katznelson and Helen V. Milner. New York: American Political Science Association.

Weyland, Kurt. 1995. "Social Movements and the State: The Politics of Health Reform in Brazil." *World Development* 23: 1699–1712.

Whiteside, Alan W. 2005. "The Economic, Social, and Political Drivers of the AIDS Epidemic in Swaziland: A Case Study." In *The African State and the AIDS Crisis*, ed. Amy S. Patterson. Burlington, Vt.: Ashgate.

Wilkinson, Steven. 2004. *Votes and Violence: Electoral Competition and Ethnic Riots in India*. New York: Cambridge University Press.

Williamson, John. 1993. "Development and the 'Washington Consensus.'" *World Development* 21: 1239–1336.

Winant, Howard. 2001. *The World Is a Ghetto: Race and Democracy since World War II*. New York: Basic Books.

Windmiller, Marshall. 1954. "Linguistic Regionalism in India." *Pacific Affairs* 27 (4): 291–318.

Wogart, J. P., and G. Calcagnotto. 2006. "Brazil's Fights against AIDS and Its Implications for Global Health Governance." *Healthcare Quarterly* 9 (1): 76–89.

World Bank. 1999. *Confronting AIDS: Public Priorities in a Global Epidemic*. Rev. ed. New York: Oxford University Press for the World Bank.

———. 2003. *Brazil: AIDS and STD Control III Project*. Project Appraisal Document, Report 5759-BR, June 4.

———. 2005. World Development Indicators. Online database.

World Bank. Operations Evaluation Department. 2004. *Brazil: First and Second AIDS and STD Control Projects: Project Performance Assessment*. April 2004.

World Health Organization (WHO). 1987. Fortieth World Health Assembly: Global Strategy for the Prevention and Control of AIDS. WHO, Geneva.

———. 1992. Forty-fifth World Health Assembly: Global Strategy for the Prevention and Control of AIDS. WHO, Geneva.

———. 2000. *The World Health Report 2000: Health Systems: Improving Performance*. Geneva: World Health Organization.

———. 2003. *The World Health Report 2003: Shaping the Future*. Geneva: World Health Organization.

————. 2004. "Antiretroviral Drugs for Treating Pregnant Women and Preventing HIV Infection in Infants: Guidelines for Care Treatment and Support for Women Living with HIV/AIDS and Their Children in Resource-Constrained Settings." WHO, Geneva.

————. 2005. *Progress on Global Access to HIV Antiretroviral Therapy: An Update on 3 by 5*. Geneva: WHO.

Young, Crawford, and Thomas Turner. 1985. *The Rise and Decline of the Zairean State*. Madison: University of Wisconsin Press.

Page references followed by *fig* indicate an illustrated figure; followed by *t* indicate a table.